QuickBooks® 2011

FOR

DUMMIES®

by Stephen L. Nelson
CPA, MBA (finance), MS (taxation)

WILEY

Wiley Publishing, Inc.

QuickBooks® 2011 For Dummies®

Published by
Wiley Publishing, Inc.
111 River Street
Hoboken, NJ 07030-5774

www.wiley.com

Copyright © 2010 by Wiley Publishing, Inc., Indianapolis, Indiana

Published by Wiley Publishing, Inc., Indianapolis, Indiana

Published simultaneously in Canada

For general information on our other products and services, please contact our Customer Care Department within the U.S. at 877-762-2974, outside the U.S. at 317-572-3993, or fax 317-572-4002.

For technical support, please visit www.wiley.com/techsupport.

Wiley also publishes its books in a variety of electronic formats. Some content that appears in print may not be available in electronic books.

Library of Congress Control Number: 2010935588

ISBN: 978-0-470-64649-6

Manufactured in the United States of America

10 9 8 7 6 5 4 3 2 1

WILEY

About the Author

Stephen L. Nelson, CPA, MBA (finance), MS (taxation), has a simple purpose in life: He wants to help you (and people like you) manage your business finances by using computers. Oh, sure, this personal mandate won't win him a Nobel Prize or anything, but it's his own little contribution to the world.

Steve's experiences mesh nicely with his special purpose. A CPA in Redmond, Washington, his past small business experience includes a stint as an adjunct professor of taxation (S corporations and limited liability companies) at Golden Gate University graduate tax school and a few years working as a senior consultant and CPA with Arthur Andersen & Co. (er, yeah, *that* Arthur Andersen — but, hey, it was nearly 30 years ago). Steve, whose books have sold more than 4 million copies in English and have been translated into 11 other languages, is also the bestselling author of *Quicken 2010 For Dummies*.

Dedication

To the entrepreneurs and small-business people of the world. You folks create most of the new jobs.

Acknowledgments

Hey, reader, lots of folks spent lots of time working on this book to make QuickBooks easier for you. You should know who these people are. You may just possibly meet one of them someday at a produce shop, squeezing cantaloupe, eating grapes, and looking for the perfect peach.

First, a huge thanks to the wonderful folks at Intuit who helped me by providing the beta software and other friendly assistance for this and past editions of this book.

Another big thank-you goes to the editorial folks at Wiley Publishing, Inc., including Kevin Kirschner (project editor), Jen Riggs (copy editor), and Bob Woerner (executive editor). Thanks also to David Ringstrom for his technical assistance and superb attention to detail. Finally, thanks, too, to the composition staff.

Publisher's Acknowledgments

We're proud of this book; please send us your comments at http://dummies.custhelp.com. For other comments, please contact our Customer Care Department within the U.S. at 877-762-2974, outside the U.S. at 317-572-3993, or fax 317-572-4002.

Some of the people who helped bring this book to market include the following:

Acquisitions, Editorial

Project Editor: Kevin Kirschner

Executive Editor: Bob Woerner

Copy Editor: Jen Riggs

Technical Editor: David H. Ringstrom

Editorial Assistant: Amanda Graham

Sr. Editorial Assistant: Cherie Case

Cartoons: Rich Tennant
(www.the5thwave.com)

Composition Services

Project Coordinator: Katie Crocker

Layout and Graphics: Samantha K. Cherolis

Proofreaders: Melissa Cossell, Cynthia Fields

Indexer: Claudia Bourbeau

Publishing and Editorial for Technology Dummies

> **Richard Swadley,** Vice President and Executive Group Publisher

> **Andy Cummings,** Vice President and Publisher

> **Mary Bednarek,** Executive Acquisitions Director

> **Mary C. Corder,** Editorial Director

Publishing for Consumer Dummies

> **Diane Graves Steele,** Vice President and Publisher

Composition Services

> **Debbie Stailey,** Director of Composition Services

Contents at a Glance

Table of Contents

Introduction

. . . .

Running or working in a small business is one of the coolest things a person can do. Really. I mean it. Sure, sometimes the environment is dangerous — kind of like the Old West — but it's an environment in which you have the opportunity to make tons of money. And it's also an environment in which you can build a company or a job that fits you. In comparison, many brothers and sisters working in big-company corporate America are furiously trying to fit their round pegs into painfully square holes. Yuck.

You're wondering, of course, what any of this has to do with this book or with QuickBooks. Quite a lot, actually. The whole purpose of this book is to make it easier for you to run or work in a small business by using QuickBooks.

About QuickBooks

Let me start off with a minor but useful point: QuickBooks comes in several different flavors, including QuickBooks Basic, QuickBooks Pro, QuickBooks Premier, QuickBooks Premier Accountants Edition, and QuickBooks Enterprise Solutions.

This book, however, talks about QuickBooks Premier Edition.

Does this mean that I somehow leave you adrift if you have one of the other flavors? No way. I wouldn't do that to you. QuickBooks Premier is a superset of QuickBooks Simple Start and QuickBooks Pro, and is identical in most areas to QuickBooks Enterprise Solutions. By describing how you use QuickBooks Premier, I also tell you how to use the other flavors of QuickBooks.

What's more, for the readers of this book, there's no discernible difference between QuickBooks Premier and QuickBooks Pro. You aren't reading this book to prepare for the CPA exam, right? Right. The extra whistles and bells that make QuickBooks Premier, well, *premier* are all things that only accountants care about: remote access to QuickBooks and your QuickBooks data, reversal of general entries, extra security for general ledger closings, and so on. So I don't talk much about those things.

The bottom line? Yes, there are several flavors of QuickBooks, but if you're just trying to get started and want to use QuickBooks, this book works for QuickBooks Pro, QuickBooks Premier, and QuickBooks Enterprise Solutions.

About This Book

This book isn't meant to be read from cover to cover, like some _Stieg Larsson_ page-turner. Instead, it's organized into tiny, no-sweat descriptions of how you do the things you need to do. If you're the sort of person who just doesn't feel right not reading a book from cover to cover, you can (of course) go ahead and read this thing from front to back. You can start reading Chapter 1 and continue all the way to the end (which means through Chapter 21 and the appendixes).

I don't think this from-start-to-finish approach is bad because I tell you a bunch of stuff (tips and tricks, for example) along the way. I tried to write the book in such a way that the experience isn't as rough as you might think, and I really do think you get good value from your reading.

But you also can use this book the way you'd use an encyclopedia. If you want to know about a subject, you can look it up in the Table of Contents or the index; then you can flip to the correct chapter or page and read as much as you need or enjoy. No muss, no fuss.

I should, however, mention one thing: Accounting software programs require you to do a certain amount of preparation before you can use them to get real work done. If you haven't started to use QuickBooks yet, I recommend that you read through the first few chapters of this book to find out what you need to do first.

Hey. There's something else I should tell you. I fiddled a bit with the Windows display settings. For example, I noodled around with the font settings and most of the colors. The benefit is that the pictures in this book are easy to read. And that's good. But the cost of all this is that my pictures look a little bit different from what you see on your screen. And that's not good. In the end, however, what the publisher found is that people are happier with increased readability. Anyway, I just thought I should mention it here, upfront, in case you have any questions about it.

What You Can Safely Ignore

Sometimes I provide step-by-step descriptions of tasks. I feel very bad about having to do this, so to make things easier for you, I describe the tasks by using bold text. That way, you know exactly what you're supposed to do. I also provide a more detailed explanation in the text that follows the step. You can skip the text that accompanies the step-by-step boldface directions if you already understand the process.

Here's an example that shows what I mean:

1. **Press Enter.**

   Find the key that's labeled Enter. Extend your index finger so that it rests ever so gently on the Enter key. In one sure, fluid motion, press the Enter key with your index finger. Then remove your finger from the key.

Okay, that example is extreme. I never go into that much detail, but you get the idea. If you know how to press Enter, you can just do that and not read further. If you need help — maybe with the finger part or something else — just read the nitty-gritty details.

Can you skip anything else? Let me see now. . . . You can skip the Technical Stuff icons, too. The information next to these icons is intended only for those of you who like that kind of technical stuff.

For that matter, I guess that you can safely ignore the stuff next to the Tip icons, too — even if the accumulated wisdom, gleaned from long hours slaving over a hot keyboard, can save you much weeping and gnashing of teeth. If you're someone who enjoys trying to do something another way, go ahead and read the tips.

Sometimes, I use made-up examples (along with examples from my own experience) to help you understand how some topic or area of QuickBooks helps you and your business, and I mark these examples with the Case Study icon. This is just my way of continuing the giving. But sure, you can skip them.

What You Should Not Ignore (Unless You're a Masochist)

Don't skip the Warning icons. They're the ones flagged with the picture of the 19th century bomb. They describe some things that you *really* shouldn't do.

Out of respect for you, I don't put advice like "Don't smoke!" next to these icons. I figure that you're an adult, and you can make your own lifestyle decisions. So I reserve the Warning icons for more urgent and immediate dangers — things akin to "Don't smoke while you're filling your car with gasoline."

This icon is a friendly reminder to do something. Not to be too pushy, but it's probably not a good idea to ignore these babies.

Three Foolish Assumptions

I make three assumptions about you:

- ✔ **You have a PC running Microsoft Windows.** (I took pictures of the QuickBooks windows and dialog boxes while using Windows 7, in case you're interested.)

- ✔ **You know a little bit about how to work with your computer.**

- ✔ **You have or will buy a copy of QuickBooks Pro or QuickBooks Premier for each computer on which you want to run the program.**

This book works for QuickBooks 2011, although in a pinch, you can probably also use it for QuickBooks 2010 or 2012. (I have to say, however, that if you have QuickBooks 2010, you may instead want to return this book and trade it in for *QuickBooks 2010 For Dummies* by yours truly.)

By the way, if you haven't already installed QuickBooks and need help, jump to Appendix A, which tells you how to install QuickBooks in ten easy steps. And, if you're just starting out with Microsoft Windows, peruse Chapter 1 of the *Windows User's Guide* or one of these books on your flavor of Windows: *Windows XP For Dummies,* 2nd Edition, *Windows Vista For Dummies,* or *Windows 7 For Dummies*, all by Andy Rathbone.

How This Book 1s Organized

This book is divided into six, mostly coherent parts.

Part 1: Quickly into QuickBooks

Part I covers some upfront tasks that you need to take care of before you can start using QuickBooks. I promise I don't waste your time here. I just want to make sure that you get off on the right foot.

Part II: Daily Entry Tasks

The second part of this book explains how to use QuickBooks for your daily financial record keeping: preparing customer invoices, recording sales, and paying bills — that kind of stuff.

Just so you know, you'll be amazed at how much easier QuickBooks makes your life. QuickBooks is a really cool program.

Part III: Stuff You Do from Time to Time

Part III talks about the kinds of things that you should do at the end of the week, the end of the month, or the end of the year. This part explains, for example, how to print checks, explore QuickBooks online resources, do payroll, and create a business budget.

While I'm on the subject, I also want to categorically deny that Part III contains any secret messages that you can decipher by reading backward. Yllaer.

Part IV: Housekeeping Chores

Part IV talks about some of the maintenance tasks that you need (or someone needs) to perform to keep your accounting system shipshape: account reconciliations, financial report generation, job-costing mechanics, file management — and, oh yes, fixed asset accounting.

Part V: The Part of Tens

Gravity isn't just a good idea; it's a law.

By tradition, the same is true for this part of a *For Dummies* book. The Part of Tens provides a collection of lists: ten things you should do if you own a business, ten things to do when you next visit Acapulco — oops, sorry — wrong book.

Also by tradition, these ten-item lists don't need to have exactly ten items. You know the concept of a baker's dozen, right? You order a dozen dough-nuts but get 13 for the same price. Well, *For Dummies* ten-item lists have *roughly* ten items. (If the Dummies Man — the bug-eyed, pale-faced guy suf-fering from triangle-shape-head syndrome who appears on the back cover of this book and on icons throughout these pages — were running the bakery, a 10-doughnut order might mean that you get anywhere from 8 to 13 dough-nuts.) Do you believe that I'm an accountant? So exacting that it's scary.

Part VI: Appendixes

An unwritten rule says that computer books have appendixes, so I include three. Appendix A tells you how to install QuickBooks in ten easy steps. Appendix B explains small business accounting, provides a short biogra-phy of an Italian monk, and explains double-entry bookkeeping. Appendix C describes how to set up QuickBooks for use by multiple users — and for mul-tiple users on a network. Yikes!

Conventions Used in This Book

To make the best use of your time and energy, you should know about the conventions that I use in this book.

When I want you to type something, such as **With a stupid grin, Martin watched the tall blonde strut into the bar and order grappa**, it's in bold type. When I want you to type something that's short and uncomplicated, such as **Jennifer**, it still appears in boldface type.

Except for passwords, you don't have to worry about the case of the letters you type in QuickBooks. If I tell you to type **Jennifer**, you can type **JENNIFER** or follow poet e. e. cummings' lead and type **jennifer**.

Whenever I tell you to choose a command from a menu, I say something like "Choose Lists⇨Items," which simply means to first choose the Lists menu and then choose Items. The ⇨ separates one part of the command from the next part.

You can choose menus, commands, and dialog box elements with the mouse. Just click the thing you want.

Part I
Quickly into
QuickBooks

The 5th Wave   By Rich Tennant

"You know kids — you can't buy them just <u>any</u>
accounting software."

In this part . . .

All accounting programs — including QuickBooks — make you do a bunch of preliminary stuff. Sure, this is sort of a bummer, but getting depressed about it won't make things go any faster. So if you want to quickly get up and go with QuickBooks, peruse the chapters in this first part. I promise that I get you through this stuff as quickly as possible.

Chapter 1

QuickBooks: The Heart of Your Business

. . . .

In This Chapter

▶ Why you truly need a tool like QuickBooks

▶ What QuickBooks actually does

▶ Why QuickBooks is a popular choice

▶ What you need to do (in general) to get started

▶ How to succeed in setting up and using QuickBooks

. . . .

1 want to start this conversation by quickly covering some basic questions concerning QuickBooks, such as "Why even use QuickBooks?" and "Where and how does a guy or gal start?" — and, most importantly, "What should I not do?"

This little orientation shouldn't take more than a few minutes. Really. And the orientation lets you understand the *really* big picture concerning QuickBooks.

Why QuickBooks?

Okay, I know you know that you need an accounting system. Somebody, maybe your accountant or spouse, has convinced you of this. And you, the team player that you are, have just accepted this conventional viewpoint as the truth.

But just between you and me, why do you *really* need QuickBooks? And what does QuickBooks do that you really, truly need done? And heck, just to be truly cynical, also ask the question "Why QuickBooks?" Why not, for example, use some other accounting software program?

Why you need an accounting system

Start with the most basic question: Why do you even need an accounting system like QuickBooks? It's a fair question, so let me supply you with the two-part answer.

The first reason is that federal law requires your business to maintain an accounting system. More specifically, Section 446 (General Rule for Methods of Accounting) of Title 26 (Internal Revenue Code) of the United States Code requires that you have the ability to compute taxable income by using some sort of common-sense accounting system that clearly reflects income.

If you decide just to blow off this requirement — after all, you got into business so that you could throw off the shackles of bureaucracy — you might get away with your omission. But if the Internal Revenue Service (IRS) examines your return and you ignored Section 446, the IRS gets to do your accounting the way *it* wants. And the IRS way means that you pay more in taxes and that you also pay taxes earlier than you would have otherwise.

Here's the second reason for maintaining an accounting system. I sort of go out on an editorial limb, but I'm going to do it anyway. My strong belief — backed by over 25 years of business experience and close-hand observations of several hundred business clients — is that you can't successfully manage your business without a decent accounting system. Success requires accurately measuring profits or losses and reasonably estimating your financial condition.

This second reason makes sense, right? If your friend Kenneth doesn't know when he's making money, which products or services are profitable, and which customers are worth keeping (and which aren't), does he really have a chance?

I don't think he does.

To summarize, your business must have a decent accounting system, no matter how you feel about accounting and regardless of how time-consuming and expensive such a system is or becomes. The law requires you to have such an accounting system. And successful business management depends on such an accounting system.

What QuickBooks does

Go on to the next question that you and I need to discuss: What does QuickBooks do to help you maintain an accounting system that measures profits and losses and other stuff like that?

QuickBooks truly makes business accounting easy by providing windows that you use to record common business transactions. For example, QuickBooks has a window (you know, a Windows window that appears on your monitor's screen) that looks like a check. To record a check you write, you fill in the blanks of the window with bits of information, such as the date, amount, and person or business you're paying.

QuickBooks also has a handful of other windows that you use in a similar fashion. For example, QuickBooks supplies an invoice window that looks like an invoice you might use to bill a customer or client. You fill in the invoice window's blanks by recording invoice information, such as the name of the client or customer, invoice amount, and date by which you want to be paid.

And here's the neat thing about these check and invoice windows: When you record business transactions by filling in the blanks shown onscreen, you collect the information that QuickBooks needs to prepare the reports that summarize your profits or losses and your financial situation.

For example, if you record two invoices (for $10,000 each) to show amounts that you billed your customers and then you record three checks (for $4,000 each) to record your advertising, rent, and supplies expenses, QuickBooks can (with two or three mouse clicks from you) prepare a report that shows your profit, as shown in Table 1-1.

Table 1-1	A Profit and Loss Report
	Amount
Revenue	$20,000
Advertising	($4,000)
Rent	($4,000)
Supplies	($4,000)
Total Expenses	($12,000)
Profit	$8,000

The parentheses, by the way, indicate negative amounts. That's an accounting thing, but back to the real point of my little narrative.

Your accounting with QuickBooks can be just as simple as I describe in the previous paragraphs. In other words, if you record just a handful of business transactions by using the correct QuickBooks windows, you can begin to prepare reports like the one shown in Table 1-1. Such reports can be used to calculate profits or (ugh) losses for last week, last month, or last year. Such reports can also be used to calculate profits and losses for particular customers and products.

I know I'm kind of harsh in the first part of this chapter — bringing up that stuff about the IRS and business failure — but this accounting stuff is neat! (For the record, that's the only exclamation point I use in this chapter.) Good accounting gives you a way to manage your business for profitability. And obviously, all sorts of good and wonderful things stem from operating your business profitably: a materially comfortable life for you and your employees; financial cushioning to get you through the tough patches; and profits that can be reinvested in your business, in other businesses, and in community charities.

Let me also mention a couple other darn handy things that QuickBooks (and other accounting systems, too) do for you, the overworked business owner or bookkeeper:

- **Forms:** QuickBooks produces, or prints, forms such as checks or invoices by using the information you enter into those check windows and invoice windows that I mention earlier. So that's neat. And a true timesaver. (See Chapter 4.)

- **Electronic banking and billing:** QuickBooks transmits and retrieves some financial transaction information electronically. For example, QuickBooks can e-mail your invoices to customers and clients. (That can save you both time and money.) And QuickBooks can share bank accounting information with most major banks, making it easy to make payments and transfer funds electronically. (See Chapter 13.)

What Explains QuickBooks' Popularity?

No question about it — you need a good accounting system if you're in business. But you know what? That fact doesn't explain why QuickBooks is so popular or why you should use QuickBooks. (I ignore for one moment that you probably already purchased QuickBooks.) Therefore, let me suggest to you three reasons why QuickBooks is an excellent choice to use as the foundation of your accounting system:

- **Ease of use:** QuickBooks historically has been the easiest or one of the easiest accounting software programs to use. Why? The whole just-enter-transaction-information-into-windows-that-resemble-forms thing (which I talk about earlier) makes the data entry a breeze. Most businesspeople already know how to fill in the blanks on these forms. That means that most people — that probably includes you, too — know almost everything they need to know to collect the information that they need to do their books with QuickBooks. Over time, other software programs have tended to become more QuickBooks-like in their ease of use. The folks at Intuit have truly figured out how to make and keep accounting easy.

I should tell you, because I'm an accountant, that the ease-of-use quality of QuickBooks is not all good. Part of the reason why QuickBooks is easy to use is because it doesn't possess all the built-in internal control mechanisms that some more traditional accounting systems have. Those internal control mechanisms, of course, make your financial data more secure, but they also make the accounting software more complicated to use.

✔ **Expense:** QuickBooks, especially compared with the hardcore accounting packages that accountants love, is pretty darn inexpensive. Different versions have different prices, but for a ballpark figure, you can get an excellent accounting software solution for a few hundred bucks. Not to go all grandfatherly on you or anything, but when I was a young CPA, inexpensive accounting software packages often cost several thousand dollars. And it was almost easy to spend tens of thousands of dollars.

✔ **Ubiquity:** The ubiquity issue relates to the ease of use of QuickBooks and the cheap price that Intuit charges for QuickBooks. But oddly enough, the ubiquity of QuickBooks becomes its own benefit, too. For example, you'll find it very easy to find a bookkeeper who knows QuickBooks. And if you can't, you can hire someone who doesn't know QuickBooks and then send them to a QuickBooks class at the local community college (because that class will be easy to find). You'll also find it very easy to find a CPA who knows QuickBooks. Now, you might choose to use some other, very good piece of accounting software. However, almost assuredly, what you'll discover is that it's tougher to find people who know the software, tougher to find classes for the software, tougher to find CPAs who know the software, and even tougher to find books on the software.

What's Next, Dude?

At this point, presumably, you know why you need accounting software and why QuickBooks is probably a reasonable and maybe even an excellent choice. In other words, you swallowed my line about QuickBooks hook, line, and sinker. That decision on your part leaves the question of what you should do next. Let me say this: In a nutshell, before you can begin working with QuickBooks, you need to do the following:

1. Install the QuickBooks software, as I describe in Appendix A.

2. Run through the EasyStep Interview I describe in Chapter 2.

3. Load the master files, as I describe in Chapter 3.

If you're thinking, "Whoa, cowboy, that seems like a bit more work than what's involved in installing spreadsheet software or a new word processor," you're right. You might as well hear from me the ugly truth about accounting software: Accounting software — all of it — requires quite a bit of setup work to get things running smoothly. For example, you need to build a list of expense categories, or accounts, to use for tracking expenses. You also need to set up a list of the customers that you invoice.

Rest assured, however, that none of the setup work is overly complex; it's just time-consuming. Also, know from the very start that QuickBooks provides a tremendous amount of hand-holding to help you step through the setup process. And remember, too, that you have your new friend — that's me — to help you whenever the setup process gets a little gnarly.

How to Succeed with QuickBooks

Before you and I wrap up the little why, what, and how discussion of this chapter, I ought to provide a handful of ideas about how to make your experience with QuickBooks a successful one.

Budget wisely, Grasshopper

Here's my first suggestion: Please plan on spending at least a few hours to get the QuickBooks software installed, set up, and running. I know you don't really want to do that. You have a business to run, a family to take care of, a dog to walk, and so on.

But here's the reality sandwich you probably need to take a big bite of: It takes half an hour just to get the software installed on your computer. (This installation isn't complicated, of course. You'll mostly just sit there, sipping coffee or whatever.)

But after the QuickBooks software is installed, unfortunately, you still have to run through the EasyStep Interview. Again, this work isn't difficult, but it does take time. For example, a very simple service business probably takes at least an hour. If your business owns inventory, or if you're a contractor with some serious job-costing requirements, the process can take several hours.

Therefore, do yourself a favor: Give yourself adequate time for the job at hand.

Don't focus on features

Now let me share another little snidbit about getting going with QuickBooks. At the point that you install the QuickBooks software and start the program, you'll be in shock about the number of commands, whistles, bells, and buttons that the QuickBooks window provides. But you know what? You can't focus on the QuickBooks features.

Your job is simply to figure out how to record a handful — probably a small handful — of transactions with QuickBooks. Therefore, what you want to do is focus on the transactions that need to be recorded for you to keep your books.

Say you're a one-person consulting business. In that case, you might need to figure out how to record only the following three transactions:

- Invoices
- Payments from customers (because you invoiced them)
- Payments to vendors (because they sent you bills)

So all you need to do is discover how to record invoices (see Chapter 4), record customer payments (see Chapter 5), and record checks (see Chapter 6). You don't need to worry about much else except maybe how to print reports, but that's easy. (See Chapter 15 for the click-by-click.)

"Oh, Steve," you're saying, "you just intentionally picked an easy business. I'm a retailer with a much more complicated situation."

Okay, well, you're right that I picked an easy business for my first example, but I stand by the same advice for retailers. If you're a retailer, you probably need to figure out how to record only four transactions. Here they are:

- Sales receipts
- Bills from your suppliers
- Payments to your vendors
- Employee payroll checks

In this example, then, all you need to do is find out how to record sales receipts — probably a separate sales receipt for each bank deposit you make (see Chapter 5) — how to record bills from vendors and how to record checks to pay your bills (see Chapter 6), and handle employee payroll (see Chapter 11).

I don't want to be cranky or careless here, but one truly good trick for getting up-to-speed with QuickBooks is to focus on the transactions that you need to record. If you identify those transactions and then figure out how to record them, you've done the hard part. Really.

Outsource payroll

Here's another suggestion for you: Go ahead and outsource your payroll. That'll probably cost you between $1,000 and $2,000 per year. I know, that's roughly the total cost of four discount tickets to Hawaii, but outsourcing payroll delivers three big benefits, even after considering the stiff price:

- ✔ **Simplicity:** Payroll is one of the most complicated areas in small business accounting and in QuickBooks. Accordingly, you'll greatly simplify your bookkeeping by moving this headache off your desk and onto the desk of your accountant (he or she may love doing your payroll) or the payroll service. (You can use a national firm, such as ADP or Paychex, or a local firm.)

- ✔ **Penalties:** Did I mention that payroll is one of the most complicated areas in small business accounting and in QuickBooks? I did? Good, because you truly need to know that payroll preparation and accounting mistakes are easy to make. And payroll mistakes often subject you to seriously annoying fines and penalties from the IRS and from state revenue and employment agencies. I grant you that paying $1,500 per year for payroll processing seems like it's way too much money, but you need to prevent only a couple of painful fines or penalties per year to drastically cut the costs of using an outside payroll service.

- ✔ **Mrs. Peabody's annual raise:** One final reason for outsourcing payroll also exists. Let me explain. You don't want to do payroll yourself. Really, you don't. As a result, you'll eventually assign the task to that nice woman who works in your office, Mrs. Peabody. Here's what will happen when you do that: Late one afternoon during the week following Mrs. Peabody's first payroll, she'll ask to meet with you — to talk about why Mrs. Raleigh makes $15,000 more per year than she (Mrs. Peabody) does, and also to ask why she (Mrs. Peabody) makes only $2 per hour more than Wayne, the idiot who works in the warehouse. Because you're a nice person, Mrs. Peabody will leave a few minutes later with a $1.50-per-hour raise. And at that point, you'll remember, vaguely, my earlier caution about the problem of saving maybe $2,000 per year in payroll service fees but then having to give Mrs. Peabody an extra $3,000 raise. Ouch.

Get professional help

A quick point: You can probably get a CPA to sit down with you for an hour or so and show you how to enter a handful of transactions in QuickBooks. In other words, for a cost that's probably somewhere between $100 and $200, you can have somebody hold your hand for the first three invoices you create, the first two bills you record, the first four checks you write, and so on.

You should try to do this if you can. You'll save yourself untold hours of headache by having someone who knows what she or he is doing provide an itty-bit of personalized training.

Use both the profit and loss statement and the balance sheet

And now, my final point: You truly want to use your *profit and loss statement* (which measures your profits) and your *balance sheet* (which lists your assets, liabilities, and owner's equity) as part of managing your business. In other words, get used to producing a QuickBooks profit and loss statement each week, or month, or whatever. Then use that statement to determine your profitability. In a similar fashion, regularly produce a balance sheet to check your cash balances, the amounts customers or clients owe, and so on.

Maybe this advice seems obvious, but there's a semihidden reason for my suggestion: If you or you and the bookkeeper do the accounting correctly, both the QuickBooks profit and loss statement and the balance sheet will show numbers that make sense. In other words, the cash balance number on the balance sheet — remember that a balance sheet lists your assets, including cash — will resemble what the bank says you hold in cash. If the QuickBooks balance sheet says instead that you're holding $34 million in cash, well, you'll know something is rotten in Denmark.

Chapter 2

Answering Mr. Wizard

In This Chapter

▶ Getting ready to do the big interview

▶ Not getting discouraged about the big interview

▶ Surviving the big interview

I know that you're eager to get started. After all, you have a business to run. But before you can start using QuickBooks, you need to do some upfront work. Specifically, you need to prepare for the QuickBooks EasyStep Interview and then you need to walk through the EasyStep Interview. (The *EasyStep Interview* is just a thorough question-and-answer session that QuickBooks uses to set itself up for you.) In this chapter, I describe how you do all this stuff.

I assume that you know how Windows works. If you don't, take the time to read Chapter 1 of your Windows user's guide or try the appropriate edition of *Windows For Dummies,* by Andy Rathbone.

Getting Ready for the Big Interview

You need to complete three tasks to get ready for the EasyStep Interview:

✔ Make an important decision about your *conversion date* (the date you convert from your old accounting system to QuickBooks).

✔ Prepare a trial balance as of the conversion date.

✔ Go on a scavenger hunt to collect a bunch of stuff that you'll need or find handy for the interview.

The big decision

Before you fiddle with your computer or the QuickBooks software, you need to choose the date — the so-called *conversion date* — on which you want to begin using QuickBooks for your financial record keeping.

This decision is hugely important because the conversion date that you choose dramatically affects both the work you have to do to get QuickBooks running smoothly and the initial usefulness of the financial information that you collect and record by using QuickBooks.

You have three basic choices:

- ✔ **The right way:** You can convert at the beginning of your accounting year (which is, in most cases, the same as the beginning of the calendar year). This way is the right way for two reasons. First, converting at the beginning of the year requires the least amount of work from you. Second, it means that you have all the current year's financial information in one system.

- ✔ **The slightly awkward way:** You can convert at the beginning of some interim accounting period (probably the beginning of some month or quarter). This approach works, but it's slightly awkward because you have to plug your year-to-date income and expenses numbers from the old system into the new system. (If you don't know what an interim accounting period is, see Appendix B.)

- ✔ **The my-way-or-the-highway way:** You can convert at some time other than what I call the right way and the slightly awkward way. Specifically, you can choose to convert whenever you jolly well feel like it. You create a bunch of unnecessary work for yourself if you take this approach, and you pull out a bunch of your hair in the process. But you also have the satisfaction of knowing that through it all, you did it your way — without any help from me.

I recommend choosing the right way. What this choice means is that if it's late in the year — say, October — you just wait until January 1 of the next year to convert. If it's still early in the year, you can also retroactively convert as of the beginning of the year. (If you do this, you need to go back and do your financial record keeping for the first part of the current year by using QuickBooks: entering sales, recording purchases, and so on.)

If it's sometime in the middle of the year — say, Memorial Day or later — you probably want to use the slightly awkward way. (I'm actually going to use the slightly awkward way in this chapter because if you see how to convert to QuickBooks by using the slightly awkward way, you know how to use both the right way and the slightly awkward way.)

The trial balance of the century

After you decide when you want to convert, you need a trial balance.

"Yikes," you say. "What's a trial balance?" A *trial balance* simply lists all your assets, liabilities, and owner's equity account balances as well as the year-to-date income and expense numbers on a specified date (which, not coincidentally, happens to be the conversion date). You need this data for the EasyStep Interview and for some fiddling around that you need to do after you complete the EasyStep Interview.

Creating a trial balance doesn't have to be as hard as it sounds. If you've been using another small business accounting system, such as the simpler Quicken product from Intuit or the Simply Accounting program from Computer Associates, you may be able to have your old system produce a trial balance on the conversion date. In that case, you can get the balances from your old system. (Consider yourself lucky if this is the case.)

Just to split hairs, the trial balance should show account balances at the very start of the first day that you'll begin using QuickBooks for actual accounting. For example, if the conversion date is 1/1/2011, the trial balance needs to show the account balances at one minute past midnight on 1/1/2011. This is also the very same thing as showing the account balances at the very end of the last day that you'll be using the old accounting system — in other words, at exactly midnight on 12/31/2010 if you're converting to QuickBooks on 1/1/2011.

If your old system is rather informal (perhaps it's a shoebox full of receipts), or if it tracks only cash (perhaps you've been using Quicken), you need to do a bit more work:

✔ **To get your cash balance:** Reconcile your bank account or bank accounts (if you have more than one bank account) as of the conversion date.

✔ **To get your accounts receivable balance:** Tally the total of all your unpaid customer invoices.

✔ **To get your other asset account balances:** Know what each asset originally costs. For depreciable fixed assets, you also need to provide any accumulated depreciation that has been claimed for that asset. (*Accumulated depreciation* is the total depreciation that you've already expensed for each asset.)

By the way, check out Appendix B if you have questions about accounting or accounting terminology, such as *depreciation*.

✔ **To get your liability account balances:** Know how much you owe on each liability. If you trust your *creditors* — the people to whom you owe the money — you may also be able to get this information from their statements.

You don't need to worry about the owner's equity accounts. QuickBooks can calculate your owner's equity account balances for you, based on the difference between your total assets and your total liabilities. This method is a bit sloppy, and accountants may not like it, but it's a pretty good compromise. (If you do have detailed account balances for your owner's equity accounts, use these figures — and know that you're one in a million.)

If you're using the slightly awkward way to convert to QuickBooks — in other words, if your conversion date is some date other than the beginning of the accounting year — you also need to provide year-to-date income and expense balances. To get your income, cost of goods sold, expenses, other income, and other expense account balances, you need to calculate the year-to-date amount of each account. If you can get this information from your old system, that's super. If not, you need to get it manually. (If you suddenly have images of yourself sitting at your desk late at night, tapping away on a ten-key, you're probably right. What's more, you probably also need to allocate half of another Saturday to getting QuickBooks up and running.)

Just for fun, I created the sample trial balance shown in Table 2-1. This table shows you what a trial balance looks like if you convert at some time other than at the beginning of the accounting year.

Table 2-1   A "Slightly Awkward Way" Sample Trial Balance

Trial Balance Information	*Debit*	*Credit*
Assets		
Checking	$5,000	
Fixed assets	$60,000	
Accumulated depreciation (fixed assets)		$2,000
Liabilities information		
Loan payable		$10,000
Owner's equity and income statement information		
Opening bal equity		$20,000
Sales		$60,000
Cost of goods sold	$20,000	
Supplies expense	$2,100	
Rent expense	$4,900	
Totals	**$92,000**	**$92,000**

About those debits and credits

Don't get freaked out about those debits and credits. You just need to keep them straight for a few minutes. Here's the scoop: For assets and expenses, a *debit balance* is the same thing as a positive balance. So, a cash debit balance of $5,000 means that you have $5,000 in your account, and $20,000 of cost of goods sold means that you incurred $20,000 of costs-of-goods expense. For assets and expenses, a *credit balance* is the same thing as a negative balance. So if you have a cash balance of –$5,000, your account is overdrawn by $5,000. In the sample trial balance shown in Table 2-1, the accumulated depreciation shows a credit balance of $2,000, which is, in effect, a negative account balance.

For liabilities, owner's equity accounts, and income accounts, things are flip-flopped. A credit balance is the same thing as a positive balance. So an accounts payable credit balance of $2,000 means that you owe your creditors $2,000. A bank loan credit balance of $10,000 means that you owe the bank $10,000. And a sales account credit balance of $60,000 means that you've enjoyed $60,000 worth of sales.

I know that I keep saying this, but do remember that those income and expense account balances are year-to-date figures. They exist *only* if the conversion date is after the start of the financial year.

If you're converting at the very beginning of the accounting year, your trial balance instead looks like the one shown in Table 2-2. Notice that this trial balance doesn't have any year-to-date income or expense balances.

Table 2-2 A "Right Way" Sample Trial Balance		
Trial Balance Information	*Debit*	*Credit*
Assets		
Checking	$5,000	
Fixed assets	$60,000	
Accumulated depreciation (fixed assets)		$2,000
Liabilities information		
Loan payable		$10,000
Owner's equity and income statement information		
Opening bal equity		$53,000
Totals	$65,000	$65,000

The mother of all scavenger hunts

Even after you decide when you want to convert to QuickBooks and you come up with a trial balance, you still need to collect a bunch of additional information. I list these items in laundry-list fashion. What you want to do is find all this stuff and then pile it up (neatly) in a big stack next to the computer:

- ✔ **Last year's federal tax return:** QuickBooks asks which federal income tax form you use to file your tax return and also about your taxpayer identification number. Last year's federal tax return is the easiest place to find this stuff.

- ✔ **Copies of all your most recent state and federal payroll tax returns:** If you prepare payroll for employees, QuickBooks wants to know about the federal and state payroll tax rates that you pay, as well as some other stuff.

- ✔ **Copies of all the unpaid invoices that your customers (or clients or patients or whatever) owe you as of the conversion date:** I guess this is probably obvious, but the total accounts receivable balance shown on your trial balance needs to match the total of the unpaid customer invoices.

- ✔ **Copies of all unpaid bills that you owe your vendors as of the conversion date:** Again, this is probably obvious, but the total accounts payable balance shown on your trial balance needs to match the total of the unpaid vendor bills.

- ✔ **A detailed listing of any inventory items you're holding for resale:** This list should include not only inventory item descriptions and quantities but also the initial purchase prices and the anticipated sales prices. In other words, if you sell porcelain wombats and you have 1,200 of these beauties in inventory, you need to know exactly what you paid for them.

- ✔ **Copies of the prior year's W-2 statements, W-4 statements for anybody you've hired since the beginning of the prior year, detailed information about any payroll tax liabilities you owe as of the conversion date, and detailed information about the payroll tax deposits you've made since the beginning of the year:** You need the information shown on these forms to adequately and accurately set up the QuickBooks payroll feature. I don't want to scare you, but this is probably the most tedious part of setting up QuickBooks.

- ✔ **If you're retroactively converting as of the beginning of the year, you need a list of all the transactions that have occurred since the beginning of the year: sales, purchases, payroll transactions, and everything and anything else:** If you do the right-way conversion retroactively, you need to re-enter each of these transactions into the new system. You actually enter the information after you complete the EasyStep Interview that I describe later in this chapter, but you might as well get all this information together now, while you're searching for the rest of the items for this scavenger hunt.

If you take the slightly awkward way, you don't need to find the last item that I describe in the preceding list. You can just use the year-to-date income and expense numbers from the trial balance.

Doing the EasyStep Interview

After you decide when you want to convert, prepare a trial balance as of the conversion date, and collect the additional raw data that you need, you're ready to step through the EasyStep Interview.

Before you begin the interview, you have to start QuickBooks 2011. To do so, click the Windows Start button and then click the menu choice that leads to QuickBooks. (For example, I choose Start➪All Programs➪QuickBooks➪ QuickBooks Premier Edition 2011.) Or double-click the QuickBooks program icon if you put one on the desktop during the installation.

QuickBooks comes in several flavors. The most common flavors are QuickBooks Simple Start, QuickBooks Pro, and QuickBooks Premier. These three programs differ in several significant ways: QuickBooks Simple Start is a special "light" version of QuickBooks, which looks completely different. (I wrote another book, *QuickBooks Simple Start For Dummies*, which you should use instead of this book if you're working with QuickBooks Simple Start.) QuickBooks Pro includes the advanced job costing and time-estimating features, which I briefly describe in Chapter 16; it also includes the capability to share a QuickBooks file over a network, as I describe in Appendix C. QuickBooks Premier has features beyond the QuickBooks Pro features for accountants and auditors who want to use QuickBooks for rather large small businesses.

I actually used another very special version of QuickBooks called QuickBooks Premier Accountants Edition to write this book. The Premier Accountants Edition of QuickBooks pretends to be another version of the QuickBooks software, and I told QuickBooks Accountants Edition to pretend to be QuickBooks Premier for writing this book. I mention all this not to confuse you but so that you understand why the figures you see here may look a wee bit different from what you see onscreen. Other than minor cosmetic differences, though, the various versions of QuickBooks all work the same way. You can use this book for any of these program versions.

If this is the first time you started QuickBooks, QuickBooks displays a dialog box that explains how QuickBooks wants to use your Internet connection (answer: so it can regularly update the QuickBooks software). QuickBooks then displays a welcome message box that asks you how you want to start. For example, you can click a button to indicate that you want to see an overview tutorial, explore QuickBooks, create a new company file, or open an existing company data file.

What I suggest you do, however, is jump right into the fray. If you've never used QuickBooks before — the likely case if you started reading here — click the Create a New Company File button, which starts the EasyStep Interview. (If you've already been using an earlier version of QuickBooks, click the Open an Existing Company File button.)

The real fun begins at this point. The EasyStep Interview starts automatically, displaying the dialog box shown in Figure 2-1.

If you aren't starting QuickBooks for the first time but you want to step through the EasyStep Interview to set up a new company anyway, choose File⇨New Company.

To begin the interview, click the Start Interview button.

I should mention that the first EasyStep Interview dialog box identifies some other setup options you can use to get started. For example, the screen suggests that you might want to upgrade from Quicken. (Basically, that upgrade just means that you want QuickBooks to try using Quicken data as a starting point for QuickBooks — something that doesn't work, in my experience.) A simple bit of advice: Don't try to "upgrade" the Quicken data. It's just as easy and usually considerably cleaner to just start from scratch.

The one group of new QuickBooks users who should probably try upgrading their Quicken data are people who've done a really good job of keeping their books with Quicken, including complete balance sheet information. No offense, but you probably aren't in this category. Sorry.

Figure 2-1:
The
EasyStep
Interview
dialog box.

You can also, if you're an accounting expert, just skip the EasyStep Interview. But you don't need to worry about that option either. You're going to want to take the setup process slow and easy.

Tip 1: Get to know the interview protocol

For the most part, to complete the EasyStep Interview, all you do is fill in text boxes with the information that QuickBooks requests (see Figure 2-2) or answer questions by clicking buttons clearly marked Yes and No. When you finish answering a page of interview questions, click the Next button to move to the following page of the interview.

If you ever decide that you want to change some piece of information that you entered on a previous page of the EasyStep Interview dialog box, you can just click the Back button to back up. If you get partway through the interview process and decide that it isn't worth the time, just click the Leave button in the lower-left corner, and QuickBooks closes the EasyStep Interview dialog box. When you next restart QuickBooks, the EasyStep Interview begins again.

Here are two other notes to keep in mind:

- ✔ The EasyStep Interview dialog box appears every time you start a new company (which you do by choosing File⇨New Company).

- ✔ QuickBooks purposely makes it difficult to delete a company that you create in QuickBooks, so don't make up an imaginary company to play with unless you're familiar enough with your operating system to delete files.

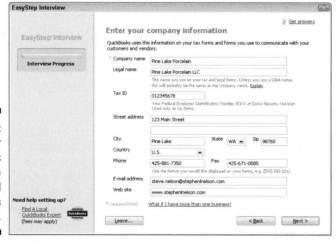

Figure 2-2: Enter your company's trade name and legal name in this dialog box.

At some point after QuickBooks starts, you see a message box that asks whether you want to register QuickBooks. If you don't register, you can use the product roughly a few times, and then — whammo! The program locks up, and you can no longer access your files. Either you register it, or you can't use it. I don't like being forced to do something, but getting worked up about having to register QuickBooks is a waste of time. The simplest option is to just register. Here's how: When QuickBooks displays the message box that asks whether you want to register, click the Online button to register online, or click the Phone button to register over the phone. If you go with the Phone option, QuickBooks displays another dialog box that gives you a telephone number to call and provides a space for you to enter your registration number.

I don't provide you a blow-by-blow account of what happens when you take the interview. Instead, I provide a handful of key tips that you can read now and use later (during the interview) to make the process as easy and as fast as possible.

Tip 2: Take your time

As you step through the interview process, the EasyStep Interview dialog box displays a bunch of different pages with suggestions, instructions, and advice. Take the time to read this information. Click the Help button if you have questions. If the EasyStep Interview suggests that you view some related document with helpful information, do so.

Tip 3: Get industry-specific advice

Industry-specific advice is one of the handiest QuickBooks features. For example, are you a rancher or a farmer? QuickBooks includes a detailed online document that describes some of the unique accounting challenges that your business faces, provides tips for making your record keeping easier, and points out QuickBooks features that might be of particular interest to someone like you. Are you a retailer? A manufacturer? A writer? A consultant? You can get this same sort of information, too.

QuickBooks displays industry-specific tips and tidbits of information throughout the interview. Keep your eyes peeled for the green arrows that mark these little hints. Let me mention one other quick pointer about this industry-specific information stuff: You may not understand everything that you read. That's okay. You still want to read the tips and maybe jot them down on a piece of paper as you go along. As you work with QuickBooks and find out more about it, you'll find that more and more of the information provided in the industry-specific tips makes sense.

To view a document of industry-specific information at any time, click the Support link on the Navigation bar and then click the Industry-Specific Information hyperlink. Click the List of Industries hyperlink and then select your industry from the list in the Help window that QuickBooks displays. To print a copy of the information, click the Options button and choose Print Topic from the drop-down list.

Some of the hyperlinks lead to resources at the `www.quickbooks.com` Web site, so QuickBooks may prompt you to make an Internet connection to access that information.

Tip 4: Accept the suggested filename and location

A few minutes into the EasyStep Interview, QuickBooks asks you whether you want to change its suggested name and location for the file that it uses to store your accounting information (see Figure 2-3). The suggested filename is normally your company name, anyway. I can think of no good reason why you need to fiddle with or change the suggested filename or location. Don't do it. Let QuickBooks name the file whatever it wants and let QuickBooks store the file wherever it wants.

Figure 2-3:
The Filename for New Company dialog box lets you change the suggested filename and location, but I don't recommend doing so.

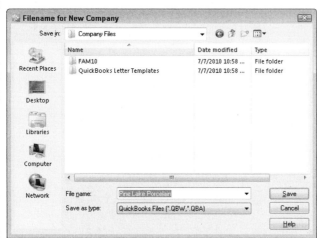

Tip 5: Go with the suggested Chart of Accounts

Immediately after you name the file that QuickBooks uses for storing your financial information, the EasyStep Interview displays a dialog box that shows a list of accounts that QuickBooks wants to use for tracking your business's financial condition. This dialog box also asks whether the list of accounts is the one that you want to use. Unless you know quite a bit about accounting and are willing to find out just as much about QuickBooks, I recommend that you accept the suggested Chart of Accounts. You make your future record keeping much easier by doing so.

Tip 6: Consider tracking all your expenses with your checkbook

You get two choices regarding how to record your expenses:

- ✔ By using just your checkbook
- ✔ By creating a bills-to-pay list

QuickBooks asks this question in the dialog box shown in Figure 2-4. I want to be careful about what I say next because the decision you make in this dialog box can really screw up your business. Here's my suggestion: Consider taking the second option — the one that says you don't want to keep track of the bills you owe.

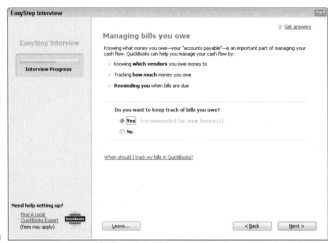

Figure 2-4: Simplify your bill paying by choosing not to track bills you owe.

Now, before you rush off to the next EasyStep Interview question, confident and happy in my suggestion, let me tell you about the implicit trade-off that you're making. If you select the no-tracking-of-bills-owed option, you do simplify your record keeping — which is why I suggest that you take this route. The predictable catch is that you can't track your unpaid bills as closely. Until you sit down to actually write checks for your bills, you don't really know (precisely) how much money you owe vendors. What's more, you can't separate the actual incurring of some expense from the cash outflow that pays the expense. So by taking the no-tracking-of-bills-owed option, you can't finely tune accrual-basis accounting (unless you pay bills when you incur them). And you can't closely monitor the money that you owe vendors.

In my business, I don't track bills I owe, and that simplifies my record keeping. My business is probably a little unusual (at least for a small business) for a couple reasons. First, almost all my expenses get negotiated upfront and then get fixed by contract. For this reason, I don't use and don't need to use QuickBooks to keep track of and remind me about my unpaid bills. In effect, the negotiations and contracts do that. Second, I've actually been in business for quite a while — 25 years, in fact. I don't have the cash-flow problems that many (most?) small businesses have, which means that if I want to produce an accurate profit and loss statement or an accurate balance sheet — one that includes all my expenses — I can just pay all my unpaid bills.

I guess the bottom line here is this: If you don't need to use QuickBooks to closely monitor your unpaid bills, and if you don't mind losing profit-calculation precision because of the lag between the time you incur an expense and the time you pay the bill by writing a check, go ahead and skip the bill tracking. This choice greatly simplifies one area of your record keeping.

Tip 7: Add accounts you need

As you step through the interview questions, QuickBooks asks a few times whether you want to add an account (see Figure 2-5). Go ahead and do this — and feel comfortable doing so. Adding accounts isn't hard. (You need an account for each individual asset, liability, income, or expense amount that you want to track.)

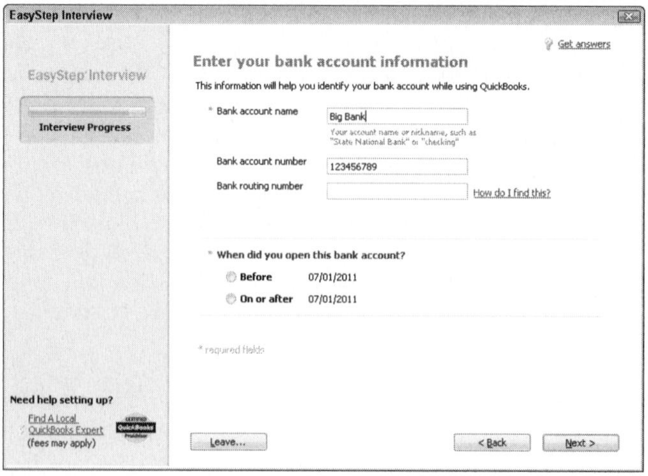

Figure 2-5:
During the
EasyStep
Interview,
QuickBooks
asks
whether
you want to
add bank
accounts.

The Rest of the Story

Throughout the preceding sections in this chapter, I describe how you pre-pare for and then step through the EasyStep Interview. When the EasyStep Interview is over, though, you need to take care of three other little jobs:

✔ You need to describe in detail your inventory, your customer receiv-ables, and (if you chose to ignore my earlier suggestion about not track-ing vendor bills you owe) your vendor payables.

✔ You need to describe your current business finances, including any year-to-date revenue and year-to-date expenses that aren't recorded as part of getting your customer receivables and vendor payables entered into QuickBooks.

✔ If you want to use accrual-basis accounting, you need to make an adjustment.

These chores aren't time-consuming, but they are the three most compli-cated tasks that you need to do to set up QuickBooks. (If you aren't sure what the big deal is about accrual-basis accounting, I respectfully suggest that you take a break here and read Appendix B.)

To set up the inventory records, you just identify the items you hold in inven-tory, as described in Chapter 3.

To set up your customer receivables and (if necessary) vendor payables, you first need to identify the customers and vendors, as described in Chapter 3. After that work, you may need to enter customer invoices that were prepared prior to the conversion date but that are still uncollected at conversion, as described in Chapter 4. Similarly, you may need to enter vendor payables that were incurred prior to the conversion date but that are still unpaid at conversion.

I talk about this stuff more in Chapter 3, so if you're still okay with doing some more installation and setup work, go ahead and flip there. However . . .

Should You Get Your Accountant's Help?

So should you get help from your accountant? Oh, shoot, I don't know. If you follow my directions carefully (both in this chapter and the next), and your business financial affairs aren't wildly complex, I think you can probably figure out all this stuff on your own.

Having said that, however, I suggest that you at least think about getting your accountant's help at this juncture. Your accountant can do a much better job of giving you advice that may be specific to your situation. In many cases, your accountant can give you beginning trial balance amounts that agree with your tax returns. The accountant probably knows your business and can keep you from making a terrible mess of things, just in case you don't follow my directions carefully.

Just so you know: One of the things that I (as a CPA) do for my clients is help them set up QuickBooks. Because I do this, I can give you a couple pieces of useful information about getting a CPA's help in setting up. First, your CPA (assuming that he or she already knows QuickBooks) should be able to help you through the setup process in an hour or two, so your CPA can do it (or help you do it) much faster than you can on your own. Second, an hour or so of tutoring from your CPA should mean that you get enough help to record all your usual transactions. With just this help, you can find out how to pay your bills, how to invoice customers exactly the way you want, and how to produce reports. I used to pooh-pooh this kind of hand-holding, but the older (and hopefully wiser) I get, the more I see that business owners and book-keepers benefit from this upfront help. A bit of planning and expert advice in the beginning can save you a whole lot of trouble later.

Chapter 3

Populating QuickBooks Lists

*T*he EasyStep Interview (which I discuss at some length in Chapter 2) doesn't actually get QuickBooks completely ready to use. You also need to enter the names of all your products, employees, customers, and vendors (and a handful of other items) into lists. In this chapter, I describe how you create and work with these lists. I also describe how you clean up some of the accounting messiness created when you enter information into these lists.

The Magic and Mystery of Items

The first QuickBooks list you need to set up is the *Item list* — the list of stuff you buy and sell. Before you start adding to your Item list, however, I need to tell you that QuickBooks isn't very smart about its view of what you buy and sell. It thinks that anything you stick on a sales invoice or a purchase order is something you're selling.

If you sell colorful coffee mugs, for example, you probably figure (and correctly so) that you need to add descriptions of each of these items to the Item list. However, if you add freight charges to an invoice, QuickBooks thinks that you're adding another mug. And if you add sales tax to an invoice, well, guess what? QuickBooks again thinks that you're adding another mug.

This wacky definition of items is confusing at first. But just remember one thing, and you'll be okay: You aren't the one who's stupid; QuickBooks is. No,

I'm not saying that QuickBooks is a bad program. It's a wonderful accounting program and a great tool. What I'm saying is that QuickBooks is only a dumb computer program; it isn't an artificial-intelligence program. It doesn't pick up on the little subtleties of business — such as the fact that even though you charge customers for freight, you aren't really in the shipping business.

Each entry on the invoice or purchase order — the mugs that you sell, the subtotal, the discount, the freight charges, and the sales tax — is an *item.* Yes, I know this setup is weird, but getting used to the wackiness now makes the discussions that follow much easier to understand.

If you want to see a sample invoice, take a peek at Figure 3-1. Just so you're not confused, to make more room for the invoice window, I removed the QuickBooks Navigation bar that typically appears along the left edge of the QuickBooks window.

Do you see those first three items: Rainbow Mugs, Yellow Mugs, and Red Mugs? You can see the sense of calling them *items,* right? These mugs are things that you sell.

But then suppose that you give frequent buyers of your merchandise a 10 percent discount. To include this discount in your accounting, you need to add a Subtotal item to tally the sale and then a Discount item to calculate the discount. Figure 3-1 also shows this. See it? Kind of weird, eh?

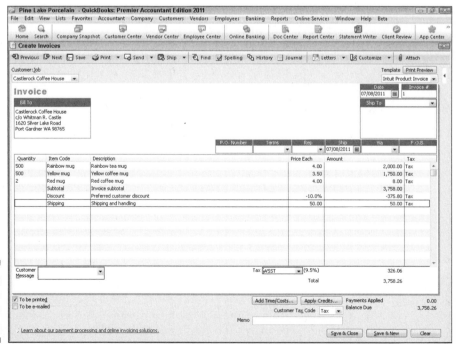

Figure 3-1:
A sample QuickBooks invoice.

Then look at the Shipping and Handling item, which charges the customer $50 for freight. Yep, that's right — another item. In sum, everything that appears on an invoice or a purchase order is an item that you need to describe in your Item list.

Just above the invoice total, if you look closely, you can see another item for including sales tax on your invoices — and that's really an item, too.

I describe creating invoices in Chapter 4 and creating purchase orders in Chapter 7.

Adding items you might include on invoices

To add invoice or purchase-order items to the Item list, follow these steps:

1. **Choose Lists⇨Item List.**

   QuickBooks, with restrained but obvious enthusiasm, displays the Item List window, as shown in Figure 3-2.

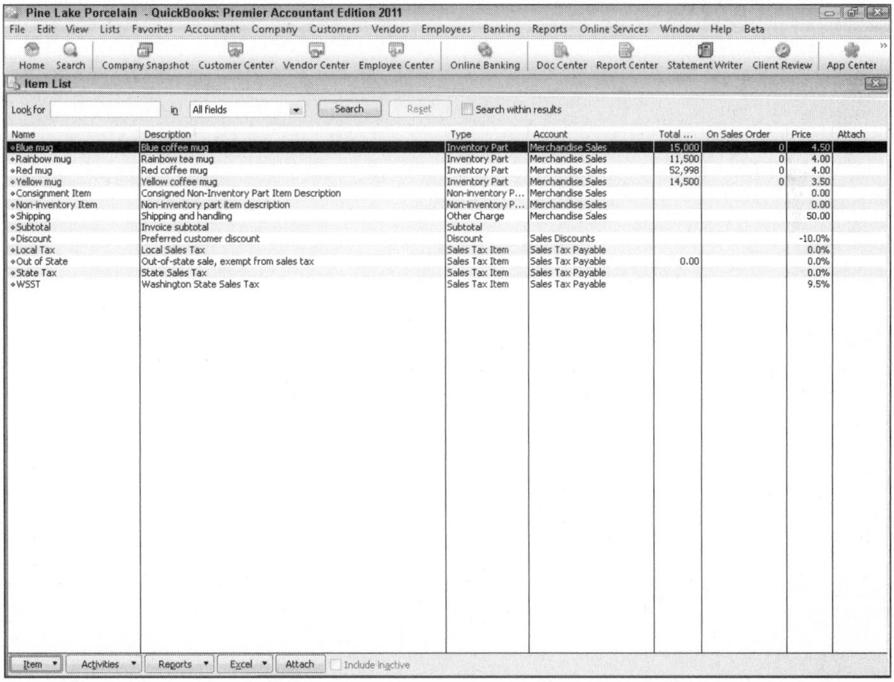

Figure 3-2: The QuickBooks Item List window.

2. **Click the Item button at the bottom of the Item List window and then choose New from the drop-down list.**

   QuickBooks displays the New Item window, as shown in Figure 3-3.

3. **Categorize the item.**

   Select an item type from the Type drop-down list. The Item list that you see is dependent on the type of business you told QuickBooks you were in when you set up the program, so use the following as a sample — the amount and type of items that you need depend on the business you're in. Select one of the following item types by clicking the name in the list:

   • *Service:* Select this type if you charge for a service — such as an hour of labor or a repair job.

   • *Inventory Part:* Select this type if what you sell is something that you buy from someone else, and you want to track your holdings of the item. If you sell thingamajigs that you purchase from the manufacturer Thingamajigs Amalgamated, for example, you specify the item type as Inventory Part. (For more information on using QuickBooks to track inventory, see Chapter 7.)

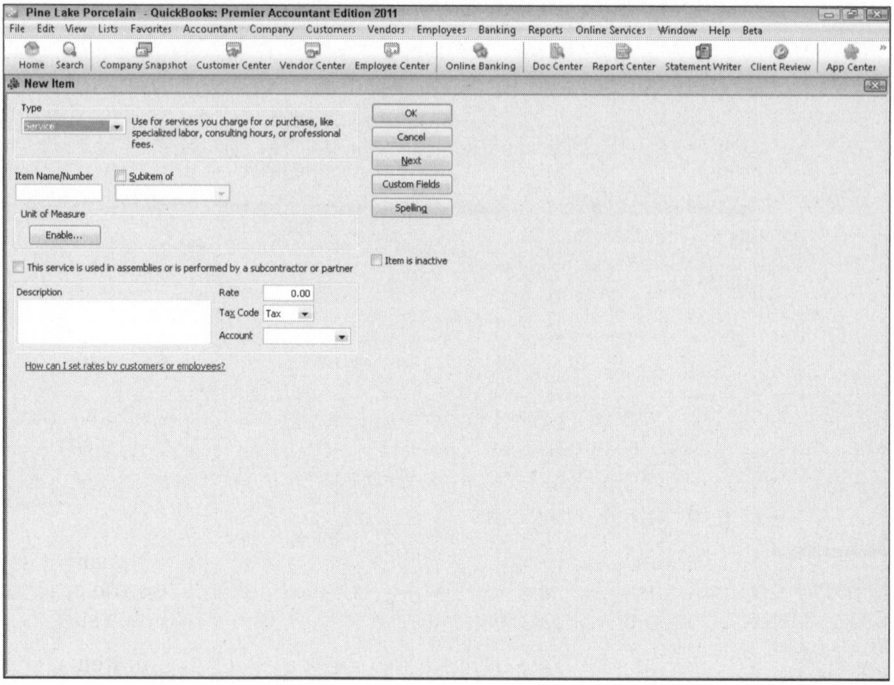

Figure 3-3: The QuickBooks New Item window.

- *Inventory Assembly:* Select this type if what you sell is something that you make from other Inventory items. In other words, if you buy raw materials or other components and then assemble these things to create your finished product, the finished product is an Inventory Assembly item.

- *Non-Inventory Part:* Select this type if what you sell is something that you don't want to track as inventory. (You usually don't use this item type for products that you sell, by the way. Instead, you use it for items that you buy for the business and need to include on purchase orders.)

- *Other Charge:* Select this item type for things such as freight and handling charges that you include on invoices.

- *Subtotal:* This item type adds everything before you subtract any discount, add the sales tax, and so on.

- *Group:* Use this item type to enter a bunch of items (which are already on the list) at one time. This item is a nice timesaver. For example, if you commonly sell sets of items, you don't have to specify those items individually every time you write an invoice.

- *Discount:* This item type calculates an amount to be subtracted from a subtotal.

- *Payment:* This option is wacky, but if your invoice sometimes includes an entry that reduces the invoice total — customer deposits at the time of sale, for example — select this item type. If this item type confuses you, just ignore it.

- *Sales Tax Item:* Select this item type for the sales tax that you include on the invoice.

- *Sales Tax Group:* This item type is similar to the Group item type, but you use it only for sales taxes that are collected in one transaction and owed to multiple agencies.

4. Type an item number or name.

Press the Tab key or use your mouse to click the Item Name/Number text box below the Type drop-down list. Then type a short description of the item.

5. (Optional) Make the item a subitem.

If you want to work with *subitems* — items that appear within other items — select the Subitem Of check box and use the corresponding drop-down list to specify the parent item to which a subitem belongs.

If you set up a parent item for coffee mugs and subitems for red, yellow, and rainbow mugs, for example, you can produce reports that show parent items (such as mugs) and subitems (such as the differently colored mugs). Subitems are just an extra complexity, so if you're new to this QuickBooks stuff, I suggest that you keep things simple by avoiding them.

6. **Describe the item in more detail.**

   Move the cursor to the Description text box and type a description. This description then appears on the invoice. Note that if you specified the item type as Inventory Part in Step 3, you see two description text boxes: Description on Purchase Transactions and Description on Sales Transactions. The purchase description appears on purchase orders, and the sales description appears on sales invoices.

7. **If the item type is Service, Non-Inventory Part, or Other Charge, tell QuickBooks how much to charge for the item, whether the item is subject to sales tax, and which income account to use for tracking the income that you receive from selling the item.**

   • *For a Service type,* use the Rate text box to specify the price you charge for one unit of the service. If you charge by the hour, for example, the rate is the charge for an hour of service. If you charge for a job — such as a repair job or the completion of a specific task — the rate is the charge for the job or task.

   • *For a Non-Inventory Part type,* use the Price text box to specify the amount you charge for the item.

   • *For an Other Charge type,* use the Amount or % text box, which replaces the Rate text box, to specify the amount you charge for the item. You can type an amount, such as **20** for $20.00, or you can type a percentage. If you type a percentage, QuickBooks calculates the Other Charge Amount as the percentage multiplied by the preceding item shown on the invoice. (You usually put in an Other Charge after using a Subtotal item — something I talk about in the "Creating other wacky items for invoices" section, later in this chapter.)

   • *For all three types,* use the Tax Code drop-down list box to indicate whether the item is taxed. (Note that the Tax Code box appears only if you told QuickBooks in the EasyStep Interview that you charge customers sales tax.)

   • *For all three types,* use the Account drop-down list to specify which income account you want to use to track the income that you receive from the sale of this item.

8. **If the item type is Inventory Part, tell QuickBooks how much to charge for the inventory part, how much the inventory part costs, and which income account to use for tracking the product sales income.**

   For an Inventory Part item type, QuickBooks displays the New Item window, as shown in Figure 3-4.

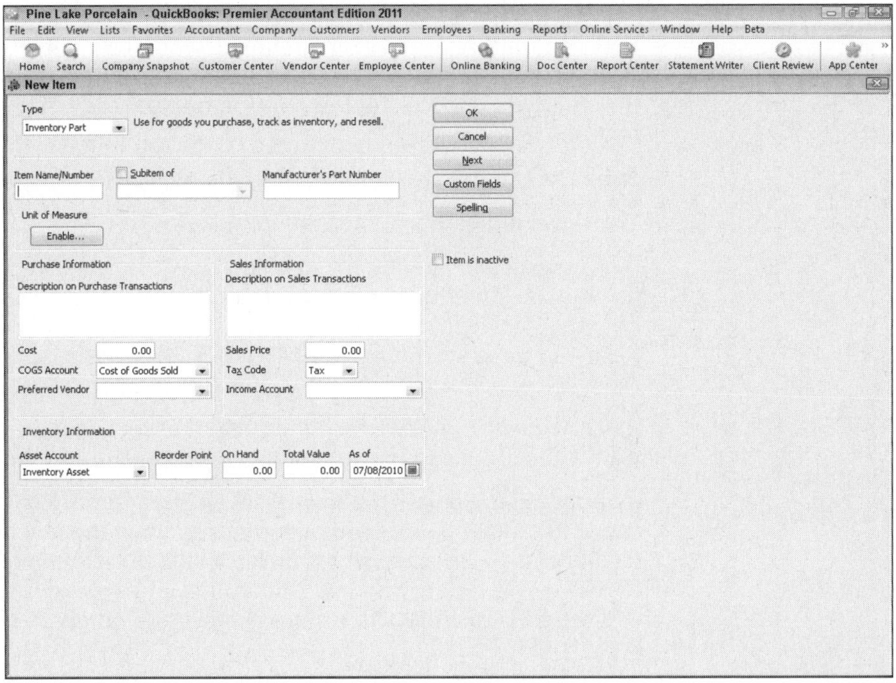

Figure 3-4:
The QuickBooks New Item window with the Inventory Part item type selected.

You use the extra fields that this special version of the window displays to record the following information:

- *Description on Purchase Transactions:* Describe the part. This description appears on the documents (such as purchase orders) that you use when you buy items for your inventory.

- *Cost:* Specify the average cost per unit of the items that you currently have. This field acts as the default rate when you enter the item on a purchase transaction.

- *COGS (Cost of Goods Sold) Account:* Specify the account that you want QuickBooks to use for tracking this item's cost when you sell it. (QuickBooks suggests the Cost of Goods Sold account. If you've created other accounts for your COGS, select the appropriate account.)

- *Preferred Vendor:* Specify your first choice when ordering the item for your business. (If the vendor isn't on your Vendor list, QuickBooks asks you to add it. If you say, "Yeah, I do want to add it," QuickBooks displays the Add Vendor window, which you can then use to describe the vendor.)

- *Description on Sales Transactions:* Type a description of the item that you want to appear on documents, such as invoices and so on, that your customers see. (QuickBooks suggests the same description that you used in the Description on Purchase Transactions text box as a default.)

- *Sales Price:* Enter the amount that you charge for the item.

- *Tax Code:* Indicate whether the item is taxed.

- *Income Account:* Specify the account that you want QuickBooks to use for tracking the income from the sale of the part. This is probably the Resale Income or Sales account. You typically use the Resale Income account to track wholesale (nontaxable) sales and the Sales account to track retail (taxable) sales.

- *Asset Account:* Specify the other current asset account that you want QuickBooks to use for tracking this Inventory item's value.

- *Reorder Point:* Specify the lowest inventory quantity of this item that can remain before you order more. When the inventory level drops to this quantity, QuickBooks adds a Reminder to the Reminders list, notifying you that you need to reorder the item. (To see the Reminders list, choose Lists⇨Reminders.)

- *On Hand:* Set this field to the physical count for the item at the conversion date if you're setting up an item for the first time as part of setting up QuickBooks. Otherwise, leave this field set to zero.

- *Total Value:* Leave this field at zero, too.

- *As Of:* Enter the current date.

9. **If the item type is Inventory Assembly, tell QuickBooks which cost-of-goods-sold and income account to use for tracking the item, how much to charge for the inventory assembly, and how to build the item from other component inventory items.**

   Note: The Inventory Assembly item is available in QuickBooks Premier and Enterprise but is not in Simple Start or QuickBooks Pro.

   For an Inventory Assembly item type, QuickBooks displays the New Item window.

   You use the extra fields that this special version of the window displays to record the following information:

   - *COGS (Cost of Goods Sold) Account:* Specify the account that you want QuickBooks to use for tracking this item's cost when you sell it. (QuickBooks suggests the Cost of Goods Sold account. If you've created other accounts for your COGS, select the appropriate account.)

- *Description:* Type a description of the item that you want to appear on documents that your customers see, such as invoices.

- *Sales Price:* Enter the amount that you charge for the item.

- *Tax Code:* Indicate whether the item is taxed.

- *Income Account:* Specify the account that you want QuickBooks to use for tracking the income from the sale of the part. This is probably the Resale Income or Sales account. You typically use the Resale Income account to track wholesale (nontaxable) sales and the Sales account to track retail (taxable) sales.

- *Bill of Materials:* Use the Bill of Materials list box to identify the component items and the quantities needed to make the inventory assembly.

- *Asset Account:* Specify the other current asset account that you want QuickBooks to use for tracking this inventory item's value.

- *Build Point:* Specify the lowest inventory quantity of this item that can remain before you manufacture more. When the inventory level drops to this quantity, QuickBooks adds a Reminder to the Reminders list, notifying you that you need to make more of the item.

- *On Hand:* Set this field to the physical count for the item at the conversion date if you're setting up an item for the first time as part of setting up QuickBooks. Otherwise, leave this field set to zero.

- *Total Value:* If you enter a value other than zero into the On Hand field, set the total value amount as the cost of the items you're holding. Otherwise, leave this field at zero.

- *As Of:* Enter the conversion date into the As Of text box if you're describing some item as part of getting QuickBooks set up. Otherwise, just enter the current date.

10. **If the item type is Sales Tax Item, tell QuickBooks what sales tax rate to charge and what government agency to pay.**

    Note: The Sales Tax Item version of the New Item window looks a little different from the window shown earlier in Figure 3-4. This is straightforward stuff, though. Enter the sales tax rate into the appropriate box and the state (or the city or other tax agency name) into the appropriate box:

    - *Sales Tax Name and Description:* Specify further details for later identification.

    - *Tax Rate:* Specify the sales tax rate as a percentage.

    - *Tax Agency:* Name the state or local tax agency that collects all the loot that you remit. If the tax agency isn't on the list, you can add it by selecting Add New from the drop-down list.

11. **If the item type is Payment, describe the payment method and how you want QuickBooks to handle the payment.**

    You use payment items to record a down payment made when the invoice is created to reduce the final balance due from the customer later. *Note:* Retainers and Advance Deposits are handled differently.

    The Payment version of the New Item window looks a little different from the window shown in Figure 3-4.

    Use the Payment Method drop-down list to specify the method of payment for a Payment. QuickBooks provides a starting list of several of the usual payment methods. You can easily add more payment types by choosing Add New from the drop-down list. When you choose this entry, QuickBooks displays the New Payment Method dialog box. In the dialog box's only text box, identify the payment method: cows, beads, shells, or some other what-have-you.

    When you're finished, use the area in the lower-left corner of the New Item window to either group the payment with other undeposited funds or, if you use the drop-down list, deposit the payment to a specific account.

12. **Click OK or Next when you're finished.**

    When you finish describing one item, click OK to add the item to the list and return to the Item List window. Click Next to add the item to the list and keep the New Item window onscreen so that you can add more items.

13. **If you added a new Inventory item, record the purchase of the item.**

    After you finish describing any new inventory items, you need to make another transaction to categorize the purchase of the items (unless they just showed up one morning on your doorstep). For an explanation of these transactions, turn to Chapter 7.

Using multiple units of measurement

If you buy and sell items of inventory with the same measurement units — for example, say that you both *buy* and *sell* individual coffee mugs — you use a single unit of measure for your purchases and sales. Some businesses, however, use multiple units of measurement. For example, say that a business purchases boxes of coffee mugs, at 24 mugs to the box, but then sells those coffee mugs singly. In this case, purchases of an item would probably be counted in boxes (one measurement unit). Yet, sales of the item would probably be counted as individual mugs (another measurement unit). To deal with this complexity, where appropriate, the New Item dialog boxes include an Enable button (see Figures 3-3 or 3-4, for example). Click the Enable button, and QuickBooks starts a little wizard that steps you through identifying the units of measure you need to use and how QuickBooks should convert from one unit of measure to another.

Creating other wacky items for invoices

In the preceding section, I don't describe all the items that you can add. For example, you can create a *Subtotal item* to calculate the subtotal of the items you list on an invoice. (You usually need this subtotal when you want to calculate a sales tax on the invoice's items.) You might want to create other wacky items for your invoices as well, such as discounts. I describe these special types of items in the next few sections.

Creating Subtotal items to stick subtotals on invoices

You need to add a Subtotal item if you ever want to apply a discount to a series of items on an invoice. (I show a Subtotal item on the invoice shown earlier in Figure 3-1.) To add a Subtotal item to your Item list, choose Lists⇨Item List, click the Item button, and select New from the drop-down list. This displays the New Item window — the same window I show several times earlier in this chapter. Specify the item type as Subtotal and then provide an item name (such as *Subtotal*).

When you want to subtotal items on an invoice, all you do is stick this Subtotal item on the invoice after the items you want to subtotal. Keep in mind, though, that QuickBooks doesn't set up a subtotal feature automatically. You have to add a Subtotal item; otherwise, you can apply a Discount item that you create only to the single item that immediately precedes the discount. A *Discount item,* by the way, calculates a discount on an invoice.

Creating Group items to batch stuff you sell together

You can create an item that puts one line on an invoice that's actually a combination of several other items. To add a Group item, display the New Item window and specify the item type as Group. QuickBooks displays the New Item window, as shown in Figure 3-5.

For example, if you sell three items — say, blue mugs, yellow mugs, and red mugs — but sometimes sell the items together in a set, you can create an item that groups the three items. Note that when you create a group, you continue to track the group member inventories individually and don't track the inventory of the group as a new item.

In the New Item window, use the Item/Description/Qty list box to list each item included in the group. When you click an item line in the Item/Description/Qty list box, QuickBooks places a down arrow at the right end of the Item column. Click this arrow to open a drop-down list of items. (If the list is longer than can be shown, you can use the scroll bar on the right to move up and down the list.) If you select the Print Items in Group check box, QuickBooks lists all the items in the group on invoices. (In the case of the mugs, invoices list the individual blue, red, and yellow mugs instead of just listing the group name, such as *Mug Set.*)

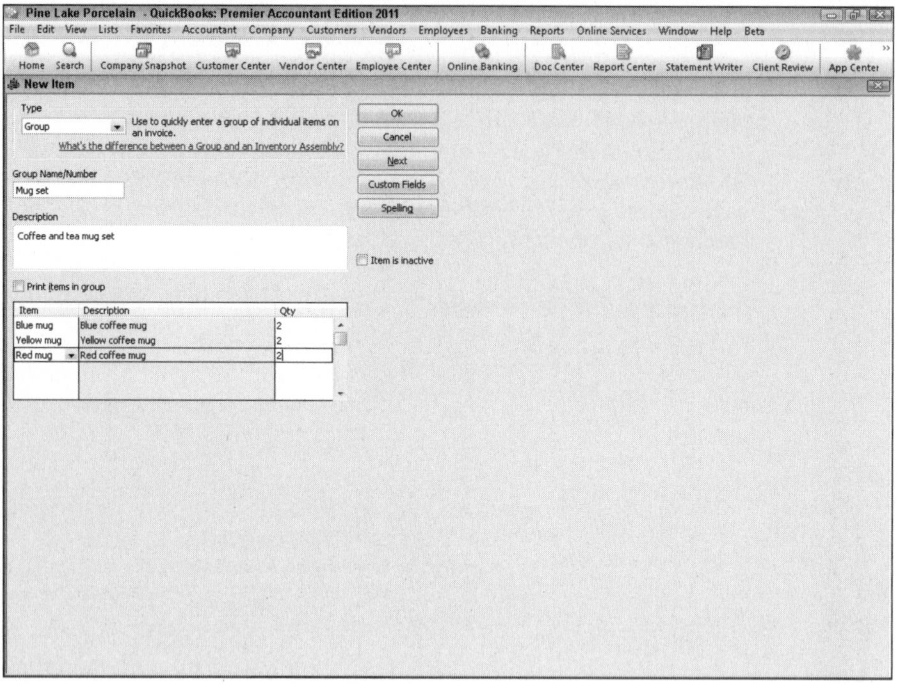

Figure 3-5:
The QuickBooks New Item window with the item type Group selected.

Creating Discount items to add discounts to invoices

You can create an item that calculates a discount and sticks the discount on an invoice as another line item. (I show a Discount item on the invoice that appears in Figure 3-1.) To add a Discount item to the list, display the New Item window, specify the item type as Discount, and provide an item name or number and a description.

Use the Amount or % text box to specify how the discount is calculated. If the discount is a set amount (such as $50.00), type the amount. If the discount is calculated as a percentage, enter the percentage, including the percent symbol. When you enter a percentage, QuickBooks calculates the discount amount as the percentage multiplied by the preceding item shown on the invoice. (If you want to apply the discount to a group of items, you need to use a Subtotal item and follow it with the discount, as Figure 3-1 shows.)

Use the Account drop-down list to specify the expense account that you want to use to track the cost of the discounts you offer.

Use the Tax Code drop-down list box to specify whether the discount gets calculated before or after any sales taxes are calculated. (This option appears only if you indicated in the EasyStep Interview that you charge sales tax.)

You probably want to check with your local sales tax revenue agency to determine whether sales tax should be calculated before or after the discount.

If you need to collect sales tax, and you didn't set up this function in the EasyStep Interview, follow these steps:

1. **Choose Edit⇨Preferences.**

   The Preferences dialog box appears.

2. **Click the Sales Tax icon in the list on the left, click the Company Preferences tab, and then select the Yes option button in the Do You Charge Sales Tax area.**

3. **Add the Sales Tax item(s) to your Item list.**

Creating Sales Tax Group items to batch sales taxes

Sales Tax Groups enable you to batch several sales taxes that you're supposed to charge as one tax so that they appear as a single sales tax on the invoice. Combining the taxes is necessary — or at least possible — when you're supposed to charge, say, a 6.5 percent state sales tax, a 1.7 percent county sales tax, and a 0.4 percent city sales tax, but you want to show one all-encompassing 8.6 percent sales tax on the invoice.

To add a Sales Tax Group item, display the New Item window and then specify the item type as Sales Tax Group. QuickBooks displays the New Item window, as shown in Figure 3-6. Use the Tax Item/Rate/Tax Agency/ Description list box to list the other sales tax items that you want to include in the group. When you click an item line in the list box, QuickBooks places a down arrow at the right end of the Tax Item column. You can click this arrow to open a drop-down list of Sales Tax items.

Editing items

If you make a mistake, you can change any piece of item information by displaying the Item List window and double-clicking the item so that QuickBooks displays the Edit Item window, which you can use to make changes.

The Item List window provides another tool you can use to edit item information. If you click the Item button and choose the Add/Edit Multiple Items command, QuickBooks displays the Add/Edit Multiple List Entries window. This window provides a spreadsheet you can use to add or edit more than one item at a time. The method I describe in the previous paragraphs often works best because it allows you to collect more information — for example, information such as item descriptions. But if you need to enter or edit a large number of items, check out the Add/Edit Multiple Items command. Sometimes the command saves you time.

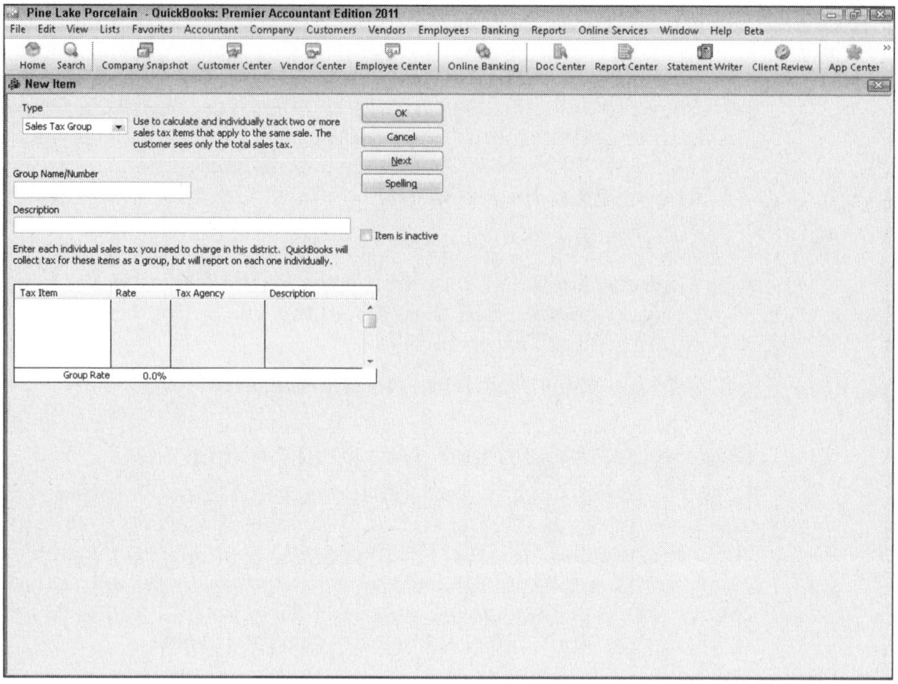

Figure 3-6:
The New
Item win-
dow for the
item type
Sales Tax
Group.

Adding Employees to Your Employee List

If you do payroll in QuickBooks, or if you track sales by employees, you need to describe each employee. Describing employees is pretty darn easy. Click the Employee Center icon at the top of the screen to display the Employee Center window. Then click the New Employee button that appears just above the list in the upper-left corner of the screen to have QuickBooks display the New Employee window, as shown in Figure 3-7.

The New Employee window is pretty straightforward, right? You just fill in the fields to describe the employee.

Lesser computer-book writers would probably provide step-by-step descriptions of how you move the cursor to the First Name text box and type the person's first name, how you move the cursor to the next text box, type something there, and so on. Not me. No way. I know that you can tell just by looking at this window that all you do is click a text box and type the obvious bit of information. Right?

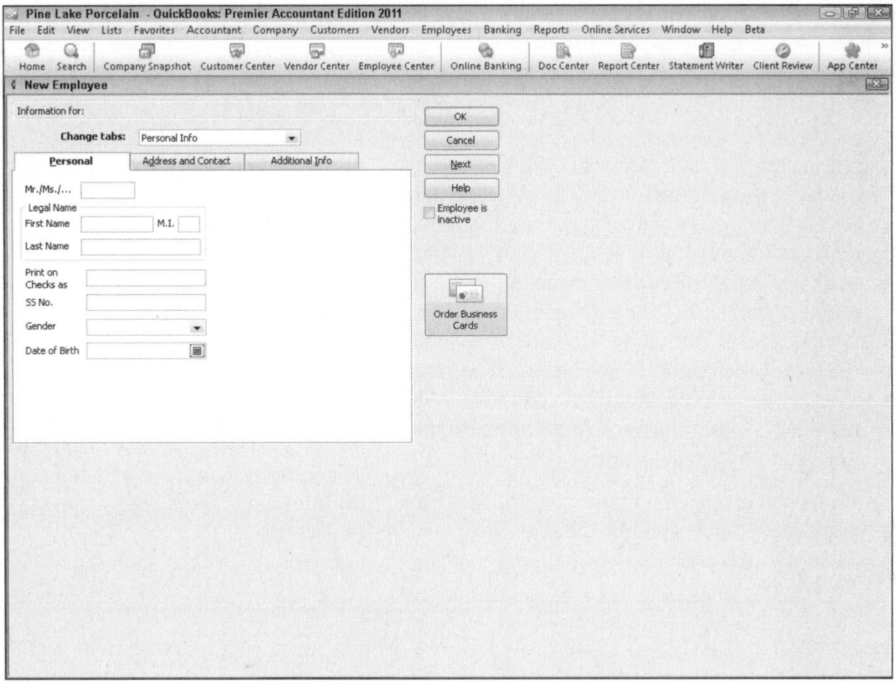

Pine Lake Porcelain - QuickBooks: Premier Accountant Edition 2011

File   Edit   View   Lists   Favorites   Accountant   Company   Customers   Vendors   Employees   Banking   Reports   Online Services   Window   Help   Beta

Home   Search   Company Snapshot   Customer Center   Vendor Center   Employee Center   Online Banking   Doc Center   Report Center   Statement Writer   Client Review   App Center

New Employee

Information for:

Change tabs: Personal Info

| Personal | Address and Contact | Additional Info |

Mr./Ms./...

Legal Name
First Name   M.I.
Last Name

Print on
Checks as

SS No.

Gender

Date of Birth

OK
Cancel
Next
Help
☐ Employee is inactive

Order Business Cards

Figure 3-7:
The New
Employee
window.

TIP

I do need to tell you a couple important things about the New Employee window:

✔ When you release an employee, it's important to enter the release date for the employee on the Employment Info tab after you write that final paycheck. (To change to a new tab, choose the new tab from the cleverly named Change Tabs drop-down list.) This way, when you process payroll in the future, you can't accidentally pay the former employee.

✔ As for the Type field (an option on the Employment Info tab), most employees probably fit the regular category. If you're uncertain whether an employee fits the guidelines for corporate officer, statutory employee, or owner, see the *Circular E* publication from the IRS. And sleep tight.

The Address and Contact tab provides boxes for you to collect and store address information. The Additional Info tab enables you to create customizable fields in case you want to keep information that isn't covered by the QuickBooks' default fields — favorite color and that type of thing. Again, what you need to do on this tab is fairly straightforward. By the way, if you've told QuickBooks that you want to do payroll, QuickBooks prompts you to enter the information it needs to calculate things like federal and state income taxes, payroll taxes, and vacation pay.

Inactivating list items

One of the neat features in QuickBooks is that it enables you to simplify your lists by hiding items that are no longer active, including those that you expect to be active again later. If you have seasonal employees, you can hide them from your Employee list during the times of the year when they don't work. Or if you sell commemorative key chains only every five years, you can keep them from cluttering your Item list in the off years. You can also inactivate customers and vendors from their respective lists.

To inactivate something from a list, all you have to do is open the list and double-click the item. When QuickBooks opens the item, employee, customer, or vendor that you want to inactivate, select the Item Is Inactive check box. (The name of the check box changes, depending on what you're trying to inactivate.) Then click OK. QuickBooks hides this member from your list. The next time you display the list, the Include Inactive box appears.

To view and edit hidden members of your list, just click the Include Inactive box. Any inactive members show up with X icons beside them. If you want to reactivate a member, all you have to do is click the X icon, and the member is reactivated.

After you finish describing an employee, click OK to add the employee to the list and return to the Employee List window, or click Next to add the employee to the list and add more employees.

You can also inactivate an employee from your list if it starts to get cluttered with names of employees who no longer work for you. Read about inactivating items, employees, customers, and vendors in the following "Inactivating list items" sidebar. I recommend waiting to inactivate them until after the year is finished and the W-2 forms have been printed.

Customers Are Your Business

Here's how you add customers to your Customer list:

1. **Choose Customers⇨Customer Center.**

   The Customer Center window appears.

2. **Click the New Customer & Job button and then click New Customer.**

   QuickBooks displays the Address Info tab of the New Customer window, as shown in Figure 3-8. Use this window to describe the customer in as much detail as possible.

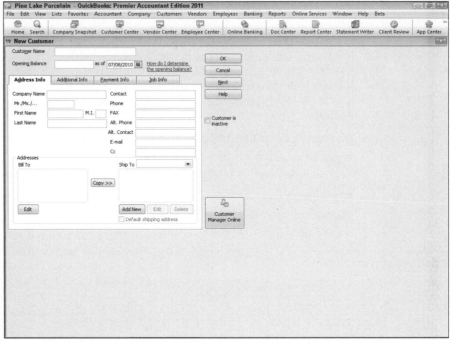

3. **Type the customer's name.**

   Enter the name of the customer as you want it to appear in the Customer list. You can list customers by company name or by the representative's last name.

4. **Enter the company name.**

5. **(Optional) Enter the name of your contact, along with other pertinent information.**

   Move the cursor to the Mr./Ms. text box and type the appropriate title. Do the same with the First Name, M.I., and Last Name text boxes. (QuickBooks automatically fills in the names in the Contact text box as you type them. Nice touch, eh?)

   Go ahead and fill in the Phone, FAX, Alt. Phone, and E-Mail text boxes while you're at it.

6. **(Really optional) Type the name of your alternative contact in the Alt. Contact text box.**

7. **Enter the billing address.**

   You can use the Bill To text box to provide the customer's billing address. QuickBooks copies the Company and Contact names to the first lines of the billing address, so you need to enter only the address. To move from the end of one line to the start of the next, press Enter.

8. **Enter the shipping address.**

   You can use the Ship To box to provide the customer's shipping address. Click the Copy button to copy the billing address to the Ship To box. If the shipping address differs from the Bill To address, simply open the Ship To list box, click Add New, and then enter the shipping address information the same way that you enter the Bill To address. You can add multiple shipping addresses. After you add a shipping address for a customer, you can select the shipping address from the Ship To list box.

9. **(Optional) Click the Additional Info tab and record more data.**

   When you click this tab, QuickBooks displays the tab shown in Figure 3-9. You can use this tab to describe the customer in more detail.

10. **(Optional) Click the Payment Info tab and record more data.**

    You can use the boxes on the Payment Info tab (see Figure 3-10) to record bits of customer information, such as the account number that should be included with any payments.

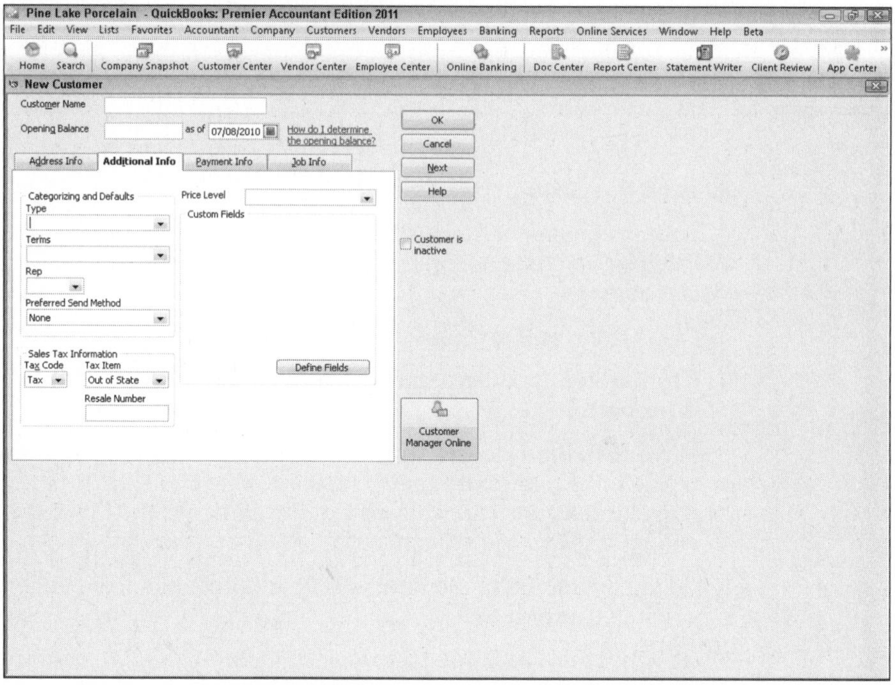

Figure 3-9:
Add more
details
on the
Additional
Info tab.

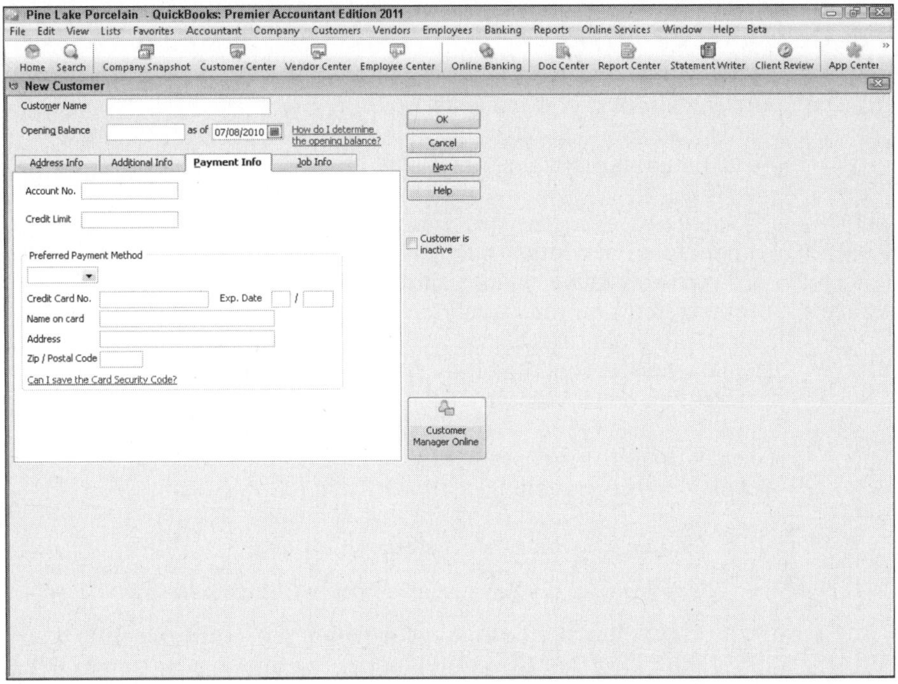

Figure 3-10:
The
Payment
Info tab.

11. (Optional) Click the Job Info tab to add specific job information.

Because you're creating a new customer account, not invoicing by jobs, I explain this step in the next section. If you're the "can't wait" type, feel free to take a look. You can add a specific job to the new customer's information.

12. Save the customer information by clicking OK or Next.

When you finish describing a customer, you can save it in one of two ways: Click OK to add the customer to the list and return to the Customer Center window, or click Next to add the customer to the list and keep the New Customer window onscreen so that you can add more customers.

If you want to change some bit of customer information, display the Customer Center window, double-click the customer name in which you want to change information, and then make changes in the Edit Customer window.

It's Just a Job

In QuickBooks, you can track invoices by customer or by customer and job. This may sound kooky, but some businesses invoice customers (perhaps several times) for specific jobs.

Take the case of a construction subcontractor who does foundation work for a handful of builders of single-family homes. This construction subcontractor probably invoices his customers by job, and he invoices each customer several times for the same job. For example, he invoices Poverty Rock Realty for the foundation job at 1113 Birch Street when he pours the footing and then again when he lays the block. At 1028 Fairview, the same foundation job takes more than one invoice, too.

To set up jobs for customers, you first need to describe the customers (as I explain in the preceding section). Then follow these steps:

1. **Choose Customers⇨Customer Center.**

   QuickBooks displays the Customer Center window.

2. **Right-click the customer for whom you want to set up a job, choose Add Job from the contextual menu that appears and click the Add Job tab.**

   QuickBooks displays the New Job window (shown in Figure 3-11). You use this window to describe the job. A great deal of the information in this window appears on the invoice.

3. **Add the job name.**

   The cursor is in the Job Name text box. Just type the name of the job or project.

4. **Identify the customer.**

   On the off chance that you selected the wrong customer in Step 2, take a peek at the Customer drop-down list. Does it name the correct customer? If not, activate the drop-down list and select the correct customer.

5. **(Optional) Name your contact and fill in other relevant information.**

   You can enter the name of your contact and alternative contact in the Mr./Ms., First Name, M.I., and Last Name text boxes. QuickBooks fills in the Contact text box for you. You probably don't need to be told this, but fill in the Phone and FAX text boxes just so that you have that information on hand. If you want to get really optional, fill in the Alt. Phone and Alt. Contact text boxes. Go ahead: Take a walk on the wild side.

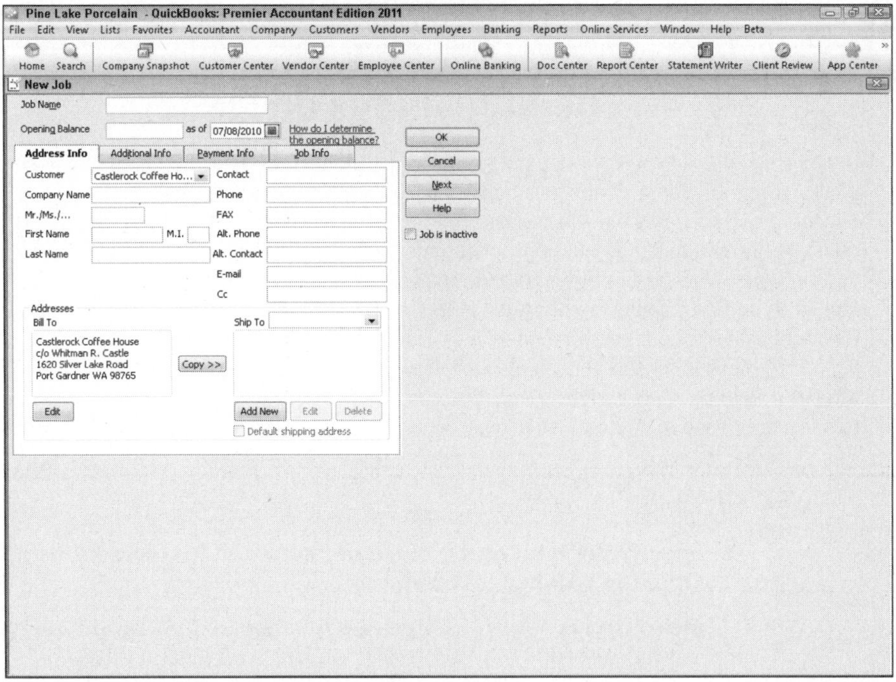

Figure 3-11:
The New
Job
window.

6. **Enter the job's billing address.**

   You can use the Bill To text box to provide the customer's job billing address. Because chances are good that the job billing address is the same as the customer billing address, QuickBooks copies the billing address from the Customer list. But if need be, make changes.

7. **Select the Ship To address.**

   You can use the Ship To text box to provide the job's shipping address. Click the Copy button if the shipping address is the same as the Bill To address.

8. **(Massively optional) Click the Additional Info tab and categorize the job.**

   You can use the Customer Type drop-down list to give the job type. The only initial types in the default list are Corporate and Referral. You can create other types by choosing Add New from the Customer Type drop-down list (so that QuickBooks displays the New Customer Type dialog box) and then filling in the blanks.

9. **Click the Payment Info tab and set the customer's credit limit (that is, if you've given the customer a credit limit).**

   You can set the customer's credit limit by using the Credit Limit box.

The little things do matter

If you aren't familiar with how payment terms work, you can get a bird's-eye view here. For the most part, payment terms just tell the customer how quickly you expect to be paid. For example, *Due on Receipt* means that you expect to be paid as soon as possible. If Net is followed by some number, as in Net 15 or Net 30, the number indicates the number of days after the invoice date within which the customer is supposed to pay. So Net 15 means that the customer is supposed to pay within 15 days of the invoice date.

Some payment terms, such as 2% 10 Net 30, include early payment discounts. In other words, the customer can deduct 2 percent from the bill if it's paid within 10 days. Either way, the customer must pay the bill within 30 days. For more information on how to make early payment discounts work for you, see Chapter 21.

10. **Specify the total of the customer's unpaid invoices by using the Opening Balance text box.**

    Move the cursor to the Opening Balance text box and type the total amount owed by the customer on the conversion date.

    QuickBooks suggests that you *not* enter a balance in the Opening Balance box as part of setting up QuickBooks. (If you're interested in the logic of QuickBooks' argument, you can view the Customer's online tutorial, which is available by choosing Help➪QuickBooks Learning Center and then clicking the How to Enter Your Customers link.) However, I've thought long and hard about this, and I think you want to enter the customer's unpaid balance into the Opening Balance box. Doing this makes setting up QuickBooks correctly much easier.

11. **Enter the current date in the As Of text box.**

12. **(Optional) Click the Job Info tab and add specific job information.**

    Figure 3-12 shows the Job Info tab. You can use the Job Status drop-down list to choose None, Pending, Awarded, In Progress, Closed, or Not Awarded, whichever is most appropriate. The Start Date is (I know that this one is hard to believe) the day you start the job. As anyone knows, the Projected End and the End Date aren't necessarily the same. Don't fill in the End Date until the job is actually finished. The Job Description field can contain any helpful information you can fit on one line, and the Job Type is an extra field you can use. (If you do use this field, you can add a new job type by choosing Add New from the Job Type list.)

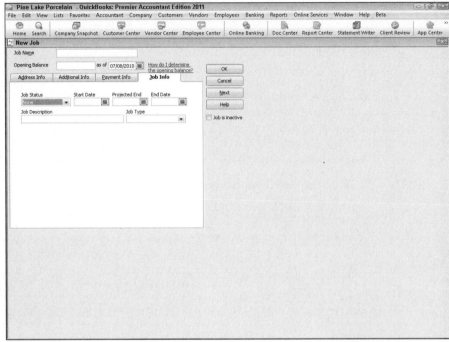

Figure 3-12:
The Job
Info tab.

13. Save the job information by clicking OK or Next.

After you finish describing the job, you have two options: You can click OK to add the job to the list and return to the Customer Center window, or you can click Next to add the job to the list and keep the New Job window onscreen so that you can add more jobs.

You can edit job information the same way that you edit customer information. Display the Customer Center window by choosing Customer➪Customer Center. When QuickBooks displays the window, double-click the job and make the changes in the Edit Job window that appears.

To add a large number of customers or jobs to the Customers list at the same time, display the Customer Center window, click the New Customer & Job button, and then choose the Add Multiple Customer:Jobs option. QuickBooks displays the Add/Edit Multiple List Entries worksheet, which lets you collect and edit all the same information that the regular customer and job windows do.

Adding Vendors to Your Vendor List

Adding vendors to your Vendor list works the same basic way as adding customers to your Customer list. Here's how to get the job done:

1. **Choose Vendors⇨Vendor Center or click the Vendor Center icon at the top of the screen.**

   QuickBooks displays the Vendor Center window. Along with listing your vendors, it lists any sales tax agencies that you identified as part of setting up Sales Tax items.

2. **Click the New Vendor button.**

   QuickBooks displays the Address Info tab of the New Vendor window, as shown in Figure 3-13. You use this window to describe the vendors and all their little idiosyncrasies.

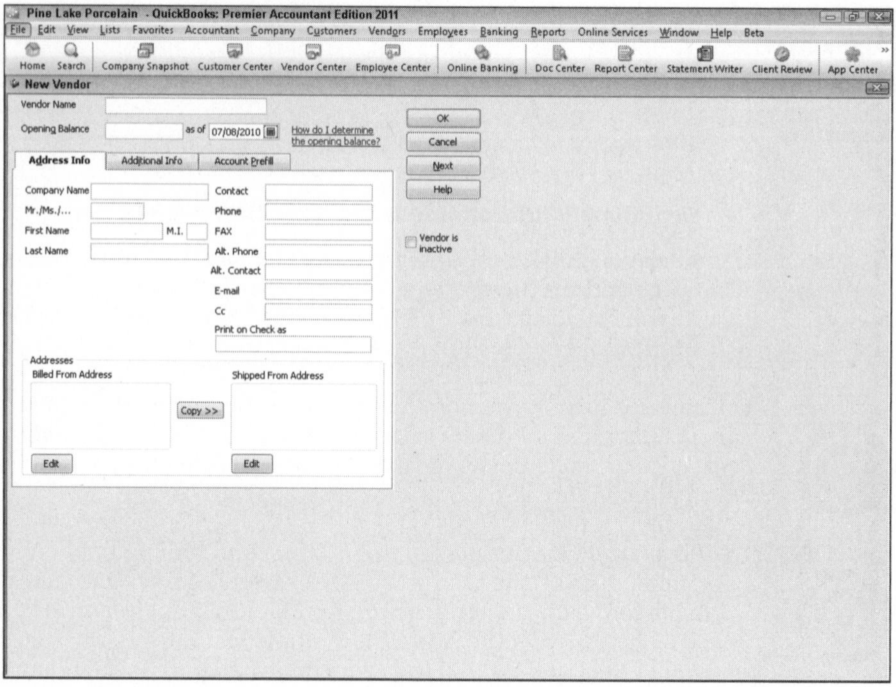

Figure 3-13:
The Address Info tab of the New Vendor window.

3. Enter the vendor's name.

The cursor is already in the Vendor Name text box. All you have to do is type the vendor's name as you want it to appear on the Vendor list. If you want to list your vendors by company name, enter the company name. To list them by the first or last name of the sales representative, enter one of these names. Just remember that the list is going to sort, alphabetically or numerically, by the information you enter in this field, not by the information below.

4. (Optional) Enter the name of your contact.

Fill in the Mr./Ms., First Name, M.I., and Last Name text boxes. QuickBooks fills in the Contact text box for you automatically.

5. Enter the address to which you're supposed to mail checks.

You can use the Addresses text box to provide the vendor's address. QuickBooks copies the Company and Contact names to the first line of the address, so you need to enter only the street address, city, state, and zip code. To move from the end of one line to the start of the next, press Enter.

6. (Optional) Enter the vendor's telephone and fax numbers, and, if available, the e-mail address.

The window also has an Alt. Phone text box for a second telephone number. They thought of everything, didn't they?

7. Verify the entry in the Print on Check As text box.

QuickBooks assumes that you want the company name to appear on any checks you write for this vendor. If not, change the text box to whatever you feel is more appropriate.

8. At this point, click the Additional Info tab.

The window you see onscreen hopefully bears an uncanny resemblance to Figure 3-14.

9. (Optional) Enter your account number in the Account No. text box.

If the vendor has assigned account numbers or customer numbers to keep track of customers, type your account or customer number in the Account No. text box. You can probably get this piece of information from the vendor's last invoice.

An account number is required if you want to use QuickBooks' online bill payment feature (which I describe in Chapter 13) to pay the vendor. QuickBooks transfers the account number to the memo field of the payment check.

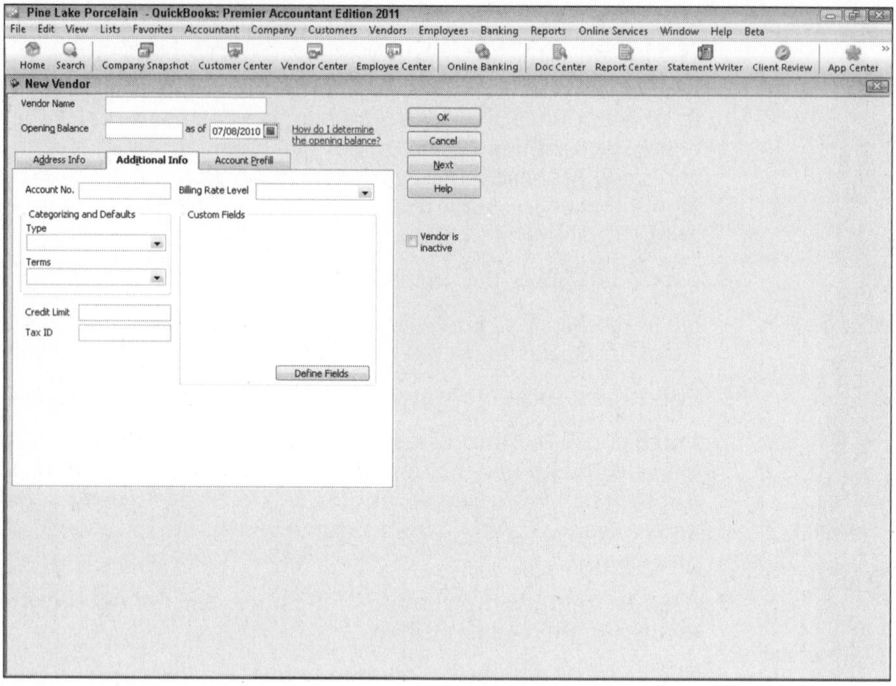

Figure 3-14:
The
Additional
Info tab
of the
New Vendor
window.

10. Categorize the vendor by selecting an option from the Type drop-down list.

See that Type drop-down list? If you open the list, you see the initial QuickBooks list of vendor types. You can pick any of these types, but my suggestion is that you diligently identify any vendor to whom you need to send a 1099 Form as a 1099 contractor. (In 2010 and 2011, a *1099 contractor* is any unincorporated business or person who performs services and to whom you pay $600 or more during the year. But starting in 2012, when this requirement falls out of the Obamacare legislation, you need to send a 1099 to everyone and anyone to whom you pay more than $600 annually. And, yes, that does mean you'll send a 1099 to the airline company, the telephone company, the bank, your insurer, and so on.)

To create a new vendor type, select Add New from the drop-down list and fill in the blanks in the New Vendor Type dialog box that QuickBooks displays. You can create as many new vendor types as you need.

11. Specify the payment terms that you're supposed to observe by selecting an option from the Terms drop-down list.

QuickBooks has already set up all the usual ones. (If you want to, you can choose Add New to set up additional payment terms.)

If a vendor offers an early payment discount, it's usually too good a deal to pass up. Interested in more information about early payment discounts? Do you have an inquiring mind that needs to know? See Chapter 21 to find out about the advantages of early payment discounts.

12. **(Optional) Specify your credit limit, if the vendor has set one.**

This procedure is obvious, right? You click in the Credit Limit text box and enter the number.

13. **(If applicable) Store the vendor's federal tax identification number and select the Vendor Eligible for 1099 check box.**

This number might be the vendor's Social Security number if the vendor is a one-person business. If the vendor has employees, the federal tax identification number is the vendor's employer identification number. You need this information only if you're required to prepare a 1099 for the vendor.

Starting in 2012, as noted in Step 10, all businesses will be required to send a 1099 to almost everyone, so it's a good idea to begin collecting taxpayer identification numbers now.

14. **Type 0 (zero) in the Opening Balance text box.**

You typically don't want to enter the amount you owe the vendor; you do that later, when you pay your bills. However, if you're using *accrual-basis accounting* for your expenses (this just means that your accounting system counts bills as expenses when you get the bill and not when you pay the bill), you need to tell QuickBooks what amounts you owe vendors at the conversion date. You can do that most easily by entering opening balances for vendors into the Opening Balance box as you set up a vendor in the Vendor list.

15. **Enter the conversion date in the As Of text box.**

What you're doing here, by the way, is providing the date on which the value shown in the Opening Balance text box is correct.

QuickBooks provides an Account Prefill tab on the New Vendor window. Use this tab to specify a set of expense accounts that QuickBooks will suggest any time you indicate you're writing a check, entering a bill, or entering a credit card charge for the vendor.

16. **Save the vendor information by clicking OK or Next.**

After you finish describing the vendor, you have two options: Click OK to add the vendor to the list and return to the Vendor Center window, or click Next to add the vendor to the list and leave the New Vendor window onscreen so that you can add more vendors.

To add a large number of vendors to the Vendor list at the same time, display the Vendor Center window, click the New Vendor button, and then choose the Add Multiple Vendors option. QuickBooks displays the Add/Edit Multiple List Entries worksheet, which lets you collect and edit all the same information that the regular vendor windows do.

The Other Lists

Throughout the preceding sections, I cover almost all the most important lists. A few others I haven't talked about yet are Fixed Asset, Price Level, Sales Tax Code, Classes, Other Names, Sales Rep, Customer Type, Vendor Type, Job Type, Terms, Customer Messages, Payment Method, Ship Via, and Memorized Transactions. I don't give blow-by-blow descriptions of how you use these lists because you don't really need them. The other QuickBooks lists are generally more than adequate. You can usually use the standard lists as is without building other lists.

Just so I don't leave you stranded, however, I want to give you quick-and-dirty descriptions of these other lists and what they do.

To see some of these lists, choose the list from the Lists menu or choose Lists⇨Customer & Vendor Profile Lists and choose the list from the submenu that QuickBooks displays.

The Fixed Asset list

If you buy *fixed assets* — things such as vehicles, various pieces of furniture, miscellaneous hunks of equipment, and so on — somebody is supposed to track this stuff in a list. Why? You need to have this information at your fingertips (or at your accountant's fingertips) to calculate depreciation. And if you later dispose of some item, you need this information to calculate the gain or loss on the sale of the item.

For these reasons, QuickBooks includes a Fixed Asset list. Figure 3-15 shows the Fixed Asset Item List window, used to describe and identify your fixed assets.

Note: I should tell you that your CPA or tax accountant already has such a list that he or she has been maintaining for you. So don't, like, totally freak out because this is the first you've heard about this fixed assets business.

Chapter 18 describes handling fixed assets in a bit more detail.

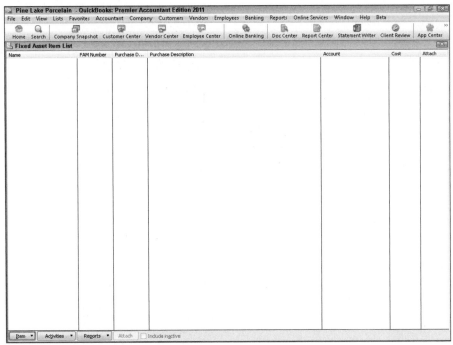

Figure 3-15:
The Fixed
Asset Item
List window.

The Price Level list

The first time I encountered the QuickBooks Price Level feature, I was sorely confused about how the feature worked. I'm still a little confused — not about how the feature works, but about who'd really want to use this feature. But heck, what do I know? Here's the deal: *Price Levels* enable you to adjust an item price as you're creating an invoice. For example, you can create a price level that increases the price for some item by 20 percent. And you create a price level that decreases the price for some item by 10 percent. You adjust a price by selecting a price level from the Price field on an invoice. (This may not make much sense until you see the Create Invoices window, which I describe in Chapter 4, but it's fairly straightforward.)

The Sales Tax Code list

The Sales Tax Code list just maintains a list of sales tax codes. These sales tax codes, when used on an invoice or bill, tell QuickBooks whether items are taxable.

The Class list

Classes enable you to classify transactions by department or location, for example, so that you can track trends and assess performance across parts of your business. Classes are cool (really cool), but they add another dimension to the accounting model that you use in QuickBooks, so I'm not going to describe them here. I urge you — nay, I implore you — to get comfortable with how the rest of QuickBooks works before you begin mucking about with classes. Here are just a handful of useful tidbits in case you want to use classes:

✔ You may need to turn on the QuickBooks Class Tracking feature. To do this, choose Edit⇨Preferences, click the Accounting icon, click the Company Preferences tab, and select the Use Class Tracking check box.

Note: The Class box appears in data entry windows only after you turn on class tracking.

✔ To display the Class list, choose Lists⇨Class List.

✔ To add classes to the Class list, display the Class List window (choose Lists⇨Class List), right-click the window, choose New to display the New Class window, and then fill in the blanks.

✔ To tag transactions as falling into a particular class — invoices, checks, bills, journal entries, and so on — select the appropriate class from the Class list box.

By the way, one other point: Before you go off and start using classes to complicate your accounting, make sure that you can't get what you want by beefing up your chart of accounts.

You won't see a Class List command in the Lists menu if you indicated during the EasyStep Interview that you don't want to use classes. But you can change your mind later and start using classes. Choose Edit⇨Preferences, click the Accounting icon, and select the Use Class Tracking check box on the Company Preferences tab.

The Other Names list

QuickBooks provides an Other Names list that works as a watered-down, wimpy Vendor and Employee list combination. You can write checks to people named on this Other Names list, but you can't do anything else. You can't create invoices or purchase orders for them, for example. And you don't get any of the other information that you want to collect for vendors or employees.

You're really better off working with good, accurate, rich Vendor and Employee lists. If you don't like this suggestion, however, just choose Lists⇨Other Names List to display the Other Names List window, click the Other Names button, choose New from the drop-down list, and then fill in the blanks in the New Name window.

The Sales Rep list

You can create a list of the sales representatives you work with and then indicate which sales rep sells to a customer or generates a sale. To do this, choose Lists⇨Customer & Vendor Profile Lists⇨Sales Rep. When you choose this command, QuickBooks displays the Sales Rep List window, which lists all the sales representatives. To add sales representatives, click the Sales Rep button, select New from the drop-down list, and then fill in the window that QuickBooks displays.

Customer, Vendor, and Job Types list

You can create lists of customer types, vendor types, and job types and then use these lists to categorize customer, vendor, and job information. This is probably no surprise, but to do this, you need to use the appropriate command:

- ✔ Lists⇨Customer & Vendor Profile Lists⇨Customer Type List
- ✔ Lists⇨Customer & Vendor Profile Lists⇨Vendor Type List
- ✔ Lists⇨Customer & Vendor Profile Lists⇨Job Type List

When you choose one of these commands, QuickBooks displays the appropriate List window, which lists all the Customer types, Vendor types, or Job types. To add types, click the Type button, select New from the drop-down list, and then fill in the window that QuickBooks displays.

How you use any of these types of lists depends on your business. In a situation in which you want to sort or segregate customers, vendors, or jobs in some unusual way, use the Customer Type, Vendor Type, or Job Type list.

 Over the last few years, I've used the Customer Type box to identify which marketing technique has brought me a client: yellow-pages advertising, newspaper advertising, professional referrals, and so on. Because QuickBooks easily prints reports that summarize client revenue by customer type, using the Customer Type field in this manner lets me easily see how much revenue different marketing activities produce — and when I'm getting a decent return on my marketing dollars.

The Terms list

QuickBooks maintains a Terms list, which you use to specify what payment terms are available. To add terms, choose Lists⇨Customer & Vendor Profile Lists⇨Terms List. When you choose this command, QuickBooks displays the Terms List window. To add more terms, click the Terms button, select New from the drop-down list, and then fill in the window that QuickBooks displays.

The Customer Message list

This list is another minor player in the QuickBooks drama. You can stick messages at the bottom of invoices if you first type the message in the Customer Message list. QuickBooks provides a handful of boilerplate messages: thank you, happy holidays, mean people suck, and so on. You can add more messages by choosing Lists⇨Customer & Vendor Profile Lists⇨Customer Message List. When QuickBooks displays the Customer Message List window, click its Customer Message button and choose New. Then use the New Customer Message window that QuickBooks displays to create a new message.

The Payment Method list

Now this will be a big surprise. (I'm just kidding.) QuickBooks provides descriptions for the usual payment methods. But, of course, you can add to these by choosing Lists⇨Customer & Vendor Profile Lists⇨Payment Method. When you choose this command, QuickBooks displays the lost city of Atlantis. Okay, not really. QuickBooks actually displays the Payment Method window. To add more methods, click the Payment Method button, select New from the drop-down list, and then fill in the window that QuickBooks displays.

The Ship Via list

QuickBooks provides descriptions for the usual shipping methods. These descriptions are probably entirely adequate. If you need to add more, however, you can do so by choosing Lists⇨Customer & Vendor Profile Lists⇨Ship Via. When you choose this command, QuickBooks displays the Ship Via List window, which lists all the shipping methods that you or QuickBooks said are available. To add more methods, click the Shipping Method button, select New from the drop-down list, and then fill in the window that QuickBooks displays. Friends, it doesn't get much easier than this.

The Vehicle list

As I describe in a bit more detail in Chapter 18, QuickBooks provides a Vehicle list that you can use to maintain a list of business vehicles. To see the Vehicle list, choose Lists➪Customer & Vendor Profile Lists➪Vehicle List. When you choose this command, QuickBooks displays the Vehicle List window, which lists all the vehicles that you previously said are available. To identify additional vehicles, click the Vehicle button, select New from the drop-down list and then fill in the window that QuickBooks displays.

To record vehicle mileage inside QuickBooks, choose Company➪Enter Vehicle Mileage. Then use the window that QuickBooks displays to identify the vehicle, the trip length in miles, the trip date, and a bit of other trip-related information.

The Memorized Transaction list

The Memorized Transaction list isn't really a list. At least, it's not like the other lists that I describe in this chapter. The Memorized Transaction list is a list of accounting transactions — invoices, bills, checks, purchase orders, and so on — that you've asked QuickBooks to memorize. To display the Memorized Transaction list, choose Lists➪Memorized Transaction List.

You can have QuickBooks memorize transactions so that you can quickly record them later or even put them on a schedule for recurring usage. This feature can save you lots of time, especially for transactions you regularly make.

The Reminders list

Here's a list that isn't accessible from the Lists menu. QuickBooks keeps track of a bunch of stuff that it knows you need to monitor. If you choose Company➪Reminders, QuickBooks displays the Reminders window. Here, you see such entries as invoices and checks that need to be printed, inventory items you should probably reorder, and so on.

Organizing Lists

To organize a list, you must be in single-user mode. (I describe multi-user mode in Appendix C.) Here are some ways that you can organize your list:

> ✔ **To move an item and all its subitems:** Click the diamond beside the item and then drag the item up or down the list to a new location.
>
> ✔ **To make a subitem its own item:** Click the diamond beside the item and then drag it to the left.
>
> ✔ **To make an item a subitem:** Move the item so that it's directly beneath the item you want it to fall under. Then click the diamond beside the item and drag it to the right.
>
> ✔ **To alphabetize a list:** Click the Name button at the top of the list window. QuickBooks alphabetizes your list of customers, vendors, accounts and so on in both "a to z" order and reverse "z to a" order.

You can't reorganize the Vendor or the Employee list.

Printing Lists

You can print customer, vendor, and employee lists by clicking the Print button at the top of the specific Center screen for the type of list you choose. The list is among the options available to print in a drop-down list.

You can print a regular list by displaying the list, clicking the button in the lower-left corner of the list window, and then choosing Print List. However, often the best way to print a list is to print a list report. You can create, customize, and print a list report by choosing Reports⇨List and then choosing the list that you want to print. You can also create one of a handful of list reports by clicking the Reports button in the list window and choosing a report from the pop-up menu. For more information on printing reports, see Chapter 15.

Click the Activities button in a list window to quickly access common activities associated with the items on that list. Or click Reports to quickly access common reports related to the items on the list.

Exporting List Items to Your Word Processor

If you use QuickBooks to store the names and addresses of your customers, vendors, and employees, you can create a text file of the contact information for these people. You can then export this file to another application, such as a word processor, to create reports that use this information.

To export list information to a text file, click the button in the lower-left corner of the list window and choose Print List. When QuickBooks displays the Print dialog box, select the File option button, click Print, and then provide a filename when prompted.

The File menu Print Forms command also provides a Labels command for producing mailing labels for customers and vendors. And before I forget, let me also mention that the last command of the Company menu — Prepare Letters with Envelopes — lets you prepare letters (and, duh, addressed envelopes) from the name and address information from the Customer, Vendor, and Employee lists discussed earlier in this chapter.

Dealing with the Chart of Accounts List

I saved the best for last. After you get done setting up your lists, you still need to finalize one list: the Chart of Accounts. The Chart of Accounts just lists the accounts you and QuickBooks use to track income and expenses, assets, liabilities, and equity.

This is kind of a funny step, however, because a bunch of Chart of Accounts stuff is already set up. So what you're really doing here is just finalizing the chart of accounts. Typically, this consists of two or possibly three separate steps: describing customer balances, describing vendor balances, and entering the rest of the trial balance.

Describing customer balances

If you entered customer unpaid invoice totals when you set up the customers — which is what I recommend — you've already described your customer balances. You, my friend, can skip ahead to the next section, "Describing vendor balances."

If you didn't enter customer unpaid invoice totals, you need to supply that information before you finalize the Chart of Account information. To do this, enter the invoice in the usual way, which I describe in Chapter 4. The one really important thing to do is use the original invoice date when you enter the invoice.

Now, I know what you're thinking: "Hey, dude. The order of your instructions is all screwed up. Here I am, slogging through Chapter 3, and now totally out of the blue, you're telling me that I have to jump ahead to Chapter 4 and read that?"

Yeah, well, that's right. This jumping around and jumping ahead is the big reason that I told you earlier to do it the way I did. Hey, sorry.

Describing vendor balances

If you entered vendor unpaid bill totals when you set up the vendors — this is also what I recommend — you described your vendor balances.

If you didn't enter vendor unpaid bill totals, you need to supply that information, as I describe in Chapter 6 in the discussion on recording your bills the accounts payable way. The one really important thing to do is to use the original vendor bill date when you enter the vendor bill.

Camouflaging some accounting goofiness

After you enter the customer and vendor balances into QuickBooks, you need to enter the rest of the trial balance, which you do by taking two big steps. In the first step, you camouflage a couple of goofy accounts, called *suspense accounts,* which QuickBooks creates when you set up the Item, Customer, and Vendor lists. The second step, which I describe in the following section, is supplying the last few missing numbers.

Figure 3-16 shows a sample trial balance after I enter the inventory, accounts receivable, and accounts payable balances. (These account balances get set up indirectly, as I note in the sidebar "For accountants only," later in this chapter.) When you set up your Item, Customer, and Vendor lists, you also create account balances for inventory, accounts receivable, and accounts payable.

You can produce your own half-complete trial balance from inside QuickBooks by clicking the Report Center icon and choosing Reports⇨Accountants & Taxes⇨Trial Balance. QuickBooks displays the trial balance report in a document window.

If you need to do so, enter the conversion date in the As Of box by clicking in the box and typing the conversion date in MM/DD/YYYY format. Figure 3-16, for example, shows the conversion date 7/1/2011 on the As Of line. You can set the From box to any value; the From and To range just needs to end with the conversion date. Make a note of the credit and debit balances shown for the Uncategorized Income and Uncategorized Expenses accounts.

If you want, you can print the report by clicking the Print button; then, when QuickBooks displays the Print Report dialog box, click its Print button. Yes, you click *two* Print buttons.

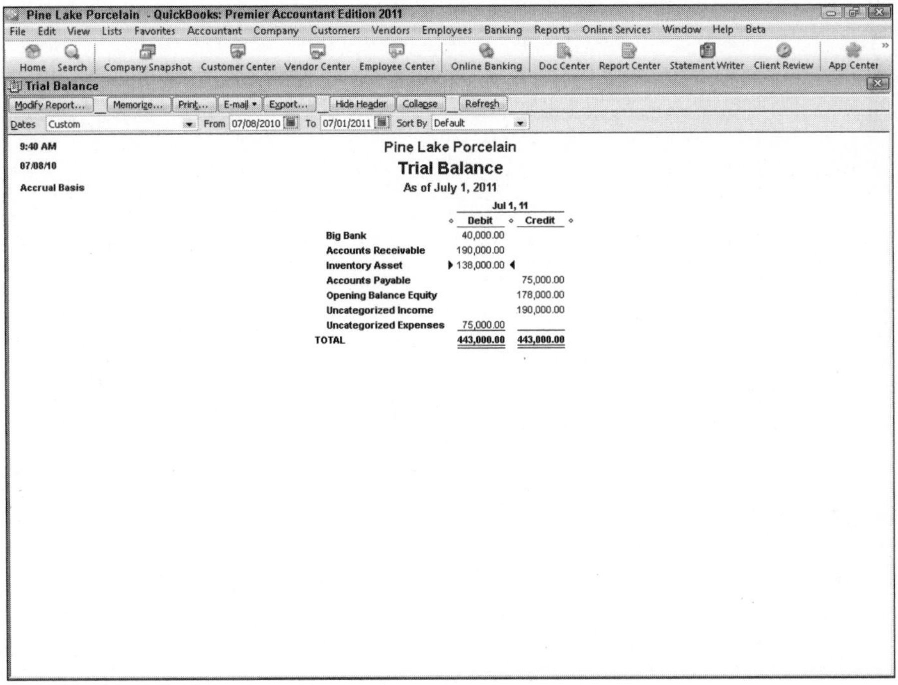

Figure 3-16:
A sample
trial
balance.

After you have the conversion date balances for the Uncategorized Income and Uncategorized Expenses accounts, you're ready to make the accrual-accounting adjustment. To do so, follow these steps:

1. **From the Home screen, either click the Chart of Accounts icon in the Company area or choose Lists⇨Chart of Accounts to display the Chart of Accounts window, as shown in Figure 3-17.**

2. **Double-click Opening Balance Equity in the Chart of Accounts list to display that account.**

   Opening Balance Equity is listed after the liability accounts. QuickBooks displays the *register* — just a list of transactions — for the Opening Balance Equity account. Figure 3-18, coincidentally, shows this register.

3. **Select the next empty row of the register if it isn't already selected (although it probably is).**

   You can select a row by clicking it, or you can use the up- or down-arrow key to move to the next empty row.

4. **Type the conversion date in the Date field.**

   Move the cursor to the Date field (if it isn't already there), and type the date. Use the MM/DD/YYYY format. For example, you can type either **06302011** or **6/30/2011** to enter June 30, 2011.

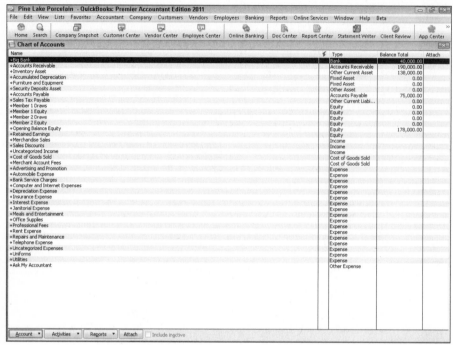

Figure 3-17:
The Chart
of Accounts
window.

5. Type the Uncategorized Income account balance (from the trial balance report) in the Increase field.

In Figure 3-16, for example, the Uncategorized Income account balance is $190,000. In this case, click the Increase field and type **190000** in the field.

You don't need to include the dollar sign or the comma; QuickBooks adds the punctuation for you.

6. Type Uncategorized Income **(the account name) in the Account field.**

Select the Account field, which is on the row under the word *Payee,* and begin typing **Uncategorized Income**, the account name. As soon as you type enough of the name for QuickBooks to figure out what you're typing, it fills in the rest of the name for you. When this happens, you can stop typing.

7. Click the Record button to record the Uncategorized Income adjustment transaction.

8. Again, select the next empty row of the register.

Click the row or use the up- or down-arrow key.

9. Type the conversion date in the Date field.

Move the cursor to the Date field (if it isn't already there), and type the date. You use the MM/DD/YYYY format. You can type **6/30/2011,** for example, to enter June 30, 2011.

10. **Type the Uncategorized Expenses account balance in the Decrease field.**

    In Figure 3-16 (shown earlier), for example, the Uncategorized Expenses account balance is $75,000. In this case, you click the Decrease field and then type **75000**. I've said this before, but I'll say it again because you're just starting out: You don't need to include any punctuation, such as a dollar sign or comma.

11. **Type** Uncategorized Expenses **(the account name) in the Account field.**

    Select the Account field, which is on the second line of the register transaction, and begin typing **Uncategorized Expenses**, the account name. As soon as you type enough of the name for QuickBooks to figure out what you're typing, it fills in the rest of the name for you.

12. **Click the Record button to record the Uncategorized Expenses adjustment transaction.**

    Figure 3-18 shows the Opening Balance Equity register with the correction transactions. The correction transactions are numbered with a 3 and a 4. See them? They're the first transactions in the register.

You can close the Opening Balance Equity register at this point. You're finished with it. One way to close it is to click the Close button in the upper-right corner of the window.

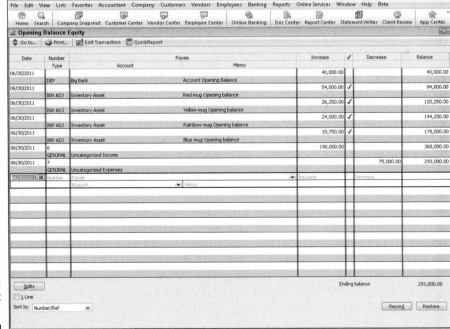

Figure 3-18: The transactions numbered 6 and 7 fix the uncategorized income and uncategorized expenses account balances.

For accountants only

If you're reading this sidebar, I assume that you're an accountant who's been asked to help your client with the last piece of the QuickBooks conversion. Of course, you understand double-entry bookkeeping, and presumably you're familiar with the general mechanics involved in converting to new accounting systems. With those two caveats, you're ready to start.

First, your client has probably already installed QuickBooks and then, by running something called the EasyStep Interview, partially set up a Chart of Accounts and loaded three master files: the Item list, the Customer list, and the Vendor list. The Item list master file describes the inventory account balances. (QuickBooks uses an average costing assumption.) The Customer list master file describes the accounts receivable balances. The Vendor list master file describes the accounts payable balances. Because your client has set up these master files, QuickBooks has made three journal entries, which I describe in the following paragraphs. (I'm using *X*s to represent numbers, in case you're not familiar with this convention.)

To set up the conversion date bank account and inventory balance (if either exists), QuickBooks created the following entry:

	Debit	Credit
Bank Account Asset	$X,XXX	
Inventory Asset	$X,XXX	
Opening Bal Equity		$X,XXX

To set up the conversion date accounts receivable (A/R) balance (if A/R exists), QuickBooks created the following entry:

	Debit	Credit
Accounts Receivable	$X,XXX	
Uncategorized Income		$X,XXX

To set up the conversion date accounts payable (A/P) balance (if A/P exists), QuickBooks created the following entry:

	Debit	Credit
Accounts Payable		$X,XXX
Uncategorized Expenses	$X,XXX	

To complete the picture, you need to do two little housekeeping chores. If your client plans to use accrual-basis accounting, you need to get rid of the credit to the Uncategorized Income account and the debit to the Uncategorized Expenses account. (These two accounts are really just suspense accounts.) And you need to load the rest of the trial balance. I describe the steps for accomplishing these tasks in the section "Supplying the missing numbers," toward the end of this chapter.

You can check your work thus far — and checking it *is* a good idea — by producing another copy of the trial balance report. What you want to check are the Uncategorized Income and Uncategorized Expenses account balances. They should both be zero, as shown in Figure 3-19.

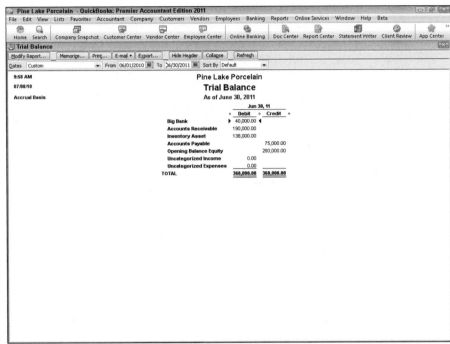

Figure 3-19:
Another
sample trial
balance.

You can produce a trial balance by choosing Reports⇨Accountant & Taxes⇨ Trial Balance. QuickBooks displays the trial balance report in a document window. If you need to enter the conversion date in the As Of line, click the box and type the conversion date in MM/DD/YYYY format.

If the Uncategorized Income and the Uncategorized Expenses account balances don't show zero, you (with my help, of course) might have botched the accrual adjustment. To fix the mistake, redisplay the Opening Balance Equity register (as noted earlier, you can double-click Opening Balance Equity in the Chart of Accounts list to display that account), select the adjustment transactions, and then check the account, amount, and field (Increase or Decrease). If one of the fields is wrong, select the field and replace its contents by typing over it.

Supplying the missing numbers

You're almost done. Really. Your last task is to enter the rest of the trial balance amounts into QuickBooks. To perform this task, you need to have a trial balance prepared as of the conversion date. If you followed my instructions in Chapter 2, you have one. Follow these steps:

1. **Choose either Company⇨Make Journal Entries or Accountant⇨Make Journal Entries.**

   QuickBooks displays the Make General Journal Entries window, as shown in Figure 3-20.

2. **Type the conversion date in the Date field.**

   Move the cursor to the Date field (if it isn't already there) and type the date. As you might know by now, you use the MM/DD/YYYY format. For example, type **6/30/2011** for June 30, 2011 (or **06302011** if you don't want to put in the slashes).

3. **Type each trial balance account and balance that isn't already in the half-completed trial balance.**

   Okay. This step sounds confusing. But remember that you've already entered your cash, accounts receivable, inventory, and accounts payable account balances, and perhaps even a few other account balances and a portion of the Opening Bal Equity account balance as part of the EasyStep Interview.

   Now you need to enter the rest of the trial balance — specifically, the year-to-date income and expense account balances, any missing assets or liabilities, and the remaining portion of the Opening Bal Equity. To enter each account and balance, use a row of the Make General Journal Entries window list box. Figure 3-21 shows how this window looks after you enter the rest of the trial balance into the list box rows.

4. **Click the Save & New button to record the general journal entries that set up the rest of your trial balance.**

Checking your work one more time

Double-checking your work is a good idea. Produce another copy of the trial balance report. Check that the QuickBooks trial balance is the same one that you wanted to enter.

You can produce a trial balance by choosing Reports⇨Accountant & Taxes⇨ Trial Balance. Be sure to enter the conversion date in the As Of text box. If the QuickBooks trial balance report agrees with what your records show, you're finished.

If the QuickBooks trial balance doesn't agree with what your records show, you need to fix the problem. Fixing it is a bit awkward but isn't complicated. Choose Reports⇨Accountant & Taxes⇨Journal. QuickBooks displays a report or journal that lists all the transactions that you or QuickBooks entered as part of setting up. (The Dates, From, and To text boxes need to specify the conversion date.) Scroll through the list of transactions until you get to the last one. The last transaction is the one that you entered to set up the rest of the trial balance; it names recognizable accounts and uses familiar debit and credit amounts. Double-click this transaction. QuickBooks redisplays the Make General Journal Entries window with the botched transaction. Find the mistake and then fix the erroneous account or amount by clicking it and typing the correct account or amount.

Congratulations! You're done.

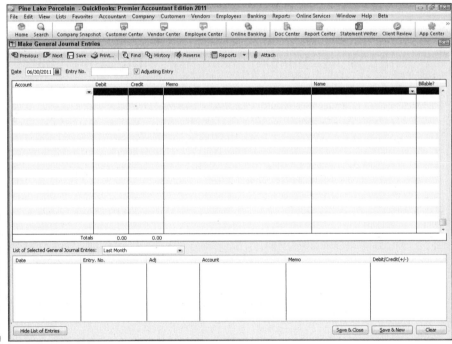

Figure 3-20:
The empty Make General Journal Entries window.

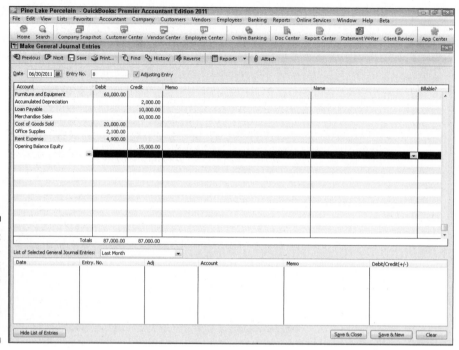

Figure 3-21:
The com-
pleted Make
General
Journal
Entries
window.

Part II
Daily Entry Tasks

The 5th Wave   By Rich Tennant

"This isn't a quantitative or a qualitative estimate of the job. This is a wish-upon-a-star estimate of the project."

In this part . . .

Okay. You have QuickBooks set up, or maybe you were lucky enough to have someone else do all the dirty work. All that doesn't matter now, though, because this part is where the rubber really hits the road. You need to start using QuickBooks to do a bunch of stuff on a regular, and maybe daily, basis. Invoice customers. Record customer payments. Pay bills. This part describes how you do all these things.

Chapter 4

Creating Invoices and Credit Memos

In this chapter (you might be surprised to discover), I describe how to create and print invoices in QuickBooks as well as how to create and print credit memos.

You use the QuickBooks invoice form to bill customers for the goods that you sell. You use its credit memos form to handle returns and canceled orders for which you've received payments.

Making Sure That You're Ready to Invoice Customers

I know that you're probably all set to go. But first, you need to check a few things, okay? Good.

You already should have installed QuickBooks, of course. (I briefly describe how in Appendix A.) You should have set up a company and a Chart of Accounts in the EasyStep Interview, as I describe in Chapter 2. You also should have entered all your lists and your starting trial balance or talked your accountant into entering it for you, as I describe in Chapter 3.

As long as you've done all this prerequisite stuff, you're ready to start. If you don't have one of the prerequisites done, you need to complete it before going any further.

Sorry. I don't make the rules. I just tell you what they are.

Preparing an Invoice

After you complete all the preliminary work, preparing an invoice with QuickBooks is a snap. If clicking buttons and filling in text boxes are becoming old hat to you, skip the following play-by-play commentary and simply display the Create Invoices window — by either choosing Customers⇨Create Invoices or clicking the Invoices icon on the Home page — and then fill in this window and click the Print button. If you want more help than a single sentence provides, keep reading for step-by-step instructions.

In the following steps, I describe how to create the most complicated and involved invoice around: a *product invoice.* Some fields on the product invoice don't appear on the *service* or *professional invoice,* but don't worry whether your business is a service or professional. Creating a service or professional invoice works basically the same way as creating a product invoice — you just fill in fewer fields. And keep in mind that you start with Steps 1 and 2 no matter what type of invoice you create. Without further ado, here's how to create an invoice:

1. **Display the Create Invoices window by choosing Customers⇨Create Invoices.**

   The Create Invoices window appears, as shown in Figure 4-1.

2. **Select the template or invoice form that you want to use from the Template drop-down list located in the upper-right corner.**

   QuickBooks comes with predefined invoice form types, including Product, Professional, Service, and (depending on how you set up QuickBooks and which version of QuickBooks you're using) a handful of other specialized invoice templates as well. Which one appears by default depends on which one you told QuickBooks that you wanted to use in the EasyStep Interview. You can even create your own custom invoice template (or modify an existing one) by clicking the Customize button. I describe customizing invoice forms in the "Customizing Your Invoices and Credit Memos" section, later in this chapter.

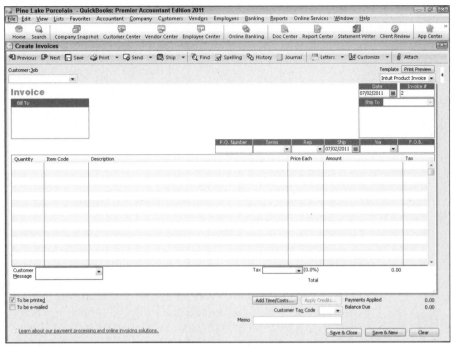

Figure 4-1:
The Create
Invoices
window.

3. **Identify the customer and, if necessary, the job by using the Customer:Job drop-down list.**

   Scroll through the Customer:Job drop-down list until you see the customer or job name that you need; then click it.

4. **(Optional) Assign a class to the invoice.**

   If you use classes to track expenses and income, activate the Class drop-down list and select an appropriate class for the invoice. To turn this handy way of categorizing transactions on or off (which is overkill for some businesses), choose Edit⇨Preferences, click Accounting on the left, click the Company Preferences tab, and then select or clear the Use Class Tracking check box. (Figure 4-1 doesn't show the Class box.)

5. **Give the invoice date.**

   Press Tab several times to move the cursor to the Date text box. Then enter the correct date in MM/DD/YYYY format. You also can use the following secret codes to change the date:

   • *Press* + (the plus symbol) to move the date ahead one day.

   • *Press* – (the minus symbol) to move the date back one day.

- *Press T* to change the date to today's date (as specified by the system time that your computer's internal clock provides).

- *Press M* to change the date to the first day of the month (because *M* is the first letter in the word *month*).

- *Press H* to change the date to the last day of the month (because *H* is the last letter in the word *month*).

- *Press Y* to change the date to the first day of the year (because, as you no doubt can guess, *Y* is the first letter in the word *year*).

- *Press R* to change the date to the last day of the year (because *R* is the last letter in the word *year*).

You can also click the button on the right side of the Date field to display a small calendar. To select a date from the calendar, just click the date you want. Click the arrows in the top-left and top-right corners of the calendar to display the previous or next month.

6. **(Optional) Enter an invoice number in the Invoice # text box.**

QuickBooks suggests an invoice number by adding 1 to the last invoice number that you used. You can accept this addition, or if you need to have it your way, you can tab to the Invoice # text box and change the number to whatever you want.

7. **Fix the Bill To address, if necessary.**

QuickBooks grabs the billing address from the Customer list. You can change the address for the invoice by replacing some portion of the usual billing address. You can, for example, insert another line that says *Attention: William Bobbins,* if that's the name of the person to whom the invoice should go.

8. **Fix the Ship To address, if necessary.**

I feel like a broken record, but here's the deal: QuickBooks also grabs the shipping address from the Customer list. So if the shipping address has something unusual about it for just this one invoice, you can change the address by replacing or adding information to the Ship To address block. Note that QuickBooks will keep track of each of the shipping addresses you use for a customer, so if you used a shipping address before, you may be able to select it from the Ship To drop-down list.

9. **(Optional . . . sort of) Provide the purchase order number in the P.O. Number text box.**

If the customer issues purchase orders (POs), enter the number of the purchase order that authorizes this purchase. (Just for the record, PO is pronounced *pee-oh,* not *poh* or *poo.*)

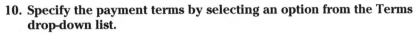

10. **Specify the payment terms by selecting an option from the Terms drop-down list.**

    I have only one request: Don't offer a customer an early payment discount without reading the first couple sections in Chapter 21. Please. I'm only looking out for your welfare. Really.

11. **(Optional) Name the sales representative.**

    Rep doesn't stand for *Reputation,* so don't put three-letter editorial comments in here (although I can't, for the life of me, imagine what you could do with three letters). If you want to track sales by sales representative, use the Rep drop-down list. Simply activate the list by clicking its arrow and then pick a name. Sales representatives can include employees, but they can also include other people that you've entered in your other lists. To quickly add a sales rep, select Add New and then use the handy-dandy dialog boxes that QuickBooks displays. To work with the Sales Rep list, choose Lists⇨Customer & Vendor Profile Lists⇨Sales Rep List.

12. **Specify the shipping date if it's something other than the invoice date.**

    To specify the date, simply move the cursor to the Ship text box and then type the date in MM/DD/YYYY format. You can move the cursor by pressing Tab or by clicking the text box.

    Oh — one other quick point: Remember all those secret codes that I talk about in Step 5 for changing the invoice date? They also work for changing the shipping date.

13. **Specify the shipping method.**

    You can probably guess how you specify the shipping method, but parallel structure and a compulsive personality force me to continue. So to specify the shipping method, move the cursor to the Via drop-down list and then select a shipping method from it.

    By the way, you can add new shipping methods to the list by selecting Add New and then filling out the cute little dialog box that QuickBooks displays. Setting up new shipping methods is really easy. Really easy.

14. **Specify the FOB point by using the F.O.B. text box.**

    FOB stands for *free-on-board.* The FOB point is more important than it first seems — at least in a business sense — because the FOB point determines when the transfer of ownership occurs, who pays freight, and who bears the risks of damage to the goods during shipping.

    If a shipment is free-on-board at the *shipping* point, the ownership of the goods being sold transfers to the purchaser as soon as the goods leave the seller's shipping dock. (Remember that you're the seller.) In this case, the purchaser pays the freight and bears the risk of shipping damage. You can specify the FOB shipping point either as FOB Shipping Point or by using the name of the city. If the shipping point is Seattle, for example, FOB Seattle is the same thing as FOB Shipping Point. Most goods are shipped as FOB Shipping Point, by the way.

If a shipment is free-on-board at the *destination* point, the ownership of the goods that are being sold transfers to the purchaser as soon as the goods arrive on the purchaser's shipping dock. The seller pays the freight and bears the risk of shipping damage. You can specify the FOB destination point either as FOB Destination Point or by using the name of the city. If the destination point is Omaha, for example, FOB Omaha is the same thing as FOB Destination Point.

15. **Enter each item that you're selling.**

Move the cursor to the first row of the Quantity/Item Code/Description/Price Each/Amount/Tax list box. Okay, I know that isn't a very good name for it, but you know what I mean, right? You need to start filling in the line items that go on the invoice. After you move the cursor to a row in the list box, QuickBooks turns the Item Code field into a drop-down list. Activate the Item Code drop-down list box of the first empty row in the list box and then select the item.

When you select the item, QuickBooks fills in the Description and Price Each text boxes with whatever sales description and sales price you've entered in the Item list. (You can edit the information for this particular invoice if you need to.) Enter the number of items sold in the Quantity text box. (After you enter this number, QuickBooks calculates the amount by multiplying Quantity by Price Each.) If you need other items on the invoice, use the remaining empty rows of the list box to enter each one. If you marked the Taxable check box when you added the item to the Item list, the word *Tax* appears in the Tax column to indicate that the item will be taxed. If the item is nontaxable (or you feel like being a tax evader for no good reason), click the Tax column and select *Non*.

You can put as many items on an invoice as you want. If you don't have enough room on a single page, QuickBooks adds as many pages as necessary to the invoice. Information about the invoice total, of course, goes only on the last page.

Click the Add Time/Costs button at the bottom of the form to display the Choose Billable Time and Costs dialog box. Use this dialog box to select costs that you've assigned to the customer or job. Use the Items tab to select items purchased for the job. Use the Expenses tab to select reimbursable expenses and enter markup information. Use the Time tab to select billable time recorded by the Timer program, the Weekly Timesheet, or in the Time/Enter Single Activity window.

16. Enter any special items that the invoice should include.

If you haven't worked much with the QuickBooks item file, you have no idea what I'm talking about. (For more information about adding to and working with lists in QuickBooks, cruise through Chapter 3.)

To describe any of the special items, activate the Item Code drop-down list of the next empty row and then select the special item. After QuickBooks fills in the Description and Price Each text boxes, edit this information (if necessary). Describe each of the other special items — subtotals, discounts, freight, and so on — that you're itemizing on the invoice by filling in the empty rows in the list box.

If you want to include a Discount item and have it apply to multiple items, you need to stick a Subtotal item on the invoice after the inventory or other items that you want to discount. Then stick a Discount item directly after the Subtotal item. QuickBooks calculates the discount as a percentage of the subtotal.

17. (Optional) Add a customer message.

Click in the Customer Message box, activate its drop-down list, and select a clever customer message. To add customer messages to the Customer Message list, choose Add New and then fill in the dialog box that QuickBooks displays. (I know that I talk about the Customer Message box in Chapter 3, but I wanted to quickly describe how to add a customer message again so that you don't have to flip back through a bunch of pages.)

18. Specify the sales tax.

If you specified a tax rate in the Customer list, QuickBooks uses it as a default. If it isn't correct, move the cursor to the Tax list box, activate the drop-down list, and select the correct sales tax.

19. (Truly optional) Add a memo.

You can add a memo description to the invoice if you want to. This memo doesn't print on invoices — only on the Customer Statement. Memo descriptions give you a way of storing information related to an invoice with that invoice. Figure 4-2 shows a completed Create Invoices window.

20. If you want to delay printing this invoice, clear the To Be Printed check box that's below the column of buttons in the lower-left area of the Create Invoices window.

I want to postpone talking about what selecting the To Be Printed check box does until I finish the discussion of invoice creation. I talk about printing invoices a little later in the chapter. I promise.

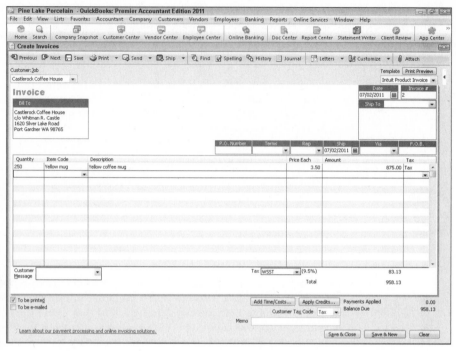

Figure 4-2:
A completed
Create
Invoices
window.

21. Save the invoice by clicking the Save & New button or the Save & Close button.

QuickBooks saves the invoice that's onscreen. If you click Save & New, QuickBooks displays an empty Create Invoices window so that you can create another invoice.

You can page back and forth through invoices that you created earlier by clicking the Next and Previous buttons.

When you're done creating invoices, you can click the invoice form's Save & Close button. Or click the Close button, also known as the Close box, which is the little red box marked with an X in the upper-right corner of the window.

Fixing Invoice Mistakes

I'm not a perfect person. You're not a perfect person. Heck, nobody is; everyone makes mistakes. You don't need to get worked up over mistakes that you make while entering information in invoices, though, because in the following sections, I show you how to fix the most common mistakes that you might make on your invoices.

If the invoice is still displayed onscreen

If the invoice is still displayed onscreen, you can just move the cursor to the box or button that's wrong and then fix the mistake. Because most of the bits of information that you enter in the Create Invoices window are short and sweet, you can easily replace the contents of some fields by typing over whatever's already there. To start all over again, just click the Clear button. To save the invoice after you've made your changes, click the Save & New button.

If you need to insert a line in the middle of the invoice, right-click to display a contextual menu and then choose Insert Line or Delete Line.

If the invoice isn't displayed onscreen

If the invoice isn't displayed onscreen and you haven't yet printed it, you can use the Next and Previous buttons to page through the invoices. When you get to the one with the error, simply fix the error as I describe in the preceding section. If you make an error fixing the invoice, you can click the Revert button to go back to the saved invoice. The Revert button replaces the Clear button when you're viewing an existing invoice — that is, an invoice that you've already saved.

If you printed the invoice, you also can make the sort of change that I describe in the preceding paragraphs. For example, you can page through the invoices until you find the one (now printed) that has the error. And you can correct the error and print the invoice again. I'm not so sure that you want to go this route, however, if you've already sent the invoice. You might want to consider fixing the invoice by issuing either a credit memo (if the original invoice overcharged) or another invoice (if the original invoice undercharged). The reason why I suggest issuing a credit memo (which I show you how to do in the appropriately titled section, "Preparing a Credit Memo," later in this chapter) or another invoice is that life gets awfully messy if you and your customer have multiple copies of the same invoice floating around and causing confusion.

Deleting an invoice

I hesitate to mention this, but you also can delete invoices. Procedurally, deleting an invoice is easy. You just display the invoice in the Create Invoices window and choose Edit⇨Delete Invoice. When QuickBooks asks you to confirm your deletion, click Yes. Read the following paragraph first, though, because you may not want to delete the invoice.

Even though deleting invoices is easy, it isn't something that you should do casually or for fun. Deleting an invoice is okay if you've just created it, only you have seen it, and you haven't yet printed it. In this case, no one needs to know that you've made a mistake. It's your secret. The rest of the time — even if you create an invoice that you don't want later — you should keep a copy of the invoice in the QuickBooks system. By doing so, you have a record that the invoice existed, which usually makes it easier to answer questions later.

"But how do I correct my books if I leave the bogus invoice?" you ask.

Good question. To correct your financial records for the invoice that you don't want to count anymore, simply *void* the invoice. The invoice remains in the QuickBooks system, but QuickBooks doesn't count it because it loses its quantity and amount information. Good news — voiding an invoice is as simple as deleting one. Just display the invoice in the Create Invoices window and then choose Edit⇨Void Invoice.

Preparing a Credit Memo

Credit memos can be a handy way to fix data-entry mistakes that you didn't find or correct earlier. Credit memos are also handy ways to handle things like customer returns and refunds. If you've prepared an invoice or two in your time, you'll find that preparing a QuickBooks credit memo is a lot easier than using old-fashioned methods.

In the following steps, I describe how to create the most complicated and involved kind of credit memo: a *product credit memo.* Creating a *service* or *professional credit memo* works basically the same way, however. You just fill in fewer fields.

1. **Choose Customers⇨Create Credit Memos/Refunds or click the Refunds & Credits icon in the Customer section of the Home page to display the Create Credit Memos/Refunds window (as shown in Figure 4-3).**

2. **Identify the customer and, if necessary, the job in the Customer:Job drop-down list.**

   You can select the customer or job from the list by clicking it.

3. **(Optional) Specify a class for the credit memo.**

   If you're using classes to categorize transactions, activate the Class drop-down list and choose the appropriate class for the credit memo.

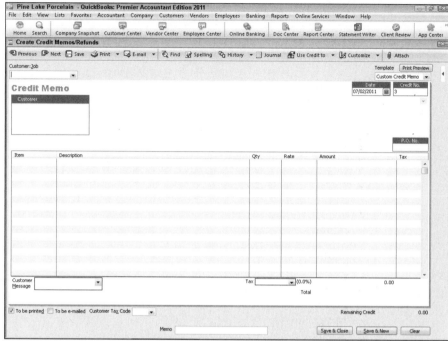

Figure 4-3:
The Create
Credit
Memos/
Refunds
window.

4. **Date the credit memo. (Going steady is optional.)**

   Press Tab to move the cursor to the Date text box. Then enter the correct date in MM/DD/YYYY format. You also can use the secret date-editing codes that I describe in the section "Preparing an Invoice," earlier in the chapter. Oh, boy.

5. **(Optional) Enter a credit memo number.**

   QuickBooks suggests a credit memo number by adding 1 to the last credit memo number you used. You can accept the number or tab to the Credit No. text box to change the number to whatever you want.

6. **Fix the Customer address, if necessary.**

   QuickBooks grabs the billing address from the Customer list. You can change the address for the credit memo by replacing some portion of the usual billing address. Typically, you should use the same address for the credit memo that you use for the original invoice or invoices.

7. (Optional . . . sort of) Provide the purchase order (PO) number.

If the credit memo adjusts the total remaining balance on a customer purchase order, you should probably enter the number of the purchase order into the P.O. No. text box.

Here's my logic on this suggestion, for those readers who care: If you billed your customer $1,000 on P.O. No. 1984, which authorizes a $1,000 purchase, you "used up" the entire purchase order — at least according to the customer's accounts payable clerk, who processes your invoices. If you make sure that a credit memo for $1,000 is identified as being related to P.O. No. 1984, however, you essentially free up the $1,000 purchase balance, which might mean that you can use, or bill on, the purchase order again.

8. If the customer returns items, describe each item.

Move the cursor to the first row of the Item/Description/Qty/Rate/Amount/Tax text box. In the first empty row of the box, activate the Item drop-down list and then select the item. After you select it, QuickBooks fills in the Description and Rate text boxes with whatever sales description and sales price you entered in the Item list. (You can edit this information if you want, but it isn't necessary.) Enter the number of items that the customer is returning (or not paying for) in the Qty text box. (After you enter this number, QuickBooks calculates the amount by multiplying Qty by Rate.) Enter each item that the customer is returning by filling in the empty rows of the list box.

In the case of inventory items, QuickBooks assumes that the items you're showing on a credit memo are returned to inventory. You want to adjust your inventory physical counts if unsold items are returned.

As with invoices, you can put as many items on a credit memo as you want. If you don't have enough room on a single page, QuickBooks keeps adding pages to the credit memo until you're finished. The total information, of course, goes on the last page.

9. Describe any special items that the credit memo should include.

If you want to issue a credit memo for other items that appear on the original invoice — freight, discounts, other charges, and so on — add descriptions of each item to the Item list.

To add descriptions of these items, activate the Item drop-down list of the next empty row and then select the special item. (You activate the list by clicking the field once to turn it into a drop-down list and then by clicking the field's down arrow to access the list box.) After QuickBooks fills in the Description and Rate text boxes, edit this information (if necessary). Enter each special item — subtotal, discount, freight, and so on — that you're itemizing on the credit memo.

If you want to include a Discount item, you need to stick a Subtotal item on the credit memo after the inventory or other items that you've discounted. Then stick a Discount item directly after the Subtotal item. In this way, QuickBooks calculates the discount as a percentage of the subtotal.

10. **(Optional) Add a customer message.**

    Activate the Customer Message list and select a clever customer message.

11. **Specify the sales tax.**

    Move the cursor to the Tax list box, activate the list box, and then select the correct sales tax.

12. **(Optional, but a really good idea . . .) Add a memo.**

    You can use the Memo text box to add a memo description to the credit memo. For example, you might use this description to explain your reasons for issuing the credit memo and to cross-reference the original invoice or invoices. Note that the Memo field prints on the Customer Statement. Figure 4-4 shows a completed Create Credit Memos/Refunds window.

13. **If you want to delay printing this credit memo, clear the To Be Printed check box.**

    I want to postpone talking about what selecting the To Be Printed check box does until I finish the discussion of credit memo creation. Coverage of printing invoices and credit memos comes up in a later section.

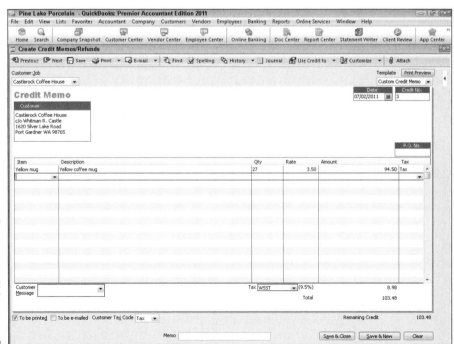

Figure 4-4: A completed Create Credit Memos/ Refunds window.

14. **Save the credit memo.**

   To save a completed credit memo, click either the Save & New or Save & Close button. QuickBooks then displays a dialog box that asks what you want to do with the credit memo: Retain the credit, give a refund, or apply the credit to an invoice. Make your choice by clicking the button that corresponds to what you want to do. If you choose Apply to Invoice, QuickBooks asks for some additional information. QuickBooks then saves the credit memo that's onscreen and, if you clicked Save & New, displays an empty Create Credit Memos/Refunds window so that you can create another credit memo. (Note that you can page back and forth through credit memos that you created earlier by clicking the Next and the Previous buttons.) When you're done creating credit memos, you can click the credit memo form's Close button.

If you indicate that you want to print a refund check, QuickBooks displays the Write Checks window and automatically fills out the check, linking it to the memo.

Fixing Credit Memo Mistakes

Sure, I can repeat the same information that I gave you in the section "Fixing Invoice Mistakes," earlier in this chapter, and leave you with a strange feeling of *déjà vu*. But I won't.

Here's everything you need to know about fixing credit memo mistakes: You can fix credit memo mistakes the same way that you fix invoice mistakes. If you need more help, refer to the earlier section "Fixing Invoice Mistakes."

History Lessons

Would you mind doing a small favor for me? Take another peek at the images shown in Figures 4-1 and 4-4, and then look at the Create Invoices window shown in Figure 4-5. See the difference? That panel of customer history information?

QuickBooks lets you add and remove historical information about a customer from the Create Invoices window, the Create Credit Memos/Refunds window, and most other "customer information" windows, too. To add historical information about a customer to a window, click the Show History button that appears in the upper-right corner of the window just to the right of the Print Preview button. Note that you click links in the historical information panel to drill down and get more information about, for example, a listed transaction.

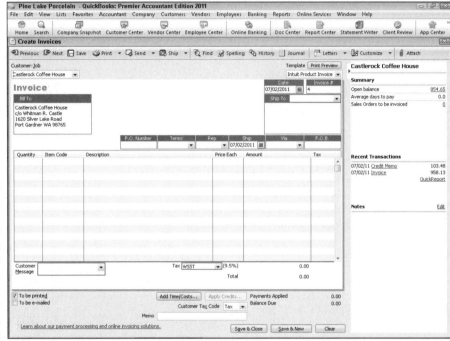

Figure 4-5:
The
Customer
Invoices
window
with the
customer
history
information.

Printing Invoices and Credit Memos

As part of setting up QuickBooks, you selected an invoice type. I assume that you have the raw paper stock for whatever invoice type you chose. If you're going to print on blank letterhead, for example, I assume that you have let-terhead lying around. If you decide to use preprinted forms, I assume that you've ordered those forms and have received them.

I also assume that you've already set up your printer. If you've ever printed anything, your printer is already set up. Really.

Loading the forms into the printer

This part is easy. Simply load the invoice forms into the printer the same way you always load paper. Because you have one of about a jillion different printers, I can't give you the precise steps that you need to take, but if you've used a printer a bit, you should have no problem.

Wait a minute. What's that? Your printer is brand new, and you've never used it before? Okay, here's one of my weird ideas: Use a pencil or something else that's heat resistant (so that it won't melt and gum up the insides of the printer) to draw an arrow on a piece of paper. (Do not, repeat, do *not* use crayon. And don't let your children watch you do this.) Draw the arrow so that it points toward the top edge of the paper. Load the paper in the printer, with the arrow face up, and note which direction the arrow is pointing. Print something. Anything. When the paper comes out, notice whether the image faces the same direction as the arrow and whether it's on the same side of the paper as the arrow. With this information and a little logic, you can figure out how to load forms correctly.

Setting up the invoice printer

You need to set up the invoice printer only once, but you need to specify a handful of general invoice-printing rules. These rules also apply to credit memos and purchase orders, by the way.

To set up your printer for invoice printing, follow these steps:

1. **Choose File⇨Printer Setup. From the Form Name drop-down list, choose Invoice.**

   QuickBooks displays the Printer Setup dialog box, as shown in Figure 4-6.

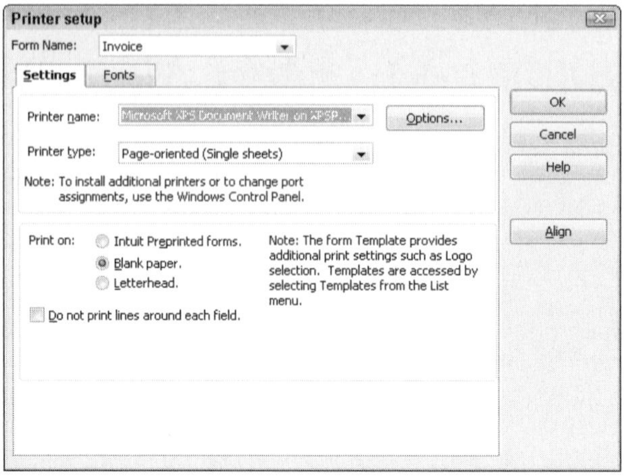

Figure 4-6:
The Printer Setup dialog box.

2. **Select the printer that you want to use to print invoices.**

   Activate the Printer Name drop-down list to see the installed printers. Select the one that you want to use for printing invoices and purchase orders.

3. **(Optional) Select the printer type.**

   The Printer Type drop-down list describes the kind of paper that your printer uses. You have two choices:

   - *Continuous:* Your paper comes as one connected ream with perforated edges.
   - *Page-Oriented:* Your paper is in single sheets.

4. **Select the type of invoice form.**

   Select the option button that describes the type of form that you want to print on: Intuit Preprinted Forms, Blank Paper, or Letterhead. Then select the Do Not Print Lines around Each Field check box if you don't like the nice little boxes that QuickBooks creates to separate each field.

   For more on these types of forms, read the sidebar, "What am I printing on?"

5. **(Optional, but a really good idea . . .) Print a test invoice on real invoice paper.**

   Click the Align button. When QuickBooks displays the Align Printer dialog box, choose the type of invoice that you want to print from the list and then click OK. When QuickBooks displays the Fine Alignment dialog box, as shown in Figure 4-7, click the Print Sample button to tell QuickBooks to print a dummy invoice on whatever paper you've loaded in the invoice printer.

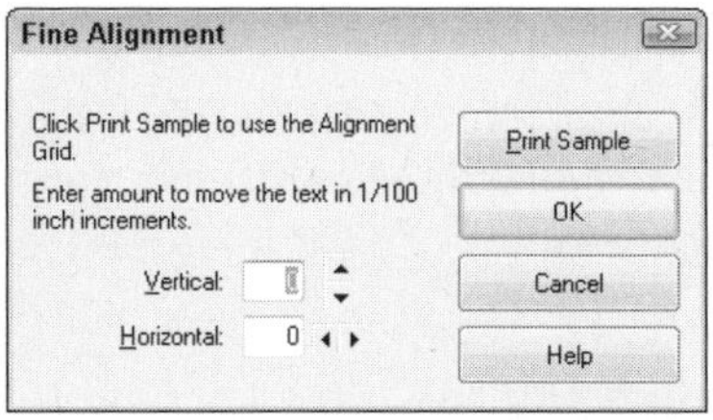

Figure 4-7:
The Fine Alignment dialog box.

The dummy invoice that QuickBooks prints gives you a chance to see what your invoices will look like. The invoice also has a set of alignment gridlines that prints over the Bill To text box. You can use these gridlines if you need to fine-align your printer.

6. **Fix any form-alignment problems.**

   If you see any alignment problems after you complete Step 5, you need to fix them. (Alignment problems usually occur only with impact printers. With laser printers or inkjet printers, sheets of paper feed into the printer the same way every time, so you almost never need to fiddle with the form alignment.)

To fix any big alignment problems — like stuff printing in the wrong place — you need to adjust how the paper feeds into the printer. When you finally get the paper loaded as best you can, be sure to note exactly how you have it loaded. You need to have the printer and paper set up the same way every time you print.

For minor (but nonetheless annoying) alignment problems, use the Fine Alignment dialog box's Vertical and Horizontal boxes to adjust the form's alignment. Then print another sample invoice. Go ahead and experiment a bit. You need to fine-tune the printing of the invoice form only once. Click OK in the Fine Alignment dialog box when you finish, to have QuickBooks redisplay the Printer Setup dialog box.

Clicking the Options button in the Printer Setup dialog box (refer to Figure 4-6) opens the selected printer's Windows printer setup information, where you can do such things as specify quality settings or print order. Because this information relates to Windows and not to QuickBooks, I'm not going to explain it. If you're the curious type or accidentally click it and then have questions about what you see, refer either to your Windows user's guide or the printer's user's guide.

7. **Save your printer settings stuff.**

    After you finish fiddling with all the Printer Setup dialog box settings, click OK to save your changes.

    If you always want to use some particular settings to print a particular form (maybe you always print two copies of an invoice, for example), see the "Customizing Your Invoices and Credit Memos" section, later in this chapter.

You can print invoices and credit memos one at a time or in a batch. How you print them makes no difference to QuickBooks or to me, your humble author. Pick whatever way seems to fit your style the best. The following sections show you how.

Printing invoices and credit memos as you create them

If you want to print invoices and credit memos as you create them, follow these steps:

1. **Click the Print button after you create the invoice or credit memo.**

    After you fill in the boxes in the Create Invoices window (refer to Figure 4-2) or the Create Credit Memos/Refunds window (refer to Figure 4-4), click the Print button. QuickBooks, ever the faithful servant, displays either the Print One Invoice dialog box (as shown in Figure 4-8) or the Print One Credit Memo/Refund dialog box (which looks almost like the Print One Invoice dialog box).

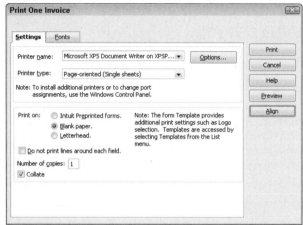

Figure 4-8:
The Print
One Invoice
dialog box.

2. (Optional) Select the type of invoice or credit memo form.

If you're using a different type of invoice or credit memo form than you've described for the invoice printer setup, select the type of form that you want to print from the Print On radio button choices. You can select Intuit Preprinted Forms, Blank Paper, or Letterhead.

You shouldn't have to worry about printing test invoice or credit memo forms or fiddling with form alignment problems if you addressed these issues when you set up the invoice printer, so I'm not going to talk about the Align button here. If you want to do this kind of stuff and you need help, refer to the preceding section, "Setting up the invoice printer," in which I describe how to print test forms and fix form-alignment problems.

3. Print the form.

Click the Print button to send the form to the printer. QuickBooks prints the form.

4. Review the invoice or credit memo and reprint the form, if necessary.

Review the invoice or credit memo to see whether QuickBooks printed it correctly. If the form looks wrong, fix whatever caused the problem (perhaps you printed it on the wrong paper, for example) and reprint the form by clicking the Print button again.

Printing invoices in a batch

If you want to print invoices in a batch, you need to mark the To Be Printed check box that appears in the lower-left corner of the Create Invoices window. This check mark tells QuickBooks to put a copy of the invoice on a special invoices-to-be-printed list.

What am I printing on?

Sometimes people get confused about the difference between preprinted forms, letterhead, and plain paper. Here's the scoop: *Preprinted forms* have your company name, perhaps your logo, and a bunch of other boxes and lines (often in another color of ink) already printed on them. Preprinted forms are often multipart forms. (Examples of preprinted forms come in the QuickBooks box.)

Letterhead is what you usually use for letters that you write. It has your company name and address on it, for example, but nothing else. To save you from having to purchase preprinted forms, QuickBooks enables you to use letterhead to create invoices and forms. (To make the letterhead look a little more bookkeeper-ish, QuickBooks draws lines and boxes on the letterhead so that it looks sort of like a preprinted invoice.)

Plain paper is, well, plain paper. Nothing is printed on it. So QuickBooks needs to print everything — your company name, all the invoice stuff, and (optionally) lines and boxes. Not that you care, but in my CPA practice, I use high-quality plain paper to bill my clients and find that approach works just great.

When you later want to print the invoices-to-be-printed list, follow these steps:

1. **Display the Create Invoices window (choose Customers⇨Create Invoices), click the arrow next to the Print button, and choose Print Batch from the drop-down list.**

   QuickBooks displays the Select Invoices to Print dialog box, as shown in Figure 4-9. This box lists all the invoices that you marked as To Be Printed that you haven't yet printed.

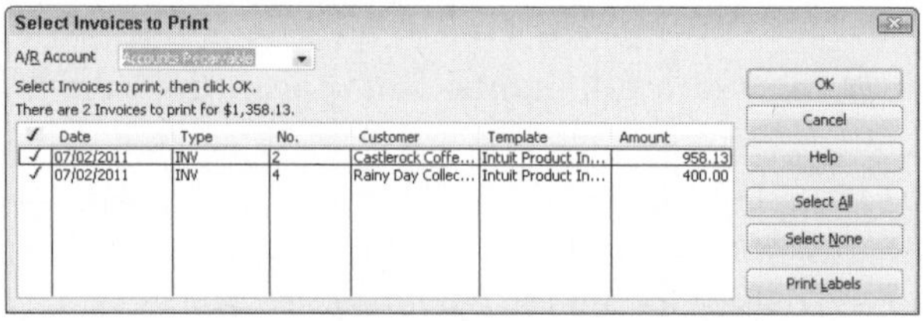

Figure 4-9:
The Select Invoices to Print dialog box.

Select Invoices to Print						
A/R Account	Accounts Payable ▾					OK
Select Invoices to print, then click OK.						Cancel
There are 2 Invoices to print for $1,358.13.						Help
✓	Date	Type	No.	Customer	Template	Amount
✓	07/02/2011	INV	2	Castlerock Coffe...	Intuit Product In...	958.13
✓	07/02/2011	INV	4	Rainy Day Collec...	Intuit Product In...	400.00

Select All
Select None
Print Labels

2. **Select the invoices that you want to print.**

   Initially, QuickBooks marks all the invoices with a check mark, indicating that they'll be printed. You can select and deselect individual invoices on the list by clicking them. You also can click the Select All button (to mark all the invoices) or the Select None button (to deselect all the invoices).

3. Click OK.

After you correctly mark all the invoices you want to print — and none of the ones you don't want to print — click OK. QuickBooks displays the Print Invoices dialog box, as shown in Figure 4-10.

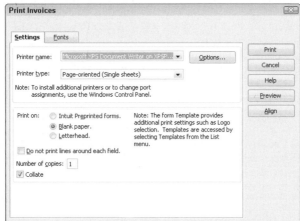

Figure 4-10: The Print Invoices dialog box.

4. (Optional) Select the type of invoice form.

If you use a different type of invoice form than you described during the invoice setup, select the type of form that you want to print on by using the Print On options. You can choose Intuit Preprinted Forms, Blank Paper, or Letterhead.

For more on these types of forms, read the sidebar, "What am I printing on?" elsewhere in this chapter.

5. Print the forms.

Click the Print button to send the selected invoice forms to the printer. QuickBooks prints the forms and then displays a message box that asks whether the forms printed correctly.

6. Review the invoice forms and reprint them if necessary.

Review the invoices to see whether QuickBooks printed them all correctly. If all the forms look okay, click OK in the message box. If one or more forms don't look okay, enter the invoice number of the first incorrect form in the message box. Then fix whatever problem fouled up the form (perhaps you printed it on the wrong paper, for example) and reprint the bad form(s) by clicking the Print button again. (The Print button is in the Print Invoices dialog box.)

Printing credit memos in a batch

If you want to print credit memos in a batch, you need to select the To Be Printed check box that appears in the lower-left corner of the Create Credit Memos/Refunds window. Selecting this box tells QuickBooks to put a copy of the credit memo on a special credit memos to-be-printed list.

Printing credit memos in a batch works similarly to printing invoices in a batch. Because I describe how to print invoices in a batch in the preceding section, here I speed through a description of printing credit memos in a batch. If you get lost or have questions, refer to the preceding section.

When you're ready to print the credit memos that are on the to-be-printed list, follow these steps:

1. **Display the Create Credit Memos/Refunds window (refer to Figure 4-4), click the down arrow next to the Print button, and choose Print Batch from the drop-down list.**

   QuickBooks displays the Select Credit Memos to Print dialog box.

2. **Select the credit memos that you want to print.**

3. **Click OK to display the Print Credit Memos dialog box.**

4. **Use the Print Credit Memos dialog box to describe how you want your credit memos to be printed.**

5. **Click the Print button to send the selected credit memos to the printer.**

   QuickBooks prints the credit memos.

Sending Invoices and Credit Memos via E-Mail

If you have e-mail already set up on your computer, you can e-mail invoices rather than print them. To e-mail an invoice or credit memo, click the Send button, which appears at the top of the Create Invoices window. (The button shows a picture of a little envelope with a green arrow.) QuickBooks displays the Send Invoice dialog box, as shown in Figure 4-11.

To send your invoice via e-mail, enter the e-mail address of the business that you want to bill or refund money to, edit the message as appropriate (make sure to click that Check Spelling button), and then click the Send Now button.

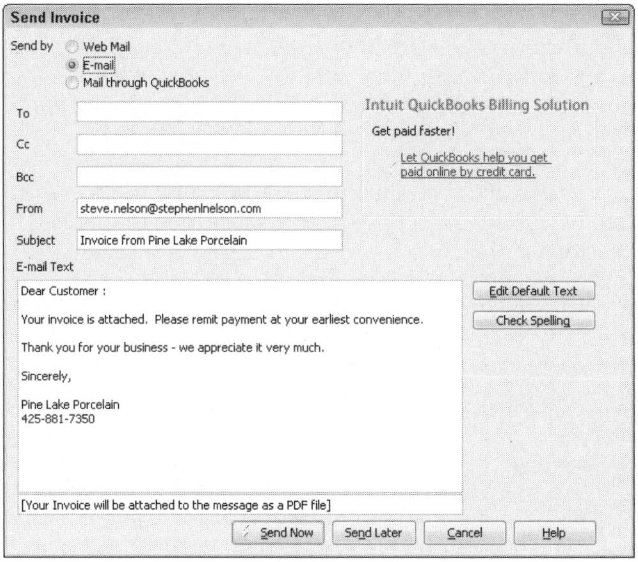

Send Invoice

Send by ○ Web Mail
         ⦿ E-mail
         ○ Mail through QuickBooks

To   [   ]   Intuit QuickBooks Billing Solution

Cc   [   ]   Get paid faster!

Bcc [   ]   Let QuickBooks help you get
                                              paid online by credit card.
From   steve.nelson@stephenlnelson.com

Subject   Invoice from Pine Lake Porcelain

E-mail Text

Dear Customer :   [Edit Default Text]

Your invoice is attached. Please remit payment at your earliest convenience.   [Check Spelling]

Thank you for your business - we appreciate it very much.

Sincerely,

Pine Lake Porcelain
425-881-7350

[Your Invoice will be attached to the message as a PDF file]

[Send Now] [Send Later] [Cancel] [Help]

Figure 4-11:
The Send
Invoice dia-
log box.

TIP

If you want to wait to send your invoice, click the Send Later button while in the Send Invoice dialog box or select the To Be E-Mailed check box in the lower-left corner of the invoice window, and QuickBooks batches your e-mail invoices. You can send the entire batch later by clicking the arrow next to the Send button and choosing the Send Batch command. Note that QuickBooks also has a mailing service that you can sign up for. To get the dirt on this option, click the Send button and choose the Mail Invoice command from the menu that QuickBooks displays.

REMEMBER

You can also fax invoices and credit memos from inside QuickBooks if you have a modem installed. To do this, click the Print button at the top of the Create Invoices or the Create Credit Memos/Refunds window, choose your fax/modem from the Printer Name drop-down list, and then use the wizard that appears to send the fax via your modem. (Long-distance charges may apply.)

Customizing Your Invoices and Credit Memos

With QuickBooks, you can easily customize the invoice and credit memo templates, or create new invoices and credit memos based on one of the existing

QuickBooks templates. All you have to do is open the form that you want to customize and click the Customize button. When QuickBooks displays the Customize Your QuickBooks Forms window, you can click the Create New Design button to go to an Intuit Web page that walks you through the steps to creating your own highly customized form (see Figure 4-12).

Alternatively, you can click the Customize Data Layout button (also available from the Customize Your QuickBooks Forms window) to display dialog boxes that supply buttons and boxes that you can use to first create a copy of the standard QuickBooks invoice or credit memo form and then modify the data that appears on the new copy of the form. Note that the customization dialog boxes provide a Preview area that shows what the customizations look like, so go hog-wild and be adventurous. (If you make a mess, just click Cancel to abandon your customization changes. Then, if you want, restart the process — perhaps a bit wiser and smarter for the experience.)

If you're creating a new invoice form using the customization dialog boxes, you can also click the Layout Designer button in the customization dialog box to open the Layout Designer window, as shown in Figure 4-13. In this window, you can become a true layout artist and observe how the overall look of your invoice changes when you move fields around the page with your mouse.

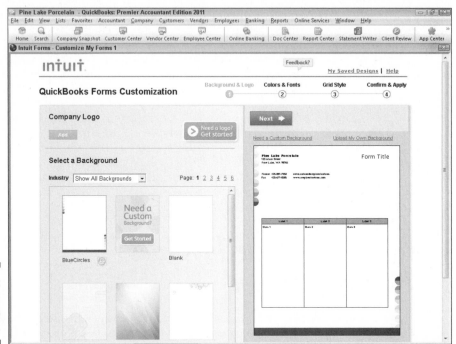

Figure 4-12:
The Create
New Design
Web page.

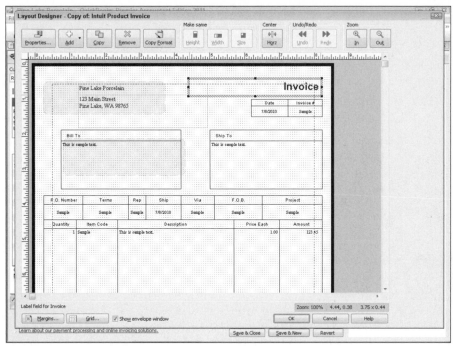

Figure 4-13:
Use Layout
Designer to
customize
an invoice.

Chapter 5

Reeling In the Dough

....

In This Chapter

▶ Recording and printing sales receipts

▶ Discovering special tips for retailers

▶ Looking at special tips for retailers

▶ Fixing sales receipt mistakes

▶ Recording customer payments

▶ Correcting mistakes in recording customer payments

▶ Making deposits

▶ Tracking customer open invoices and collections

▶ Assessing finance charges

....

You need to record the amounts that customers pay you when they fork over cash, at the time of a sale or after you invoice them. In this chapter, I describe how to record these payments and explain how to make bank deposits, track the amounts that customers owe and pay, and assess finance charges.

If you've been using QuickBooks to prepare customer invoices, you're ready to begin recording payments. You'll have no problem. If you haven't been invoicing customers, you need to make sure that you have a couple things ready to go before you can record cash sales.

First, you need to make sure that your lists are up-to-date. (I describe updating these lists in Chapter 3.) And second, if you want to print sales receipts, you need to have your printer set up to print them. You do so by choosing File⇨Printer Setup and then selecting Sales Receipt from the Form Name drop-down list. Setting up your printer to print sales receipts works just like setting it up to print invoices and credit memos (as I describe in Chapter 4).

Recording a Sales Receipt

You record a *sales receipt* when a customer pays you in full for the goods at the point of sale. Sales receipts work similarly to regular sales (for which you first invoice a customer and then later receive payment on the invoice). In fact, the big difference between the two types of sales is that sales receipts are recorded in a way that changes your cash balance rather than your accounts receivable balance.

In the following steps, I describe how to record sales receipts for products, which are the most complicated type of cash sale. Recording sales receipts for services works basically the same way, however. You simply fill in fewer fields.

1. **Choose Customers⇨Enter Sales Receipt.**

   Or, on the Home screen, click the Create Sales Receipts icon. Or, in the Customer Center, choose the customer from the list and then choose New Transactions⇨Sales Receipts. The Sales Receipt Template appears with the customer already selected at the top.

   The Enter Sales Receipts window appears, as shown in Figure 5-1.

   Your Enter Sales Receipts window may not look exactly like mine for a couple reasons. The first is that QuickBooks customizes (and you can customize) its forms to fit your particular type of business. The second reason is that QuickBooks may initially display a Payment toolbar on the sales receipt form and on the Receive Payment form. You can turn off the Payment toolbar by clicking its Close Toolbar button. You can turn on the Payment toolbar by choosing Edit⇨Preferences, selecting Sales & Customers, clicking My Preferences, and checking the Show Payment Toolbar box.

   Customizing sales receipt forms works in a similar way to customizing invoices and credit memos, as I describe in Chapter 4. If your Enter Sales Receipts window includes more fields than I describe here, you can also turn to that chapter for help on how to fill out the additional fields or turn them off.

2. **Identify the customer and, if necessary, the job.**

   Activate the Customer:Job drop-down list by clicking the down arrow to the right of the box. Scroll through the Customer:Job list until you see the customer or job name that you want and then click it. Note that unlike with invoices, the Customer:Job field isn't required for cash sales.

3. **(Optional) Specify a class for the sales receipt.**

   If you're using classes to categorize transactions, activate the Class drop-down list and select the appropriate class for the sales receipt. (I don't show the Class list box in Figure 5-1, so don't look for it there.)

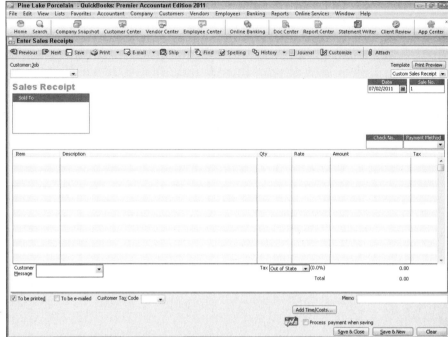

Figure 5-1:
The Enter
Sales
Receipts
window,
strangely
empty and
perhaps a
bit lonely.

4. **Date the sales receipt.**

   Press Tab to move the cursor to the Date text box. Then type the correct date in MM/DD/YYYY format. You can change the date by using any of the date-editing codes. (You can find these codes in Chapter 4 and on the online Cheat Sheet for this book at www.dummies.com/cheatsheet/quickbooks2011.)

5. **(Optional) Enter a sale number.**

   QuickBooks suggests a cash sale number by adding 1 to the last cash sale number you used. Use this number or tab to the Sale No. text box and change the number to whatever you want.

6. **Fix the Sold To address, if necessary.**

   QuickBooks grabs the billing address from the Customer list and uses the billing address as the Sold To address. You can change the address for the cash sale, however, by replacing the appropriate part of the usual billing address.

7. **Record the check number.**

   Enter the customer's check number in the Check No. text box. If the customer is paying you with cold hard cash, you can leave the Check No. text box empty.

8. **Specify the payment method.**

   To specify the payment method, activate the Payment Method drop-down list and select something from it: cash, check, Visa, MasterCard, or whatever. If you don't see the payment method that you want to use, you can add the method to the Payment Method list. Choose Add New to display the New Payment Method dialog box. Enter a description of the payment method in the text box and click OK.

9. **Describe each item that you're selling.**

   Move the cursor to the first row of the Item/Description/Qty/Rate/Amount/Tax list box. When you do, QuickBooks turns the Item field into a drop-down list. Activate the Item drop-down list of the first empty row in the list box and then select the item. When you do, QuickBooks fills in the Description and Rate text boxes with whatever sales description and sales price you entered in the Item list. (You can edit this information if you want, but that probably isn't necessary.) Enter the number of items sold in the Qty text box. Describe each of the other items you're selling by filling in the next empty rows of the list box.

   If you add an inventory item to an invoice, QuickBooks adds a small button to the Quantity field when the cursor rests on the Quantity field. If you click the button, QuickBooks displays a window that describes the on-hand quantities of the inventory item.

   If you've already read the chapter on invoicing customers (Chapter 4), what I'm about to tell you will seem very familiar: You can put as many items on a sales receipt as you want. If you don't have enough room on a single page, QuickBooks adds as many pages as you need to the receipt. The sales receipt total, of course, goes on the last page.

10. **Describe any special items that the sales receipt should include.**

    If you didn't set up the QuickBooks item file, you have no idea what I'm talking about. Here's the scoop: QuickBooks thinks that anything that you stick on a receipt (or an invoice, for that matter) is something that you're selling. If you sell blue, yellow, and red thingamajigs, you obviously need to add each of these items to the Item list. But if you add freight charges to your receipt, QuickBooks thinks that these charges are just another thingamajig and requires you to enter another item in the list. The same is true for a volume discount that you want to stick on the receipt. And if you add sales tax to your receipt, well, guess what? QuickBooks thinks that the sales tax is just another item that needs to be included in the Item list. (For more information about working with your Item list and adding new items, refer to Chapter 3.)

    To include one of these special items, move the cursor to the next empty row in the Item box, activate the drop-down list by clicking the arrow on the right side of the box, and then select the special item. After QuickBooks fills in the Description and Rate text boxes, you might need to edit this information. Enter each special item — subtotals, discounts, freight, and so on — that you're itemizing on the receipt by filling in the next empty rows of the list box.

If you selected the Taxable check box when you added the item to the Item list, the word *Tax* appears in the Tax column to indicate that the item will be taxed.

If you want to include a discount item (so that all the listed items are discounted), you need to stick a subtotal item on the receipt after the inventory items or other items you want to discount. Then stick the discount item directly after the subtotal item. In this way, QuickBooks calculates the discount as a percentage of the subtotal.

11. (Optional) Add a customer message.

Click in the Customer Message box, activate its drop-down list, and choose a clever customer message. To add customer messages to the customer message list, select Add New. When QuickBooks displays the New Customer Message box, fill it in and then click OK.

12. Specify the sales tax.

If you specify tax information when you create your company file during the EasyStep Interview — remember how QuickBooks asked whether you charge sales tax? — QuickBooks fills in the default tax information by adding the taxable items (which are indicated by the word *Tax* in the Tax column) and multiplying by the percentage you indicated when you created your company file. If the information is okay, move on to Step 13. If not, move the cursor to the Tax box that's to the right of the Customer Message box, activate the drop-down list, and choose the correct sales tax. For more information about setting a default sales tax for a customer on the Customer list, read Chapter 3.

13. (Truly optional and probably unnecessary for cash sales) Add a memo in the Memo text box.

You can include a memo description with the cash sale information. This memo isn't for your customer. It doesn't even print on the cash receipt, should you decide to print one. The memo is for your eyes only. Memo descriptions give you a way to store information that's related to a sale with the sales receipt information.

14. Decide whether you're going to print the receipt.

If you aren't going to print the receipt, make sure that the To Be Printed check box is empty — if not, click it to remove the check.

Figure 5-2 shows a completed Enter Sales Receipts window.

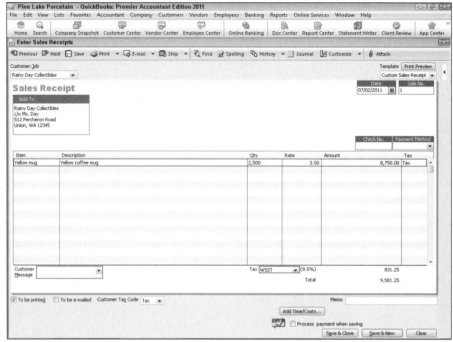

Figure 5-2:
The
completed
Enter Sales
Receipts
window.

15. Save the sales receipt.

To save a completed sales receipt, click either the Save & Close button or the Save & New button. QuickBooks saves the sales receipt that's onscreen and then, if you clicked Save & New, displays an empty Enter Sales Receipts window so that you can create another sales receipt. (Note that you can page back and forth through receipts that you created earlier by clicking the Next and Previous buttons and display and remove historical information for the selected customer by clicking the Show History button. The Show History button is the little arrow to the right of the Print Preview button in the upper right-hand corner of the screen.) When you're done creating sales receipts, you can click the Enter Sales Receipts window's Close button.

Printing a Sales Receipt

To print a single sales receipt as you're recording the information, click the Print button in the Enter Sales Receipts window. The Print One Sales Receipt dialog box appears, as shown in Figure 5-3. The following steps tell you how to complete this dialog box:

Figure 5-3:
The Print
One Sales
Receipt dia-
log box.

1. **Select the type of sales receipt form.**

   If you're using a different sales receipt form type than you described for the invoice/purchase order (PO) printer setup, select the type of form that you want to print on by selecting a radio button in the Print On section. You can choose Intuit Preprinted Forms, Blank Paper, or Letterhead. (See Chapter 4 for more on these printer options.)

   You shouldn't have to worry about printing test receipts or fiddling with form alignment problems if you addressed these issues during the invoice/PO printer setup, so I'm not going to talk about the Align button here. If you want to print a test receipt or need to change the alignment, read Chapter 4 for how to proceed.

2. **Print that puppy!**

   Click the Print button to send the form to the printer. QuickBooks prints the sales receipt.

3. **Review the sales receipt and reprint the form, if necessary.**

   Review the sales receipt to see whether QuickBooks printed it correctly. If the form doesn't look okay, fix whatever problem fouled up the printing; perhaps you forgot to include the company name and address, for example. Then reprint the form by clicking the Print button (in the Enter Sales Receipts window) again, selecting the form on which you want to print (again), and then clicking the Print button in the Print One Sales Receipt dialog box (you got it — again).

To print a batch of receipts, make sure that you select the To Be Printed check box on each receipt that you want to print and then display the Enter Sales Receipts window, click the arrow beside the Print button, and choose Print Batch from the drop-down list. QuickBooks displays the Select Receipts to Print dialog box, which enables you to choose which receipts to print. Select the desired receipts by putting a check mark in the first column and then click OK.

The Print Sales Receipts dialog box appears. This dialog box resembles the Print One Sales Receipt dialog box in just about every way, and the instructions work in exactly the same manner. For help with this dialog box, refer to the sections on printing invoices and credit memos in batches in Chapter 4.

Special Tips for Retailers

Are you a retailer? If so, you're probably saying, "Hey, idiot, what you just described is way too much work to do every time someone walks into the store and buys some $3 item."

You know what? You're right. So here's what retailers do to record their sales. Retailers record the day's sales by using one, two, or three sales receipt transactions. Retailers don't record each individual sales receipt transaction.

Say that some coffee mug retailer sold 2,500 red coffee mugs for the day for $3.50 each. In that case, at the end of the day, the retailer needs to record total sales of $8,750 and then the sales tax. (In my example here, sales tax is 9.5 percent.) With these example numbers, the *daily* sales would be recorded using a sales receipt transaction like the one shown earlier in Figure 5-2.

Pretty straightforward, right? And that's not too much work, all things considered.

Let me share a handful of other tips for recording retail sales:

- ✔ **You probably want to record a sales receipt transaction for each deposit you make.** In this manner, you can indicate that a particular sales receipt transaction (really a batch of sales) is deposited at one time into your bank account — which makes reconciling your bank account relatively easy.

- ✔ **You probably want to separate cash sales from credit card sales because often credit card sales are handled differently.** Your credit card processing company, for example, might hold on to credit card sales for a few days, or it might deduct a fee before depositing the money into your bank account. You want to record a separate sales receipt transaction for each deposit that you make (or some other company makes) into the bank account — again, to make reconciling the bank account easier.

- ✔ **If you don't use the Item list to monitor your inventory (because you have way too many items to store in the QuickBooks Item list), use items that are designated as non-inventory parts.** For example, you might use non-inventory part items, such as *daily cash sales, daily AmEx sales,* and *daily Visa/MC sales* if you make three deposits every day for cash and check sales, for American Express sales, and for Visa and MasterCard sales. If you don't track inventory in your items file, your

CPA handles the inventory and cost of goods sold calculations on your tax return. He or she probably also records a journal entry transaction to get your account balances correct as of the end of your fiscal year.

✔ **You may want to look at the QuickBooks Point of Sale system.** The QuickBooks Point of Sale system makes it easy to quickly record cash register sales. In fact, the more expensive version of the QuickBooks Point of Sale system comes with a scanner, a receipt printer, and a cash drawer. When you ring up a sale with the QuickBooks Point of Sale system, the software automatically records your sales and the effect on inventory and cost of goods sold.

✔ **You also may not want to use inventory items to track your inventory if you're a retailer.** You may instead want to use non–inventory part items or generic non-inventory part items. In this way, QuickBooks won't track the quantity of items that sell — only the dollar amounts of your sales.

Correcting Sales Receipt Mistakes

If you make a mistake in entering a sales receipt (cash sale), don't worry. Here's a list of common problems and how to fix them:

✔ **If the sales receipt is still displayed onscreen:** If the sales receipt is still onscreen, you can move the cursor to the box or button that's incorrect and then fix the mistake. Most of the bits of information that you enter in the Enter Sales Receipts window are fairly short or are entries that you've selected from a list. You can usually replace the contents of some field by typing over whatever's already there or by making a couple quick clicks. If you really messed up and want to start over from scratch, you can click the Clear button. To save a receipt after you've entered it correctly, click either the Save & Close button or the Save & New button.

If you need to insert a line in the middle of a sales receipt, right-click where you want to insert the line and choose Insert Line from the short-cut menu. To delete a line, right-click it and then choose Delete Line from the shortcut menu.

✔ **If the sales receipt isn't displayed onscreen:** If the sales receipt isn't onscreen, and you haven't yet printed it, you can use the Next and Previous buttons to page through the sales receipts. When you get to the one with the error, fix the error as I describe in the preceding bullet. If you make a mistake while editing a receipt, you can click the Revert button to go back to the saved receipt and not save your changes. Note that Clear toggles to Revert after you edit a transaction.

Even if you printed the customer's receipt, you can make the sort of change that I just described. For example, you can page through the sales receipts by using the Next and Previous buttons until you find the receipt (now printed) with the error. And you can correct the error and print the receipt again. I'm not so sure that you want to go this route, however. Things will be much cleaner if you void the cash sale by displaying the sales receipt and choosing Edit⇨Void Sales Receipt. Then enter a new, correct cash sales transaction.

✔ **If you don't want the sales receipt:** You usually won't want to delete sales receipts, but you can delete them. (You'll almost always be in much better shape if you just void the sales receipt.) To delete the receipt, display it in the Enter Sales Receipts window (choose Customers⇨Enter Sales Receipt and then page through the sales receipts by using the Next and Previous buttons until you see the cash sale that you want to delete) and then choose Edit⇨Delete Sales Receipt. When QuickBooks asks you to confirm the deletion, click Yes.

If you want to see a list of all your cash sales, choose Edit⇨Find, and the Simple Find screen appears. Select Transaction Type⇨Sales Receipt and then click Find. Select the receipt you want to see from the list that appears. If you're already viewing a sales receipt, choose Edit⇨Find Sales Receipts. When you click the Find button, another screen pops up and asks for details of the sales receipt that you're looking for. Click the Find button on that screen, and QuickBooks gives you a list of your cash sales for the criteria you selected.

Recording Customer Payments

If your customers don't always pay you upfront for their purchases, you need to record another type of payment: the payments that customers make to pay off or pay down what you've invoiced them. To record the payments, of course, you first need to record invoices for the customer. If you issue credit memos that customers can use to reduce the amounts they owe, you also first need to record credit memos for each customer. (Check out Chapter 4 to find out how to create and record these items.) The rest is easy.

To access a wealth of customer information all on one page, click the Customer Center icon at the top of the screen or choose Customers⇨ Customer Center. The Customer Center appears, listing outstanding balances for all customers and detailed information for the customer selected in the Customers & Jobs list.

To display the Receive Payments window, click the Receive Payments icon on the Home screen or click the Customer Center icon and select the customer you need. Click New Transactions and Receive Payments or choose Customers⇨Receive Payments from the top menus. Then describe the customer payment and the invoices paid. If you want the gory details, read through the following steps:

1. **Choose Customers⇨Receive Payments.**

   The Receive Payments window appears, as shown in Figure 5-4. (The window may ask whether your company accepts credit cards; click Yes or No to close the dialog box.)

2. **Identify the customer and, if necessary, the job.**

   Activate the Received From drop-down list and select the customer (and job, if necessary) by clicking its name. QuickBooks lists the open, or unpaid, invoices for the customer in the list box at the bottom of the window.

3. **Specify the payment date.**

   Press Tab to move the cursor to the Date text box (the one right above the Reference # text box), and type the correct date in MM/DD/YYYY format. To edit the date, you can use the secret date-editing codes that I describe in Chapter 4 and on the online Cheat Sheet for this book at www.dummies.com/cheatsheet/quickbooks2011.

4. **Enter the amount of the payment.**

   Move the cursor to the Amount field and type the customer payment amount. *Note:* If the customer is paying with a credit card and your merchant bank deducts a fee from the individual payments, record the full amount of the payment on this payment screen and the merchant fee later on the Deposit screen.

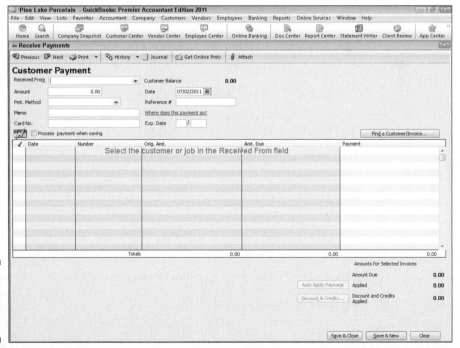

Figure 5-4:
The Receive
Payments
window.

5. **(Optional) Specify the payment method.**

   Activate the Pmt. Method drop-down list and choose the payment method.

6. **(Optional) Enter the check number.**

   You can guess how this works, right? You move the cursor to the Reference # field. Then you type the check number from the customer's check. Do you need to complete this step? Naw. But this bit of information might be useful if you or the customer later ends up with questions about what checks paid for what invoices. So I'd go ahead and enter the check number.

7. **(Optional) Add a memo description.**

   Use the Memo description for storing some bit of information that will help you in some way. Note that this field prints on the Customer Statement.

8. **If the customer has any outstanding credits, decide whether to apply them in this payment.**

   QuickBooks totals the amounts of any of the customer's existing credits. They can be anything from an overpayment on a previous invoice to a return credit or anything else.

   When you create a new invoice, QuickBooks notifies you that there are credits available on the customer's account and asks whether you want to apply any of them to the new invoice.

   If you want to apply a credit memo to a specific open invoice, select the invoice and then click the Discounts & Credits button. When QuickBooks displays the Credits tab of the Discount and Credits dialog box, as shown in Figure 5-5, click the credit memo that you want to apply and then click Done.

9. **Identify which open invoices the customer is paying.**

   By default, QuickBooks automatically applies the payment to the open invoices, starting with the oldest open invoice. You can change this application by entering amounts in the Payment column. Simply click the open invoice's payment amount and enter the correct amount.

   You can leave a portion of the payment unapplied, if you want to. QuickBooks then asks what you want to do with the overpayment: You can leave the amount on account to be applied or refund the amount to the customer or client. By the way, if you record an underpayment, QuickBooks asks whether you want to just leave the unpaid amount sitting there or want to instead write off the remaining balance.

   If you want to apply the customer payment to the oldest open invoices, click the Auto Apply Payment button. If you want to unapply payments that you've already applied to open invoices, click the Clear Selections button. Clear Selections and Auto Apply Payment are the same button. QuickBooks changes the name of the button, depending on whether you've already applied payments.

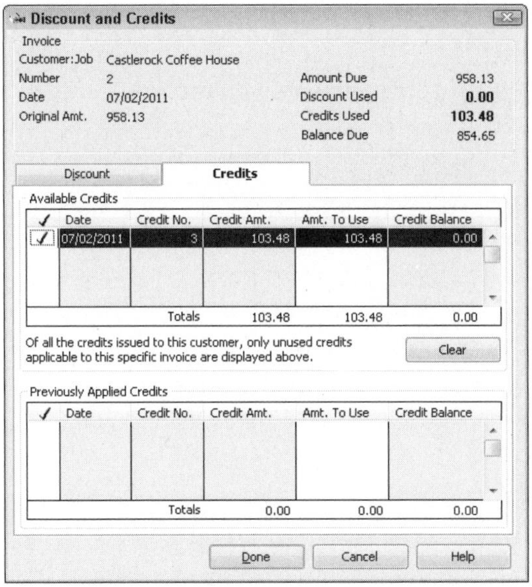

Figure 5-5:
The Credits
tab of the
Discount
and Credits
dialog box.

10. **Adjust the early payment or other discounts, if necessary.**

    If you offer payment terms that include an early payment discount, QuickBooks automatically reduces the open invoice original amount (shown in the Orig. Amt. column) by the early payment discount that you specify to calculate the adjusted amount due (shown in the Amt. Due column) if the payment is dated within the discount period.

    To specify any other discounts, select the open invoice that you want to adjust. Then click the Discount & Credits button. With little or no hesitation, the Discount tab of the Discount and Credits dialog box appears, as shown in Figure 5-6. Type the dollar amount of the discount in the Amount of Discount text box. Then specify the expense account that you want to use to track discounts by activating the Discount Account drop-down list and selecting one of the accounts. (Interest Expense is probably a good account to use unless you want to set up a special expense account called something like *Discount Expense* or *Discounts Given*.)

    When you're finished, click Done to return to the Receive Payments window. (For more information on the costs and benefits of early payment discounts, see Chapter 21.)

11. **Record the customer payment information.**

    After you identify which invoices the customer is paying — the unapplied amount should probably show as zero — you're ready to record the customer payment information. You can do so by clicking either the Save & New button or the Save & Close button. QuickBooks saves the customer payment shown onscreen. If you click Save & New, QuickBooks displays an empty Receive Payments window so that you can enter another payment.

You can return to customer payments you recorded earlier by clicking the Previous button.

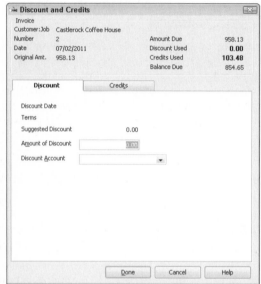

Figure 5-6:
The
Discount
tab of the
Discount
and Credits
dialog box.

Correcting Mistakes in Customer Payments Entries

You can correct mistakes that you make in entering customer payments in basically the same way that you correct mistakes that you make in entering cash sales.

First, you display the window you used to enter the transaction. In the case of customer payments, click the Customer Center icon and select the customer you need. You see a list of that customer's transactions on the right side. Double-click the payment transaction you want to change, and the original payments screen appears. And then you make your changes. Then you click Save & Close. Pretty straightforward, right?

If you already recorded a deposit that includes the payment you want to delete or edit, you need to delete the deposit before you can delete or edit the payment.

Making Bank Deposits

Whenever you record a cash sale or a customer payment on an invoice, QuickBooks adds the cash to its list of undeposited funds. These undeposited funds could be a bunch of checks that you haven't yet deposited, or they could consist of *coinage* (currency and coins) or even credit card payments, if you accept those.

You can also tell QuickBooks to give you the choice of indicating that a particular payment or sales receipt is deposited directly into a specified account. To tell QuickBooks to give you this choice, choose Edit⇨Preferences, scroll down to the Payments icon, click the Company Preferences tab, and then deselect the Use Undeposited Funds as a Default Deposit to Account option. After you make this change, QuickBooks adds buttons and a box to the lower-left corner of the Enter Sales Receipt and Receive Payment windows so that you can indicate into which bank account the money is deposited.

Eventually, though, you'll want to take the money out from under your mattress and deposit it in the bank. To do so, follow these steps:

1. **Choose Banking⇨Make Deposits.**

   Alternatively, select Record Deposits on the Home screen in the Banking section.

   The Payments to Deposit dialog box appears, as shown in Figure 5-7. This dialog box initially lists all the payments, regardless of the payment method. You can, however, use the View Payment Method Type drop-down list to indicate that you want to see payments only of a particular type — such as credit card payments. (This feature can be pretty handy because it lets you batch all your credit card transactions together.)

2. **Select the payments that you want to deposit.**

   Click a payment or cash receipt to place a check mark in front of it, marking it for deposit. If you want to deselect a payment, click it again. To deselect all the payments, click the Select None button. To select all the payments, click the Select All button. If you have gobs of payments to look through, you can also filter the list by clicking View Payment Method Type at the top and see only the Cash or Credit Cards to select among. If you're recording credit card payments deposited, you don't need to sort through the check payments, also. They aren't gone; they just don't appear until you select that type of payment or All.

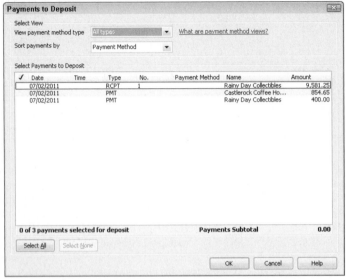

Figure 5-7:
The
Payments
to Deposit
dialog box.

3. Click OK.

After you indicate which payments you want to deposit, click OK. QuickBooks displays the Make Deposits window, as shown in Figure 5-8.

If you need to redisplay the Payments to Deposit dialog box — maybe you made a mistake or something, and now you need to go back and fix it — click the Payments button at the top of the Make Deposits screen. Note, though, that QuickBooks won't display the Payments to Deposit dialog box unless the undeposited funds list still has undeposited payments in it.

4. Tell QuickBooks into which bank account you want to deposit the money.

Activate the Deposit To drop-down list and choose the bank account in which you want to place the funds.

5. Specify the deposit date.

Press Tab to move the cursor to the Date text box and then type the correct date in MM/DD/YYYY format. Use the secret date-editing codes if you need to edit the date. (Get these codes from Chapter 4 or from the online Cheat Sheet at www.dummies.com/cheatsheet/ quickbooks2011 if you don't know them.)

6. (Optional) Add a memo description if you want to.

I don't know what sort of memo description you'd add for a deposit. Sorry. A bank deposit is a bank deposit. At least to me.

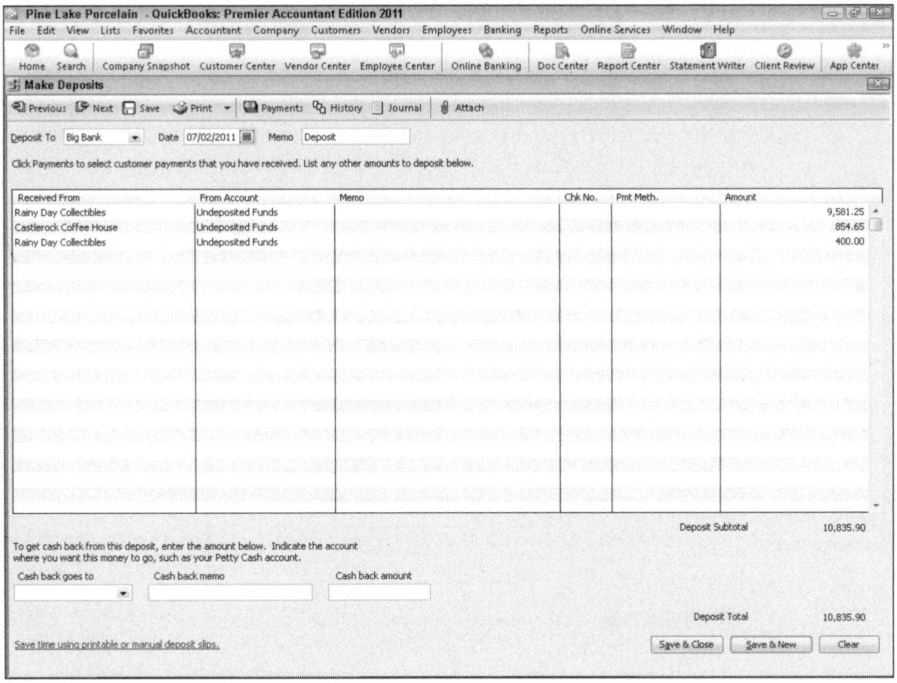

Figure 5-8:
The Make
Deposits
window.

[Screenshot of the QuickBooks Make Deposits window]

Pine Lake Porcelain - QuickBooks: Premier Accountant Edition 2011

Received From	From Account	Memo	Chk No.	Pmt Meth.	Amount
Rainy Day Collectibles	Undeposited Funds				9,581.25
Castlerock Coffee House	Undeposited Funds				854.65
Rainy Day Collectibles	Undeposited Funds				400.00

Deposit Subtotal 10,835.90
Deposit Total 10,835.90

7. Specify the cash-back amount.

If you want cash back from the deposit, activate the Cash Back Goes To drop-down list and choose a cash account, such as Petty Cash. Then enter a memo in the Cash Back Memo text box and the amount of cash back you're taking in the Cash Back Amount text box.

8. Record the deposit by clicking the Save & Close button or the Save & New button.

If you click Save & New, QuickBooks displays a new blank Make Deposits window.

TIP

If you sometimes take cash from the register or from the day's collections to spend on business supplies, for COD (collect on delivery) payments, and even for salaries, you enter the cash payment transaction as another transaction line in the Make Deposits window (refer to Figure 5-8). For example, if you use $50 from the cash register to pay for office supplies from Acme Office Store, you enter another line into the Make Deposits window. You enter **Acme Office Store** into the Received From column, your office supplies expense account into the From Account column, and **–50** into the Amount column. You use a *negative* amount to reduce the total deposit to the correct amount that is actually deposited into the checking account and to charge the expense account for the amount paid out. This is also where you record the Merchant Fees deducted from your credit card deposits I mention earlier in this section.

Improving Your Cash Inflow

I'm not going to provide a lengthy discussion of how to go about collecting cash from your customers. I do, however, want to quickly tell you about a couple other details. You need to know how to monitor what your customers owe you and how to assess finance charges. Don't worry, though. I explain these two things as briefly as I can.

Tracking what your customers owe

You can track what a customer owes in a couple ways. Probably the simplest method is to display the Customer Center by choosing Customer⇨Customer Center. Next, select the customer from the Customers & Jobs list (which appears along the left edge of the window). QuickBooks whips up a page that lists transactions for the customer. It also shows the customer's contact information. Figure 5-9 shows the Customer Center information for a customer.

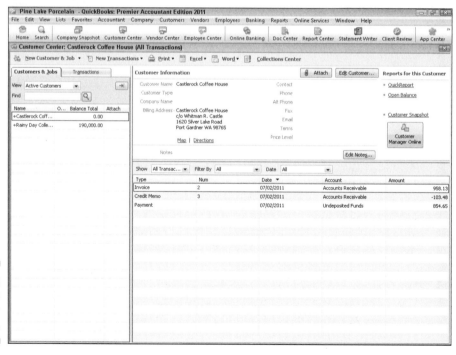

Figure 5-9:
The Customer Center.

Using QuickBooks to write a letter

You can seamlessly integrate your QuickBooks data to create collection letters in Microsoft Word. You can also use the QuickBooks business letter templates to speed the process of writing business letters. To have QuickBooks help you write a letter, choose Company⇨Prepare Letters with Envelopes. Then choose the submenu command for the type of letter you want to create or edit. Or from the Customer Center, click the Word icon and choose the letter from the menu there.

If you're creating a collection letter, you can specify which customers and jobs you want QuickBooks to search for money owed to you. You can tell QuickBooks whether you want to create a separate letter for each customer who owes you money or each job on which you're owed money. You can also specify the limit for how overdue an invoice must be to warrant a

collection letter. After you set the parameters and click Next, QuickBooks searches for overdue invoices that fit your criteria.

If you're creating a type of letter other than a collection letter, QuickBooks offers many choices based on whether you're sending the letter to a customer, a vendor, an employee, or someone else. For example, you can create credit approval, credit denial, or credit request letters. You can create birthday or apology letters. And you can create faxes or bounced check letters, just to name a few.

After you specify the information about the type of letter that you want to create, QuickBooks asks you a few questions about how you want to sign the letter. Then it creates the letter and displays it in Microsoft Word so that you can edit the letter as necessary and then print or save it.

You also should be aware that QuickBooks provides several nifty accounts receivable (A/R) reports. You get to these reports by clicking the Report Center icon and choosing Customers & Receivables. Or you can choose Reports⇨Customers & Receivables. QuickBooks then displays a submenu of about a half-dozen reports that describe how much money customers owe you. Some reports, for example, organize open invoices into different groups based on how old the invoices are. (These reports are called *agings*.) Some reports summarize only invoices or payments. And some reports show each customer's open, or unpaid, balance.

In Chapter 15, I describe, in general terms, how you go about producing and printing QuickBooks reports. So read Chapter 15 if you have questions. Let me also say that you can't hurt anything or foul up your financial records just by printing reports. So go ahead and noodle around.

You can print a statement to send to a customer by choosing Customers⇨ Create Statements. Use the Create Statements dialog box to describe which customers you want to print statements for and the date ranges you want the statements to show, and then click Print or E-Mail to print or e-mail the statements. Statements are a handy way to remind forgetful customers or clients about overdue amounts. You don't, by the way, need to send statements to everybody for every month. In my CPA practice, I send out statements a couple times a year to clients with past-due accounts. This friendly reminder always produces a handful of quick payments and awkward apologies.

Assessing finance charges

I wasn't exactly sure where to stick this discussion of finance charges. Because finance charges seem to relate to collecting the cash your customers owe, I figure that I'm okay talking about assessing finance charges here.

QuickBooks assesses finance charges on unpaid open invoices without considering any unapplied payments. Accordingly, you'll want to make sure that you apply any payments and credit memos to open invoices before assessing finance charges.

To assess finance charges, follow these steps:

1. **Choose Edit⇨Preferences, click the Finance Charge icon in the list on the left, and then click the Company Preferences tab.**

   To be able to assess finance charges, you first need to set them up.

   Only the QuickBooks administrator can change the company finance charge settings, and he or she can do so only in single-user mode.

   QuickBooks displays the Preferences dialog box, as shown in Figure 5-10. (If you've assessed finance charges before, QuickBooks displays the Assess Finance Charges window. You can display the Preferences dialog box and check or edit your finance charge settings by clicking the Settings button in the Assess Finance Charges window.)

2. **Enter the annual interest rate that you want to use to calculate finance charges.**

   Move the cursor to the Annual Interest Rate (%) text box and enter the annual interest rate.

3. **(Optional) Enter the minimum finance charge — if one exists.**

   Move the cursor to the Minimum Finance Charge text box and enter the minimum charge. If you always charge at least $25.00 on a past-due invoice, for example, type **25**.

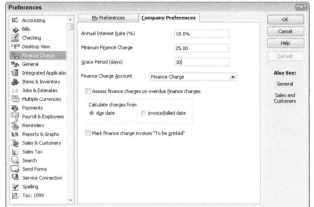

Figure 5-10:
The
Preferences
dialog box
for finance
charges.

4. **Enter the number of days of grace that you give.**

   Days of Grace. That sounds kind of like an artsy movie or serious novel, doesn't it? Basically, this number is how many days of slack you're willing to cut people. If you type **30** in the Grace Period (Days) text box, QuickBooks doesn't start assessing finance charges until 30 days after the invoice is past due.

5. **Specify which account you want to use to track the finance charges.**

   Activate the Finance Charge Account drop-down list, and select an Income or Other Income type account.

6. **Indicate whether you want to charge finance charges on finance charges.**

   Does this statement make sense? If you charge somebody a finance charge, and he or she doesn't pay the finance charge, eventually it becomes past due, too. So then what do you do the next time you assess finance charges? Do you calculate a finance charge on the finance charge? If you want to do this — and if state and local laws permit you to — select the Assess Finance Charges on Overdue Finance Charges check box.

7. **Tell QuickBooks whether it should calculate finance charges from the due date or the invoice date.**

   Select either the Due Date or Invoice/Billed Date option button. As you might guess, you calculate bigger finance charges if you start accruing interest on the invoice date.

8. **Tell QuickBooks whether it should print finance charge invoices.**

   Select the check box for Mark Finance Charge Invoices "To Be Printed" if you want to print invoices later for the finance charges that you calculate.

9. **Click OK.**

   After you use the Preferences dialog box to tell QuickBooks how the finance charges should be calculated, click OK.

10. **Choose Customers⇨Assess Finance Charges.**

    Alternatively, click the Finance Charges icon on the Home screen. The Assess Finance Charges window appears, as shown in Figure 5-11. This window shows all the finance charges that QuickBooks has calculated, organized by customer.

11. **Give the finance charge assessment date.**

    Move the cursor to the Assessment Date text box and enter the date when you're assessing the finance charges, which I'm willing to bet is the current date. (This date is also the invoice date that will be used on the finance charge invoices, if you create them.)

12. **Confirm which customers you want to be assessed finance charges.**

    QuickBooks initially marks all the finance charges, which means that it sets up a new invoice for each finance charge. (QuickBooks marks finance charges with a little check mark.) If you want to unmark (or, later, mark) a finance charge, click it. To unmark all the charges, click the Unmark All button. To mark all the charges, click the Mark All button.

    You can produce a collections report for any of the customers or jobs listed in the Assess Finance Charges window by selecting the customer name and then clicking the Collection History button.

13. **Click the Assess Charges button.**

    When the Assess Finance Charges window correctly describes the finance charges that you want to assess, click Assess Charges. You're finished with the finance charge calculations and assessments.

I don't describe how to print invoices that contain finance charges because I already slogged through invoice printing in painstaking detail in Chapter 4. If you have questions about how to print the invoices, you might want to visit that chapter.

Dealing with deposits

While I'm on the subject of improving your cash flow, let me briefly mention one other powerful cash flow technique — and discuss the bookkeeping required for that technique.

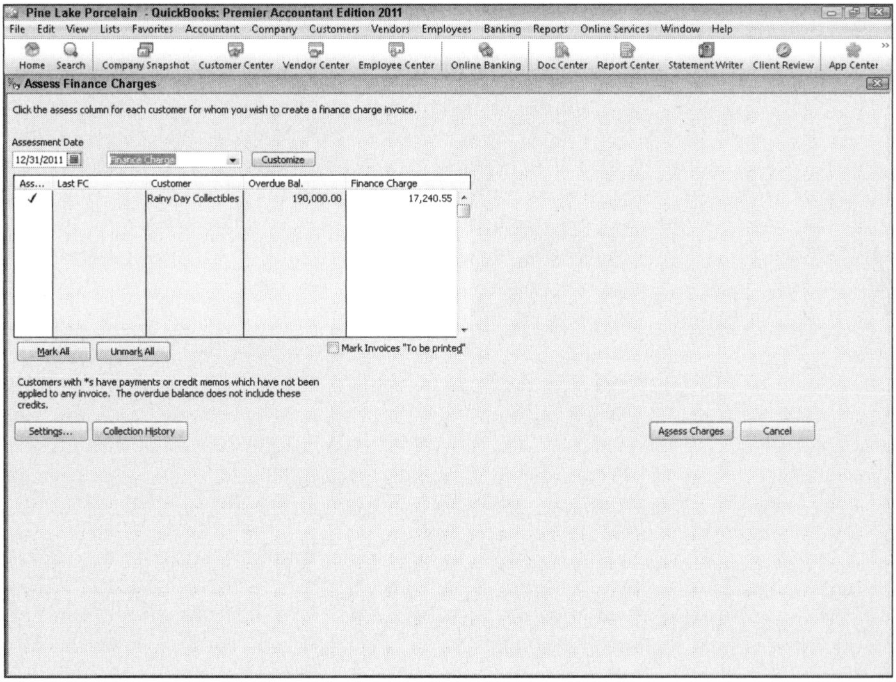

Figure 5-11:
The Assess
Finance
Charges
window.

One easy way to improve your cash flow is to accept or require upfront deposits or retainers from clients or customers before you do the actual work. In other words, before you begin work or order inventory or do whatever is the first step in your business for completing a sale, you collect cold, hard cash.

Unfortunately, these *customer deposits,* as they're called, create a bit of bookkeeping trouble. The question becomes, basically, how do you record a check or cash deposit for stuff that you haven't yet done or sold? You have two basic options:

✔ **The Easy Way:** You can just record a sales receipt for the service or product. (See "Recording a Sales Receipt" at the beginning of this chapter.) In this way, you count the cash coming into your business. And you recognize the revenue. Note, too, that if the deposit is nonrefundable — and for cash flow purposes, the deposit should be nonrefundable — you probably should count the revenue when you receive the deposit if you're a cash-basis taxpayer. (You probably are a cash-basis taxpayer, but ask your tax advisor if you aren't sure.)

> ✔ **The Precise Way:** You can recognize the deposit as a new liability. You do this by creating a journal entry that records the increase in your cash account and that records the increase in your Customer Deposits current liability account. (For help on entering journal entries, refer to Chapter 20.) If the deposit is refundable and you're a cash-basis taxpayer, or if you're an accrual-basis taxpayer, you probably should use this method. When your sale is completed and invoiced later, use the Customer Deposit item as a minus amount on the sales invoice to move the amount from the liability account and apply it to the invoice balance due.

A word of advice from an accountant

While I'm on the subject of tracking what your customers owe you, let me share a thought about collecting this money. You should have firm collection procedures that you follow faithfully. For example, as soon as an invoice is a week or so past due, it's very reasonable to place a friendly telephone call to the customer's accounts payable department to verify whether the customer has received the invoice and is in the process of paying. You have no reason to be embarrassed because some customer is late paying you! What's more, you may find out something surprising and essential to your collection. You may discover, for example, that the customer didn't receive the invoice. Or you may find out that something was wrong with the gizmo you sold or the service you provided.

As soon as an invoice is a month or so past due, you need to crank up the pressure. A firm letter asking that the customer call you to explain the past-due amount is very reasonable — especially if the customer assured you only a few weeks ago that payment was forthcoming.

When an invoice is a couple months past due, you need to get pretty serious. You'll probably want to stop selling the customer anything more because it's unclear whether you'll be paid. And you may want to start a formal collection process. (Ask your attorney about starting such a process.)

Chapter 6

Paying the Bills

. . . .

In This Chapter

▶ Using the Write Checks window to pay bills

▶ Using the accounts payable method to pay bills

▶ Deleting and editing bill payments

▶ Reminding yourself to pay bills

▶ Tracking vehicle mileage

▶ Paying sales tax

. . . .

*Q*uickBooks gives you two ways to pay and record your bills. And you have many options when it comes to deciding when to pay your bills, how to pay your bills, and how to record your bills for the purposes of tracking inventory and expenses.

In this chapter, I explain not only how to pay vendor bills but also how to pay that all-important bill that so many businesses owe to their state and local governments. I'm talking, of course, about sales tax.

Pay Now or Pay Later?

When it comes to paying bills, you have a fundamental choice to make. You can either record and pay your bills simultaneously or record your bills as they come in but then pay them when they're due. The first method is easiest, as you might guess, because you do everything at once. The second method, called the *accounts payable method,* gives you more accurate financial records and makes for more precise management of your cash and outstanding bills.

If you have a small business with little overhead, you may just as well record and pay bills simultaneously. If you need precise measurement of your expenses and bills, though — if you want to use what's termed *accrual-basis accounting* — you should use the accounts payable method of paying bills. I should note, too, that using the accounts payable method with QuickBooks isn't as difficult as it may seem at first.

And now you're ready to begin. In the next section, I describe how to pay bills by writing checks. A little later in the chapter, in the "Recording Your Bills the Accounts Payable Way" section, you find out how to pay bills by using the accounts payable method.

Recording Your Bills by Writing Checks

When you record bills by writing checks, you're doing *cash-basis accounting.* In a nutshell, this means that you count bills as expenses when you write the check to pay the bill.

I talk a little bit about cash-basis accounting in Appendix B, but let me say here that a trade-off is implicit in the choice to use cash-basis accounting. If you use cash-basis accounting — which is what I do in my little business — you greatly simplify your bookkeeping, but you lose precision in your measurement of your expenses. And you don't keep track of your unpaid bills inside QuickBooks. They just stack up in a pile next to your desk.

As long as you understand this trade-off and are comfortable with it, you're ready to begin using this method, which you do by following the steps I provide in the paragraphs that follow.

The slow way to write checks

You can write checks either from the register or from the Write Checks window. Using the Write Checks window is the slow way, but it enables you to record your expenses and the items (if any) that you purchase. Using the Write Checks window is the best choice in the following situations:

- You're paying for an inventory item.
- You're paying for something for which you have a purchase order.
- You plan to be reimbursed for the bill that you're paying.
- You want to record what job or class the bill falls under.

To use the Write Checks window to write checks, follow these steps:

1. **Choose Banking⇨Write Checks.**

   Alternatively, click the Write Checks icon in the Banking section of the Home screen. The Write Checks window appears, as shown in Figure 6-1. Notice that this window has three parts:

   - *The check part on the top,* which you no doubt recognize from having written thousands of checks in the past.

- *The buttons* on the top and bottom.
- *The Expenses and Items tabs* near the bottom of the window. This part is for recording what the check is for, as I explain in Steps 7, 8, and 9.

2. Click the Bank Account drop-down list and choose the account from which you want to write this check.

This step is very important if you have more than one account. Make sure that you choose the correct account; otherwise, your account balances in QuickBooks will be incorrect.

3. Specify the check date.

Click the Date box and type the check date. I don't keep reminding you about this, but because I'm still in the early part of this book, remember that you can enter today's date by pressing the T key. You can also click the button to the right of the Date box to get a pop-up calendar. To select a date from the pop-up calendar, click the calendar day that you want to use.

4. Fill in the Pay to the Order Of line.

If you've written a check to this person or party before, the AutoFill feature fills in the name of the payee in the Pay to the Order Of line for you after you start typing the name. (AutoFill does so by comparing what you type with names shown in the Customer, Vendor, Employee, and Other Names lists.) AutoFill also puts the payee's address in the Address text box.

The AutoRecall feature can even fill out the entire check for you, based on the last check that you wrote to this vendor. (You can enable AutoRecall by choosing Edit⇨Preferences, clicking the General icon, and using the Automatically Recall Information box and buttons.)

Does the check look all right? Maybe all you need to do is tab around, adjusting numbers. Otherwise, read the next 12 steps. (Another 12-step program?) In these steps, I explain how to record information about a new vendor and pay a check to that vendor in one fell swoop.

If you've never paid anything to this person before, the program displays a Name Not Found message box after you enter the name on the Pay to the Order Of line. You can click either Quick Add or Set Up to add the payee name to one of your lists. (To find out how to do so, check out the "To Quick Add or to Set Up?" sidebar, elsewhere in this chapter.)

5. Type the amount of the check.

Now comes my favorite part. I've always found it a big bother to write out the amount of checks. I mean, if you write a check for $21,457.00, how do you fit "twenty-one thousand, four hundred fifty-seven dollars, and no cents" on the line? Where do you put those hyphens, anyway?

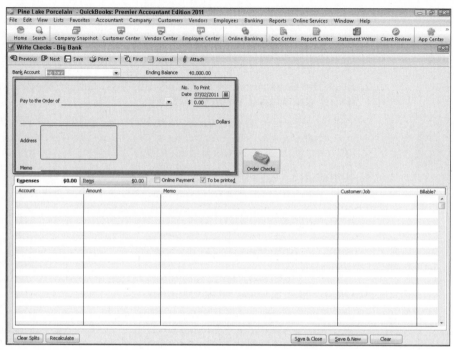

Figure 6-1:
The Write
Checks
window.

All you have to do with QuickBooks is enter the amount next to the dollar sign and press Tab. When you press Tab, QuickBooks writes the amount for you on the Dollars line. At moments like this, I'm grateful to be alive in the 21st century, when computer technology can do these marvelous things for me.

6. (Optional) Fill in the Address text box.

You need to fill in this box only if the address isn't there already and if you intend to send the check by mail in a window envelope.

7. (Optional) Fill in the Memo line.

You can put a message to the payee on the Memo line — a message such as *Quit bleeding me dry.* But you usually put an account number on the Memo line so that the payee can record your account number.

If you try to click the Save & New button and close the dialog box now, QuickBooks tells you that you can't and tries to bite your leg off. Why? Because you can't write a check unless you fill out the Expenses and Items tabs. You use these tabs to describe what the check pays.

8. Move the cursor down to the Account column of the Expenses tab and then enter an expense account name.

Chances are that you want to enter the name of an account that's already on the Chart of Accounts. If that's the case, move the cursor to a field in the Account column; QuickBooks turns the field into a drop-down list. Click the down arrow to see a list of all your accounts. You'll probably have to scroll down the list to get to the expense accounts. Click the one that this check applies to — perhaps it's Rent. If you need to create a new expense account category for this check, choose Add New from the top of the list to see the New Account dialog box. Fill in the information and then click OK.

What if the money that you're paying with this check can be distributed across two, three, or four expense accounts? Simply click below the account that you just entered. The down arrow shoots down next to the cursor. Click the down arrow and enter another expense account, and another, and another, if you need to.

9. Tab over to the Amount column, if necessary, and change around the numbers.

If you're distributing this check across more than one account, make sure that the numbers in the Amount column correctly distribute the check to the appropriate accounts. Figure 6-2 shows a completed check.

10. (Optional) Enter words of explanation or encouragement in the Memo column.

Someday, you may have to go back to this check and try to figure out what these expenses mean. The Memo column may be your only clue. Enter some wise words here such as *August rent, copier repair,* or *company party.*

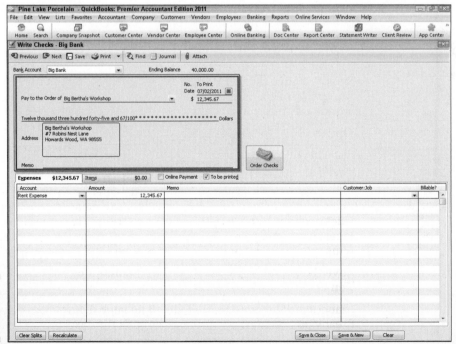

Figure 6-2:
A completed check.

To Quick Add or to Set Up?

If you click Quick Add in the Name Not Found message box, you see a Select Name Type message box asking whether the payee is a Vendor, Customer, Employee, or Other. Most likely, the payee is a vendor, in which case you click Vendor (but you can, of course, click one of the other three options). The address information that you write on the check goes in the Vendor list — or Customer, Employee, or Other Names list, depending on what you clicked. (Read through Chapter 3 if you're in the dark about adding to your lists.)

Selecting the Set Up option in the Name Not Found message box is a little more interesting.

When you select this option, you also see the Select Name Type box. Click Vendor, Customer, Employee, or Other. Click OK, and then you see the New *Whatever* window (as I discuss in Chapter 3) if you've already added new vendors, customers, or employees to your lists.

By the way, my long-suffering technical editor, David, wants me to point out that using the Quick Add method is sort of lazy. With Quick Add, QuickBooks requires you to collect only a minimal amount of information.

---

11. (Optional) Assign the expense to the Customer:Job column.

If you plan to be reimbursed for these expenses, or if you just want to track your expenses by job, enter the name of the customer who is going to reimburse you. Click the down arrow to find the customer. Enter an amount for each customer or job, if necessary.

12. (Optional) Assign the expense to a class.

You also can track expenses by class by making entries in the Class column. Notice the usual down arrow, which you click to see a list of classes. You won't see the Class column, however, unless you told QuickBooks that you wanted to use classes when you created your company. (You create the company when you work your way through the EasyStep Interview; refer to Chapter 2.)

If you want to have QuickBooks track expenses by class, you have to set it up to do so. To set up QuickBooks to track expenses, choose Edit⇨Preferences. When QuickBooks displays the Preferences dialog box, click the Accounting icon, click the Company Preferences tab, and then check the Use Class Tracking check box.

13. Use the Items tab to record what you're purchasing.

You may be purchasing inventory items, or you may already have filled out a purchase order for the items for which you're paying. If either of these cases is so, click the Items tab. If you don't have a purchase order for the items, go on to Step 14. If you do have a purchase order for the items, click the Select PO button to see a list of purchases on order with this vendor. Check those for which you're paying, and click OK.

QuickBooks doesn't show its purchase order (PO) feature unless you told it during the EasyStep Interview that you want to use purchase orders. If you now think you want to use them, choose Edit➪Preferences. When QuickBooks displays the Preferences dialog box, click the Items & Inventory button, click the Company Preferences tab, and then select the Inventory and Purchase Orders Are Active check box.

14. Move the cursor to the Item column and enter a name for the item.

Notice the down arrow in this column. Click the arrow to see the Items list. Does the item that you're paying for appear on this list? If so, click it. If not, choose Add New from the top of the list and fill out the New Item window. (Read about this in Chapter 3.)

15. Fill in the rest of the rows of items on the Items tab.

You can enter all the items that you're purchasing on this tab. Make sure that the Items tab accurately shows the items that you're purchasing, their cost, and the quantity.

When you finish adding items, you may want to use one of the following options that appear in the Write Checks window:

- Click the *Print button* to print the check in the Write Checks window. This option doesn't print all the checks that you have written and marked to be printed, however. (I explain how to print more than one check at a time in Chapter 10.)

- The *Clear Splits button* deletes any individual amounts that you entered for separate expenses or items on the Expenses and Items tabs. Then QuickBooks enters the total amount of the check in the Amount column on the Expenses tab.

- The *Recalculate button* totals the items and expenses in the window. It also puts the total on both the numeric and text amount lines of the check.

- The *To Be Printed check box* designates the check for printing. Select this check box if you want to print the check with QuickBooks by using your printer and preprinted check forms. Clear this check box if you're recording a handwritten check.

- The *Online Payment check box* (if you've enabled online bill pay) lets you specify that you want to specify that the particular check you're describing an "online payment." See Chapter 13 for more information about online banking.

16. Click the Save & New button or the Save & Close button to finish writing the check.

Click Save & Close to tell QuickBooks that you want to save the check and close the check form. Click Save & New to tell QuickBooks that you want to save the check and then display another blank check form. If you don't want to save the check, close the dialog box and then click No when QuickBooks asks whether you want to save the check.

You can also use the Next and Previous buttons to move to previously written checks or to a blank check form. If you write check number 101, for example, clicking Next takes you to check 102 so that you can write that one. (Clicking Previous moves you to check 100, in case you need to edit a check that you've written earlier.)

Well, that's over with. For a minute there, I thought that it would never end.

The fast way to write checks

If you want to pay a bill that isn't for inventory, that you won't be reimbursed for, or that you don't need to track in any way, shape, or form, you can write your check directly from the Checking register. This method is the fast and easy way to go. Follow these steps:

1. **Choose Banking⇨Use Register.**

   Alternatively, click the Check Register icon in the Banking section on the Home page. The register appears, as shown in Figure 6-3. (If you have more than one bank account, you have to choose the proper account from the drop-down list and click OK.) The cursor is at the end of the register, ready and waiting for you to enter check information.

2. **Fill in the information for the check.**

   Notice that the entries you make are the same ones that you'd make on a check. You need to note three things about the register:

   • If you enter a Payee name that QuickBooks doesn't recognize, you see the Name Not Found message box, and you're asked to give information about this new, mysterious vendor. To see what to do next, read the preceding set of instructions on writing a check the slow way.

   • You have to choose an account name. Chances are good that you can find the right one in the Account drop-down list; if you can't, enter one of your own. QuickBooks displays the Account Not Found message box and asks you to fill in the information about this new account.

   • To record a check that pays more than a single expense, click the Splits button (in the bottom-left corner of the window) to display a little box that you can use to input multiple expense accounts and amounts.

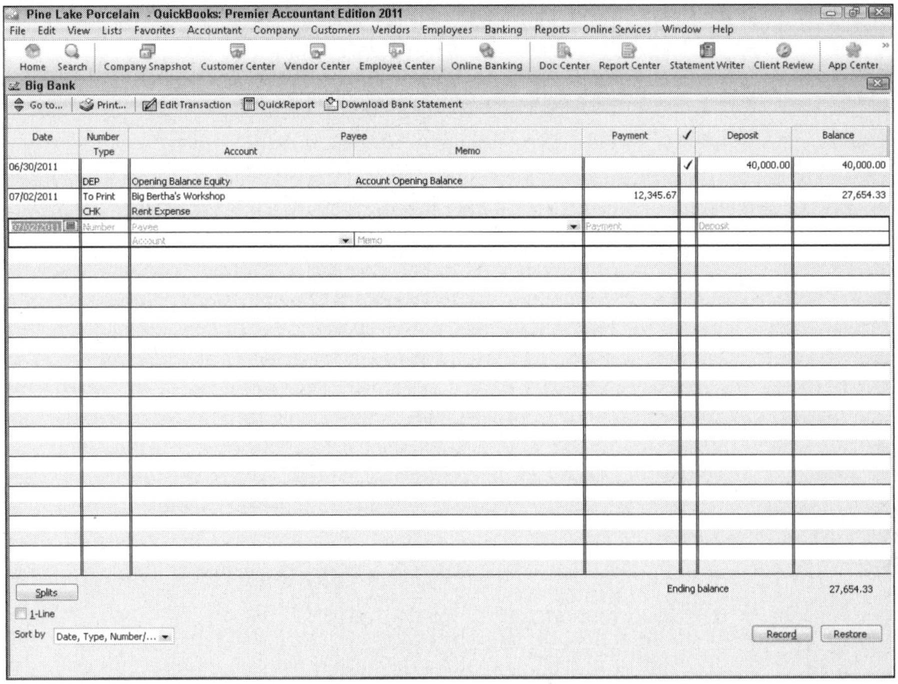

Figure 6-3:
The register.

As you fill out the register, if you decide that you want to be reimbursed for this check or that you want to track expenses and items, click the Edit Transaction button. You see the Write Checks window; refer to Figure 6-1. Follow Steps 3–14 in the preceding section on how to write a check the slow way to fill in the Write Checks window. When you finish filling in the Write Checks window, click Save & New. You're back where you started, in the register window.

3. When you finish filling in the check information, click the Record button.

You click Record, of course, to record the check.

By the way, if you realize that you made a mistake and haven't yet clicked Record to record the check, you can click the Restore button to go back to square one. Clicking Restore blanks out what you just entered so that you can start over again.

If you want to print the check (or checks) that you've just entered, flip to Chapter 10 for details. In the meantime, in Chapter 8, I give you the lowdown on keeping your checkbook — so turn there if this discussion of checks has you really excited.

Recording Your Bills the Accounts Payable Way

The accounts payable (A/P) way of paying bills involves two steps. The first is a trifle on the difficult side, and the second step is as easy as pie. First, you record your bills. If you read the section earlier in this chapter on writing checks the slow way, you're already familiar with using the Expenses tab and the Items tab to record bills. You need to fill out those tabs for the A/P method as well if you want to distribute a bill to accounts, customers, jobs, classes, and items. If you read the first half of this chapter, some of what follows will be old hat.

After you record your bills, you can go on to the second step: telling QuickBooks which bills to pay. Then QuickBooks writes the checks. You print them. You mail them.

To make the A/P method work, you have to record your bills as they come in. That doesn't mean that you have to pay them right away. By recording your bills, you can keep track of how much money you owe and how much money your business really has. QuickBooks reminds you when your bills are due so that you don't have to worry about forgetting to pay a bill.

When you record bills the accounts payable way, you're using accrual-basis accounting. I explain accrual-basis accounting in Appendix B.

Recording your bills

When a bill comes in, the first thing to do is record it. You can record bills through the Enter Bills window or the Accounts Payable register. If you plan to track bills by expense and item, you need to use the Enter Bills window. I describe that method first. If you have a simple bill to pay that doesn't need to be reimbursed or tracked, skip ahead to the "Paying Your Bills" section, later in this chapter.

To record a bill through the Enter Bills window, follow these steps:

1. **Choose Vendors⇨Enter Bills.**

   Alternatively, click the Enter Bills icon in the Vendors area on the Home page. Figure 6-4 shows the Enter Bills window. You no doubt notice that the top half of this window looks a great deal like a check — that's because much of the information that you put here ends up on the check that you write to pay your bill. (If you see the word *Credit* at the top of the form rather than *Bill,* select the Bill radio button in the top-left corner. You also can use this screen to enter credit memos from vendors.)

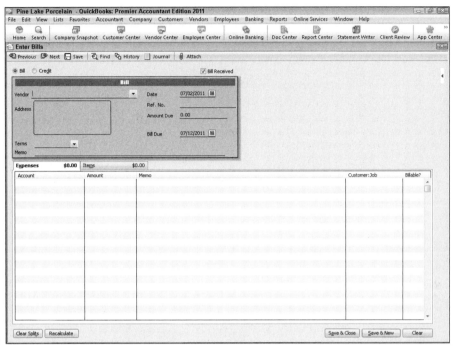

Figure 6-4:
The Enter
Bills
window.

2. Select the name of the vendor whom you're paying.

If you want to pay this bill to a vendor who's already on the Vendor list, click the down arrow at the end of the Vendor line and choose the vendor. (Then QuickBooks automatically fills the Enter Bills window with as much information as it can remember.) If this vendor is new, QuickBooks asks you to Quick Add or Set Up some information about the vendor: the address, credit limit, payment terms, and so on. You provide this information in the New Vendor window. If you aren't familiar with this window, make a brief visit to Chapter 3.

If you have one or more unfilled purchase orders with the vendor that you select, QuickBooks asks you whether you want to receive against a purchase order. Click Yes if you do or No if you don't. If you choose to receive against a purchase order, QuickBooks displays the Open Purchase Orders dialog box, as shown in Figure 6-5. It lists the open purchase orders you've recorded. When you select one or more purchase orders to receive against, QuickBooks fills in the items and amounts from these orders for you, which you can modify as necessary. When you finish with the Purchase Orders dialog box, click OK to get back to the Enter Bills window.

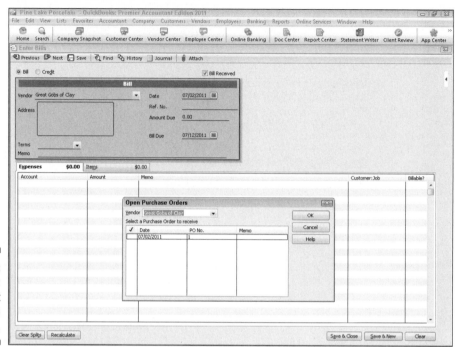

Figure 6-5:
Paying a
bill against
a purchase
order.

Hey, you know what? I don't talk about purchase orders until Chapter 7. But here's the *CliffsNotes* version: To create a *purchase order,* which is a record of items you order from vendors, choose Vendors➪Create Purchase Orders. When QuickBooks displays the Create Purchase Orders window, describe your order. You print and edit purchase orders, by the way, in the same manner as you print invoices and credit memos.

3. Select the payment terms that describe when the bill is due.

In the Terms line, open the drop-down list and choose the payment terms (if the information isn't already there from when you set up the vendor).

4. (Optional) Enter the vendor's reference number.

If you enter the vendor's reference number for the bill — this is probably just the invoice number or your account number — the reference number prints on the voucher that's part of the printed check.

5. (Optional) Enter a memo to describe the bill.

You can enter a note in the Memo text box. The note that you enter appears on the A/P register.

6. **Move the cursor down to the Account column of the Expenses tab and enter an expense account name.**

   Chances are good that you want to enter the name of an expense account that's already on the chart of accounts. If that's the case, click the down arrow to see a list of all your accounts. You probably have to scroll down the list to get to the expense accounts. (A fast way to move down the list is to start typing the account name; you go straight down the list.) Click the account that this bill represents. (Most likely, it's Supplies or something like that.)

   If you need to create a new expense account category for this bill, choose Add New from the top of the list. You see the New Account dialog box. Fill in the information, and click OK.

   What if the money that you're paying out because of this bill can be split among two, three, or four expense accounts? Simply click below the account that you just entered. The down arrow appears. Click it to enter another expense account, and another, and another, if you need to.

7. **Tab over to the Amount column, if necessary, and change the numbers.**

   If you're splitting this bill among several accounts, make sure that the numbers in the Amount column add to the total of the bill.

8. **(Optional) Enter words of explanation or wisdom in the Memo column.**

9. **(Optional) Assign the expense to a Customer:Job.**

   If you plan to be reimbursed for these expenses, or if you just want to track your expenses by job, enter the customer who is going to reimburse you. Enter an amount for each account if necessary. You can use the down arrow to find customers and then click them.

10. **(Optional) Assign the expense to a class.**

    You also can track expenses by class by making entries in the Class column. Notice the usual down arrow, and click it to see a list of classes. (You don't see a Class column unless you told QuickBooks that you want to use classes.)

    If you want to have QuickBooks track expenses by class, you can set it up to do so. To set up QuickBooks to track expenses, choose Edit⇨Preferences. When QuickBooks displays the Preferences dialog box, click the Accounting icon, click the Company Preferences tab, and then select the Use Class Tracking check box.

    If you want, click the Recalculate button to total the expenses.

11. **Use the Items tab to record the various items that the bill represents.**

    Click the Items tab. Enter the items you purchased and the prices you paid for them.

If you realize after partially completing the bill that the bill does indeed pay a purchase order, click the Select PO button, which appears on the Items tab of the Enter Bills window.

From the Vendor drop-down list, choose the name of the vendor who sent you the bill. In the list of open purchase orders, click in the column on the left to put a check mark next to the purchase order (or orders) for which you're paying. Easy enough? Click OK when you're done; QuickBooks fills out the Items tab for you automatically.

 12. **Move to the Item column and enter a name for the item.**

Notice the down arrow in this column. Click it to see the Item list. Does the item that you're paying for appear on this list? If so, click that item. If not, choose Add New from the top of the list and fill out the New Item window. (Refer to Chapter 3.)

 13. **Fill in the rest of the rows of items on the Items tab.**

You can enter all the items you're purchasing here. Make sure that the Items tab accurately shows the items that you're purchasing, their costs, and their quantities. If you want to, click the Recalculate button to total the items.

 14. **Save the bill.**

Click Save & New to save your record of the bill and then enter another bill. Or click Save & Close to record your bill but not enter another bill.

Just as in the case with customer-related windows (like the Create Invoices window), QuickBooks lets you add and remove historical information about a vendor from and to the Enter Bills window and many other "vendor information" windows. To add historical vendor information to a window, click the Show History button that appears in the upper-right corner of the window. You click links in the Show History panel to drill down and get even more information about, for example, a listed transaction.

Entering your bills the fast way

You also can enter bills directly in the Accounts Payable register. This method is faster, but it makes tracking expenses and items more difficult.

If you want to enter bills directly in the Accounts Payable register, follow these steps:

 1. **Choose Lists⇨Chart of Accounts or click the Chart of Accounts icon on the Home page.**

The Chart of Accounts opens.

2. **Open the Accounts Payable account.**

   When QuickBooks displays your Chart of Accounts, double-click the Accounts Payable account in the list. You see the Accounts Payable register window, as shown in Figure 6-6. The cursor is at the end of the register, ready and waiting for you to enter the next bill.

3. **Fill in the information for your bill.**

   Enter the same information that you would if you were filling in the Enter Bills window that I describe at the beginning of this chapter. In the Vendor text box, click the down arrow and choose a name from the Vendor list.

   If you enter a vendor name that QuickBooks doesn't recognize, you see the Vendor Not Found message box, and QuickBooks asks you to give information about this new, mysterious vendor. Either click Quick Add to have the program collect the information from the register as you fill it out or click Set Up to see the New Vendor dialog box. (I describe the choice between Quick Add and Set Up in the "To Quick Add or to Set Up?" sidebar, elsewhere in this chapter. I explain how to set up new vendors in Chapter 3.)

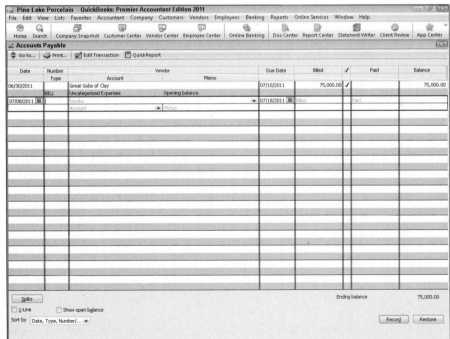

Figure 6-6: The Accounts Payable register window.

You have to select an account name. You can probably find the right one in the Account drop-down list; if you can't, enter one of your own. You see the Account Not Found message box, and QuickBooks asks you to fill in information about this new account.

If you decide while you fill out the register that you want to be reimbursed for this check or that you want to track expenses and items, click the Edit Transaction button to see the Enter Bills window (as shown in Figure 6-4). Follow Steps 2–12 in the "Recording your bills" section (earlier in this chapter) to fill in the Enter Bills window. When you finish filling in the window, click Save & New. You're back where you started: in the Accounts Payable window.

See the Splits button? This Splits button works the same as the Splits button in the bank account register window. When you click Splits, QuickBooks provides additional rows for inputting expense and class information.

4. **When you fill in all the information, click Record.**

The Restore button, located just right of Record, is there in case you fill out the register but decide that you want to start all over again before you've recorded the transaction. Click Restore to clear the information onscreen, and you have a clean slate.

Deleting a bill

Suppose that you accidentally enter the same bill twice or enter a bill that was really meant for the business next door. (Just because you're tracking bills by computer doesn't mean that you don't have to look over things carefully anymore.) Here's how to delete a bill that you entered in the Accounts Payable register:

1. **Locate the bill in the Accounts Payable register by using one of the following methods:**

   • *If you know roughly what day you entered the bill,* you can scroll through the list to find it. The entries are listed in date order. (Select the 1-Line check box to display each bill on one line rather than on two lines to make the scrolling go faster.)

   • *If you don't remember the date,* use the Edit menu's Find command.

   And now, back to the Accounts Payable register window that you have in progress. . . .

2. **Select the bill that you want to delete by clicking anywhere in the bill.**

3. **Choose Edit➪Delete Bill.**

   QuickBooks confirms that you really, truly want to delete the transaction. If you click OK, it dutifully deletes the bill from the A/P register.

Using the Find dialog box

When you can't remember the information that you need to find a particular entry or transaction, you can search for the information by using the Find dialog box. For example, if you can't recall when you entered the bill, choose Edit⇨Find to open the Find dialog box. Choose a *filter* (the category to search by). The box to the right changes to include drop-down lists or text boxes that you can use to specify what you want to search for.

Choose as many filters as you like, but be careful to enter information accurately, or QuickBooks will look for the wrong information.

Also, try to strike a balance, choosing only as many filters as you really need to find your information. The more filters you choose, the more searching QuickBooks does, and the longer the search takes.

After you finish choosing filters, click the Find button, and the transactions that match all your filters appear in the list at the bottom of the window. Click the transaction that you want to examine more closely and then click Go To. QuickBooks opens the appropriate window and takes you right to the transaction. Very snazzy, I do believe.

Remind me to pay that bill, will you?

You could tie a string around your finger, but the best way to make sure that you pay your bills on time is to have QuickBooks remind you. In fact, you can make the Reminders message box the first thing that you see when you start QuickBooks.

To adjust the QuickBooks reminder options, you must be logged on as the administrator in single-user mode. Then choose Edit⇨Preferences. When QuickBooks displays the Preferences dialog box, click the Reminders icon from the list on the left and then click the Company Preferences tab to access the dialog box shown in Figure 6-7, with the Reminders item on the list.

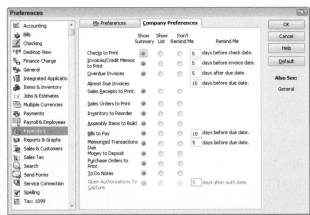

Figure 6-7:
The Preferences dialog box.

Make sure that its Show Summary or Show List option button is selected and then give yourself several days' notice before you need to pay bills by typing a number (10 is the default and usually works well) in the Days Before Due Date text box, in the Remind Me column.

If you select the Show Summary option (the first button to the right of the option), you get a summary of the bills that you owe each time you start QuickBooks. If you select Show List (the second button to the right of the option), you get the details about each bill.

Be sure to review the Reminders window when you start QuickBooks or open a new company file. The window lists reminders (such as forms you need to print and payments you need to transmit) and tells you which unpaid bills you're supposed to pay. You can see this list by choosing Company⇨Reminders.

Paying Your Bills

If you've done everything right and recorded your bills correctly, writing checks is a snap. Just follow these steps:

1. **Choose Vendors⇨Pay Bills.**

   Alternatively, click the Pay Bills icon located on the home page. You see the Pay Bills window, as shown in Figure 6-8.

2. **Change the Payment Date box (at the bottom) to the date that you want to appear on the checks.**

   By default, this box shows today's date. If you want another date on the payment check — for example, if you're postdating the check — change this date. (See the online Cheat Sheet at www.dummies.com/ cheatsheet/quickbooks2011 for some secret date-editing codes.)

3. **Set a cutoff date for showing bills.**

   In the Show Bills Due On or Before date box, tell QuickBooks which bills to show by entering a date. If you want to see all the bills, select the Show All Bills radio button.

4. **Use the Sort By drop-down list to tell QuickBooks how to sort the bills.**

   You can arrange bills by due date with the oldest bills listed first, arrange them alphabetically by vendor, or arrange them from largest to smallest.

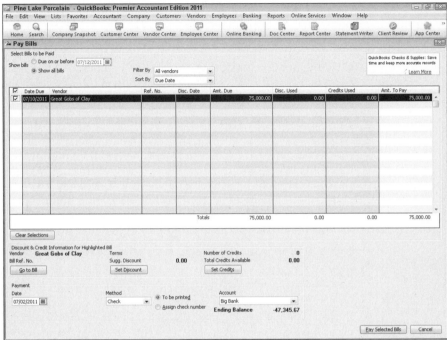

5. Identify which bills to pay.

If you want to pay all the bills in the dialog box, click the Select All Bills button. If you want to clear all the bills you marked, click the Clear Selections button. If you want to pick and choose, click to the left of the bill's due date to pay the bill. A check mark appears where you click. Note that after you apply a payment, the Clear Selections button replaces the Select All Bills button.

6. Change the Amt. to Pay figure if you want to pay only part of a bill.

That's right — you can pay only part of a bill by changing the number in the Amt. to Pay column. (Of course, they can always just send you another bill. . . .)

7. Get the early payment discount rate on your bills, if any.

You may be eligible for an early payment discount on some bills. To find out how much of a discount you get, click the Amt. to Pay field and then click the Set Discount button to see the Discount tab of the Discount and Credits dialog box. Use the Discount tab's Amount of Discount box to give the dollar amount of the discount. Use the Discount tab's Discount

Account box to specify which account should be used for recording the money saved through the discount.

8. **Get a list of credit memos that you can apply to the payment.**

   Click the Set Credits button to see the Credits tab of the Discount and Credits dialog box. If you want to use one of the credits listed to reduce the amount of the bill, click it and then click Done.

9. **Select a payment date, method, and bank account.**

   Use the Payment area's Date box to specify when the bill should be paid, the Method drop-down list to select the payment method you want to use (Check or Credit Card), and the Account drop-down list to select the bank account from which payment will be made. (***Note:*** If you've subscribed to and set up the QuickBooks online bill payment feature, you have another payment method choice: online payment. I describe making online payments in Chapter 13.)

10. **If you plan to print the check, select the To Be Printed option button.**

    Many businesses use QuickBooks to keep track of checks, but instead of printing the checks, they have employees write them by hand. If your business uses this method, select the Assign Check Number radio button. Then, when QuickBooks asks how it should number the check, either give the number by typing it into the appropriate box or tell QuickBooks to automatically number the check.

11. **Click the Pay Selected Bills button to pay the bills and close the Pay Bills window.**

    QuickBooks goes into the Accounts Payable register and notes that you paid these bills; then it goes into the Checking register and "writes" the check or checks. Figures 6-9 and 6-10 show you exactly what I mean. (The two figures show a $75,000 bill from Great Gobs of Clay being paid.)

QuickBooks shows the original bill amount as the amount that's paid, not the original bill amount minus the early payment discount. It needs to use this method to completely pay off the bill.

In the Accounts Payable register, you see BILLPMT in the Type column and the amount paid in the Paid column. The Due Date and Billed columns are now empty.

In the Checking register, you again see BILLPMT in the Type column.

But don't kid yourself — these bills aren't really paid yet. Sure, they're paid in the mind of QuickBooks, but the mind of QuickBooks extends only as far as the metal (or trendy plastic) box that holds your computer. You still have to write or print the checks and deliver them to the payees.

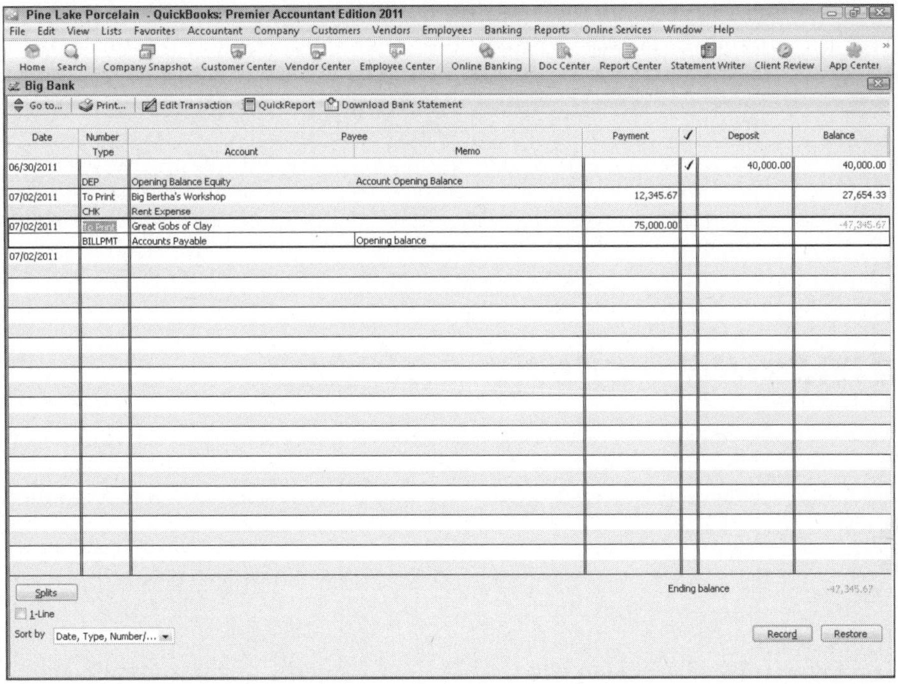

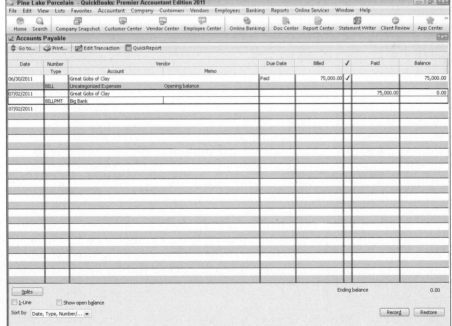

Figure 6-9:
How a paid
bill looks in
the register.
Oooh. Cool.

Figure 6-10:
How the
check that
pays a bill
looks in the
Accounts
Payable
register.

If you're going to write the checks by hand, enter the check numbers from your own checkbook into the QuickBooks register Number column. You want these numbers to jibe, not jive. (I know: A pun is the lowest form of humor.)

If you plan to print the checks, see Chapter 10.

And another thing: If you enter a bill, you absolutely must use the Pay Bills command to record the payment that pays off the bill. If you don't do this, the unpaid bill just sits there forever, lonely and forlorn.

Tracking Vehicle Mileage

QuickBooks includes a vehicle mileage-tracking feature that lets you track your business miles. To track vehicle mileage in QuickBooks, choose Company➪Enter Vehicle Mileage. Then, in the Enter Vehicle Mileage dialog box that appears, record the vehicle, date, miles driven, odometer settings, and reason for the trip. (I talk a bit more about tracking vehicle mileage in Chapter 18, so you may want to refer to it if this is something you're really interested in.)

May I briefly tell you the IRS rules for deducting business miles? Essentially, you have two approaches to choose between. The easier method — and the one that I use, because I'm lazy — is to record as a business expense an amount per business mile driven. The rate per mile is roughly $0.50, which is far less than the actual cost of driving most cars. But, hey — that's the price of slothfulness.

The hard method for tracking business miles is to track all your vehicle expenses — including gas, oil, repairs, insurance, and vehicle depreciation — and then record as a business expense the business-use portion of these expenses.

To get the business-use portion of your vehicle, use the ratio of business miles to total miles. For example, if over the year, you drive 6,000 business miles and your total miles are 12,000, your business-use percentage equals 50 percent. In this case, you can record as a business expense 50 percent of your vehicle expenses.

Usually with the hard "actual expenses" method, you get a higher business vehicle expense deduction. However, you should note that the IRS limits the amount that you can include as vehicle depreciation, so you don't get as high a deduction as you might at first think. (You may want to consult your tax advisor for details.)

No matter which method you use, you want a record of your actual business miles, which the Enter Vehicle Mileage command enables you to do. By law, you need a good record of business mileage to legitimately claim the deduction.

Paying Sales Tax

To ingratiate itself with you retailers, QuickBooks includes a special dialog box for paying sales tax. However, to use this dialog box, you must have sales tax items or a sales tax group already set up. See Chapter 3 for a thorough explanation of items and groups.

To see how much sales tax you owe and to write checks to government agencies in one fell swoop, choose Vendors⇨Sales Tax⇨Pay Sales Tax to access the Pay Sales Tax dialog box, as shown in Figure 6-11. Alternatively, click the Pay Sales Tax icon on the Home page in the Vendors area.

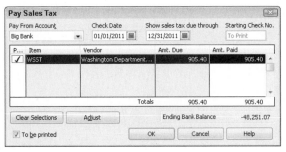

Figure 6-11: The Pay Sales Tax dialog box.

This dialog box is similar to the Pay Bills window (refer to Figure 6-8). The buttons basically work the same way.

Click in the Pay column to add check marks next to all the items that you want to pay. QuickBooks automatically writes checks in the Checking register. Your payments are likewise recorded in the Sales Tax Payable register.

If in your area the state or local tax agency allows a discount for timely sales tax remittals, you should know about the Vendors⇨Sales Tax⇨Adjust Sales Tax command. When you choose this command, QuickBooks displays the Sales Tax Adjustment dialog box, which lets you adjust the sales tax liability you owe some government agency for something like a discount.

A Quick Word on the Vendor Center Window

If you choose Vendors⇨Vendor Center or click the Vendor Center icon, QuickBooks displays a window that summarizes a bunch of information about the vendor in question. This feature doesn't actually provide you with new information. But — and this is noteworthy — it does give you a slick way to get all the information you have regarding a particular vendor. Note that you can select which vendor's information appears in the Vendor Center window by selecting the vendor from the vendor list that appears at the left edge of the window.

Chapter 7

Inventory Magic

*F*or small and growing businesses, inventory is one of the toughest assets to manage. First, of course, you need to physically care for stuff. Second, you have to make sure that you don't run out of some item or have too much of some other item.

QuickBooks (fortunately) provides elegant sophistication in its inventory management features, making inventory management easy. With a little jiggering, you can probably get it to work in any simple case — and even in many more complex cases.

If you want to make inventory accounting really easy and don't care about a bit of imprecision, take a peek at the last section of this chapter, "The Lazy Person's Approach to Inventory."

Setting Up Inventory Items

Before you can track your inventory, you need to do two things. First, you need to tell QuickBooks that you want to track inventory. To do this, choose Edit➪Preferences. When QuickBooks displays the Preferences dialog box, click the Items & Inventory icon in the list on the left. Your screen should look remarkably similar to the one in Figure 7-1. (You might have to click the Company Preferences tab first.) Make sure that the Inventory and Purchase Orders Are Active check box is marked and that one of the Warn If Not Enough Inventory to Sell radio buttons is marked.

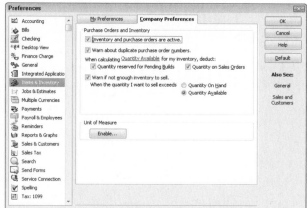

Figure 7-1:
The
Preferences
dialog
box for
Items and
Inventory.

Here's the second thing that you need to do: Create an *Item list*. This list is a description of all items that you might conceivably put on an invoice. In other words, all items that you order and sell belong on the Item list.

You should've set up your initial Item list in the EasyStep Interview (refer to Chapter 2). If you need to add an item to your list, choose Lists➪Item List. Then click the Item button, choose New from the drop-down list, and fill in the New Item window. If you want the blow-by-blow, go to Chapter 3 and get it straight from the horse's mouth.

After you turn on the inventory stuff and set up (or update) your Item list, you can track your inventory.

When You Buy Stuff

As you unload items from a truck, receive them in the mail, or buy them from a street peddler, you have to record the items so that QuickBooks can track your inventory. How you record the items and pay for them depends on whether you pay cash on the barrelhead, receive a bill along with the items, or receive the items without a bill (in which case, you pay for the items later).

And you may have filled out a purchase order (PO) for the items that you're receiving. If that's the case, receiving the items gets a little easier. If you receive items for which you already filled out a PO, see the section, "How Purchase Orders Work," later in this chapter. I strongly recommend filling out a PO when you order items that you're going to receive and pay for later.

Recording items that you pay for upfront

Okay, you just bought three porcelain chickens in the bazaar at Marrakech, and now you want to add them to your inventory and record the purchase. How do you record inventory you paid for over the counter? By using the Write Checks window, of course — the same way you record any other bills you pay for upfront. Just make sure that you fill out the Items column as I describe in Chapter 6.

Recording items that don't come with a bill

What happens if the items come before the invoice? Lucky you — you have the stuff, and you don't have to pay for it yet. However, you do have to record the inventory you just received so that you know you have it on hand. You can't do that in the Write Checks window because you won't be writing a check to pay for the stuff — at least not for a while. How do you record items that you receive before paying for them? Read on:

1. **Either Choose Vendors⇨Receive Items or click the Receive Inventory icon on the Home screen, and select the option to Receive Inventory without a bill.**

   You see the Create Item Receipts window, as shown in Figure 7-2. This window is similar to the Enter Bills window that I describe in Chapter 6, but it reads Item Receipt Only. (You see the Enter Bills window again when you receive the bill for items.)

2. **Fill in the top part of the window.**

   If you want to record items from a vendor who's already on the Vendor list, click the down arrow and then choose the vendor. If the vendor is a new vendor, choose Add New from the drop-down list and then, in the New Vendor dialog box that appears, click Set Up to set up information about the vendor: the address, the credit limit, payment terms, and so on. When you're done with the New Vendor dialog box, click Save & Close.

3. **Click the Items tab.**

   You need to click the Items tab only if it isn't already displayed. It probably is. But the computer book writers' code of honor and a compulsive personality require me to tell you that there's another tab — the Expenses tab — and you could possibly display it instead.

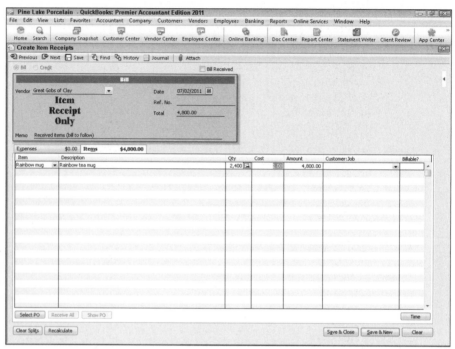

Figure 7-2:
The Create
Item
Receipts
window.

4. **Move to the Item column and type a name for the item.**

   Notice the down arrow in the Item column. Click it to see the Item list.
   Does the item that you're paying for appear on this list? If so, click it. If
   not, enter a new item name. You see the Item Not Found message box.
   Click Set Up, fill out the New Item dialog box and then click Save & Close.
   (See Chapter 3 for help with describing new items.)

   You may just as well go down the packing slip, entering the items on
   the Items tab. Make sure that the Items tab accurately shows what's on
   the packing slip. And put a brief description of the items in the Memo
   field because that description might prove useful later when you want
   to match up your item receipt with the bill. When you finish, the Create
   Item Receipts window should look something like what you see in Figure
   7-2 (shown earlier).

5. **Click the Save & New button or the Save & Close button to record the
   items that you just received.**

   The items are officially part of your inventory. The item receipt has been
   entered on the Accounts Payable register. Not only that, but also, you're
   all ready for when the bill comes.

Paying for items when you get the bill

The items arrive, and you fill out an item receipt. Three weeks pass. What's this in your mailbox? Why, it's the bill, of course! Now you have to enter a bill for the items that you received three weeks ago. This job is easy:

1. **Choose Vendors⇨Enter Bill for Received Items.**

   Or, from the Home screen, click the Enter Bills Against Inventory icon. If you're on the Vendor Center, click New Transactions and then Enter Bill for Received Items. The Select Item Receipt dialog box appears, as shown in Figure 7-3.

Figure 7-3:
The Select
Item Receipt
dialog box.

2. **Click the Vendor drop-down list and choose the name of the vendor who sent you the bill.**

   You see one or more item receipts in the box, with the date you put on the receipt, its reference number, and the memo that you wrote on the receipt.

3. **Select the item receipt for which you want to enter a bill and then click OK.**

   The Enter Bills window appears, as shown in Figure 7-4. Does this information look familiar? It should — it's the same information that you put in the Create Item Receipts window, only now you're working with a bill, not a receipt.

4. **Compare the Items tab in the window with the bill.**

   Are you paying for what you received earlier? Shipping charges and sales tax may have been added to your bill. You may also need to adjust the price because you may have been guessing when you recorded receiving the items. If so, add to and adjust the original receipt information by using the Items tab. (You can click the Recalculate button to add the new items.)

How many days do you have to pay this bill? Is it due now? Take a look at the Terms line to see what this vendor's payment terms are. Change the payment terms if they're incorrect by selecting a different entry from the drop-down list. Remember, you want to pay your bills at the best possible time, but for you to do so, the terms in the Enter Bills window must match the vendor's payment terms.

5. **Click Save & New or Save & Close to record the bill.**

Of course, you still need to pay the vendor's bill. Fair enough. Take a look at Chapter 6 if you need help.

Recording items and paying the bill all at once

Suppose that you receive the bill when you receive the goods. The items are unloaded from the elephant's back, and the elephant driver takes a bow and hands you the bill. Here are the steps you follow:

1. **Choose Vendors⇨Receive Items and Enter Bill.**

Or, from the Home screen, click Receive Inventory and then select the Receive Inventory with Bill option there. Or, from the Vendor Center, click New Transactions and then Enter Bill for Received Items. You see the Enter Bills window (refer to Figure 7-4). If you've been reading this chapter from its beginning, you're familiar with this window, and you know exactly what it is and what it does. If you landed cold turkey on this page by way of the index, you need to know, for inventory purposes, how to record the items you're paying for.

2. **Fill out the top part of the window.**

This stuff is pretty basic. Choose a vendor from the drop-down list and make sure that the vendor's terms for paying this bill are shown correctly. If this vendor is new, choose Add New. QuickBooks asks you to fill in an information dialog box about the vendor. Do it. Make sure that you fill out the Bill Due line correctly.

3. **Click the Items tab and list all the items that you're paying for.**

To see the Item list, move the cursor to the Item column and click the down arrow that appears. Make sure that the quantity and cost of the items are listed correctly on the Items tab.

4. **Click Save & New or Save & Close.**

QuickBooks adds the items you listed to the Item list and makes them an official part of your inventory.

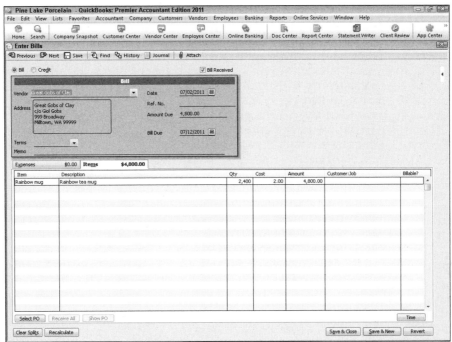

Figure 7-4:
The Enter
Bills
window.

When You Sell Stuff

In Chapter 4, I tell you how to list the items on the invoice. Maybe you noticed the similarities between the Items tab in the Enter Bills window and the Quantity/Item Code/Description/Price/Each/Amount box at the bottom of an invoice. QuickBooks uses both for keeping inventory.

When you sell stuff, QuickBooks automatically adjusts your inventory. In other words, if you buy 400 porcelain chickens and sell 350 of them, you have only 50 on hand. QuickBooks updates records for this change. No muss, no fuss. Gosh, isn't this great? No more lying awake at night, wondering whether you have enough chickens or wombats or whatever. The same thing happens when you make cash sales. When you list the items on the sales receipt, QuickBooks assumes that they're leaving your hands and subtracts them from your inventory.

One moral of this story is "Keep a good, descriptive Item list." And the other moral is "Enter items carefully on the Items tab of checks and bills and in the Item/Description/Qty/Rate/Amount box of sales receipts and invoices."

How Purchase Orders Work

If you have to order stuff for your business, consider using POs. Create QuickBooks POs even if you order goods by phone or by telegraph or even via the World Wide Web — that is, whenever you don't request goods in writing. Filling out POs enables you to determine what items you have on order and when the items will arrive. All you'll have to do is ask QuickBooks, "What's on order, and when's it coming, anyway?" Never again will you have to rack your brain to remember whether you've ordered those thingamajigs and doohickeys.

And when the bill comes, you'll already have it itemized on the PO form. Guess what? Having written all the items on your PO, you don't have to fill out an Items tab on your check when you pay the bill. Or, if you're paying bills with the accounts payable method, you don't have to fill out the Items tab in the Enter Bills window. (Look at Chapter 6 if you don't know what I'm talking about here.) When the items arrive, all you have to do is let QuickBooks know; the items are immediately added to your inventory list.

Use POs for items that you order — that is, for items that you'll receive and pay for in the future. If you buy items over the counter or receive items that you didn't order, you obviously don't need a PO. What you need to do is just pay the bill and inventory the items that you just bought, as I explain in the first half of this chapter.

Customizing a purchase order form

QuickBooks allows you to customize your purchase order form, either working from scratch to create an entirely new purchase order form or working from an existing purchase order template.

To create a new "from scratch" purchase order form, choose Vendors⇨Create Purchase Orders, click the Customize button and then, when QuickBooks displays the Customize Your QuickBooks Forms window, click the Create New Design button. QuickBooks displays an Intuit Web page that walks you through the steps to creating your own highly customized form.

To customize an existing purchase order form, choose Vendors⇨Create Purchase Orders, click the Customize button and then, when QuickBooks displays the Customize Your QuickBooks Forms window, click the Customize Data Layout button. QuickBooks, in this case, displays the Additional Customization dialog box (not shown) that supplies buttons and boxes that you can use to create a copy of the standard QuickBooks purchase order form and then modify the data that appears on the new copy of the form.

The Additional Customization dialog box provides a Preview area you can use to see what your changes look like and a Cancel button if things get terribly out of hand. Furthermore, the Additional Customization dialog box also provides a Layout Designer button, which you can click to open the Layout Designer window. The Layout Designer window allows you to become a true layout artist and make all sorts of changes to the overall look of your purchase order simply by moving fields around the page with your mouse.

Filling out a purchase order

Perhaps you're running low on gizmos, or doohickeys, or some other item on your Item list, and you're ready to reorder these things — whatever they are. Follow these steps to fill out a PO:

1. **Choose Vendors⇨Create Purchase Orders.**

   Or click the Purchase Orders icon on the Home screen; or click the New Transactions area of the Vendor Center and then select Purchase Orders. You see the Create Purchase Orders window, which is similar to what's shown in Figure 7-5. Note that the exact details of this window depend on how you customize your PO form.

2. **Choose a vendor from the Vendor drop-down list.**

   Click the down arrow to see a list of your vendors. Click a vendor to see its name and address in the Vendor box. If you can't find the name of the vendor on your list, click Add New from the list and then fill in the information about the vendor in the resulting New Vendor dialog box. Click Save & Close when you're done with the dialog box.

3. **If you track your inventory by class, select a class from the Class drop-down list.**

   The Create Purchase Orders window may not have a Class drop-down list. If it doesn't and you want it to have one, you have to set up QuickBooks to track expenses by Class. To do so, open the QuickBooks file in single-user mode as the administrator. Then choose Edit⇨Preferences and click the Accounting icon in the list on the left. (You may also need to click the Company Preferences tab.) Finally, select the Use Class Tracking check box and then click OK.

4. **(Optional) Select a Rep, an Expected Date, and a FOB (which I describe in Chapter 4) if you're using them on your PO.**

   You may have to fill in other fields before you get to the item-by-item descriptions at the bottom. Again, these fields may not appear if you haven't indicated that you want them on your form.

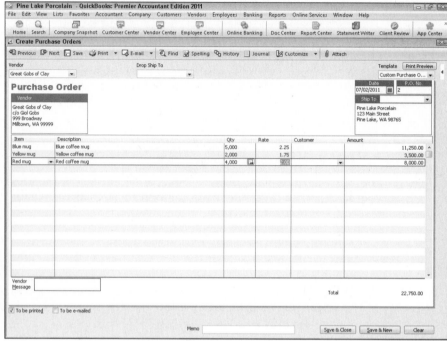

Figure 7-5:
The Create
Purchase
Orders
window.

5. Move to the Item column and start entering the items you're ordering.

Entering the items is the most important part of creating a PO. When you move into the Item column, it turns into a drop-down list. Click its down arrow to see the Item list. You may need to scroll to the item that you want to enter. A fast way to scroll to the item is to type the first few letters of the item name. If you type the name of an item that isn't on the Item list, QuickBooks asks whether you want to set up this item. If so, click Set Up and then fill in the New Item dialog box.

Enter as many items as you want in the Item column. QuickBooks fills in an item description for you, but you can edit whatever it puts into the Description column, if need be. In the Qty column, indicate how many of each item you need.

6. If you want to, fill in the Vendor Message field — and definitely fill in the Memo field.

The Vendor Message field is where you put a message to the party receiving your order. You could write, "Get me this stuff pronto!"

No matter what you do, be sure to fill in the Memo field. What you write in this field appears in the Open Purchase Orders dialog box and is the surest way for you to identify what this PO is for. Write something meaningful that you can understand two weeks, three weeks, or a month from now, when you pay for the items that you're ordering.

At the bottom of the Create Purchase Orders window is the To Be Printed check box, which tells you whether you printed this PO. If you want to print the PO, make sure that this check box is selected. After you print the PO, the check disappears from the box.

7. **Click Print to print the PO.**

If this PO is one of many that you've been filling out and you want to print several at once, click the arrow beside the Print button and choose Print Batch from the drop-down list. Before you print the PO, however, you may want to click the down arrow beside the Print button and choose Preview to see what the PO will look like when you print it. QuickBooks shows you an onscreen replica of the PO. I hope it looks okay.

You use the History button after you receive the items you've so carefully listed on the PO. After you receive the items and record their receipt, clicking this button tells QuickBooks to give you the entire history of an item — when you ordered it and when you received it.

As for the other buttons at the top, I think that you know what those are.

8. **Click Save & New or Save & Close to record the PO.**

QuickBooks saves the PO and displays a new, blank PO window in which you can enter another order.

Checking up on purchase orders

You record the POs. A couple weeks go by, and you ask yourself, "Did I order those doohickeys from Acme?" Choose Reports➪Purchases➪Open Purchase Orders to see a report that lists outstanding POs. Or click the Reports Center, select Purchases in the left column, click the List view button in the top-right corner to get an actual list of purchasing reports, and then click the Open Purchase Orders report. Alternatively, you can also use the Report Center carousel to "page" through the reports in a category: To use the carousel, select Purchases in the left column, click the Carousel view button (next to the List view button), and then click the stack-of-reports image that appears to the left or the right of the picture of the selected report.

Receiving purchase order items

After your doohickeys and gizmos have arrived by camel train, you need to record the receipt of the items and add them to your Item list.

The first two things to do are to note whether the stuff came with a bill and then decide how you want to pay for it. These decisions are the same ones that you have to make if you receive goods without having first filled out a PO.

You record PO items that you receive the same way you record other items you receive:

- ✔ If you pay for PO items with a check, use the Write Checks window.
- ✔ If you receive the PO items without a bill, use the Create Item Receipts window.
- ✔ If you receive the PO items with a bill, use the Enter Bills window.

Regardless of the window you're using, when you select the vendor who sold you the PO items, QuickBooks alerts you that open POs exist for the vendor and asks you whether you want to receive against a PO. Of course you do. (*Receive against* simply means to compare what you ordered with what you received.) When you click Yes, QuickBooks displays the Open Purchase Orders dialog box, as shown in Figure 7-6. Select the PO(s) that you're receiving against and then click OK. QuickBooks fills out the Items tab to show all the stuff you ordered. If what QuickBooks shows isn't what you received, you may have to make adjustments.

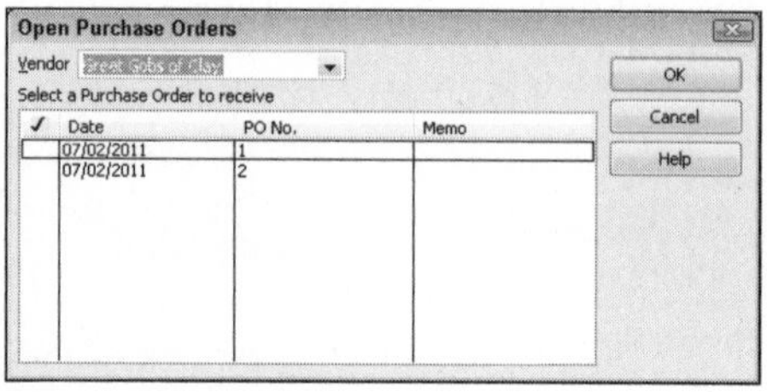

Figure 7-6:
The Open
Purchase
Orders
dialog box.

Assembling a Product

QuickBooks Premier and Enterprise include a cool tool for accounting for the manufacture of items. Suppose that Pine Lake Porcelain, the example business I use in this book, mostly just buys and resells coffee mugs and other porcelain doodads. But also suppose that once a year, Pine Lake Porcelain assembles a romantic collection of red coffee mugs into a boxed St. Valentine's Day gift set. In this case, QuickBooks can record the assembly of a boxed gift set that combines, for example, six red coffee mugs, a cardboard box clad in shiny red foil, and some red tissue paper.

Identifying the components

Each component that makes up the assembly — in this example, the St. Valentine's Day boxed gift set — needs to be an item on your Item list. Chapter 3 describes how to add items to the Item list, so I don't repeat that information here. The weird thing about assembly items, however, is that the New Item window identifies the parts that make up the assembly. For example, the St. Valentine's Day boxed gift set assembly includes these items: six red coffee mugs, a cardboard gift box, and some tissue paper that loved ones can use when they become emotionally overwhelmed by the generosity of this thoughtful gift. These items get listed as the pieces that make up the boxed gift set.

Building the assembly

To build an assembly, choose Vendors⇨Inventory Activities⇨Build Assemblies. Or, if you're on the Home screen, click the Build Assemblies icon in the Company area. QuickBooks displays the Build Assemblies window, as shown in Figure 7-7. All you do is choose the item that you want to build from the Assembly Item drop-down list and then the quantity that you (or some hapless co-worker) entered in the Quantity to Build text box (in the lower-right corner). Then you click either the Build & Close button or the Build & New button. (Click Build & New if you want to record the assembly of some other items.)

While I'm on the subject, let me make a handful of observations about the Build Assemblies window and the Build Assemblies command:

✔ In the top-middle portion of the window, QuickBooks shows the quantities of the assembly that you have on hand and for which customers have placed orders. That's pretty useful information to have, so, hey — remember that it's there.

✔ The main part of the Build Assemblies window shows you what goes into your product. Not that you care, but this is called a *bill of materials*.

✔ At the bottom of the bill of materials list, QuickBooks shows you the maximum number of assemblies you can make, given your current inventory holdings.

✔ When you build an item, QuickBooks adjusts the inventory item counts. For example, in the case of boxed gift sets — each with six red coffee mugs, one piece of wrapping tissue, and a cardboard box — QuickBooks reduces the item counts of red coffee mugs, wrapping tissues, and boxes, and increases the item counts of the boxed gift sets when you record building the assembly.

✔ Some of the components used in an assembly may not be inventory items. When you use non-inventory parts in an assembly, QuickBooks doesn't care about the item counts.

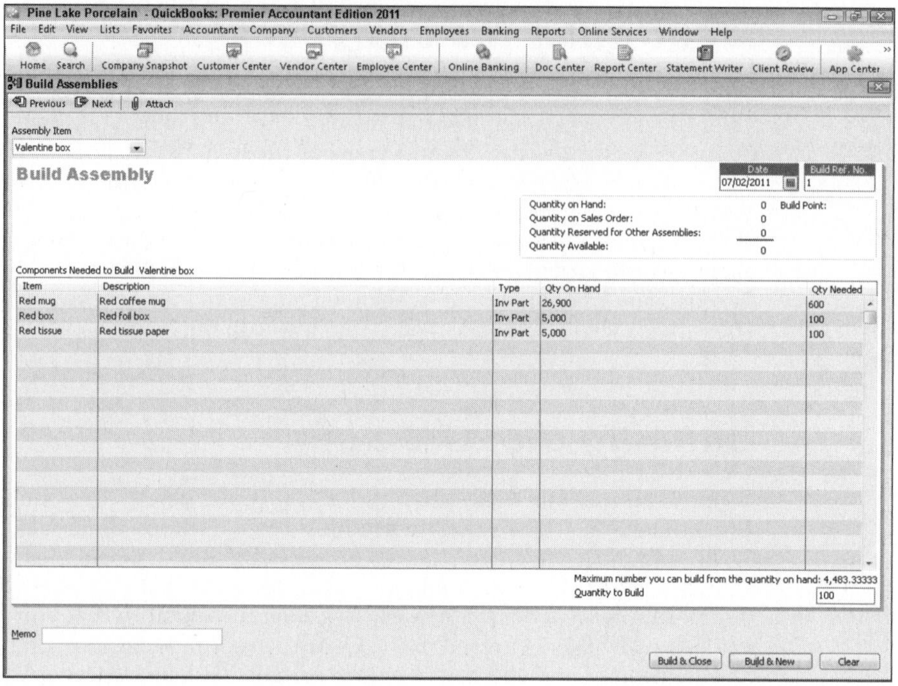

Pine Lake Porcelain - QuickBooks: Premier Accountant Edition 2011

File Edit View Lists Favorites Accountant Company Customers Vendors Employees Banking Reports Online Services Window Help

Home Search Company Snapshot Customer Center Vendor Center Employee Center Online Banking Doc Center Report Center Statement Writer Client Review App Center

Build Assemblies

Previous Next Attach

Assembly Item
Valentine box

Build Assembly

	Date	Build Ref. No.
	07/02/2011	1

Quantity on Hand:	0	Build Point:
Quantity on Sales Order:	0	
Quantity Reserved for Other Assemblies:	0	
Quantity Available:	0	

Components Needed to Build Valentine box

Item	Description	Type	Qty On Hand	Qty Needed
Red mug	Red coffee mug	Inv Part	26,900	600
Red box	Red foil box	Inv Part	5,000	100
Red tissue	Red tissue paper	Inv Part	5,000	100

Maximum number you can build from the quantity on hand: 4,483.33333

Quantity to Build   100

Memo

Build & Close   Build & New   Clear

Figure 7-7:
The Build
Assemblies
window.

Time for a Reality Check

QuickBooks does a pretty good job of tracking inventory, but you're still going to have to make that complete annual inventory of what you have in stock. What I'm saying here is that you're going to have to go over everything and count it by hand. Sorry. You just can't avoid that chore.

QuickBooks will produce a handy physical inventory worksheet that you and your minions can use to count inventory. To produce this report, choose Vendors➪Inventory Activities➪Physical Inventory Worksheet. Then, after QuickBooks produces an onscreen version of this worksheet report, click the Print button to print hard copies of the worksheet. You can use the printed worksheet to record actual physical counts of the inventory items you hold.

After you make your count, what happens if your inventory figures differ from those QuickBooks has? First, you have to decide who's right: you or a computer program. You're right, probably. Products get dropped. They break. And that means that you have to adjust the QuickBooks inventory numbers.

Choose Vendors⇨Inventory Activities⇨Adjust Quantity/Value on Hand. Or click the Adjust Quantity On Hand icon in the Company section of the Home screen. The Adjust Quantity/Value on Hand window appears, as shown in Figure 7-8.

The first thing to do is choose an account for storing your inventory adjustments. Choose it from the Adjustment Account drop-down list. You also can select a class from the Class drop-down list.

For what it's worth, some accountants like to use a special inventory adjustments expense account to provide a way to see the total inventory adjustments over the year.

Go down the Item column, selecting items from the Item list whose counts you need to update. When you select an item, QuickBooks shows the item count that it thinks is correct in the Quantity on Hand column. If this count is wrong, enter the correct count in the New Quantity column. Click Save & Close when you're done.

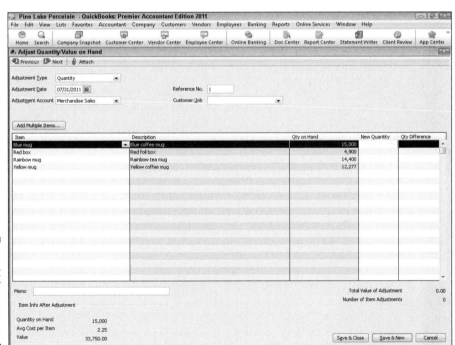

Figure 7-8:
The Adjust
Quantity/
Value
on Hand
window.

Dealing with Multiple Inventory Locations

If you've read this chapter to this point, you've seen now how QuickBooks handles your inventory. With rather elegant simplicity, but for many businesses, QuickBooks gets the job done.

Unfortunately, I've encountered a real headache when using the most common versions of QuickBooks for inventory. What if you store inventory in multiple locations — for example, in a Michigan warehouse and in a Chicago distribution facility? Or in a couple retail locations — one on the right side of the tracks and the other one on the wrong side of the tracks?

The problem is that QuickBooks is set up to deal with a single inventory location. So although you can know how much inventory you have in total, if you aren't careful, you won't know how much is in Michigan and how much is in Chicago. And you can't even really check on inventory shrinkage because QuickBooks' records don't tie to location-specific inventory counts.

Now I need to tell you upfront that you don't have any *cheap, good way* to deal with this in QuickBooks. Throughout the following sections, though, I explain a couple sloppy fixes and one rather expensive but very robust fix you can do.

Manually keep separate inventory-by-location counts

If you have only a handful of items in your little business — say, a few dozen — it's pretty easy to keep a simple manual running tab on what you have in the Michigan warehouse and what's in the Chicago distribution facility.

Such a system is very . . . er, crude. It may just be a couple sticky notes taped to your computer monitor. No kidding. Still, it lets you know how much inventory you have (roughly) and where it's stored. And for some purposes, that works okay.

Use different item numbers for different locations

The embarrassingly crude approach that I describe in the preceding section doesn't work if you have a lot of items, so the approach won't work for a multiple-location retailer. Accordingly, if you're a retailer with a large number of items, I'm sorry, but I think you probably need to create sets of item numbers for each inventory location. This means a lot more work for you, of course, but it's really the only practical way to handle your inventory if you have more than a handful of items.

Upgrade to QuickBooks Enterprise Solutions

In past editions, oh, ten editions of this book, I've half jokingly suggested that fellow QuickBooks users start a letter-writing campaign, pleading with Intuit to support a multiple-stores or multiple-inventory locations feature.

I'm not sure if this collective letter-writing campaign explains the new feature, but starting with QuickBooks Enterprise Solutions 2011, you can effectively deal with situations where you're holding inventory in multiple locations and transferring inventory between locations with the Advanced Inventory feature. I don't discuss it here. But you can (if you have the Enterprise version of QuickBooks) read the online help.

Note: QuickBooks Enterprise Solutions costs considerably more than QuickBooks Pro and QuickBooks Premier. At the time of this writing, for example, the Intuit Web site quotes the price for up to five users as roughly $3,000.

The Lazy Person's Approach to Inventory

The inventory accounting approach that I describe in the previous paragraphs of this chapter is the textbook approach. What's more, the approach is a really good one because it lets you accurately calculate your cost of goods sold and accurately estimate the value of the inventory you're holding. To paraphrase Martha Stewart, these are Good Things.

You should know, however, that you can also use a simpler approach to inventory accounting. Specifically, rather than keeping track of individual inventory items by using a *perpetual inventory system* — this simply means that you track each item when it moves into your business and out into a customer's car or minivan — you can use a simple periodic system. In the sections that follow, I tell you how a periodic inventory system works in QuickBooks. Then I tell you what's bad and what's good about using a periodic inventory system.

How periodic inventory systems work in QuickBooks

If you use a periodic inventory system, you set up an Other Current Asset type account called *Inventory.* Then, whenever you purchase inventory, you categorize the inventory purchase as falling into this "fake" inventory account. (I'm calling the account a fake inventory account because it isn't a real inventory account to QuickBooks.)

To record your cost of goods sold each month, you use a journal entry to move an appropriate portion out of the fake inventory account and into your cost of goods sold account. How do you know what portion you should move? Good question. In a nutshell, you guess based on what your historical cost of goods sold percentage is.

Here's an example of how this works: Suppose that since time immemorial, your cost of goods sold has run 45 percent of your sales revenue, and that last month, you sold $10,000 of stuff. In this case, you'd figure that 45 percent of $10,000 ($4,500) equals the cost of the inventory that you sold. Accordingly, you'd move $4,500 out of the fake inventory account and into cost of goods sold.

Predictably, this rough-and-ready approach means that your inventory and cost of goods sold numbers are going to be wrong. So, at the end of the year, you still perform a physical inventory count to figure out exactly what you truly hold in inventory. At that point, you'd adjust the inventory and cost of goods sold balances so that they match what your physical inventory shows.

For example, it may be that over the course of the year, your rough 45 percent number has meant that you moved $5,000 too much from inventory to cost of goods sold. In this case, you'd move $5,000 out of cost of goods sold and back to inventory.

Or you may find that you moved $5,000 too little from inventory to cost of goods sold. To fix that problem, you move another $5,000 from inventory to cost of goods sold.

A final quick point about using a periodic inventory: As I note in this little discussion, you don't use inventory items if you're using a periodic inventory. So what you put on invoices or sales receipts is just a generic, non-inventory part item.

The good and bad of a periodic inventory

A periodic inventory system is good for some types of businesses. For example, if you have too many items to track with the QuickBooks Item list, the approach that I describe here can be a lifesaver.

However, periodic inventory systems create some problems. Here are the four biggest and baddest problems in my mind:

✔ You won't really know which items are selling well and which aren't because you won't be tracking sales by inventory items. This means that you can't stock more of the hot-selling stuff and less of stuff that's not selling.

✔ You won't know what you really hold in your inventory except when you take that year-end physical inventory. (You won't know how many dollars of inventory you're holding, nor will you know which item quantities you're holding.)

✔ Because you won't make item-level adjustments based on your physical inventory, you won't know which items are prone to shrinkage from problems such as theft, breakage, and spoilage.

✔ You'll need to make the journal entries that record the dollars moving out of inventory and into cost of goods sold. These journal entries aren't terribly difficult, but they can be a little bit tricky to figure out the first few times.

You'll need to decide whether you want or need to go with a simpler periodic inventory system in spite of the problems such a system presents. The one final thought that I'll leave you with is this: Many small businesses — especially small retailers — successfully use periodic inventory systems.

Chapter 8

Keeping Your Checkbook

. . . .

In This Chapter

▶ Writing checks from the Write Checks window or the register

▶ Recording deposits and transfers

▶ Working with several currencies

▶ Voiding and deleting transactions

▶ Handling NSF checks

▶ Searching for transactions

. . . .

*I*n a sense, a small business's finances and cash flows revolve about the business's checkbook. Which means this chapter is mighty important. Here, you're finally going to see how to do those everyday checkbook things using QuickBooks: entering checks, deposits, and transfers. Along the way, you also find out about some neat tools that QuickBooks provides for making these tasks easier, faster, and more precise.

Writing Checks

Chapter 6 shows you the two ways to write checks: from the Write Checks window and from the register. In case you were asleep in the back row of the class, here's the short version of the instructions for writing checks.

You can record debit card and ATM transactions the same way that you record checks that you write.

Writing checks from the Write Checks window

You can record handwritten checks and other checks that you want to print with QuickBooks by describing the checks in the Write Checks window.

To write a check from the Write Checks window, follow these steps:

1. **Choose Banking⇨Write Checks.**

   You can also click the Write Checks icon located in the Banking section of the Home screen. QuickBooks displays the Write Checks window, as shown in Figure 8-1.

2. **Click the Bank Account drop-down list at the top of the window and choose the account from which you want to write this check.**

   This step is really important and is something that you should always remember to do before you write a check if you have multiple bank accounts.

3. **Enter a check number or mark the check for printing.**

   Select the To Be Printed check box if you plan on printing the check with QuickBooks, using your printer and preprinted check forms that you've purchased. (I describe this process in Chapter 10.) If you're recording a check you wrote by hand, enter the check number you used for the check in the No. text box.

4. **Fill in the check.**

   If you've written a check to this person or party before, the AutoFill feature fills in the name of the payee in the Pay to the Order Of line for you after you start typing the name. How QuickBooks manages this feat may seem akin to magic, but it's really not that tough. QuickBooks just compares what you've typed so far with names on your lists of customers, employees, and others. As soon as QuickBooks can match the letters that you've typed with a name on one of these lists, it grabs the name.

   If you haven't written a check to this person or party before, QuickBooks asks you to add the payee name. Do that. (If you're not sure whether you want to add a payee or how to add a payee, read through Chapter 6.)

   Enter the amount of the check next to the dollar sign and then press Tab. QuickBooks writes the amount for you on the Dollars line. It also writes the address if it's been filled out in the payee's master file.

5. **Fill in the Expenses and Items tabs, if necessary.**

   Don't know what these are? Chapter 6 explains them in minute detail.

6. **Click the Save & Close button or the Save & New button to finish writing the check.**

   There you have it. Your check is written and entered in the register, ready to be printed and mailed.

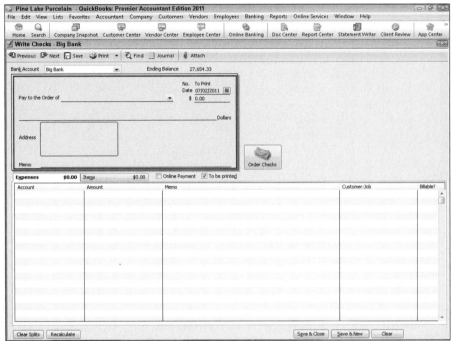

Figure 8-1:
The Write
Checks
window.

Writing checks from the Checking register

People who've grown accustomed to *Quicken,* a cousin of QuickBooks, might want to use the register window to write checks. (Quicken users like the register metaphor better, I guess.)

To write a check from the register, follow these steps:

1. **Open the register.**

   Choose Banking⇨Use Register or click the Check Register icon in the Banking area of the Home screen. If you have more than one bank account, QuickBooks displays the Use Register dialog box so that you can select the proper account.

   From the drop-down list, choose the checking account against which you want to write the check and then click OK. You see the register window (see Figure 8-2). The cursor is at the end of the register, ready for you to enter check information. (QuickBooks automatically fills in today's date.)

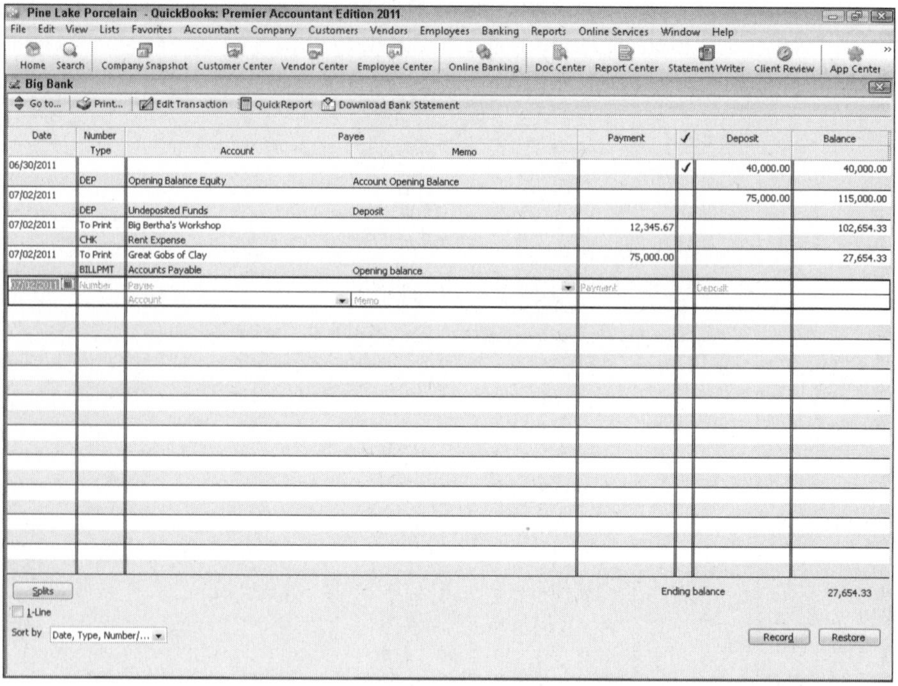

Figure 8-2:
The register
window.

QuickBooks uses the account name in the window title. This is why Figure 8-2 refers to *Big Bank* Account. That's the name of the fictitious bank account that I set up.

2. Fill in the information for your check.

Notice that the entries you make in this register are the same ones that you'd make in the Write Checks window. If you're more comfortable entering checks in that window, you can click the Edit Transaction button, which is at the top of the register window, to see the Write Checks window in all its glory and write a check there. In fact, if you want to enter expenses or itemize what you're paying for with the check, you have to click the Edit Transaction button and get into the Write Checks window.

Otherwise, just go from field to field and enter the information in the register. Once again, use the drop-down lists to enter the Payee and Account names. If you enter a Payee or Account name that QuickBooks doesn't recognize, the program asks you to give more information.

Here's sort of a trick question: What if the check you're writing pays more than one category of expense? For example, say you pay your landlord both for your rent and for a share of the utilities. Are you limited to one expense account? Do you face the mother of all accounting dilemmas — choosing between two correct accounts? Well, no, you don't. You can just click the Splits button. QuickBooks displays a splits area that you can use to split a check across several different accounts. For example, a $1,500 check that pays $1,200 of rent and $300 of utilities can split onto two separate lines: one that records the $1,200 of rent expense and one that records the $300 of utilities expense.

3. **When you finish filling in the check information, click the Record button.**

   You can also click the Restore button if you decide that you want to go back to start over again. Clicking Restore blanks out what you just entered.

 If you write checks by hand, as opposed to printing them with QuickBooks, make sure that the check numbers in the register and the check numbers in your checkbook match. You may need to go into the QuickBooks register and change numbers in the Number column. When your bank statement comes, reconciling your bank statement and your checkbook is much easier if you enter check numbers correctly.

Changing a check that you've written

What if you need to change a check after you've already entered it? Perhaps you made a terrible mistake, such as recording a $52.50 check as $25.20. Can you fix it? Sure. Just go into the register and find the check that you want to change. Go to the Payment or Deposit field and make the change.

If you have more extensive changes to make (for instance, if the check is a split transaction), put the cursor where the check is and click Edit Transaction. QuickBooks displays the Write Checks window with the original check in it. Make the changes. (Don't forget to make changes on the Items and Expenses tabs, too, if necessary.)

When you finish, click Save & Close. You go back to the register, where you see the changes to the check.

 If you have the Write Checks window displayed, you can also use the Next and Previous buttons to page through your checks and make any changes.

Packing more checks into the register

Usually, QuickBooks displays two rows of information about each check you enter. It also displays two rows of information about each type of transaction that you enter. If you want to pack more checks into a visible portion of the register, select the 1-Line check box at the bottom of the register window. When you select this check box, QuickBooks uses a single-line format to display all the information in the register except the Memo field. (See Figure 8-3.)

TIP

Paying for items with cash

To track petty cash purchases, you need a petty cash account. You can set up a petty cash account (which works just like a bank account) by following the steps in "Setting up a second bank account," later in this chapter. To record purchases that you make from the money in that coffee can beside your desk, use the petty cash register. You can record cash purchases just like you record checks. (Of course, you don't need to worry about using the correct check numbers when you record cash purchases; you can just use the numbers 1, 2, 3, and so on.) To record cashed checking withdrawals to be used for petty cash in the office, just record the withdrawal as a transfer to your petty cash account, as I describe later in the chapter.

Compare Figure 8-2 with Figure 8-3 to see what the 1-Line display looks like. Checking registers can get awfully long, and the 1-Line display is helpful when you're looking through a long register for a check or transaction.

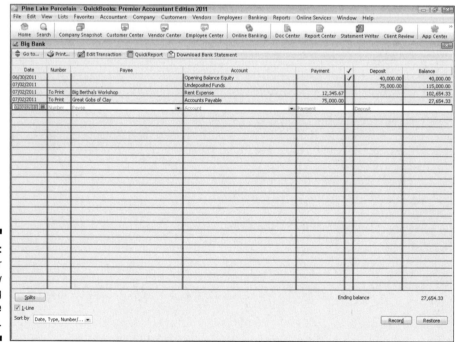

Figure 8-3:
The register window when using 1-Line display.

Depositing Money into a Checking Account

You can't write checks unless you deposit some money in your checking account. You didn't know that? Well, the next time you're taking your exercise in the prison yard, give it some serious thought. From time to time, you must deposit money in your checking account and record those deposits in the register.

You can record deposits in two ways. Find out about those ways in the following sections.

Recording simple deposits

If you have a simple deposit to make — a sum of money that didn't come from one of your customers — just make the deposit directly in the Checking register.

Suppose that your elderly Aunt Iris sends you $100 with a note explaining how more than 80 years ago, Great-Uncle Bert started his hammock manufacturing business with only $100, and for good luck, she's sending you $100 to help you along.

Recording a simple deposit is, well, pretty simple. Follow these steps:

1. **Open the Checking register.**

   Choose Banking⇨Use Register, or click the Check Register icon in the Banking section of the Home screen. If you have more than one bank account, QuickBooks displays the Use Register dialog box. Select the checking account into which you want to make the deposit, and click OK. QuickBooks displays the register window (refer to Figure 8-2).

2. **In the Date column, enter the date on which you made the deposit.**

3. **In the Payee column, enter the name of the person or business that sent you money.**

   Don't worry if QuickBooks adds a check number in the Number field when you move to the Payee column. When you enter a deposit amount, QuickBooks changes the Number field to DEP (for deposit, of course).

4. **Enter the amount that you're depositing.**

   Move the cursor to the Deposit column and enter the amount.

5. **Enter an account for this deposit.**

Move to the Account field, click the down arrow, and choose an account from the list. For a gift like this, you'll likely choose an account like Uncategorized Income.

6. **Click the Record button.**

Your deposit is entered, and your checking account's balance is fattened accordingly. Note that all entries in the register are made in chronological order, with deposits first and checks next.

Depositing income from customers

Depositing income from customers is a little more complicated if you issue invoices and receive payments because it involves using the Payments to Deposit dialog box. Have you been recording customer payments as they come in? (You do so by choosing Customers⇨Receive Payments or Customers⇨Enter Sales Receipt, as I describe in Chapter 5; or by selecting the Create Sales Receipts or Receive Payments icon on the Home screen; or by clicking the Customer Center and selecting New Transactions, Sales Receipts, or Receive Payments.) If you've recorded customer payments and told QuickBooks to group them with your other undeposited funds, QuickBooks places these payments in your Undeposited Funds account. Now all you have to do is transfer the undeposited funds to your checking account. Here's how:

1. **Choose Banking⇨Make Deposits.**

You can also click the Record Deposits icon in the Banking section of the Home screen. Because you have undeposited funds, you see the Payments to Deposit dialog box, as shown in Figure 8-4. This dialog box lists the checks that you've received but haven't put in a checking account or other bank account yet.

The View Payment Method Type drop-down list lets you see payments of only a particular type: cash, check, American Express, and so on. If you group deposits by payment type, this list works as a slick tool to group transactions that you'll deposit together.

2. **Select the checks that you want to deposit and then click OK.**

Place a check mark (click the column) next to the checks that you want to deposit. If you want to deposit all the checks, click the Select All button.

The Make Deposits window appears, as shown in Figure 8-5. Do you recognize the information in the middle of the window? It describes the checks that you just selected to be deposited.

You want to make sure that the Deposit Total shown in the Make Deposits window is the right deposit amount — in other words, the actual amount truly deposited into the bank account. When you attempt to reconcile the bank account, you'll compare the deposit total shown here with your bank statement's cleared deposits amount.

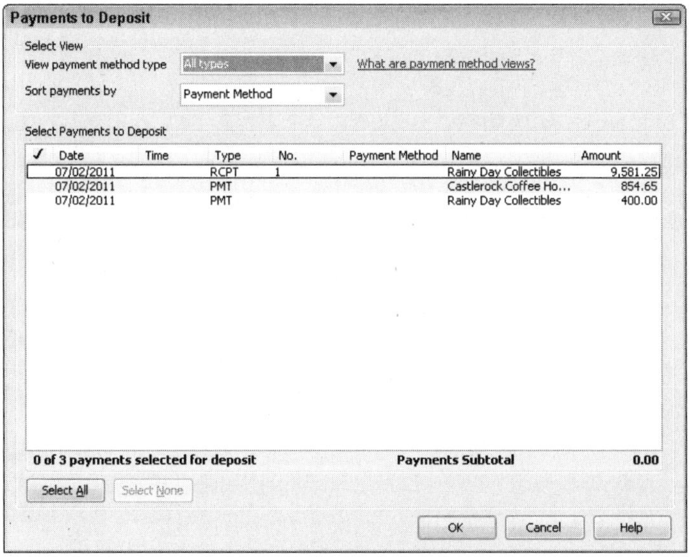

Figure 8-4:
The Payments to Deposit dialog box.

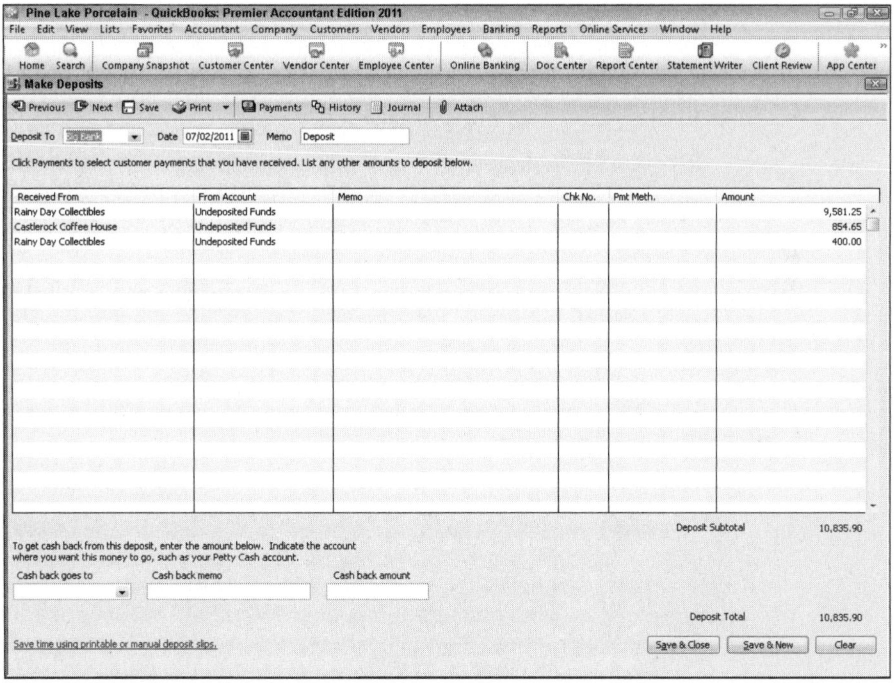

Figure 8-5:
The Make Deposits window.

3. **Select the checking account to receive these deposits.**

   Select the account from the Deposit To drop-down list at the top of the window. And while you're at it, check the Date text box to make sure that it shows the date you'll deposit these checks in your checking account. In other words, if you're not going to make it to the bank or the ATM until tomorrow, put tomorrow's date in the Date text box.

4. **Add any other noncustomer deposits to include on the deposit slip.**

   If your grandma (bless her heart) gave you 1,000 pennies in 20 rolls, for example, that's an extra $10 that you can record on this deposit slip. At the bottom of the list of payments, enter the name of the person who gave you the cash, the account, a memo, a check number, the payment method (cash, in this case), a class if you're using classes, and the amount.

5. **(Optional) Write a note to yourself in the Memo box to describe this deposit.**

6. **Click the Print button to get a hard copy of the deposit slip.**

   Many banks accept this deposit slip, so you can print it and put it in the envelope with your ATM deposit or hand it to the bank clerk. Whatever you write on the memo appears on the register. (You should probably write a memo to yourself in case you need to know what this deposit is years from now, when you're old and dotty.)

7. **Record any cash back that you plan to get with the deposit.**

   If you need to get cash to replenish your petty cash account, select the account from the Cash Back Goes To drop-down list, write a memo, and then record the amount of cash that you want to get back from the deposit.

8. **Click the Save & Close button at the bottom of the Make Deposits window.**

   The deposit is recorded in QuickBooks. It appears in your register next to the letters DEP.

Transferring Money between Accounts

Account transfers occur when you move money from one account to another — for example, from your savings account to your checking account. But jeepers, why am I telling you this? If you have one of those combined savings and checking accounts, you probably do this sort of thing all the time.

Oh, now I remember why I brought this up: QuickBooks makes quick work of account transfers as long as you've already set up both accounts.

Setting up a second bank account

If you haven't set up a second account, you need to set one up. To do so, open the Chart of Accounts by choosing Lists➪Chart of Accounts, or just click the Chart of Accounts icon on the Home screen in the Company section. Click the Account button and then choose New. Fill in the name of the account and, if you want to, the account number or a description of the account. Then fill in the As Of box with the date that you opened the account. Enter the opening balance as zero so that you can record your initial deposit or transfer of money into the account. You record initial deposits the way I describe earlier in this chapter (either as simple deposits or as customer deposits, whatever the case may be). You record an initial transfer by completing the following steps:

1. **Choose Banking➪Transfer Funds.**

   You see the Transfer Funds Between Accounts window, as shown in Figure 8-6.

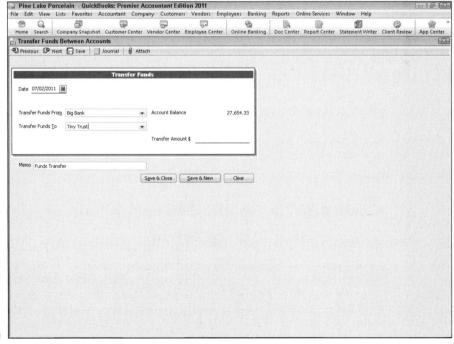

Figure 8-6:
The Transfer Funds Between Accounts window.

2. **Select the bank account from which you're going to transfer the money.**

   From the Transfer Funds From drop-down list at the top of the window, choose the account.

3. **Select the bank account to which you want to transfer the money.**

   From the Transfer Funds To drop-down list, select the account that receives the funds.

4. **Enter the amount that you want to transfer and, optionally, fill in the Memo box.**

   Provide the transfer amount for the obvious reason: QuickBooks can't read your mind.

5. **Click the Save & New button or the Save & Close button.**

   QuickBooks records the transfer, which you can confirm by opening your register. You see that the transfer has the letters TRANSFR in the Type column and the name of the account to which you transferred the money in the Account column. The amount that you transferred shows in the Payment column (because you transferred the funds out of this account). Figure 8-7 shows a $5,000 transfer — in the figure, the selected transaction is the one I'm talking about — from a checking account called Big Bank to a savings account called Tiny Trust. You can tell this transaction is a transfer because the other account name shows up in the Account box.

About the other half of the transfer

Here's the cool thing about transfer transactions: QuickBooks automatically records the other half of the transfer for you. Figure 8-8 shows the other half of the transfer from Figure 8-7. This register is for a savings account called Tiny Trust. The $5,000 transfer from your checking account actually made it into your savings account. The transfer once again shows up as a TRANSFR.

Changing a transfer that you've already entered

Big surprise here, but changing a transfer that you already entered works just like changing a check. First, you find the transfer in the account register, and then you click the Edit Transaction button. You see the Transfer Funds Between Accounts window with the transfer check that you wrote. Make changes to the check and then click Save & New or Save & Close. You return to the register, where your deposit is adjusted accordingly.

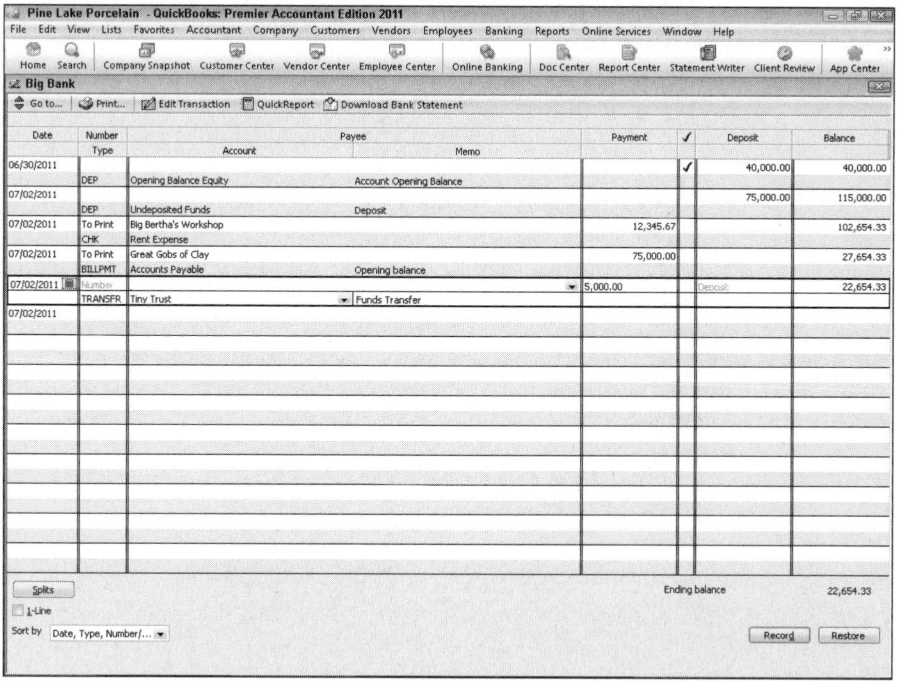

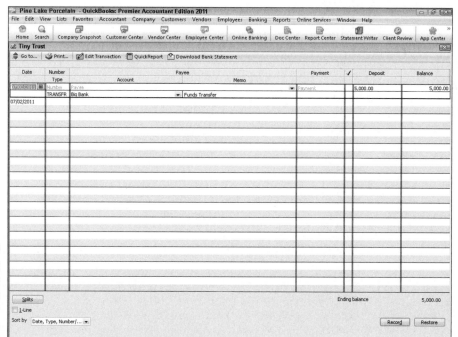

Figure 8-7:
A transfer transaction in the register.

Figure 8-8:
The other half of the transfer transaction.

Working with Multiple Currencies

If you tell QuickBooks that you need to do your accounting in multiple currencies — something you do by choosing Edit⇨Preferences, selecting Multiple Currencies, clicking the Company Preferences tab, and then clicking the Yes I Use More Than One Currency button — QuickBooks reconfigures its operation and appearance so you can work with more than one currency.

As you might expect, given this is QuickBooks I'm talking about, working with multiple currencies isn't that complicated. To go "multiple currencies," you simply identify the currency that you'll use for specific bank accounts, customers, and vendors. And then QuickBooks assumes, when you're recording transactions for these bank accounts, customers, and vendors, that you're working in the specified currency. QuickBooks clearly identifies the specified currency in windows and dialog boxes next to amount boxes.

To allow you to convert foreign currencies to your home currency, QuickBooks also adds a Currency List command to the Lists menu, which you use to track currencies and their exchange rates so you can translate transactions denominated in a foreign currency into your home currency.

To Delete or to Void?

What happens if you put a transaction — a deposit, check, or transfer payment — in a register and later decide that it shouldn't be there? You have two ways of handling this situation. If you want to keep a record of the transaction but render it moot, meaningless, or nada, you void the transaction. But if you want to obliterate the transaction from the face of the Earth as though it never happened, you delete it.

Decide whether you want to void or delete the transaction and then follow these steps:

1. **Find the transaction in the register.**

   In the upcoming section, "The Big Register Phenomenon," I tell you some quick ways to find transactions.

2. **Choose either Edit⇨Delete Check or Edit⇨Void Check and then click the Record button.**

   There; the deed is done. Figure 8-9 shows a register window with a voided check. The voided transaction is the one selected. Notice the word VOID in the Memo column. If this check had been deleted, it wouldn't even show up in the register. An alternative method is to select the check in the register or on the check screen and then right-click and choose Void Check from there.

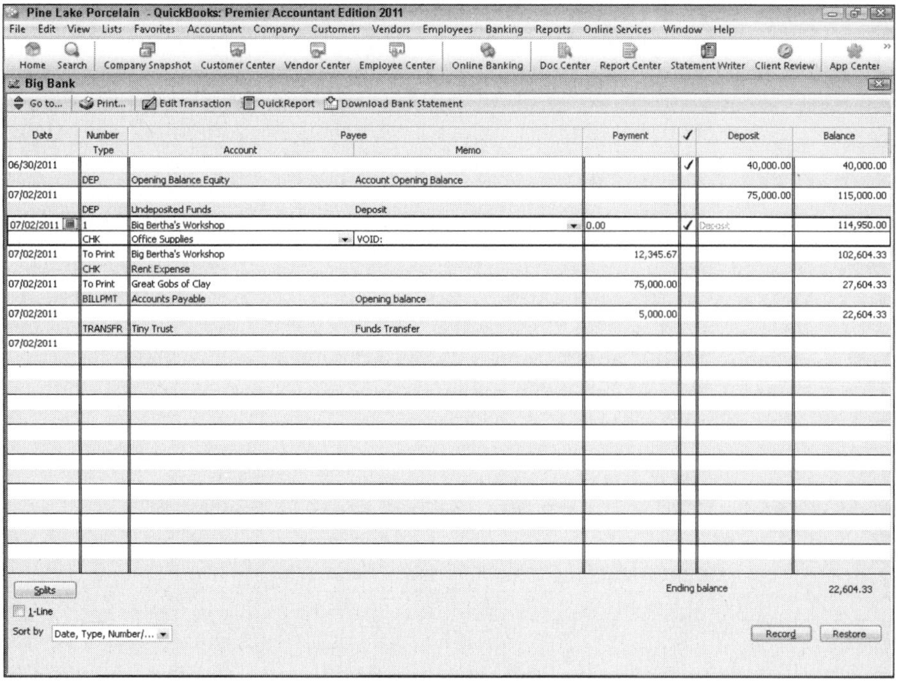

Pine Lake Porcelain - QuickBooks: Premier Accountant Edition 2011

File Edit View Lists Favorites Accountant Company Customers Vendors Employees Banking Reports Online Services Window Help

Home Search | Company Snapshot Customer Center Vendor Center Employee Center | Online Banking | Doc Center Report Center Statement Writer Client Review | App Center

Big Bank

Go to... | Print... | Edit Transaction | QuickReport | Download Bank Statement

Date	Number / Type	Account	Payee Memo	Payment	✓	Deposit	Balance
06/30/2011	DEP	Opening Balance Equity	Account Opening Balance		✓	40,000.00	40,000.00
07/02/2011	DEP	Undeposited Funds	Deposit			75,000.00	115,000.00
07/02/2011	1 / CHK	Big Bertha's Workshop / Office Supplies	VOID:	0.00	✓	Deposit	114,950.00
07/02/2011	To Print / CHK	Big Bertha's Workshop / Rent Expense		12,345.67			102,604.33
07/02/2011	To Print / BILLPMT	Great Gobs of Clay / Accounts Payable	Opening balance	75,000.00			27,604.33
07/02/2011	TRANSFR	Tiny Trust	Funds Transfer	5,000.00			22,604.33
07/02/2011							

Splits

☐ 1-Line

Sort by Date, Type, Number/... ▾

Ending balance   22,604.33

Record | Restore

Figure 8-9:
The register shows a voided check.

The Edit menu changes depending on what kind of transaction shows or is selected in the open window (that is, Void Deposit, Void Check, and so on).

Handling NSF Checks from Customers

I've had a handful of reader questions about how to handle insufficient-funds (NSF) check transactions. Here's how I suggest handling this situation:

1. **Record the service charge that the bank charges you for handling the bounced check, just like any other bank service charge.**

   You can enter a transaction directly into the register, for example. Or you can even record the bank service fee as though it's a check that you just wrote. Anything coming out of your account is entered just like a check. (Refer to the earlier discussions in this chapter for information on entering transactions in the register or on recording checks.)

2. **Record the adjustment to your bank account balance because the customer's check didn't clear as a withdrawal or payment.**

   You can use a bad-debt expense account to categorize the expense of the bounced check if you're on the accrual basis for taxes; otherwise, cash-basis companies should directly charge their sales income account to reduce their income.

3. **(Optional) Try to collect on the check again.**

   Try running by the customer's bank. You might also try to assess the customer a bounced-check fee. (See Chapter 4 for information on invoicing customers.) But be honest: You're probably not going to be able to collect, are you? So write a Note in the Customer's master file that says not to take any checks. It will appear right in the middle of the Customer Center screen when you select that customer to record the next sale.

4. **Post a huge copy of the check in your cash register area so the deadbeat customer's friends and family see the check.**

   I'm just joking about this. But you know that.

The Big Register Phenomenon

If you start entering checks, deposits, and transfers into your registers, you soon find yourself with registers that contain hundreds, and even thousands, of transactions. You can still work with one of these big registers by using the tools and techniques that I talk about in the preceding paragraphs. Nevertheless, let me give you some more help for dealing with . . . (drum roll, please) . . . the big register phenomenon.

Moving through a big register

You can use the Page Up and Page Down keys to move up and down through your register a screenfull of transactions at a time. Some people call this activity *scrolling*. You can call it whatever you want.

You can also use the Home key to move through the register. Press the Home key once to move to the front of the field you're currently in. Press the Home key twice to move to the first field of the transaction you're on (the Date field), or press it three times to move to the first transaction in the register.

The End key works in a similar fashion. Bet you can guess how this works. Press the End key once to move to the end of the field you're in, press it twice to move to the last field of the transaction you're on (the Memo field), or press it three times to move to the last transaction in the register.

Of course, you can use the vertical scroll bar along the right edge of the register, too. Click the arrows at either end of the vertical scroll bar to select the next or previous transaction. Click either above or below the square scroll box to page back and forth through the register. Or, if you have no qualms about dragging the mouse around, you can drag the scroll box up and down the scroll bar.

QuickBooks lets you sort your register in different ways, which makes scrolling through and finding transactions much easier. To sort your register the way you prefer, choose an option from the Sort By drop-down list in the lower-left corner of the register window.

Finding that darn transaction

Want to find that one check, deposit, or transfer? No problem. I discuss this technique elsewhere in the book, but it's appropriate here, too. The Edit menu's Find command provides a handy way for doing just such a thing. Here's what you do:

1. **Choose Edit⇨Find and then click the Advanced tab.**

   QuickBooks, with restrained but obvious enthusiasm, displays the Advanced tab of the Find window (see Figure 8-10). You use this window to describe — in as much detail as possible — the transaction that you want to find.

   Choose Edit⇨Find to display the Simple tab of the Find window. The Simple tab enables you to search for transactions by using the transaction type, customer or job name, date, number, or amount. You can easily switch to an advanced search by clicking the Advanced tab.

2. **Choose a filter that describes the information that you already have.**

   In the figure, the Name filter is chosen. When you click different filters, the Find window changes.

3. **Describe the filter that identifies the transaction that you want to locate.**

   In the upper-left box, which is set to Name in Figure 8-10, choose the filter that describes the subject of your search from the drop-down list. In case of an account-based filter, for example, you can select to look at all accounts, just income accounts, just expense accounts, and so on. Other filters provide different boxes for setting the filter.

   By the way, the case of the text doesn't matter. If you type **rainy**, for example, QuickBooks finds *RAINY* as well as *Rainy*.

4. **Repeat Steps 2 and 3 as necessary.**

   Yes, you can filter through as many fields as you want. In fact, you can filter so much that nothing matches your specification.

5. Click Find to let the search begin.

Click the Find button to begin looking. If QuickBooks finds transactions that match the one you described, QuickBooks lists them in the bottom half of the window.

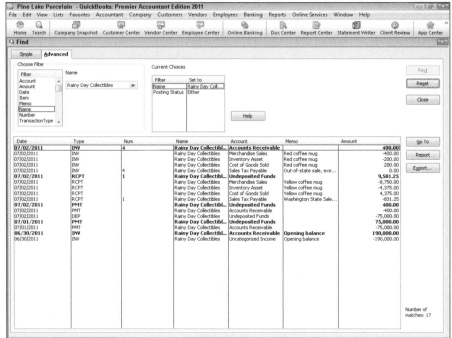

Figure 8-10:
The
Advanced
tab of the
Find
window.

Chapter 9

Paying with Plastic

· ·

In This Chapter

▶ Setting up and selecting credit card accounts

▶ Entering credit card charges

▶ Changing charges that you've entered already

▶ Reconciling credit card statements

▶ Paying the monthly credit card bill

▶ Handling debit cards

▶ Handling customer credit cards

· ·

*Y*ou can use QuickBooks to track your business credit cards in much the same way that you use it to keep a checkbook. The process is almost the same but with a few wrinkles.

By the way, although this chapter is really about you charging money on your credit cards, at the very end of the chapter, I talk about how to handle the tricky problem of your customers paying with credit cards.

Tracking Business Credit Cards

If you want to track credit card spending and balances with QuickBooks, you need to set up a credit card account — if you didn't already do so in the EasyStep Interview, which you can read about in Chapter 2. (In comparison, you use bank accounts to track things such as the money that flows into and out of a checking, savings, or petty cash account.)

Setting up a credit card account

To set up a credit card account, you follow roughly the same steps that you use to set up a bank account:

1. **Choose Lists⇨Chart of Accounts.**

   Or click the Chart of Accounts icon on the Home screen. QuickBooks displays the Chart of Accounts window, as shown in Figure 9-1.

2. **Click the Account button in the lower-left corner of the Chart of Accounts window and then choose New.**

   QuickBooks displays the first Add New Account window, which simply displays a list of option buttons corresponding to the different types of accounts QuickBooks allows.

3. **Select the Credit Card option.**

   Selecting Credit Card tells QuickBooks that you want to set up a credit card account. I'm sure that you're surprised. Click Continue. QuickBooks displays the second Add New Account window, as shown in Figure 9-2.

4. **Type a name for the account in the Account Name text box.**

   Why not do it right? Move the cursor to the Account Name text box and then enter the name of your credit card.

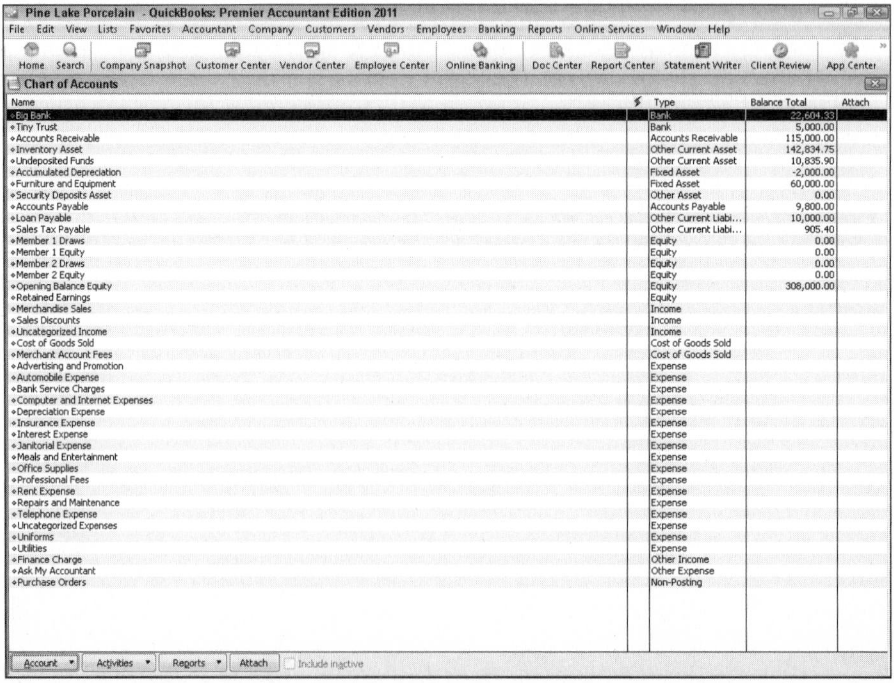

Figure 9-1:
The Chart
of Accounts
window.

5. **Type the card number in the Credit Card Acct. No. text box.**

    If you're creating a general Credit Card account for more than one card, leave the Credit Card Acct. No. text box empty. While you're at it, you can describe the card, too. You might want to type **Usury!** in the Description text box, depending on your card's interest rate.

6. **Click the Save & Close button.**

    QuickBooks redisplays the Chart of Accounts window (refer to Figure 9-1). Now, the window lists an additional account: the credit card account that you just created.

Selecting a credit card account so that you can use it

To tell QuickBooks that you want to work with a credit card account, you use the Chart of Accounts window (shown earlier in Figure 9-1). Choose Lists⇨Chart of Accounts. After you display the window, double-click the credit card account that you want to use. QuickBooks displays the Credit Card register so that you can begin recording transactions.

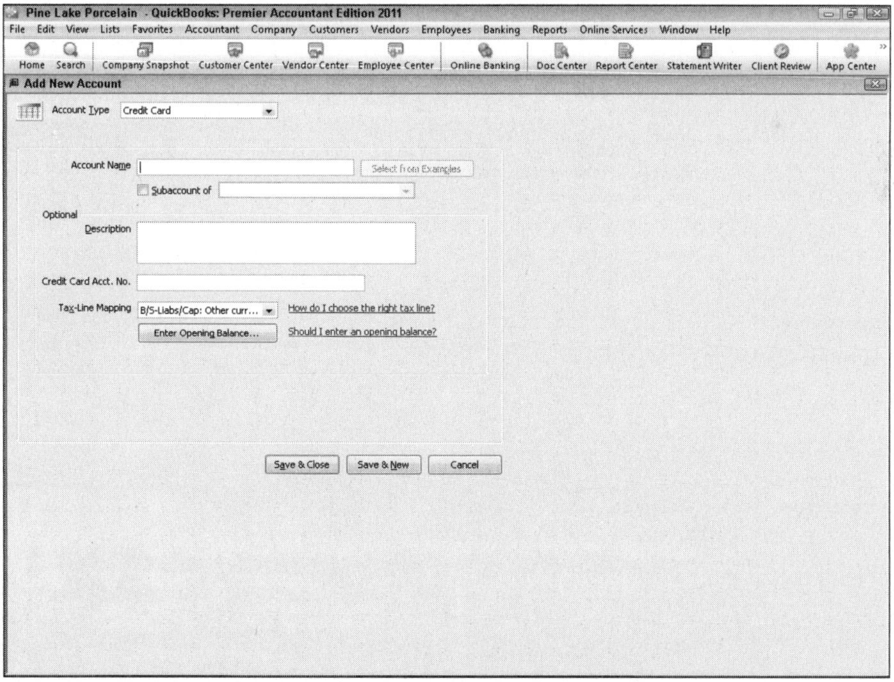

Figure 9-2:
The second
Add New
Account
window.

As an alternative to the Chart of Accounts window, you can click the Enter Credit Card Charges icon in the Banking area of the Home screen. Or you can also choose Banking➪Enter Credit Card Charges.

Entering Credit Card Transactions

After you select a credit card account, QuickBooks displays the Credit Card register. Figure 9-3 shows the register for a credit card account I've named *FrequentFlyer*. It looks a lot like a Checking register, doesn't it?

The Credit Card register works like the regular register window that you use for a checking account. You enter transactions in the rows of the register. When you record a charge, QuickBooks updates the credit card balance and the remaining credit limit.

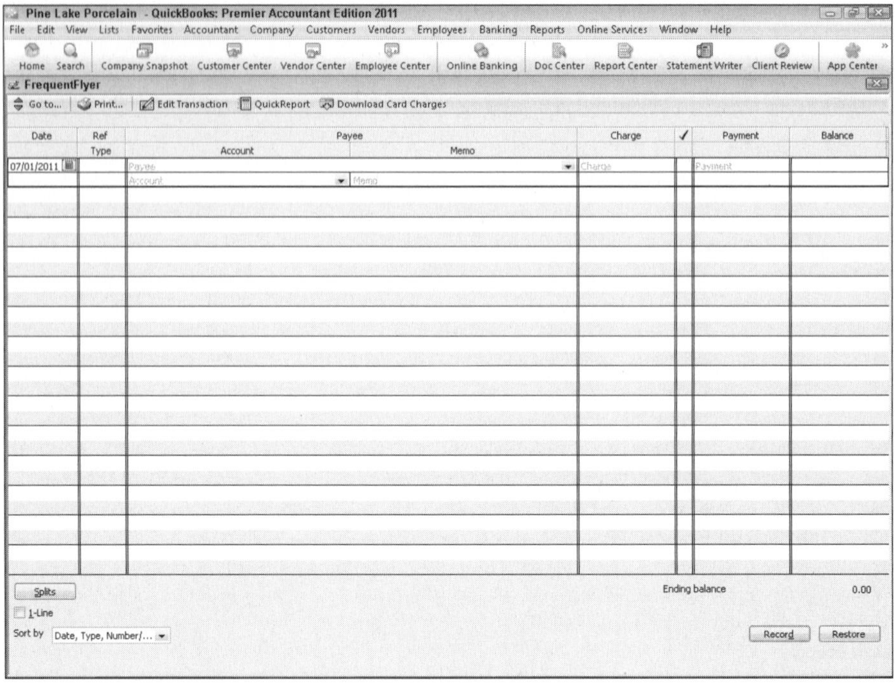

Figure 9-3:
The Credit Card Register window.

Recording a credit card charge

Recording a credit card charge is similar to recording a check or bank account withdrawal. For the sake of illustration, suppose that you charged $50.00 worth of burritos and margaritas to your favorite Mexican restaurant, La Cantina. Here's how you record this charge:

1. **Choose Banking⇨Enter Credit Card Charges.**

   The Enter Credit Card Charges window appears, as shown in Figure 9-4.

2. **From the Credit Card drop-down list, select the credit card that you charged the expense against.**

   Click the down arrow next to the Credit Card list and then select a card from the drop-down list.

3. **In the Purchased From field, record the name of the business that you paid with a credit card.**

   Move the cursor to the Purchased From line and click the down arrow. You see a list of names. Choose one from the list.

   If you've never dined at this fine establishment before, choose Add New. Then add the business name.

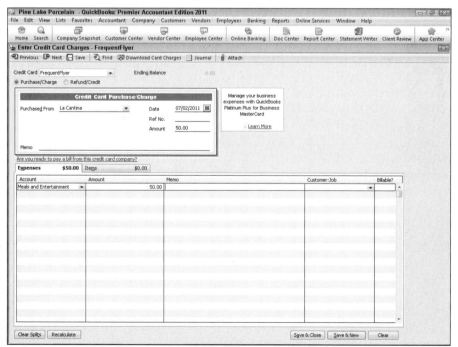

Figure 9-4:
The Enter Credit Card Charges window.

4. **Select the appropriate radio button to indicate whether the transaction is a purchase or a credit.**

   Select the Purchase/Charge radio button if you want to record a purchase (which is what you do most of the time and what this example shows you). Select the Refund/Credit radio button if you want to record a credit on your account (if you returned something, for example).

5. **Enter the charge date in the Date field.**

   Move the cursor to the Date line (if the cursor isn't already there), and type the date, using the MM/DD/YYYY format. For example, type either **07022011** or **7/2/11** for July 1, 2011. If you're entering this charge two or three days after the fact, don't enter today's date. Enter the date when the charge was made. Using that date makes reconciling your records with your credit card company's records easier when you get your monthly statement.

6. **Type the charge amount in the Amount field.**

   Move the cursor to the Amount line and enter the total charge amount. Don't type a dollar sign but do type the period to indicate the decimal place.

7. **(Optional) Enter a memo description in the Memo text box.**

   Move the cursor to the Memo text box and type the specific reason that you're charging the item. In this case, you could type **Important Business Meeting** or something like that.

   Wait. You know what? Let me be more serious. No joking for a minute, okay? This memo description box is a good place to document the business purpose for a charge, which is a tax law requirement if you're recording a travel, meal, or entertainment business credit card charge.

8. **Fill in the Expenses tab.**

   I'm hoping that you have read Chapters 6 and 8 so that you know all about the Expenses tab — and that you're thoroughly bored by the topic. However, if you opened the book right to this page, you use the Expenses tab to record business expenses.

   Move to the Account column of the Expenses tab, click the down arrow, and choose an Expense account from the list (most likely, Travel & Ent:Meals if this were a business lunch). If you enter a name here that QuickBooks doesn't already know, it asks you to set up an expense account.

   QuickBooks automatically fills in the Amount column when you enter a sum in the Amount field. Type something in the Memo column and assign this expense to a Customer:Job and Class if you want to. You need to turn on class tracking if you want to assign the expense to a class.

9. **Fill in the Items tab.**

   Because this charge is for a meal at a restaurant, you don't itemize the charge. However, if you were charging inventory items such as lumber, paper supplies, and so on, you'd fill in the Items tab.

If you have a purchase order (PO) on file with the vendor that you entered in the Purchased From line, QuickBooks tells you so. Click the Select PO button to see a list of your outstanding purchase orders with the vendor. If you don't know how to handle purchase orders, see Chapter 7.

10. **Record the charge by clicking the Save & New button or the Save & Close button.**

    The charge is recorded in the Credit Card register. Figure 9-5 shows what the Credit Card register looks like after I enter a handful of charges.

Changing charges that you've already entered

Perhaps you record a credit card charge and then realize that you recorded it incorrectly. Or perhaps you shouldn't have recorded it at all because you didn't pay for the business lunch. (Someone else paid for it after one of those friendly arguments over who should pay the bill. You know the type of argument I mean: "No, I insist." "On the contrary, I insist." You get the picture.)

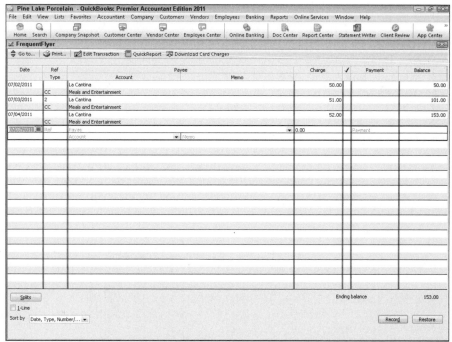

Figure 9-5: The Credit Card Register window with some transactions.

You have to go into the Credit Card register and either edit or delete the charge by following these steps:

1. **Choose Lists⇨Chart of Accounts.**

   You see the Chart of Accounts window.

2. **Double-click the credit card account where the faulty charge is.**

   Like magic, the Credit Card register appears onscreen.

3. **Select the credit card transaction that you want to delete or change.**

   That's easy. Just move the cursor to the transaction.

4. **Void, delete, or edit the transaction:**

   - *To void the credit card transaction,* choose Edit⇨Void Credit Card Charge and then click OK.

   - *To delete the transaction,* choose Edit⇨Delete Credit Card Charge. QuickBooks displays a message box that asks whether you really want to delete the transaction. Click OK.

   - *To edit the transaction,* click the Edit Transaction button at the top of the window. You return to the Enter Credit Card Charges window. Make your changes there and then click Save & New or Save & Close. You also can make changes inside the Credit Card register and then click Record when you're done.

Reconciling Your Credit Card Statement and Paying the Bill

You *reconcile,* or balance, a credit card account the same way you balance a bank account. (For help with this task, see Chapter 14.) After you successfully get the account to balance and click Reconcile Now, QuickBooks displays the Make Payment dialog box, asking how you want to pay the bill. You can either pay by check or enter a bill to be paid later. (The second option is the accounts payable method, remember?)

If you opt to pay the bill by writing a check, you go straight to the Write Checks window, and the Expenses tab is all filled out for you. Fill in the name of the card issuer, the date, and so on. Click Save & New or Save & Close when you're done. The payment is recorded in both the Checking register and the Credit Card register because you charge the credit card liability account with the check total.

If you opt to enter the payment as a bill to be paid at a later date, you go to the Enter Bills window. Fill everything out just as you would if you were in the Write Checks window. When you click Save & New, the transaction is recorded in the Accounts Payable register and the Credit Card register.

See Chapter 6 if you need to know more about either the Enter Bills window or the Write Checks window.

So What about Debit Cards?

Debit cards, when you get right down to it, aren't really credit cards at all. Using a debit card is more akin to writing a check than anything else. Rather than withdrawing money by writing a check, however, you withdraw money by using a debit card.

Although a debit card transaction looks (at least to your friends and the merchants you shop with) like a credit card transaction, you should treat a debit card transaction like you treat a check. In a nutshell, here's what you need to do:

- When you charge something to a debit card, record the transaction just like you record a regular check. You may want to enter the transaction number as the check number or in the Memo line so that you can keep track of the transaction.

- When you withdraw cash by using a debit card, record the transaction as a regular withdrawal (or transfer to a petty cash account) as if you went to the bank with a withdrawal slip.

- When you make a deposit through a cash machine by using a debit card, record the transaction just like you record a regular deposit.

So What about Customer Credit Cards?

I want to talk about an awkward subject before you and I close our discussion about how to work with credit cards. Here I — gulp — talk about how to handle customer credit card payments.

Okay, if you don't already know this, although your customers probably love to pay you with credit cards, customer credit cards create a headache for you. The reason is that your merchant bank or credit card processor aggregates customer credit card charges and then — maybe on a daily basis or maybe every few days — deposits a big wad of cash into your bank account. The cash represents the sum of the recent credit card charges minus a (hopefully modest) fee.

This all sounds innocuous enough, but here's an example of how this works: Customers A, B, and C come in on Monday and spend $5, $10, and $15, respectively. Then, on Tuesday, customers D, E, and F come in and spend $10, $50, and $30, respectively. On Wednesday, say that you don't sell anything to someone who uses a credit card, but you do see a $105 deposit into your bank account from the credit card company.

The problem is that you're looking at the last two days of credit card transactions, and you know they total $120 because that's the total you sold to customers A, B, C, D, E, and F. So what's with the $105? Is the missing $15 a service fee? Oh, no, wait. Maybe Customer A called his credit card company and blocked that first $5 charge . . . or maybe it was Customer B?

If you accept a credit card, you know how this works, right? It's a royal headache.

I think you probably have two reasonable approaches for dealing with this madness:

- ✓ **The Good Accountant's Way:** You can record customer credit card payments in the usual way — the way that QuickBooks expects. The Good Accountant's Way produces nice accurate records but at the cost of enormous bookkeeping hassles. Interested in more information? Great! Use the QuickBooks Help command to search the QuickBooks online help for the topic *recording a credit card payment.*

- ✓ **The Bad Accountant's Way:** You can just record sales receipt transactions when the credit card company deposits net charges amounts into your bank account. In other words, using the example numbers given in an earlier paragraph, rather than recording individual transactions for customers A, B, C, D, E, and F when the sales occur, you can record a $105 transaction when the credit card company deposits $105 into your bank account. If you know the credit card company's service charge, you can record that, too, using a journal entry. (You'll probably want to ask your accountant for help on this.)

I should tell you something. The Bad Accountant's Way probably isn't justified unless you're in a high-volume situation — such as a retail store — and when you're using a periodic inventory system or when you don't sell inventory. If you have only a handful of credit card transactions — say, one every few days — or you're trying to use a perpetual inventory system, you should use the Good Accountant's Way.

Part III
Stuff You Do from Time to Time

"I think if you subtract the figure in the 'Days I Go Home Early' column from the figure in the 'Snippy Attitude' column you'll reach a zero-sum figure."

In this part . . .

After you start using QuickBooks, you need to complete some tasks at the end of every week, month, or year. This part describes these tasks: printing checks, payroll, budgeting, and so on. The list goes on and on. Fortunately, QuickBooks comes with some nifty online features to help you get the job done.

Chapter 10

Printing Checks

. . . .

In This Chapter

▶ Getting your printer ready to print checks

▶ Printing checks one at a time

▶ Printing several checks at a time

▶ Printing a register

. . . .

*T*his chapter covers the reductivity of the postcolonial implications in Joseph Conrad's *Heart of Darkness.* Just kidding. It covers how to print checks and checking registers.

Printing checks in QuickBooks is quick — well, it's quick after you set up your printer correctly. If you have a continuous-feed printer, you know by now that these printers have problems printing anything on a form. The alignment always gets messed up.

QuickBooks has check forms that you can buy, and I recommend using them if you print checks. After all, the QuickBooks checks were made to work with this program. And all banks accept these checks.

If you want help with printing reports, check out Chapter 15, where I cover this topic in almost too much detail.

Getting the Printer Ready

Before you can start printing checks, you have to make sure that your printer is set up to print them. You also have to tell QuickBooks what to put on the checks: your company name, address, logo, and so on. And you might try running a few sample checks through the wringer to see whether they come out all right.

Follow these steps to set up the printer:

1. **Choose File⇨Printer Setup.**

   After you choose this command, you see the Printer Setup dialog box, as shown in Figure 10-1.

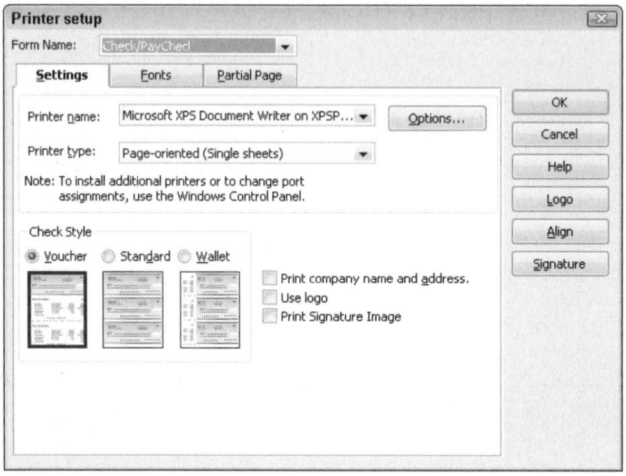

Figure 10-1:
The Printer
Setup dialog
box.

2. **Select Check/PayCheck from the Form Name drop-down list.**

   QuickBooks sets your printing options differently depending on which form you want to print. For printing checks, you want to select the Check/PayCheck form from the Form Name drop-down list at the top of the dialog box.

3. **From the Printer Name drop-down list, select your printer.**

   From the Printer Name drop-down list, click the down arrow and look at the printer names. When you installed QuickBooks, it had a frank, software-to-software talk with Windows to find out what kind of printer(s) you have, among other things. Your printer is probably already selected; if it isn't, select the correct printer.

4. **Set the correct Printer Type option, if necessary.**

   This box is probably already filled in, too, thanks to that frank discussion that I mention in Step 3. But if it isn't, click the down arrow and then choose Continuous or Page-Oriented. (The former is generally for dot-matrix printers, and the latter for laser and inkjet printers, but it really just depends on what kind of paper you use for your printer.)

5. **Select the appropriate Check Style.**

Now you're cooking. This step is where you get to make a real choice.

- *Voucher checks* are the same width as standard checks, but they're much longer. When you select the Voucher option, QuickBooks prints voucher information as well: the items and expenses tabulations from the bottom of the Write Checks window. QuickBooks also provides information about the checking account that you're writing this check on.

- *Standard checks* are sized to fit in legal envelopes.

- The *Wallet option* is for printing checks that are small enough to fit in — you guessed it — a wallet.

6. **(Optional) Click the Options button and then adjust your printer options; when you're finished, click OK to return to the Printer Setup dialog box.**

   After you click the Options button, QuickBooks displays your printer's Properties dialog box. Use this dialog box to specify print quality, number of copies, and other options specific to your printer.

7. **Click the Fonts tab of the Printer Setup dialog box and then the Fonts button on that tab to customize the fonts on your checks.**

   When you click either the Font button or the Address Font button on this tab, you see the Select Font dialog box (as shown in Figure 10-2) or the Select Address Font dialog box. You use the Address Font button to designate how your company's name and address look and the Font button to designate what all other print on your checks looks like. Here's your chance to spruce up your checks and make your company's name stand out.

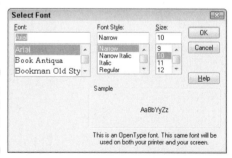

Figure 10-2:
The Select Font dialog box.

Experiment for a while with the Font, Font Style, and Size settings. For example, if you have a bookstore, choose the Bookman font (maybe using bold for your company's name and address); if you run a messenger service, choose Courier; Italian mathematicians can use Times New Roman (just kidding). You can see what your choices look like in the Sample box.

   8. **When you finish fooling around with the fonts, click OK to go back to the Printer Setup dialog box.**

   9. **Click the Partial Page tab of the Printer Setup dialog box and then select a Partial Page Printing Style.**

      Fortunately, some graphics appear; otherwise, you wouldn't have a clue what these options are, would you? These options are for the environmentally friendly among you. Suppose that you feed two checks to the printer, but the check sheets have three checks each. You have a leftover check.

      Thanks to this option, you can use the extra check. Select one of the options to tell QuickBooks how you plan to feed the check to the printer — vertically on the left (the Left option), vertically in the middle (the Centered option), or horizontally (the Portrait option). You feed checks to the printer the same way that you feed envelopes to it.

   10. **(Optional) Click the Logo button and then enter a company logo or some clip art.**

      In the Logo dialog box, click File and find the directory and BMP (bitmap) graphic file that you want to load. Click OK. Only graphics that are in BMP format can be used on your checks, and Intuit recommends that the logo be square.

   11. **(Optional) Click the Signature button and then enter a check signature image.**

      Want to get really adventurous? Click the Signature button that appears in the Printer Setup dialog box. When QuickBooks displays the Signature dialog box, click File and then find the directory and BMP (bitmap) graphic file with the signature that you want to load. Click OK. Only graphics that are in BMP format can be used as signatures on your checks.

   12. **Click OK when you're finished.**

      That setup was no Sunday picnic, was it? But your checks are all ready to be printed, and you'll probably never have to go through that ordeal again.

Printing a Check

For some reason, when I get to this part of the discussion, my pulse quickens. Actually writing a check for real money seems terribly serious. I get the same feeling whenever I mail someone cash, even if the amount is nominal.

I think that the best way to lower my heart rate (and yours, if you're like me) is to just print the darn check and be done with it. QuickBooks can print checks in two ways: as you write them or in bunches.

First things first, however. Before you can print checks, you have to load some blank checks into your printer. This process works the same way as loading any paper into your printer. If you have questions, refer to your printer's documentation. (Sorry I can't help more on this process, but a million different printers exist, and I can't tell which one you have, even when I look into my crystal ball.)

A few words about printing checks

Check printing is kind of complicated, isn't it? For the record, I'm with you on this one. I really wish it weren't so much work, but you'll find that printing checks gets easier after the first few times.

Pretty soon, you'll be running rather than walking through the steps. Pretty soon, you'll just skate around roadblocks such as check-form alignment problems. Pretty soon, in fact, you'll know all this stuff and never have to read *pretty soon* again.

Printing a check as you write it

If you're in the Write Checks window and you just finished filling out a check, you can print it. The only drawback is that you have to print checks one at a time with this method. Here's how:

1. **Fill out your check.**

   Yes, I strongly recommend filling out the check before printing it. And make sure that the To Be Printed check box is selected. Turn to Chapter 6 for help with writing checks with QuickBooks.

2. **Click the Print button in the Write Checks window.**

   You see the Print Check dialog box, as shown in Figure 10-3.

Figure 10-3:
The Print Check dialog box.

3. **Enter a check number in the Printed Check Number text box and then click OK.**

After you click OK, you see the similarly named Print Checks dialog box, as shown in Figure 10-4. The settings that you see in this dialog box are the ones that you chose when you first told QuickBooks how to print checks. If you change the settings in the Print Checks dialog box, the changes affect only this particular check. The next time you print a check, you'll see your original settings again.

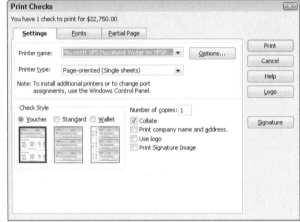

Figure 10-4:
The other
Print Checks
dialog box.

4. **Either click Print to accept the default settings or make changes in the dialog box and then click Print.**

   In the Printer Name text box, specify which printer you want to print to. In the Check Style area, indicate whether you want to print a Voucher, Standard, or Wallet check.

   If you're printing a partial page of forms on a laser printer, use the Partial Page tab to indicate both the number of check forms on the partial page and how you'll feed them through your printer.

   If you want your company's name and address to appear on the check, select the Print Company Name and Address check box on the Settings tab.

   After you click Print, QuickBooks prints the check, and you see the Print Checks – Confirmation dialog box (see Figure 10-5). Nothing tricky here — just a list of the checks that you just tried to print.

5. **If the check didn't print correctly, click the check listed in the Print Checks – Confirmation dialog box to select it and then click OK to return to the Write Checks window. Then click the Write Checks window Print button again, enter the new check number, and click Print again.**

   QuickBooks doesn't automatically keep track of incorrectly printed check forms, so you have to. If you botch a check form, be sure to write **VOID** in large letters and permanent ink across the face of the check. Then file the check away for your reference. Don't throw away the check.

Figure 10-5:
The Print
Checks –
Confirmation
dialog box.

If you still have questions about how to check any mistakes, see the section "What if I make a mistake?" later in this chapter.

6. **If your check looks good, click OK.**

   You return to the Write Checks window. Don't forget to sign the check.

Printing checks by the bushel

What if you write a mess of checks and then decide to print them? That's how the process is done usually. Here's how to print a bushel of checks:

1. **Go into the register and make sure that the checks that you want to print are marked To Print.**

   The quickest way to get into the register is to choose Banking⇨Use Register. If you have more than one bank account, select the Checking Account register that you want to open and then click OK. Do the checks that you want to print have *To Print* in the Number line? If not, tab to the Number line, press T, and then click the Record button. QuickBooks automatically fills the Number field with *To Print* and then moves on. (If the check you want to print already has a number, you need to replace the number with *T*.)

2. **Choose File⇨Print Forms⇨Checks.**

   You see the Select Checks to Print dialog box, in which you select the checks to print (see Figure 10-6).

3. **Click the check marks next to the checks that you don't want to print and then click OK.**

   All the checks are selected at first. If you want to print them all, fine. If not, click the check marks next to the checks that you don't want to print so that QuickBooks removes the check marks. Or if you want to print only a few of the checks, click the Select None button and then click next to the checks that you want to print so that QuickBooks places a check mark in the column.

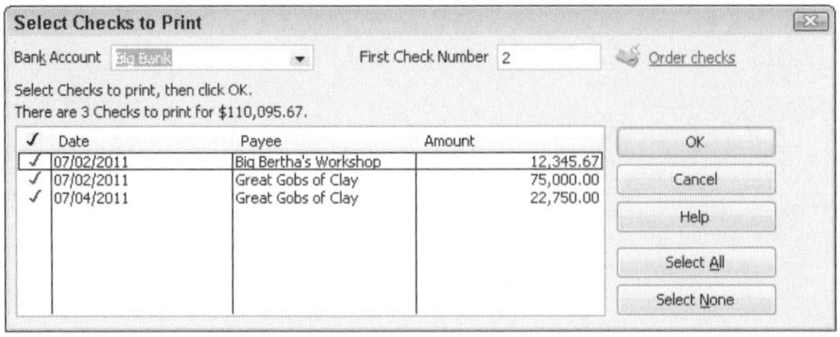

Figure 10-6:
The Select
Checks to
Print dialog
box.

When only the checks that you want to print have check marks, click OK to continue with this crazy little thing called check printing. QuickBooks, happy with your progress, displays the Print Checks dialog box (refer to Figure 10-4). Here, you see the settings that you chose when you first told QuickBooks how to print checks.

4. **Either click Print to accept the default settings, or make changes in the dialog box and then click Print.**

   You can change the settings in this dialog box if you want them to be different. Any changes that you make for a particular batch of checks don't affect the default settings. The next time you print a check, your original settings appear again.

   In the Check Style box, indicate whether you want to print Voucher, Standard, or Wallet checks. If you're printing a partial page of checks, enter the number of checks on the first page in the Number of Checks on First Page text box.

   If you want your company's name and address to appear on the checks, select the Print Company Name and Address check box on the Settings tab.

   Note that the Number of Copies text box is grayed out. If you want to change this setting, you need to choose File⇨Printer Setup.

   QuickBooks prints the checks, and then you see the Print Checks – Confirmation dialog box (refer to Figure 10-5).

5. **Review the checks that QuickBooks printed; then do one of the following:**

   • *If QuickBooks printed the checks correctly,* answer the Did Check(s) Print OK? question by clicking OK. (QuickBooks, apparently thinking that you now want to do nothing but print checks, redisplays the nearly exhausted Write Checks window.)

   • *If QuickBooks didn't print a check correctly,* type the number of the first incorrectly printed check in the text box and then click OK. In this case, repeat the steps for check printing. Note, though, that you need to reprint only the first bad check and the checks that follow it. You don't need to reprint good checks that precede the first bad check.

Don't forget to write **VOID** in large letters and permanent ink across the front of incorrectly printed check forms. Then file the checks for safekeeping. (Don't throw them away.) To record the voided check in QuickBooks, see the next section, "What if I make a mistake?"

If the numbers of the checks that you need to reprint aren't sequential and are, in fact, spread all over creation, make it easy on yourself. Click OK to clear the list of checks to be printed, go into the register, click the Number line of the checks that you need to print, and then press T. QuickBooks automatically fills these with To Print. Then choose File➪Print Forms➪Checks, as in Step 2, and continue from there.

If your checks came out all right, take the rest of the day off. Give yourself a raise while you're at it.

6. **Sign the printed checks.**

   Then — and I guess you probably don't need my help here — put the checks in the mail.

What if I make a mistake?

If you discover a mistake after you print a check, the problem may not be as big as you think.

If you already mailed the check, however, you can't do much. You can try to get the check back (if the person you paid hasn't cashed it already) and replace it with a check that's correct. (Good luck on this one.)

If the person cashed the check, you can't get the check back. If you overpaid the person by writing the check for more than you should have, you need to ask the person to pay you the overpayment amount. If you underpaid the person, you need to write another check for the amount of the underpayment.

If you printed the check but haven't mailed it, void the printed check. This operation has two parts. First, write **VOID** in large letters across the face of the check form. (Use a ballpoint pen if you're using multipart forms so that the second and third parts also show as VOID.) Second, display the register, highlight the check, and then choose Edit➪Void Check. (This option marks the check as one that's been voided in the system so that QuickBooks doesn't use the check in calculating the account balance.) If you're voiding an incorrectly printed check, you first need to create a transaction for the check number that printed incorrectly and then void that transaction.

Of course, if you want to reissue a voided check, just enter the check all over again — only this time, try to be more careful.

A big, bad warning concerning check voiding

In general, you shouldn't void checks from a previous year. (You'd do this by choosing Edit⇨Void Check.) If you do, you'll adjust the previous year's expenses, which sounds okay, but you don't want to do this because (a) it means that you can no longer prepare income statements and balance sheets that correspond to your financial statements and tax returns, and (b) you've already presumably included the check in your deductions for the previous year. If you do have a check that should be voided —

say, it's outstanding and has never been cashed or was a mistake in the first place — record a journal entry in the current year that undoes the effect of the check. Normally, the entry is a Debit to the Checking account and a Credit to the Miscellaneous Income account in the current year for the amount of the check if it was expensed in a prior tax year. If it was for something other than an expense, just reverse the check to the same account it was originally charged.

If you notice only after clicking OK in the Print Checks – Confirmation dialog box that a check printed incorrectly, you can tell QuickBooks you want to reprint the check in one of two ways. If you have the register window displayed, you can change the check's number from 007, for example, to To Print. If you have the Write Checks window displayed, you can select the To Be Printed check box.

Oh where, oh where do unprinted checks go?

Unprinted checks — those that you entered by using the Write Checks window but haven't yet printed — are stored in the register. To identify them as unprinted checks, QuickBooks puts *To Print* in the Number line. What's more, when you tell QuickBooks to print the unprinted checks, what it really does is print the checks in the register that have *To Print* in the Number line. All this knowledge is of little practical value in most instances, but it results in several interesting possibilities.

For example, you can enter the checks that you want to print directly into the register; all you need to do is type **To Print** in the Number line.

Printing a Checking Register

You can print a Checking register, or a register for any other account, too. Follow these steps to print a register:

1. **Open the account register you want to print.**

Choose Banking➪Use Register or click the Check Register icon on the Home screen and then click the Print icon. If you have more than one bank account, choose the account register you want to print from the drop-down list and then click OK.

2. **Choose File➪Print Register. Or click the Print button at the top of the register.**

   You see the Print Register dialog box, as shown in Figure 10-7. This option is available whenever you have a register open for an account.

Figure 10-7:
The Print
Register
dialog box.

3. **Fill in the Date Range text boxes.**

   To print a register of something other than the current year-to-date transactions, use the From and Through text boxes. This step is pretty darn obvious, isn't it? You just move the cursor to the From and Through text boxes and type the range of months that the register should include.

4. **(Optional) Select the Print Splits Detail check box.**

   As you know, a register doesn't show all the messy details, such as the Items and Expenses tab information, but you can select this check box to include all this stuff on your printed register.

5. **Click OK.**

   You see the Print Lists dialog box, as shown in Figure 10-8.

6. **If everything is cool, click the Print button and skip the remaining steps. If you want to change options in the Print Lists dialog box, proceed to the next step.**

   You don't have to fool around with the Print Lists dialog box. If you want to print a register *pronto,* just click Print and then QuickBooks sends the register on its merry way to your printer. Then again, if you're the sort of person who likes to fool around with this kind of stuff, carry on with the rest of these steps.

   If you want to see the effect that the different settings in this dialog box have, just experiment. You can't hurt anything or anybody.

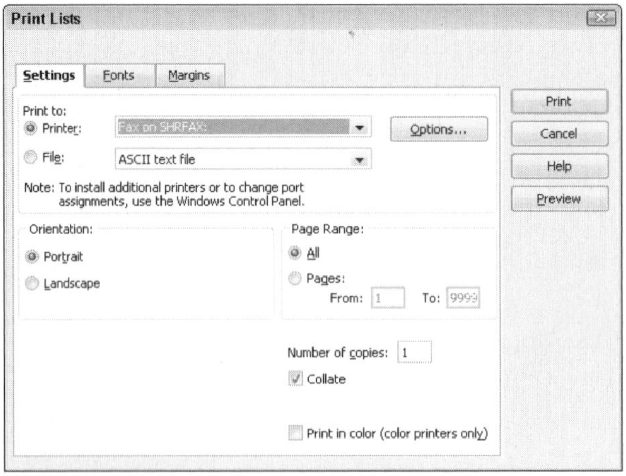

Figure 10-8:
The Print
Lists dialog
box.

7. (Optional) Print the report to disk.

To print the report to disk as a text file, select the File radio button and then choose one of the following Print To options:

- Choose *ASCII Text File* if you want to create a text file (for example, when you want to import the register into a word processing program).

- Choose *Comma Delimited File* if you'll later import the register into a spreadsheet program, such as Microsoft Excel.

- Choose *Tab Delimited File* to, for example, import the register into a database program like Access. (Oooh . . . fancy.)

8. Choose the paper orientation.

In which direction do you want the report to be printed: Portrait (regular) or Landscape (sideways)? Just select the appropriate radio button.

9. (Optional) Tell QuickBooks which pages to print.

Use the Print Range radio buttons and text boxes to limit the pages for QuickBooks to print.

10. (Optional) Color your world: Print your report in color.

If you have a color printer and want to print the register in color, select the Print in Color (Color Printers Only) check box.

11. (Optional) Preview the report.

To see how your settings will affect the report before you actually print it, click Preview. QuickBooks shows you the results onscreen. This feature has probably saved more trees than you can imagine.

12. Click Print.

After you have the report exactly the way you want it (and not one moment before!), click Print, and QuickBooks finally prints the register.

Chapter 11

Payroll

. . . .

In This Chapter

▶ Requesting an employer ID number

▶ Obtaining withholding information

▶ Computing an employee's gross wages, payroll deductions, and net wages

▶ Recording a payroll check in QuickBooks

▶ Making federal tax deposits

▶ Preparing quarterly and annual payroll tax returns

▶ Producing annual wage statements, such as W-2s

▶ Handling state payroll taxes

. . . .

*P*ayroll is one of the major headaches of running a small business. When I think of all the time that I've seen clients waste figuring out withholding amounts, writing checks, and trying to fill out comically confusing payroll tax returns, it just makes me want to scream. Fortunately, QuickBooks helps. And in a big way. In this chapter, I explain how.

Getting Ready to Do Payroll without Help from QuickBooks

However, before I launch into a discussion of doing payroll using QuickBooks, I want to share an accounting thought that's almost heretical. You may *not* want to do payroll yourself using QuickBooks. No, wait, hear me out.

The easiest way to do payroll, quite frankly, is to sign up with an outside service bureau, such as ADP or Paychex. If you have an accountant, you might also want to ask him or her about other less-expensive, local payroll services.

Of course, the easiest route is often the most expensive, and payroll services are no exception. In my experience, these full-meal-deal services tend to run about twice the price of the most expensive QuickBooks Payroll service after you add everything, but all you need to do is make a phone call. (Check your telephone book for a local number.) The payroll service will send someone nice out to your office. A few days later, all you need to do is make a phone call or send a fax when you want to pay employees.

Doing Taxes the Right Way

One thing I need to mention: Even before you set up QuickBooks for payroll, you need a few other items if you want to do payroll the right way. (If you want to do payroll the wrong way, you're reading the wrong book.)

- A federal employer identification (ID) number
- A state employer ID number (if you withhold state income taxes)
- An unemployment tax ID number
- W-4 tax forms

Getting an employer ID number

To get an employer ID number, you need to file an SS-4, Application for Employer Identification Number form, with the Internal Revenue Service (IRS). You can get this form at the IRS Web site (www.irs.gov) or by calling the IRS and asking for one.

You can also apply for and receive an employer identification number over the telephone. You still need to fill out the SS-4 form before you call, however, so that you can answer the questions that the IRS asks during the short telephone application process. (You also need to mail or fax the form to the IRS after you have your little telephone conversation.)

Or, even easier, you can just do it all online. Here's the current URL:

```
https://sa1.www4.irs.gov/modiein/individual
```

Having employees do their part

You also need to do something else before you can know how to handle all those taxes: You need to have your employees fill out W-4 forms to tell you what filing status they'll use and how many personal exemptions they'll claim. Guess where you get blank W-4s? From your friendly IRS agent or the IRS Web site (www.irs.gov) in the Forms & Publications area.

Getting Ready to Do Payroll with QuickBooks

If you want to use one of the QuickBooks Payroll service options because you want to save money, you aren't scared of a little paperwork, or maybe you want the extra flexibility that comes with doing it yourself, you need to sign up for the appropriate flavor of service.

Costs of the QuickBooks Payroll services vary based on the number of employees you have and on how much work you want the nice folks at QuickBooks to do. Figure on spending at least $100 to $200 per year for the most basic package. And note that if you want the full-meal-deal, you're looking at a current cost of between $700 and $1000 or more per year. (In addition, if past history is any guide, you'll need to more regularly upgrade your QuickBooks software.) To set up for a payroll service option, get ready to hop on the Internet. Follow these steps:

1. **Choose Employees⇨Payroll⇨Order Payroll Service.**

   QuickBooks connects to the Internet and displays the first page of a multiple-page Web form that enables you to sign and set up the QuickBooks Payroll service.

2. **Follow the onscreen instructions.**

   I don't repeat the onscreen instructions for setting up the payroll service. Providing that kind of information would be . . . well, extremely redundant. Just carefully follow the instructions, and you'll have no trouble.

   Note: Setting up the QuickBooks Payroll service requires that you have accurate year-to-date payroll information for all your employees as well as state withholding rate information. You want to collect all this information before you begin. The process of setting up payroll — assuming that you have the information at hand and that you have only a handful of employees — shouldn't take much more than half an hour.

3. **Schedule your payroll.**

   After you sign up for (and indirectly set up) the QuickBooks Payroll service, you need to schedule your upcoming payroll activities. To do this, choose Employees⇨Add or Edit Payroll Schedules. When QuickBooks displays the Payroll Schedule List window, click the Payroll Schedule button and then click New. When prompted by QuickBooks, describe the payroll you're scheduling. For example, if you're setting up a weekly payroll, name the payroll something like *Friday payroll.* Furthermore, describe the frequency as weekly, biweekly, semimonthly, and so on.

4. **Describe your employees.**

   You need to describe each of your employees and identify which payroll schedule they belong to. To do this, choose Employees⇨Employee Center. Click the New Employee button. Then, use the tabs of the window that QuickBooks displays to provide the employee's name, address, Social Security number, and so on. Note that you use the Payroll and Compensation tab to specify the employee's wage or salary and to assign the employee to a scheduled payroll.

Paying Your Employees

After you subscribe to the QuickBooks Payroll service and set up your payroll schedule, you're ready to pay someone. This section is going to blow your mind, especially if you've been doing payroll manually. The process makes your whole decision to use QuickBooks to do your payroll worthwhile. Here's how:

1. **Start the payroll process by choosing Employees⇨Pay Employees⇨Scheduled Payroll.**

   QuickBooks displays the Employee Center: Payroll Center window (see Figure 11-1). The Payroll Center window identifies any payroll schedules you set up. (The Payroll Center window also shows any payroll tax liabilities that you accrued because of past payroll activity.) Select the scheduled payroll you want to, well, do. Then click the Start Scheduled Payroll button. QuickBooks displays Enter Payroll Income window, which lists the employees who participate in the scheduled payroll. Initially, all the listed employees have a check mark beside their name, but you can click to remove a check mark and to remove an employee from the scheduled payroll.

2. **Create the paychecks.**

   When the Enter Payroll Income window correctly lists which employees should be paid, click Continue. QuickBooks calculates employee gross wages, deductions, and net wages, and the calculations appear in the Review and Create Paychecks window.

3. **(Optional) Review a payroll check.**

   You can preview any employee's payroll data by clicking his or her name in the Review and Create Paychecks window. When you click an employee's name, QuickBooks displays the Preview Paycheck window for the employee.

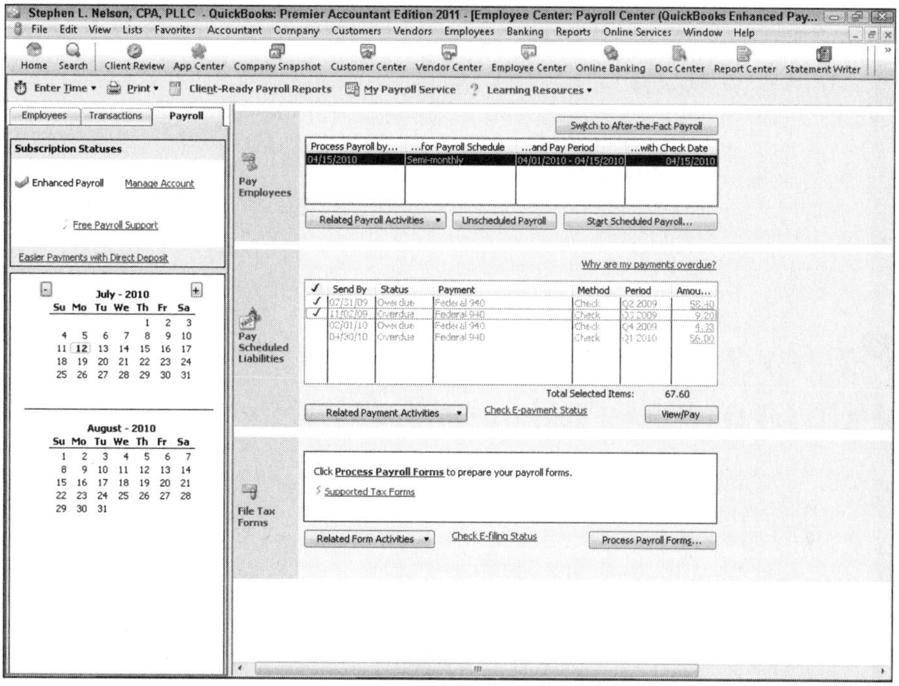

Figure 11-1:
The
Employee
Center:
Payroll
Center
window.

The main thing to pay attention to in the Preview Paycheck window is the Earnings text box. It shows what QuickBooks assumes you'll pay an employee. In the Earnings text box, you fill in the number of hours the person worked and apply these hours to a customer or job, if necessary.

The Preview Paycheck window also includes an Other Payroll Items input area. In the Other Payroll Items text box, you enter commissions; additions, such as tips, bonuses, and expense reimbursements; deductions, such as union dues and 401(k) contributions; and company contributions, such as insurance benefits and 401(k) matching amounts. You also can change the payroll item or rate or add another payroll item, if you need to.

Watch out for this: QuickBooks calculates the company taxes, the employee taxes, and the amount of the net check; this information appears in the Employee Summary area and the Company Summary area of the Preview Paycheck window. If some information is inaccurate, click the amount and change it, either by deleting it or replacing it with the correct information.

You might also note that QuickBooks keeps totals for both the current check and the year to date.

4. **Print the payroll checks.**

   When you're ready to print the payroll checks, click the Create Paychecks button. QuickBooks lets you either print payroll checks from QuickBooks or print paycheck stubs (which means you'd then hand-write payroll checks). If you direct QuickBooks to print the checks, you print the payroll checks in the same way that you print other, nonpay-roll checks. (Got a question about printing checks? Refer to Chapter 10.) If you want to print paycheck stubs and will later handwrite payroll checks, give QuickBooks the first check number so it knows how to number the checks that it records into your register.

Paying Payroll Liabilities

Make no mistake: Big Brother wants the money that you withhold from an employee's payroll check for federal income taxes, Social Security, and Medicare. Big Brother also wants the payroll taxes you owe: the matching Social Security and Medicare taxes, federal unemployment taxes, and so on. So every so often, you need to pay Big Brother the amounts that you owe.

If you withhold money from employees' checks for other reasons (perhaps for health insurance or retirement savings), these amounts are payroll liabilities that need to be paid to the appropriate parties.

Paying tax liabilities if you use the full-meal-deal Payroll service

Fortunately, if you're using the QuickBooks full-meal-deal Payroll service — this is the most expensive payroll option QuickBooks provides — your federal tax liabilities and most (perhaps all) of your state tax liabilities are paid as part of the service. In other words, Intuit withdraws money from your bank account and uses this money to pay the appropriate federal or state government agency.

Be sure to check which state payroll taxes QuickBooks calculates and pays. In Washington, which is where my business is located, QuickBooks won't calculate a couple of state payroll taxes, so I have to calculate these myself (on the state payroll tax form) and pay them with a check.

Paying tax liabilities if you don't use the full-meal-deal Payroll service

If you don't use the full-meal-deal payroll service, you need to pay the payroll liabilities yourself. To do this, choose Employees⇨Payroll Taxes and Liabilities⇨Pay Scheduled Liabilities. When QuickBooks displays the Employee Center: Payroll Center window (and its list of scheduled payrolls and the associated liabilities), choose the payroll liability you want to pay and then click the View/Pay button.

QuickBooks writes the check and puts it in your register. QuickBooks also gives the check the appropriate date and schedules it to pop up in your reminders window at the right time. Also, if you're enrolled in the Electronic Federal Tax Payment System (EFTPS) online, the check is created the same way, and the check number can be changed to EFTPS and not actually printed. (Keep reading for more on EFTPS.)

When do you make payroll tax deposits? That question frequently comes up. The general rule about U.S. federal tax deposits is this: If your accumulated payroll taxes are less than $2,500 for the quarter, you can just pay those taxes with your quarterly 941 return. This law is called the De Minimis rule. (My understanding is that the law was named after Congresswoman Dee Minimis.) If you owe more than $2,500, other special rules come into play that determine whether you pay deposits monthly, semimonthly, weekly, or even immediately. The IRS tells you, by the way, how often you're supposed to make payments.

If you owe a large amount of money, you're required to deposit it almost immediately. For example, if you owe $100,000 or more, you need to make the payroll tax deposit by the next banking day. Some nuances apply to these rules, so unless you don't owe very much (and, therefore, can fall back on the De Minimis rule), you might want to consult a tax advisor (or call the IRS).

The general rule when writing payroll checks is to make the last checks that you write the ones that pay your federal and state tax deposits when they come due. You'll never get into late-payment trouble if you follow this approach. It will also make your life a lot easier when it comes time to fill out Schedule B of Form 941, if you have to do so.

To make a payroll tax deposit, just deliver your check with an 8109 federal tax deposit coupon to a financial institution that's qualified as a depository for federal taxes or to the Federal Reserve Bank that serves your geographical area. The IRS should have already sent you a book of coupons as a result of your asking for an employer ID number. And one other thing: Make your check payable to the depository or to the Federal Reserve Bank. Note, too, that the U.S. Treasury makes it very easy to make payroll tax deposits electronically by using the EFTPS. (The Treasury will send you information on this when you start making deposits, so keep your eyes peeled for this easy way to save yourself some time.) You can visit the www.eftps.gov Web site for more information.

Paying other nontax liabilities

If you're paying nontax liabilities for things such as employee health insurance or retirement savings — it doesn't matter whether you're using the cheapo payroll service or the full-meal-deal payroll service — you also choose Employees⇨Payroll Taxes and Liabilities⇨Create Custom Liability Payment. (When you choose that command, you'll need to indicate which liabilities you want to pay.)

You need to pay all your payroll liabilities via Employees⇨Payroll Taxes and Liabilities⇨Create Custom Liability Payment if you want QuickBooks to keep your payroll liabilities straight. I mention this because people commonly just pay these liabilities by using the Write Checks window. That creates a mess.

Preparing Quarterly Payroll Tax Returns

At the end of every quarter, you need to file a quarterly payroll tax return. (By *quarters* here, I refer to calendar quarters.) If you're a business owner, for example, you must file a Form 941, which states how much you paid in gross wages, how much you withheld in federal taxes, and how much you owe for employer payroll taxes for the quarter.

You'll find that QuickBooks makes filling out these forms darn simple.

If you have household employees, such as a nanny, you must file a Form 942. Again, you fill out Form 942 to list how much you paid in gross wages, withheld in federal taxes, and owe in payroll taxes. Unfortunately, QuickBooks doesn't do a 942 for you. Apparently, it thinks you don't need domestic help.

If your accountant fills out Form 941 or 942 for you, you don't need to read this section of this chapter. Your accountant won't have any problem completing the quarterly payroll tax return by using the QuickBooks Payroll report, and in fact — I kid you not — your accountant will probably even enjoy doing it.

Using the QuickBooks full-meal-deal Payroll service

If you're using the top-of-the-line QuickBooks Payroll service, the service fills out and sends the quarterly payroll tax forms for you.

Using the other QuickBooks Payroll services

If you're using one of the other Payroll services — again, by this, I mean a payroll service other than the full-meal-deal service — you need to fill out and send the payroll tax forms, but don't worry — QuickBooks prepares the 941 for you. If you need to fill out the 942 or a state payroll tax form, QuickBooks can also be of great help. All you really need to know for these other forms is what the gross-wages totals are.

Note: QuickBooks frequently changes the names of the non-full-meal-deal payroll services. At the time I'm writing this, QuickBooks calls its least expensive option *Basic Payroll* and its second-to-least-expensive option *Enhanced Payroll.*

To get the gross-wages totals and the balances in each of the payroll tax liability accounts at the end of the quarter, print the Payroll Summary report. Choose Reports⇨Employees & Payroll⇨Payroll Summary. QuickBooks displays the Payroll Summary report. Specify the range of dates as the quarter for which you're preparing a quarterly report. Scroll across to the Total column, which shows the gross wages upon which your employer payroll taxes are calculated.

The *withholding account amounts* are the amounts that you recorded to date for the employee's federal income taxes withheld and the employee's Social Security and Medicare taxes, so QuickBooks needs to double these figures to get the actual Social Security and Medicare taxes owed. Choose Reports⇨Employees & Payroll⇨Payroll Liability Balances. QuickBooks creates a report that tallies these amounts.

QuickBooks will create and print a copy of Form 941 for you, so you don't have to get out your calculator or mess around with lining up the red form in your typewriter. Just choose Employees⇨Payroll Forms⇨Process Payroll Forms. QuickBooks runs you through a wizard that asks you for your state and the number of employees that you had over the quarter. Then QuickBooks summarizes each line of the form. When QuickBooks is done, all you have to do is print the form.

Filing Annual Returns and Wage Statements

At the end of the year, you need to file some annual returns — such as the 940 Federal Unemployment (FUTA) Tax Return — and the W-2 and W-3 wages statements.

You need to prepare any state unemployment annual summary before you prepare the 940 because the 940 requires information from the state returns.

Using the QuickBooks full-meal-deal Payroll service

If you're using the full-meal-deal payroll service, the service automatically fills out and sends these forms for you.

Using the QuickBooks economy Payroll services

If you're using one of the economy payroll service options, you need to fill out and send these forms in-house, but you get lots of help from QuickBooks. QuickBooks creates and prints the 940 and W-2s/W-3s for you. All you have to do is choose Employees⇨Payroll Tax Forms & W-2s⇨Process Payroll Forms. QuickBooks asks you for a little information, and then it calculates for you. Just check the QuickBooks records against your own, and if everything matches, print that puppy. To look over the QuickBooks data included in the form and verify its integrity, it helps to print an Employee Earnings Summary report.

If you have a little trouble, call the IRS. If you have a great deal of trouble, splurge and have someone else fill out the forms for you. Filling out these forms doesn't take a rocket scientist, by the way. Any experienced bookkeeper can do it for you.

Please don't construe my "rocket scientist" comment as personal criticism if this payroll-taxes business seems terribly complicated. My experience is that some people — and you may very well be one of them — just don't have an interest in things such as payroll accounting. If, on the other hand, you're a "numbers are my friend" kind of person, you'll have no trouble at all after you learn the ropes.

The State Wants Some Money, Too

Yeah. I haven't talked about state payroll taxes — at least not in great detail. I wish that I could provide this sort of detailed, state-specific help to you. Unfortunately, doing so would make this chapter about 150 pages long. It'd also cause me to go stark-raving mad.

My sanity and laziness aside, you still need to deal with state payroll taxes. Let me say, however, that you apply the same basic mechanics to state payroll taxes that you apply to federal payroll taxes. For example, a state income tax works the same way as the federal income tax; employer-paid state unemployment taxes work like the employer-paid federal taxes; and employee-paid state taxes work like the employee-paid Social Security and Medicare taxes.

If you're tuned in to how federal payroll taxes work in QuickBooks, you really shouldn't have a problem with the state payroll taxes — at least not in terms of mechanics. Also, note that QuickBooks can now print most state forms for most states. Check the `www.quickbooks.com` Web site for more information about this.

The one thing you need to figure out is what your state wants. To do that, you need to get the state's payroll tax reporting instructions. You may need to call the state. Or with a little luck, you may find online instructions at your state government's Web site. If that isn't much help, you can probably look up the state tax people's telephone number in your local phone book.

Chapter 12

Building the Perfect Budget

I don't think that a budget amounts to financial handcuffs, and neither should you. A *budget* is just a plan that outlines how you intend to generate sales, how you should spend your money, and your ideas about how you can best organize your firm's financial affairs.

Is This a Game You Want to Play?

If you created a good, workable Chart of Accounts, you're halfway to a good, solid budget. (In fact, for 99 out of 100 businesses, the only step left is to specify how much you earn in each income account and how much you spend in each expense account.)

Does every business need a budget? No, of course not. Maybe you have a simple financial plan that you can monitor some other way. Maybe in your business, you make money so effortlessly that you don't need to plan your income and outgo. Maybe Elvis Presley really is still alive and living somewhere in the Midwest.

For everyone else, though, a budget improves your chances of getting your business wherever you want it to go financially. It gives you a way to "plan your work and work your plan." In fact, I'll stop calling it a budget. The word has such negative connotations. I know — I'll call it *The Secret Plan*.

All Joking Aside: Some Basic Budgeting Tips

Before I walk you through the mechanics of outlining your Secret Plan, I want to give you a few tips. After that, I want to tell you a secret. A very special secret.

Here are five ways to increase the chances that your Secret Plan works:

- ✔ **Plan your income and expenses as a team, if that's possible.** For this sort of planning, two heads are invariably better than one. What's more, although I don't really want to get into marriage counseling or partnership counseling here, the budget of a business — oops, I mean its Secret Plan — needs to reflect the priorities and feelings of everyone who has to live within the plan: partners, partners' spouses, key employees, and so on. So don't use a Secret Plan as a way to minimize what your partner spends on marketing or on long-distance telephone charges talking to pseudocustomers and relatives in the old country. You need to resolve such issues before you finalize your Secret Plan.

- ✔ **Include some cushion in your plan.** In other words, don't budget to spend every last dollar. If you plan from the start to spend every dollar you make, you'll undoubtedly have to fight the mother of all financial battles: paying for unexpected expenses when you don't have any money. (You know the sort of things I mean: the repair bill when the delivery truck breaks down, a new piece of essential equipment, or that cocktail dress or tuxedo you absolutely must have for a special party.)

- ✔ **Regularly compare your actual income and outgo with your planned income and outgo.** This comparison is probably the most important part of budgeting, and it's what QuickBooks can help you with the most. As long as you use QuickBooks to record what you receive and spend and to describe your budget, you can print reports that show what you planned and what actually occurred.

  If you find that you've budgeted $1,000 per month for shipping costs, but you discover that you consistently spend twice that amount, you may need to shift some money from your monthly cocktail dress-and-tuxedo allowance . . . unless you *like* coming in over budget on shipping charges.

- ✔ **Make adjustments as necessary.** When you encounter problems with your Secret Plan — and you will — you'll know that part of your plan isn't working. Then you can make adjustments (by spending a little less on calling the old country, for example).

> ✔ **A word to the wise: Don't gear up your business overhead or your personal living and lifestyle when you have a great year (or even a few great years) in the business.** When you have a good year or even a few good years, keep your overhead and expenses modest. Stash the extra cash. If you can, build up some financial wealth that's independent and apart from your business assets. (One great way to do this, for example, is by contributing to an IRA or by setting up a Simple-IRA or a SEP/IRA for yourself and any employees.)

A Budgeting Secret You Won't Learn in College

I also have a secret tip for you. (I'm going to write very quietly now so that no one else hears. . . .)

Here's the secret tip: Go to the library and ask for the *Robert Morris & Associates Survey,* the *Risk Management Association* (or *RMA*) *Reference,* the *Dun & Bradstreet Annual Financial Statement Survey,* and any similar references of business financial statistics. After you get these references, find a nice, quiet corner of the library and look up how other businesses like yours (that is, businesses that are the same size, sell the same stuff or services, and have the same gross and net profits) spend money.

These references are really cool. For example, Robert Morris & Associates surveys bank lending officers, creates a summary of the information that these bankers receive from their customers, and publishes the results. You can look up, for example, what percentage of sales the average tavern spends on beer and peanuts.

Plan to spend an hour or so at the library. Getting used to the way that the Robert Morris & Associates report displays information takes a while. The taverns page doesn't actually have a line for beer and peanuts, for example. Instead, you see some vague accounting term like *cost of goods sold.*

Make a few notes so that you can use the information you glean to better plan your own business financial affairs. If you spend about the same amount on beer and peanuts every year as the average tavern, you're in good shape — well, unless you own a shoe store.

The point is that you can and should use this information to get a better handle on what businesses like yours earn and spend.

A final, tangential point: Have you ever heard businesspeople talk about *bench-marking?* The idea is that to compete in a market, you need to do at least as well as your competitors or similar firms in other markets. And one way to assess how you're doing compared with competitors is to compare financial ratios, or benchmarks. For example, if you compare what you spend as a percentage of revenue on advertising with what similar firms spend, you can often glean real insights into what you should do to better your business. You'll discover, for example, where you're spending too much and where you're spending too little. You'll also sometimes see competitive advantages that you possess of which you were not aware earlier.

Setting Up a Secret Plan

Okay, enough background stuff. The time has come to set up your budget — er, your Secret Plan — in QuickBooks. Follow these steps:

1. **Choose Company⇨Planning & Budgeting⇨Set Up Budgets.**

   If you haven't yet set up a budget, QuickBooks displays the Create New Budget window, as shown in Figure 12-1. If you already set up a budget, another window appears, and you need to click the Create New Budget button to get to the Create New Budget window.

Create New Budget

Create a New Budget

Begin by specifying the year and type for the new budget.

2012

Choose the budget type

◉ Profit and Loss (reflects all activity for the year)

◯ Balance Sheet (reflects ending balance)

Back | Next | Finish | Cancel

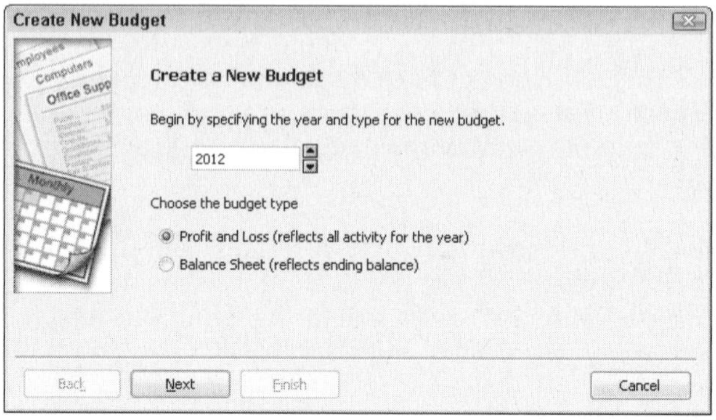

Figure 12-1:
The Create
New Budget
window.

---

2. **Select the year that you want to budget.**

   Use the box to specify the fiscal year. You use the arrows at the end of the box to adjust the year number incrementally.

3. **Select the type of budget that you want to create.**

   See those two option buttons on the Create New Budget window? They let you tell QuickBooks whether you want to create a budget of income

Chapter 12: Building the Perfect Budget *233*

and expense amounts (done with a *pro forma* profit and loss statement) or a budget of year-end asset, liability, and owner's equity account balances (done with a *pro forma* balance sheet). Typically, you want to budget income and expense amounts.

After you indicate for what year you want to budget and whether you want to budget income statement amounts or balance sheet amounts, click Next.

4. Provide any additional budgeting criteria and instructions.

QuickBooks asks next whether you want to budget using additional criteria, such as Customer:Job information or class information. You answer this question by selecting the option button that corresponds to the budgeting criteria you want and then clicking Next. (If you're just starting out, don't worry about specifying additional criteria. Keep things simple to start.)

5. Indicate whether you want to start from scratch; then click Next.

QuickBooks asks whether you want it to create a first cut at your budget by using last year's numbers or whether you just want to start from scratch. To answer this question, select the option button that corresponds to your choice. For example, to budget from scratch, select the Create Budget from Scratch radio button.

QuickBooks displays the Set Up Budgets window (see Figure 12-2).

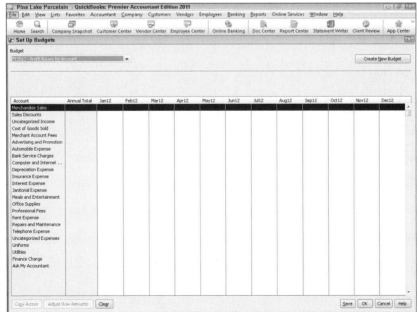

Figure 12-2:
The Set Up Budgets window.

6. Do your budget.

You use the Set Up Budgets window to identify the budgeted amounts that you plan for each account. Just click the monthly amount you want to budget and enter a value. If you say that you want to budget from scratch, by the way, QuickBooks shows a window with a bunch of empty columns (refer to the window in Figure 12-2). If you say that you want to base the coming year's budget on last year's real numbers, you see numbers in the columns.

If your Set Up Budgets window is too big for the monitor, QuickBooks shows only a few months of budgeted data at a time. Then you need to click the Show Next 6 Months button to move to the next part of the budget year. To move back to the first part of the year, click the Show Prev 6 Months button. (Only one of these Show buttons appears at a time.)

The Budget drop-down list, at the top-left corner of the Set Up Budgets window, lets you select the budget you want to work with. Why? You can work with several different versions of your budget. (To create a new budget, click the Create New Budget button, which steps you through the process described previously.)

To copy the amount shown in the selected box across the row, click the Copy Across button. (This lets you copy, for example, some amount you budgeted for January into February, March, April, May, and so on.)

If you want to be a little fancier, you can also select some budgeted amount and click the Adjust Row Amounts button. QuickBooks displays the Adjust Row Amounts dialog box (see Figure 12-3), which lets you adjust the selected amount by some specified percentage increase or decrease. If you want to increase the budgeted amount by, say, 25% per month, you use the Adjust Row Amounts window.

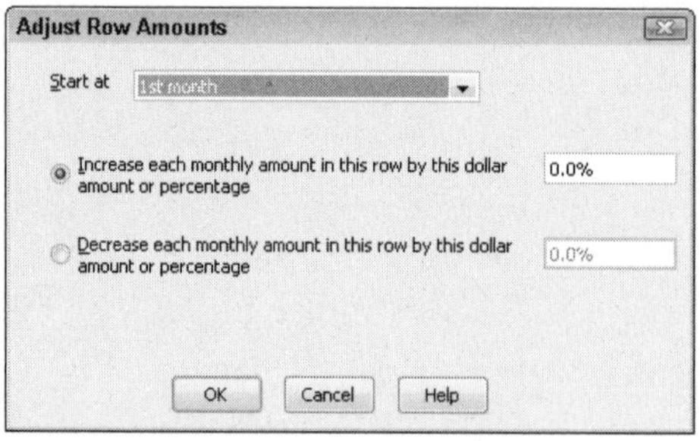

Figure 12-3:
The Adjust
Row
Amounts
dialog box.

Adjust Row Amounts

Start at   1st month

○ Increase each monthly amount in this row by this dollar   0.0%
   amount or percentage

○ Decrease each monthly amount in this row by this dollar   0.0%
   amount or percentage

OK   Cancel   Help

7. **Save your budgeting work.**

> After you enter your Secret Plan, click Save to save your work and leave the Set Up Budgets window open. Or click OK to save your work but close the Set Up Budgets window.

> I should mention, too, that you can just click Cancel if you don't want to save your work (in case you've just been noodling around).

Adjusting a Secret Plan

To later make additional changes to a budget, choose Company⇨Planning & Budgeting⇨Set Up Budgets. QuickBooks displays the Set Up Budgets window. Select the budget that you want to work with from the Budget drop-down list and then make your changes. All the same tools that you had for initially setting up your forecast (which I describe in the preceding section) are available for editing your budget.

Forecasting Profits and Losses

QuickBooks can also prepare a forecast of a year's profits (or losses) by calculating what your income statement will look like based either on the previous year's income and expenses or based on using actual numbers that you enter very similar to how you budget. (See the previous section's description of how to create a budget.)

To tell QuickBooks to forecast profits and losses, choose Company⇨Planning & Budgeting⇨Set Up Forecast. Then, when QuickBooks starts its clever little wizard, you follow the onscreen instructions. If you have questions, you can refer to the chapter's earlier discussion of setting up a budget.

Projecting Cash Flows

If you tell it to, QuickBooks attempts to project your business's cash flows. To tell QuickBooks to do this, choose Company⇨Planning & Budgeting⇨Cash Flow Projector. Then, when QuickBooks starts its clever little wizard, you follow the onscreen instructions. (This cash flow projector essentially automates the same process that you'd step through on a scratch pad or the back of an envelope.)

Using the Business Planner Tools

Depending on the version of QuickBooks that you use, one other command may be available on the Planning & Budgeting submenu: Use Business Plan Tool. The Use Business Plan Tool command starts another software program called QuickBooks Business Planner that steps you through writing a business plan. When you choose the command, QuickBooks starts the business plan software, and you write your business plan by following the onscreen steps. If you're interested in using this tool, just experiment. You can't do any damage to the QuickBooks data file.

If you didn't buy a version of QuickBooks that supplies the Business Planner software and you're now totally bummed out, let me mention that I have quite a bit of free business-planning information available at my www.stephenl nelson.com Web site, including Excel business-planning templates that you can use.

Chapter 13

Online with QuickBooks

*I*n this chapter, I start by discussing the QuickBooks online banking and bill payment features, which are pretty cool tools for some businesses. At the end of the chapter, I also briefly discuss some of the other online services that Intuit provides for QuickBooks users.

Doing the Electronic Banking Thing

Before I discuss using the QuickBooks online banking and payment services, you need to consider whether these features even make sense for you and your business. Online banking does make sense for some people — maybe even you. But then again, it might be more like the fins on a '62 Cadillac: cool, but not that cool.

So what's the commotion about?

For QuickBooks, online banking includes two parts: online banking itself and online bill payment. Basically, online banking enables you to transmit account transfer instructions to your bank and download (retrieve) account information electronically by using your computer and the Internet. Online bill payment allows you to transmit payment instructions electronically. (You basically tell your bank to write, stamp, and mail a check so that you don't have to.)

And that, my friend, is about all there is to online banking.

Finding a bank you can trust

Say you want to use the Intuit online banking services, but your bank isn't signed up. In response to this problem, many people might say, "Well, dodo-brain, just switch banks." But not you. You know that switching banks is harder than it sounds, especially for small businesses — and often is not a smart move. Many factors go into a successful small business banking relationship:

✔ **Convenience:** Doing your banking should be easy.

✔ **Trust based on a long history:** With this in hand, you can borrow money or set up mer-

chant credit card accounts without using your children for collateral.

✔ **Good rapport with a personal banker or loan officer:** If you ever have a problem — and I hope that doesn't happen — you have someone to whom you can talk.

Sure, online banking is neat. Like Cadillac fins. But online banking is neither the only nor the most important feature you need to look at when you consider a bank.

A thousand reasons not to bank online

I don't know whether you should bank online, really, but I'll share some thoughts with you. And no kidding, I've had my reservations over the years about this feature. Is it safe? Is it easy? Is it just another way for a software company and my bank to make more money off of me?

Here's my latest thinking on the matter: You ought to use online banking. It is safe if you don't share your personal identification number (PIN), and it saves you tons of time. In fact, online banking should allow many business owners to do their books themselves for just a few minutes of work at the end of the week.

That being said, I should quickly point out the few flies in the ointment, so to speak:

✔ **Your bank needs to use the Intuit service.** To use the full-blown online banking service, you need to use a bank that has signed up for this Intuit service. Many, many big banks have signed up. More banks sign up all the time, of course, but some haven't yet. So if your bank hasn't jumped on the bandwagon — that is, the Intuit bandwagon — you can't really jump on the bandwagon either. Or at least not as a full-fledged member of the band.

To find out whether your bank provides online banking, choose Banking⇨Online Banking⇨Participating Financial Institutions. After you're connected to the Internet, QuickBooks displays a list of the banks that support the Intuit flavor of online banking.

✔ **It isn't totally paperless.** Although a totally electronic system sounds really efficient and very slick, you need to realize that online bill payment (a key component of online banking) often isn't that efficient or slick because, to be quite honest, the system isn't totally electronic.

"What the . . . ?" you're saying. "I thought that was the point." Let me explain: For better or worse, most businesses are still set up to — and still expect to — receive paper checks with remittance advices. What often happens when you transmit payment instructions is that the bank or online payment service simply prints a check for you. Think about that for a minute. If the bank is printing your check, you still have all the disadvantages of a printed check, including the following:

- *You still need to allow extra time for mailing.*

- *You still have the possibility that the check will get lost.*

- *You still have the possibility that the check will be misapplied.* In other words, the check to pay your power bill might instead be applied to your neighbor's account.

✔ **There's a greater chance for error.** What's more, you have the extra complication of having your bank, rather than you, mucking up all this stuff.

✔ **It ain't free.** Best of all, the bank most likely charges for this service. And so does Intuit. (Remember that banks and software companies think that online banking is an exciting new way for them to make money.)

✔ **You might run into possible vendor confusion.** Receiving payments from your bank, as opposed to directly from you, might confuse your vendors. The confusion occurs because the checks that they receive come all bundled up in these cute little envelopes that must be torn along the perforation on just about all sides. And because you can't send a remittance slip with an online payment, vendors can easily credit your account incorrectly, which can lead to problems. (My power company regularly threatens to turn off the gas to my office because even though my electric and gas charges are included on the same bill, the power company doesn't like me to send one check via the QuickBooks online bill payment system. It needs two checks: one for the electric bill and one for the gas bill.)

One other problem bears mentioning. When you use online banking, you create a complex system without clear responsibilities for problem-solving and technical support. And that means that when you have problems, you often can't call someone to get help. (No kidding. Just the other day, some poor guy e-mailed me because his online banking stuff wasn't working: Intuit blamed the bank, the bank blamed his PC hardware, the PC company blamed

Intuit. . . . This guy has a problem that nobody can solve or will solve.) This is important to understand, so let me briefly outline the steps that an online payment might take:

1. You enter the transaction in QuickBooks.

2. You make, or QuickBooks makes, an Internet connection.

3. QuickBooks uses the Internet connection to send the transaction to the bank.

4. The bank receives the transaction information and typically creates a check, which it mails to the person you're paying.

5. The person you're paying gets the check, hopefully, and credits your account.

Five simple steps, right? Wrong. Any of these five steps can go wrong — and if one does, you don't actually make the payment or transfer, and you won't know why:

✔ **Bugs happen.** If QuickBooks or your computer has a bug, it might say that you entered and transmitted a transaction when in fact you haven't. This has happened to me.

✔ **Ya gotta get online.** If your Internet connection doesn't work or doesn't work dependably, you can't send the online transaction. I've had problems both with online banking at home over a dialup Internet connection (bad telephone cord) and at work when using a network and a DSL connection (either an incorrectly configured network or a bad DSL).

✔ **Banks are fallible.** If the bank screws up printing or mailing the check, well, of course your check won't get there. (I've had this happen, too — no kidding. QuickBooks lets you enter a five-line address on a check, but the check printed by the bank or online payment service can have only four lines. So QuickBooks just removes the fifth line of the address block.)

I don't mean to rant here, but whenever any of these problems occurs, you won't actually know *what's* gone wrong — only that *something* has gone wrong. And you'll be responsible for solving the problem even though it might be the fault of your bank, Intuit, your Internet service provider, the telephone company, or somebody else.

Making sense of online banking

So what should you do? Let me make a suggestion: If you use a bank that provides online banking, go ahead and try the service. Absolutely! It isn't very expensive — probably a few dollars per month. If you decide later on that you don't like the service, you can always go back to banking the old-fashioned way.

If you use a bank that doesn't provide online banking services and you're really bummed out about it, you can try the online bill payment component of online banking by using the Intuit online bill payment service. *Online bill payment* is the part where you send instructions either to your bank (if it provides the service) or to Intuit to write and mail checks for you. You can use the online bill payment service with any account — in essence, you just give Intuit permission to automatically deduct money from your account to make payments for you.

If you use a bank that doesn't provide online banking and you couldn't care less, don't try the online banking stuff, don't read any more of this chapter, and consider taking the rest of the afternoon off.

Signing up for the service

All you need to do to sign up for online banking service is to choose Banking⇨Online Banking⇨Set Up Account for Online Services. QuickBooks starts an online application wizard that walks you through the steps to apply for the online banking services. Just follow the onscreen instructions, and *voilà!* That's it. Another benefit of being literate.

To actually begin transmitting online payments or making account inquiries, you need to complete the application and have that application processed. Note, too, that you can also usually complete the application by filling out paperwork from your bank and turning that in. You might not have to use the online application process.

Making an online payment

Plan to create and send online payments a good week before they're due. Processing your request and then printing and sending a check takes time for the online bill payment service. And a check that your bank sends doesn't go through the mail any faster than a check you send yourself. So don't expect online bill payment to save you any time over sending checks that you print or hand-write yourself.

After you sign up for online banking, making payments is easy. Just follow these steps:

1. **Choose Banking⇨Write Checks.**

   You can also click the Write Checks icon on the Home screen. If you've written checks with QuickBooks before, you probably recognize your old familiar friend, the Write Checks window, as shown in Figure 13-1.

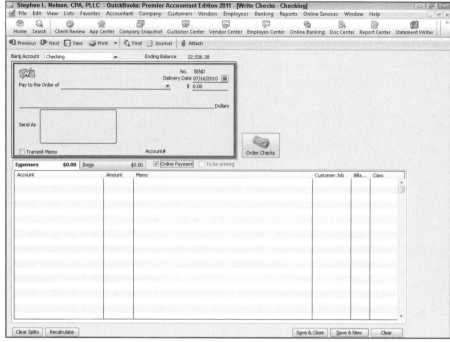

Figure 13-1:
The Write
Checks win-
dow. Hey,
this looks
familiar,
doesn't it?

2. **Click the Bank Account drop-down list at the top of the window and then choose the account from which you want to write this check.**

   Choosing the account is a really important step. Make sure that you're accessing the correct account before you write a check.

3. **Select the Online Payment check box.**

   Selecting this check box is another important step. If you don't select this check box, you aren't making an online payment; rather, you're just writing a regular check that you need to print or hand-write.

4. **Fill in the check.**

   If the payee appears on one of your name lists, the AutoFill feature fills in the name of the payee in the Pay to the Order Of line after you type a few letters. For online bill payment, you must have the correct address. If the address is incomplete, QuickBooks warns you and asks you to correct it. If you haven't entered a transaction for this person or party before or added them to a list, QuickBooks asks you to Quick Add or Set Up the payee name. Do that.

   By the way, QuickBooks makes you collect more information about anyone you're going to pay with an online payment.

Enter the amount of the check next to the dollar sign and then press Tab. QuickBooks writes out the amount for you on the Dollars line.

5. **Fill in the Expenses and Items tabs, if necessary.**

   Don't know what these tabs are? Chapter 6 explains them in minute detail. Start turning those pages.

6. **Click the Save & New button or the Save & Close button to finish writing the check.**

   Click Save & New to write another check, or click Save & Close if you're finished writing checks for the moment. There you have it. Your check is written, entered in the Checking register, and ready to be sent so that your bank or Intuit can print and mail it.

   And you thought this stuff was going to be tough, didn't you?

People who have grown accustomed to Quicken, a cousin product of QuickBooks, may want to use the Register window to make online payments. You can use the Register window in QuickBooks, too, although doing so isn't quite as slick. You just enter the payment in the usual way, except that you type the word **SEND** in the Check Number text box.

Transferring money electronically

You can electronically transfer money between bank accounts, too, as long as the accounts are at the same bank. (Both accounts, of course, also need to be set for online banking.) Here's what you need to do:

1. **Choose Banking⇨Transfer Funds.**

   You see the Transfer Funds Between Accounts window.

2. **From the Transfer Funds From drop-down list, choose the bank account that you're going to transfer the money from.**

3. **From the Transfer Funds To drop-down list, choose the bank account to which you want to transfer the money.**

   Select the account that you want to receive the funds.

4. **Select the Online Funds Transfer check box.**

   Doing so tells QuickBooks that you want to make this transfer electronically. (This box doesn't appear if you're not set up for online banking.)

5. **Enter the amount that you want to transfer in the Transfer Amount field and then fill in the Memo text box.**

   Someday, you might go into the register for the account that you're transferring money from and wonder where you transferred this money and why. Filling in the Memo line solves this little mystery beforehand.

6. **Click Save & Close.**

   The transfer is recorded. After you transmit the transfer instructions (which I describe a little later in this chapter), the transfer transaction is posted to your account — maybe not immediately, but as fast as a telephone transfer or an ATM transfer is posted.

Changing instructions

QuickBooks doesn't actually send, or transmit, your payment and transfer instructions until you tell it to. This little fact means that you can change or edit your payment instructions (what you enter with the Write Checks window) and your transfer instructions (what you enter with the Transfer Funds Between Accounts window) until you actually transmit them. You edit online payments and account transfers in the same way that you edit regular payments and account transfers. Read Chapter 8 if you need more information.

Transmitting instructions

After you describe the online payments and account transfers that you want QuickBooks to make, you transmit that information to the bank. To do so, follow these steps:

1. **Choose Banking➪Online Banking Center or click the Online Banking icon on the Home screen.**

   You see the Online Banking Center window, as shown in Figure 13-2.

2. **From the Financial Institution drop-down list at the top of the screen, choose the bank to which you're transmitting payment and transfer instructions.**

3. **Review the payment and transfer instructions one last time.**

   Take one last peek at the Items to Send list to make sure that any payment and transfer instructions that you're sending are correct. If you have questions about a particular instruction, click it and then click the Edit button. If you know that a particular payment instruction is incorrect, click it and then click the Delete button.

4. **Click the Send/Receive button to transmit the payment and transfer instructions.**

   QuickBooks prompts you to provide a PIN (personal identification number) with a cute little dialog box. If you're transmitting payment and transfer instructions for the first time, QuickBooks probably prompts you to change your PIN.

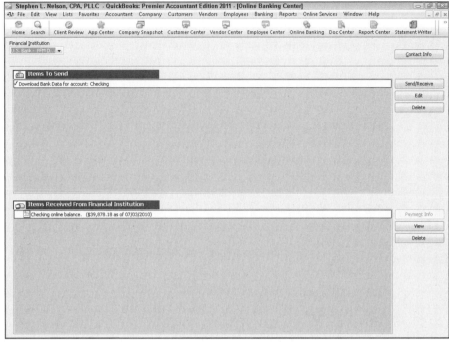

Figure 13-2:
The Online
Banking
Center
window.

5. **Review any transactions that the bank tells you about.**

   After QuickBooks makes the connection and sends and receives transactions, QuickBooks updates the information shown in the Online Banking Center window. You can get more information about many of the items listed by clicking. You can add transactions that Quickbooks downloads from the bank but which are not yet in your bank account registers by clicking the Add Transactions to QuickBooks button (which appears at the bottom of the window.)

6. **Click the Close box.**

   Hey, when you're done, you're done.

Message in a bottle

Doing all your banking electronically can be a little unsettling when you're starting out. What if, for example, you have a question? All you do is send an e-mail to the bank, asking the people there whatever question you would normally ask in a telephone call or at the drive-through window. To do so, follow these steps:

1. **Choose the Banking⇨Online Banking⇨Create Online Banking Message command.**

   QuickBooks displays the Create Message screen (see Figure 13-3) and fills in the bank name (as long as you use online banking services with only one bank). If you use online banking services with more than one bank, choose the name of the bank to which you want to send a message from the Message To drop-down list.

2. **Click the Subject box and then type a brief description of your message's subject.**

   I may be telling you something you already know, but most e-mail programs simply display a list of messages that includes the sender, the message subject, and the date. Therefore, the message subject that you use is one of the first bits of message information that the bank folks see.

3. **Select the online account that you're going to discuss in the message.**

4. **Click in the Message text box and then type your message.**

   You're on your own here.

5. **(Optional) Click the Print button to print a copy of your message.**

6. **Click OK.**

   When you click OK, you add the message to the list of stuff that's ready to send the next time you go online with your bank. You can send the instructions immediately by following the steps in the "Transmitting instructions" section, earlier in this chapter.

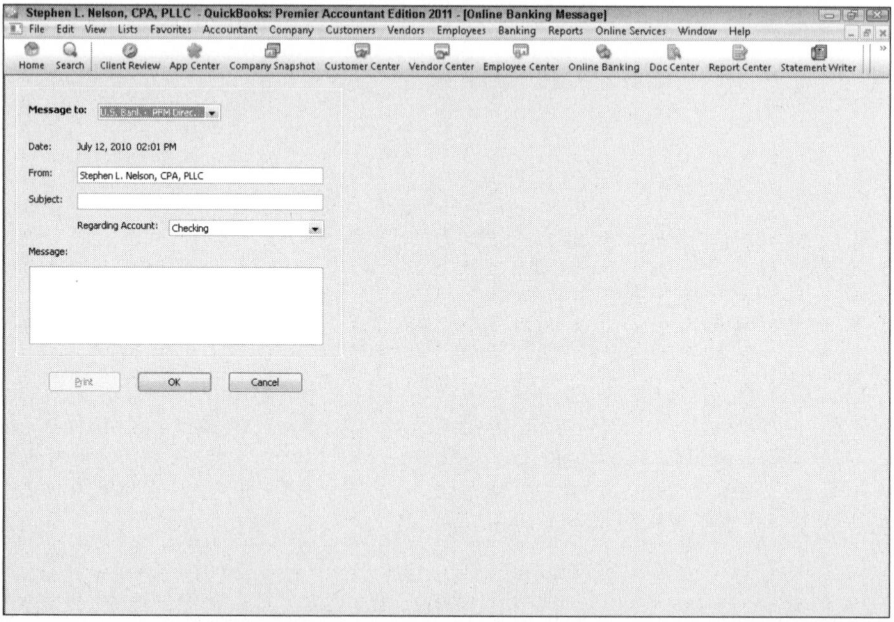

Figure 13-3:
The Online Banking Message dialog box.

A Quick Review of the Other Online Opportunities

Intuit provides several other small business–type online services to QuickBooks users. For example, Intuit has also arranged for a merchant credit card service, which you can apply for online and then use online for receiving payments and even getting charge authorizations. Through its Web site, Intuit also says it provides a small business purchasing service that makes price shopping over the Internet easy, or at least easier. QuickBooks will automatically connect you to its online incorporation service as well as help you with online search marketing. And finally, as I hint in Chapter 11, some of QuickBooks payroll services are very online-ish.

If you have questions about the current state of any of these products or services, visit the QuickBooks.com Web site and search for the name of the service. Alternatively, choose the related command from the QuickBooks Online Services menu and read the sales literature that QuickBooks displays.

Part IV
Housekeeping Chores

The 5th Wave   By Rich Tennant

"So...did you find the money that was
missing from the bottom line?"

In this part . . .

1 hope this doesn't surprise you, but your accounting system requires a bit of tender loving care. Oh, no, don't worry. Nothing unexpected. . . .

But you will want to know how to reconcile accounts (to keep your books squeaky clean), how to keep your files dust-free, and how to deal with some of the more tedious accounting chores, including fixed assets accounting and job costing.

Chapter 14

The Balancing Act

In This Chapter

▶ Balancing your bank account

▶ Troubleshooting when your account doesn't balance

1 want to start this chapter with an important point: Balancing a bank account in QuickBooks is easy and quick.

I'm not just trying to get you pumped up about an otherwise painfully boring topic. I don't think that balancing a bank account is any more exciting than you do.

My point is simply this: Because bank account balancing can be tedious and boring, use QuickBooks to reduce the drudgery.

Balancing a Bank Account

As I said, balancing a bank account is remarkably easy in QuickBooks. In fact, I'll go so far as to say that if you have any problems, they stem from . . . well, sloppy record-keeping that preceded your use of QuickBooks.

Enough of this blather; I get started by describing how you reconcile an account.

Giving QuickBooks information from the bank statement

In a *reconciliation,* as you probably know, you compare your records of a bank account with the bank's records of the same account. You should be able to explain any difference between the two accounts — usually by point-ing to checks you wrote which haven't yet cleared. (Sometimes deposits fall into the same category; you record a deposit and mail it, but the bank hasn't yet credited your account.)

The first step, then, is to supply QuickBooks the bank's account information. You get this information from your monthly statement. Supply QuickBooks the figures it needs, as follows:

1. **Choose Banking⇨Reconcile or click the Reconcile icon on the Home screen.**

   QuickBooks displays the Begin Reconciliation dialog box, as shown in Figure 14-1.

If you have several bank accounts, you may have to select which account you want to reconcile.

2. **If the bank account shown isn't the one you want to reconcile, open the Account list and choose the correct account.**

3. **Enter the bank statement date into the Statement Date text box.**

   You can adjust a date one day at a time by using the plus (+) and minus (–) keys. You can also click the Calendar button on the right side of the Statement Date text box to select a date from the calendar. See the online Cheat Sheet at www.dummies.com/cheatsheet/ quickbooks2011 for a list of other secret date-editing tricks.

4. **Verify the bank statement opening balance.**

   QuickBooks displays an amount in the Beginning Balance text box (refer to Figure 14-1).

   If the opening balance isn't correct, see the sidebar, "Why isn't my opening balance the same as the one in QuickBooks?" later in this chapter.

5. **Enter the ending balance from your bank statement into the Ending Balance text box.**

6. **Enter the bank's service charge.**

   If the bank statement shows a service charge and you haven't already entered it, move the cursor to the Service Charge text box and type the amount. (For example, type **50** for a $50 service charge.)

7. **Enter a transaction date for the service charge transaction.**

   QuickBooks adds one month to the service charge date from the last time you reconciled. If this date isn't correct, type the correct one.

8. **Assign the bank's service charge to an account.**

   Enter the expense account to which you assign bank service charges in the first Account text box — the one beside the Date text box. Activate the drop-down list by clicking the down arrow, highlight the category by using the arrow keys, and then press Enter. I'll bet anything that you record these charges in the Bank Service Charges account that QuickBooks sets up by default.

   If you told QuickBooks that you also want to track income and expense amounts by using classes, QuickBooks adds Class boxes to the Begin Reconciliation dialog box so that you can collect this information.

9. **Enter the account's interest income.**

   If the account earned interest for the month and you haven't already entered this figure, type an amount in the Interest Earned text box.

10. **Enter a transaction date for the interest income transaction.**

    You already know how to enter dates. I won't bore you by explaining it again (but see Step 3 if you have trouble).

11. **Assign the interest to an account.**

    In the second Account text box, enter the account to which this account's interest should be assigned. I bet that you record this one under the Interest Income account, which is near the bottom of the Account drop-down list. To select a category from the Account list, activate the drop-down list by clicking the down arrow, highlight the category, and then press Enter.

12. **Click the Continue button.**

    QuickBooks displays the Reconcile window, as shown in Figure 14-2.

Marking cleared checks and deposits

From the Reconcile window, shown in Figure 14-2, you tell QuickBooks which deposits and checks have cleared at the bank. (Refer to your bank statement for this information.) Follow these steps:

1. **Identify the first deposit that has cleared.**

   You know how to do this, I'm sure. Just leaf through the bank statement and find the first deposit listed.

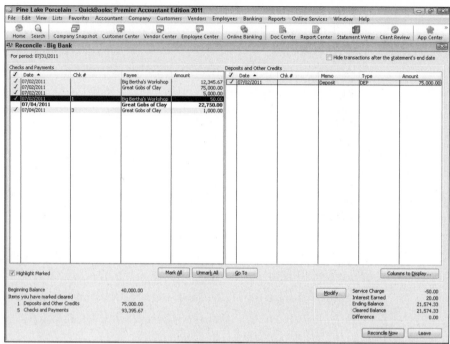

2. **Mark the first cleared deposit as cleared.**

   Scroll through the transactions listed in the Deposits and Other Credits section of the Reconcile window, find the deposit, and then click it. You also can highlight the deposit by using the Tab or arrow keys and then pressing the spacebar. QuickBooks places a check mark in front of the deposit to mark it as cleared and updates the cleared statement balance.

   If you have a large number of deposits to clear and you can identify them quickly, click the Mark All button and then simply unmark the transactions that aren't on the bank statement. To unmark a transaction, click it. The check mark disappears.

3. **Record any cleared but missing deposits.**

   If you can't find a deposit in the Reconcile window, you haven't entered it into the register yet. I can only guess why you haven't entered it. Maybe you just forgot. Close or deactivate the Reconcile window by clicking the Leave button. Now open the register and enter the deposit in the register in the usual way. To return to the Reconcile window, either reopen it or reactivate it. Or you can just choose Banking⇨Make Deposits and open the deposit screen right on top of the Reconcile window, if you like. Record the deposit and then click the Save & Close button. When you open the Reconcile window again, the deposit appears in the Deposits and Other Credits area.

4. **Repeat Steps 1–3 for all deposits listed on the bank statement.**

   Make sure that the dates match and that the amounts of the deposits are correct. If they're not, go back to the transactions and correct them. To get to a transaction, click the Go To button. You see the Write Checks or Make Deposits window where the transaction was originally recorded. Make the corrections there and then click Save & Close. You return to the Reconcile window.

5. **Identify the first check that has cleared.**

   No sweat, right? Just find the first check or withdrawal listed on the bank statement.

   QuickBooks enables you to sort the transactions listed on the Reconcile window by clicking the column headings in the Checks and Payments section and in the Deposits and Other Credits section. You might want to experiment a bit with this handy feature. Sorting and re-sorting transactions — particularly in high-transaction volume bank accounts — often eases the work of reconciling a bank account.

6. **Mark the first cleared check as cleared.**

   Scroll through the transactions listed in the Checks and Payments section of the Reconcile window; find the first check; and then click it. You also can highlight it by pressing Tab and an arrow key. Then press the spacebar. QuickBooks inserts a check mark to label this transaction as cleared and updates the cleared statement balance.

7. **Record any missing but cleared checks.**

   If you can't find a check or withdrawal in QuickBooks, guess what? You haven't entered it in the register yet. Close or deactivate the Reconcile window by clicking its Leave button or by activating another window. Then display the register and enter the check or withdrawal. To return to the Reconcile window, reopen or reactivate it. Or you can just choose Banking➪Write Checks, create the check right on top of the Reconcile window, and then click Save & Close to return to the Reconcile screen and carry on from where you left off.

8. **Repeat Steps 5–7 for all withdrawals listed on the bank statement.**

These steps don't take very long. Reconciling my account each month takes me about two minutes. And I'm not joking or exaggerating. By two minutes, I really mean two minutes.

If the difference equals zero

After you mark all the cleared checks and deposits, the difference between the Cleared Balance for the account and the bank statement's Ending Balance should equal zero. Notice that I said *should* — not *will*. Refer to Figure 14-2, which, fortunately, shows a Reconcile window in which everything is hunky-dory. If the difference is small, look for small differences between the amount of the checks in the register and the actual cleared checks on the bank statement. If you find a discrepancy with a particular check, just click the Go To button to go to the check and change the amount. Click Save & Close to go right back to the Reconcile window.

If the difference does equal zero, you're finished. Just click the Reconcile Now button. QuickBooks displays a congratulatory message box telling you that the reconciliation is complete. As a reward for being such a good boy or girl, the message box asks whether you want to print a free, all-expenses-paid Summary or Full reconciliation report. Click Summary or Full and then click OK if you want to print the report. Otherwise, just click OK.

Can't decide whether to print the reconciliation report? Unless you're a business bookkeeper or an accountant who is reconciling a bank account for someone else — your employer or a client, for example — you don't need to print the reconciliation report. All that printing does is prove that you reconciled the account. (Basically, this proof is the reason why you should print the report if you're a bookkeeper or an accountant. The person for whom you're reconciling the account will know that you did your job and will have a piece of paper to refer to later with any questions.) Also, you can always come back and print the report later, if necessary. QuickBooks saves the Reconciliation reports under Reports, Banking, Previous Reconciliation.

Now each deposit, withdrawal, and check that you just cleared is marked with a check mark in your register. If you don't believe me, open the register and find out.

If the difference doesn't equal zero

If the difference doesn't equal zero, you have a problem. If you click the Reconcile Now button, QuickBooks shows you the Reconcile Adjustment dialog box, as shown in Figure 14-3. This dialog box tells you how unbalanced your account is and asks whether you want to adjust your maladjusted account.

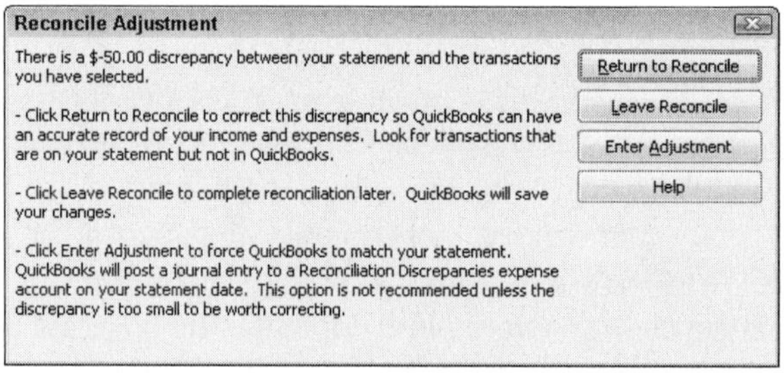

Figure 14-3:
The Reconcile Adjustment dialog box.

> **Reconcile Adjustment**
>
> There is a $-50.00 discrepancy between your statement and the transactions you have selected.
>
> - Click Return to Reconcile to correct this discrepancy so QuickBooks can have an accurate record of your income and expenses. Look for transactions that are on your statement but not in QuickBooks.
>
> - Click Leave Reconcile to complete reconciliation later. QuickBooks will save your changes.
>
> - Click Enter Adjustment to force QuickBooks to match your statement. QuickBooks will post a journal entry to a Reconciliation Discrepancies expense account on your statement date. This option is not recommended unless the discrepancy is too small to be worth correcting.
>
> [Return to Reconcile] [Leave Reconcile] [Enter Adjustment] [Help]

Click the Return to Reconcile button if you want to go back to the Reconcile window and start the search for the missing or incorrectly entered transaction.

Why isn't my opening balance the same as the one in QuickBooks?

An opening balance that isn't the same as the one shown in the Opening Balance text box can mean a couple things.

First, you may have mistakenly cleared a transaction the last time you reconciled. If you cleared a transaction last month that didn't go through until this month, your opening balance is wrong. Go back to the register and examine transactions. Each one that's cleared has a check mark next to it in the narrow column between the Payment and Deposit columns. If one of the checks that appears on this month's statement has a check mark, you made a booboo last month. From the register, click the check mark to remove it. You're asked to confirm your actions. The check now appears in the Reconcile window.

The other reason why the opening balance can be different is that a transaction that you cleared in the past got changed. If you deleted a transaction that occurred before this reconciliation period, for example, it threw off your balance. Why? Because the transaction that you deleted helped balance your account the last time around, but now that transaction is gone.

Whatever happens, don't fret. If you can't track down the faulty transaction, you can just have QuickBooks adjust the balance for you, which I explain elsewhere in this chapter. If you frequently find that your accounts don't balance, consider using the QuickBooks Audit Trail report, which lists changes to the QuickBooks data, when it's time to reconcile your accounts.

If you want to force the two amounts to agree, click OK. Forcing the two amounts to agree isn't a very good idea. To do so, QuickBooks adds a cleared transaction equal to the difference. (I talk about this transaction a little later in the chapter.)

Postponing a reconciliation (by clicking the Leave Reconcile button) and not choosing to adjust the bank account balance is usually the best approach because then you can locate and correct the problem. (The next section contains some ideas that can help you determine what the problem is.) Then you can restart the reconciliation and finish your work. (You restart a reconciliation the same way that you originate one.)

Eleven Things to Do If Your Non-Online Account Doesn't Balance

I want to give you some suggestions for reconciling an account when you're having problems. If you're sitting in front of your computer, wringing your hands, try the tips in this section:

✔ **Make sure that you're working with the right account.** Sounds dumb, doesn't it? If you have several bank accounts, however, ending up in the wrong account is darn easy. So go ahead and confirm, for example, that you're trying to reconcile your checking account at Mammoth International Bank by using the Mammoth International Bank checking account statement.

✔ **Look for transactions that the bank has recorded but you haven't.** Go through the bank statement to make sure that you recorded every transaction that your bank has recorded. You can easily overlook cash-machine withdrawals, special fees, or service charges (such as charges for checks or your safe deposit box), automatic withdrawals, direct deposits, and so on.

If the difference is positive — that is, the bank thinks that you have less money than you think that you should have — you may be missing a withdrawal transaction. If the difference is negative, you may be missing a deposit transaction.

✔ **Look for reversed transactions.** Here's a tricky one: If you accidentally enter a transaction backward — a deposit as a withdrawal or a withdrawal as a deposit — your account doesn't balance. And the error can be difficult to find. The Reconcile window shows all the correct transactions, but a transaction amount appears in the wrong list. (The amount appears in the Deposits and Other Credits list when it belongs in the Checks and Payments list, or vice versa.) The check that you wrote to Acme Housewreckers for the demolition of your carport appears in the Deposits and Other Credits list, for example.

✔ **Look for a transaction that's equal to half the difference.** One handy way to find the transaction that you entered backward — if you have only one — is to look for a transaction that's equal to half the irreconcilable difference. If the difference is $200, for example, you may have entered a $100 deposit as a withdrawal or a $100 withdrawal as a deposit.

✔ **Look for a transaction that's equal to the difference.** While I'm on the subject of explaining the difference by looking at individual transactions, I'll make an obvious point: If the difference between the bank's records and yours equals one of the transactions listed in your register, you may have incorrectly marked the transaction as cleared or incorrectly left the transaction unmarked (shown as uncleared). I don't know. Maybe that was too obvious. Naaaah.

✔ **Check for transposed numbers.** Transposed numbers are flip-flopped digits. For example, you enter $45.89 as $48.59. These turkeys always cause headaches for accountants and bookkeepers. If you look at the numbers, detecting an error is often difficult because the digits are the same. For example, when you compare a check amount of $45.89 in your register with a check for $48.59 shown on your bank statement, both check amounts show the same digits: 4, 5, 8, and 9. They just show them in a different order.

Transposed numbers are tough to find, but here's a trick that you can try: Divide the difference shown in the Reconcile window by 9. If the result is an even number of dollars or cents, chances are good that you have a transposed number somewhere.

✓ **Use the Locate Discrepancies button.** Would you mind, terribly, taking a peek back at Figure 14-1? The dialog box shown in that figure includes a Locate Discrepancies button, which you can click to display another dialog box that prints reports that may help you reconcile your account. In particular, the dialog box lets you view a report of changes made to previously cleared transactions (which would be pretty suspicious bookkeeping activity and would definitely foul up your reconciliation). It also shows a report that lists transactions marked as cleared during previous reconciliations, which might be interesting because maybe you erroneously marked a transaction as cleared before it really was cleared.

✓ **Have someone else look over your work.** This idea may seem pretty obvious, but I'm amazed by how often a second pair of eyes can find something that I overlooked. Ask one of your co-workers or employees (preferably that one person who always seems to have way too much free time) to look over everything for you.

✓ **Be on the lookout for multiple errors.** If you find an error by using this laundry list and you still have a difference, start checking at the top of the list again. You may discover, for example, after you find a transposed number that you entered another transaction backward, or incorrectly cleared or uncleared a transaction.

✓ **Try again next month (and maybe the month after that).** If the difference isn't huge in relation to the size of your bank account, you may want to wait until next month and attempt to reconcile your account again.

Before my carefree attitude puts you in a panic, consider the following example: In January, you reconcile your account, and the difference is $24.02. Then you reconcile the account in February, and the difference is $24.02. You reconcile the account in March, and — surprise, surprise — the difference is still $24.02. What's going on here? Well, your starting account balance was probably off by $24.02. (The more months you try to reconcile your account and find that you're always mysteriously $24.02 off, the more likely that this type of error is to blame.) After the second or third month, I think that having QuickBooks enter an adjusting transaction of $24.02 is pretty reasonable so that your account balances. (In my opinion, this circumstance is the only one that merits your adjusting an account to match the bank's figure.)

If you successfully reconciled your account with QuickBooks before, your work may not be at fault. The mistake may be (drum roll, please) the bank's! And in this case, you should do something else. . . .

✔ **Get in your car, drive to the bank, and beg for help.** As an alternative to the preceding idea — which supposes that the bank's statement is correct and that your records are incorrect — I propose this idea: Ask the bank to help you reconcile the account. Hint that you think the mistake is probably the bank's, but in a very nice, cordial way. Smile a lot. And one other thing: Be sure to ask about whatever product the bank is currently advertising in the lobby (which encourages the staff to think that you're interested in that 180-month certificate of deposit, causing them to be extra-nice to you).

In general, the bank's record-keeping is usually pretty darn good. I've never had a problem either with my business or personal accounts. (I've also been lucky enough to deal with big, well-run banks.) Nevertheless, your bank quite possibly has made a mistake, so ask for help. Be sure to ask for an explanation of any transactions that you discover only by seeing them on your bank statement. By the way, you'll probably pay for this help.

Chapter 15

Reporting on the State of Affairs

. . . .

In This Chapter

▶ Printing QuickBooks reports

▶ Using the Reports menu commands

▶ QuickZooming report totals

▶ Sharing information with a spreadsheet

▶ Editing and rearranging report information

▶ Processing multiple reports

▶ Using QuickReports

. . . .

*T*o find out whether your business is thriving or diving, you use the QuickBooks Reports feature. The different kinds of reports in QuickBooks cover everything from cash flow to missing checks, not to mention QuickReports. *QuickReports* are summary reports that you can get from the information on forms, account registers, or lists by merely clicking the mouse.

In this chapter, I tell you how to prepare reports, how to print them, and how to customize reports for your special needs.

What Kinds of Reports Are There, Anyway?

If you run a small business, you don't need all the reports that QuickBooks offers, but many of these reports are extremely useful. Reports show you how healthy or unhealthy your business is, where your profits are, and where you're wasting time and squandering resources.

To make sense of what might otherwise become mass confusion, QuickBooks organizes all its reports in categories. You can see what all the categories are by pulling down the Reports menu or by clicking the Report Center icon. The names of the reports read a bit like public television documentary names, don't they? "Tonight, Joob Taylor explores the mazelike federal budget in Budget Reports." You select a report category to see a list of report names.

In Table 15-1, I describe reports by category and give a short description of the major reports in each category. To get a thorough description of a particular report, go to the Help feature. To find out what a standard profit and loss report does, for example, choose Help➪QuickBooks Help and then click the Index tab. Type **financial statements** in the text box. (The Help information includes a wonderful discussion about how to understand the profit and loss and balance sheet financial statements.) Or, from the Reports Center, select the type of report on the left; you see a list of the different reports available on the right side, with a description of the information contained in each one. To read the details about a topic, click that topic in the list.

Table 15-1	QuickBooks Report Categories
Report Category	*Description*
Company & Financial	These reports give you a bird's-eye view of your company's health and cash flow. They give you a snapshot of your assets, liabilities, and equity, showing income, expenses, and net profit or loss over time.
Customers & Receivables	These accounts receivable reports are great for finding out where you stand in regard to your customer invoices. You can list unpaid invoices and group them in various ways, including by customer, job, and aging status.
Sales	These reports show what you sold and who your customers are. You can see your sales by item, by customer, or by sales representative.
Jobs, Time & Mileage	These reports let you see job and item profitability, compare job estimates versus actual costs, view time recorded on jobs and activities, and look at vehicle mileage.
Vendors & Payables	These accounts payable reports tell you everything you need to know about your unpaid bills. You can list bills in a variety of ways, including by vendor and by aging status. This category also includes a report for determining sales tax liability.
Purchases	If you enable the Items and Purchases option within QuickBooks, these reports show from whom you bought, what you bought, and how much you paid. You can list purchases by item or by vendor. One handy report shows any outstanding purchase orders.

Report Category	Description
Inventory	These reports help answer the ever-important question, "What items do I have in stock?" You can get an enormous amount of detail from these reports. For example, you can find out how many of an item you have on hand and how many you have on order. You can group inventory by vendor or by item. If you need price lists, you can print them by using a special report from your QuickBooks file.
Employees & Payroll	These reports, available if you've signed up for one of the QuickBooks payroll options, offer ways to track payroll or check your payroll liability accounts. Believe me: These reports come in handy.
Banking	These reports list checks and deposits.
Accountant & Taxes	These reports include income tax reports, journal and general ledger reports, and a trial balance.
Budgets & Forecasts	These reports show you once and for all whether your budgeting skills are realistic. You can view budgets by job, by month, or by balance sheet account. Then you can compare the budgets with actual income and expense totals. (You need to have a budget already set up to use this report — something I discuss in Chapter 12.)
List	These reports let you see your lists in detail. For example, you can see the contacts, phone numbers, and addresses on your Customer, Vendor, or Other Names lists. You also can create a detailed report of your inventory.
Industry Specific	Some versions of QuickBooks also supply industry-specific reports under the Industry Specific submenu command. QuickBooks, at the time of this writing, provides industry-specific versions of QuickBooks for accountants, contractors, manufacturers, wholesalers, professional service firms, retailers, and nonprofit organizations.

If you're not sure which specific report you want, you can use the Report Center. Just choose Reports⇨Report Center and choose a report category from the list along the left edge of the Report Center window (see Figure 15-1). QuickBooks displays a picture of the most common reports within the category in the Report Center window.

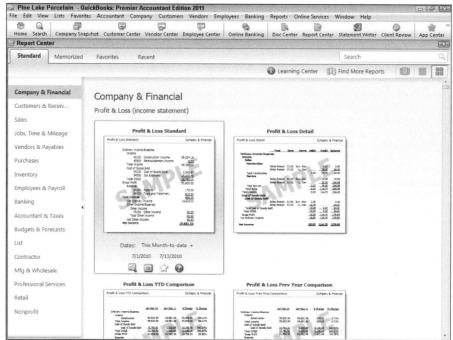

Figure 15-1:
The Report
Center
window.

Creating and Printing a Report

After you decide what report you need, all you have to do is select it from the appropriate menu or from the Report Center window. To create a standard profit and loss report, for example, choose Reports⇨Company & Financial⇨Profit & Loss Standard or select it from the Report Center.

Depending on how much data QuickBooks has to process, you may see a Building Report box before the report appears onscreen in all its glory. Figure 15-2 shows a standard profit and loss report, or an *income statement*.

If you see a Customize Report dialog box instead of a report, you can tell QuickBooks to change this option. To do so, choose Edit⇨Preferences and then click the Reports & Graphs icon in the list on the left. Click the My Preferences tab, if you have one and it isn't already selected. Remove the check mark from the Prompt Me to Modify Report Options Before Opening a Report check box.

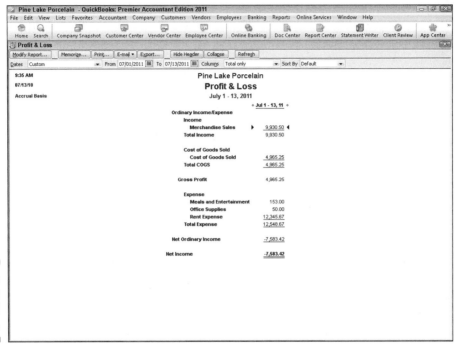

Figure 15-2:
A standard
profit and
loss report.

You can't see the entire onscreen version of a report unless your report is very small (or your screen is monstrously large). Use the Page Up and Page Down keys on your keyboard to scroll up and down, and use the Tab and Shift+Tab keys to move left and right. Or, if you're a mouse lover, you can use the scroll bar.

To print a report, click the Print button at the top of the report. QuickBooks displays the Print Reports dialog box, as shown in Figure 15-3. To accept the given specifications, which are almost always fine, click the Print button. You'll never guess what happens next: QuickBooks prints the report!

The first time you print a report, QuickBooks displays a Printing Features dialog box that explains a few things about the mechanics of choosing and printing reports.

Before I forget, I want to tell you that you can select the File radio button in the Print To panel to tell QuickBooks to save the report as a file instead of printing it. You can then choose the file format: ASCII Text File, Comma Delimited File, or Tab Delimited File. You can use either delimited-file format if you want to open the file later with a spreadsheet program, such as Microsoft Excel. After you click Print, use the Create Disk File dialog box to specify the filename and storage location.

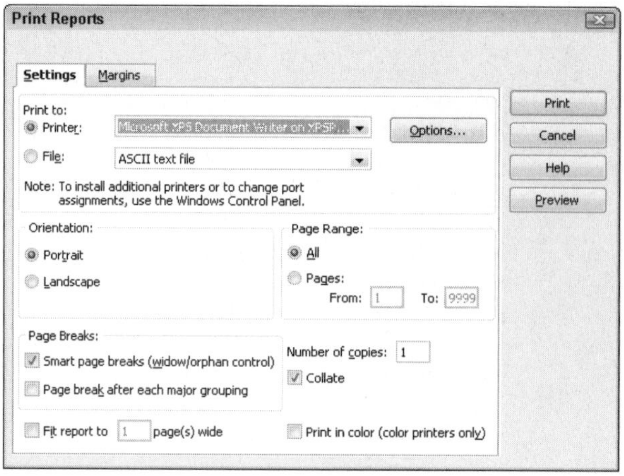

Figure 15-3:
The Print
Reports
dialog box.

Another really popular option is to "print" your report to your desktop as a PDF file that can be attached to an e-mail and sent to anyone you choose. After sending, you can drag the file to your Recycle Bin. Anything that you can print can be processed this way and e-mailed. Some documents in QuickBooks, such as Invoices, have an icon that supports PDF e-mailing; these documents are processed online through the Intuit servers. If you "print" them to the desktop and send them manually, you use your own e-mail server and send them as attachments. You need to have a PDF printer driver installed on your computer to use this function. These can be down-loaded online for free if you don't have one already, such as from www. primopdf.com.

The Orientation settings tell QuickBooks how the report is supposed to appear on the paper. The Page Range settings specify the pages that you want to print. The Fit Report to *xx* Page(s) Wide check box enables you to shrink the report so that it fits on the number of pages you specify. The purpose of the Print in Color (Color Printers Only) check box is pretty self-evident.

QuickBooks includes two page-break options for creating easier-to-read reports:

 ✔ Select the first check box (smart page breaks) to keep items that belong in the same group on the same page.

 ✔ Select the second check box to give each major group its own page.

You also can preview the report by clicking the Preview button.

Visiting the report dog-and-pony show

You can do some neat things with the reports you create. Here's a quick run-down of some of the most valuable tricks:

- **QuickZooming mysterious figures:** If you don't understand where a number in a report comes from, point to it with the mouse. As you point to numbers, QuickBooks changes the mouse pointer to a magnifying glass marked with a *Z*. Double-click the mouse to have QuickBooks display a list of all the transactions that make up that number.

    This feature, called *QuickZoom,* is extremely handy for understanding the figures that appear on reports. All you have to do is double-click any mysterious-looking figure in a report. QuickBooks immediately tells you exactly how it arrived at that figure.

- **Sharing report data with Microsoft Excel:** You can export report data to an Excel spreadsheet by clicking the Export button in the report window. QuickBooks displays the Export Report to Excel dialog box. You can use this dialog box to specify whether you want to create a new spreadsheet for the report data or whether you want to add the report data to an existing spreadsheet.

Editing and rearranging reports

You may have noticed that when QuickBooks displays the report document window, it also displays a row of buttons: Modify Report, Memorize, Print, E-Mail, Export, and so on (refer to Figure 15-2). Below this toolbar are some drop-down lists that have to do with dates, a drop-down list called Columns, and a drop-down list called Sort By. (Not all these lists are available in every report document window. I don't know why, really. Maybe just to keep you guessing.)

You don't need to worry about these buttons and lists. Read through the discussion that follows only if you're feeling comfortable, relaxed, and truly mellow, okay?

Modifying

When you click the Modify Report button, QuickBooks displays the Modify Report dialog box, as shown in Figure 15-4. From this dialog box, you can change the information displayed on a report and the way that information is arranged (by using the Display tab); the data used to generate the report (by using the Filters tab); the header and footer information (by using, predictably, the Header/Footer tab); and the typeface and size of print used for a report (by using the Fonts & Numbers tab).

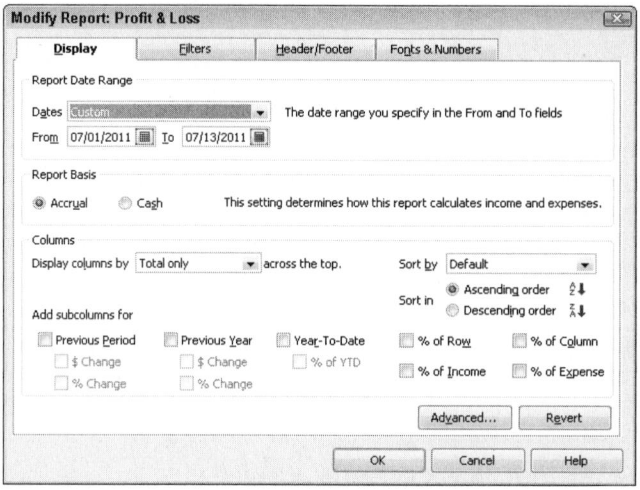

Figure 15-4:
The Modify
Report
dialog box.

Memorizing

If you do play around with the remaining buttons, you can save any custom report specifications that you create. Just click the Memorize button. QuickBooks displays the Memorize Report dialog box (shown in Figure 15-5), which asks you to supply a name for the customized report and assign the memorized report to a report group. After you name and assign the customized report, QuickBooks lists it whenever you choose Reports⇨Memorized Reports and then click the report group. You can also access Memorized Reports from the top of the Report Center screen. Whenever you want to use your special report, all you need to do is choose it from the list and click the Report button.

Figure 15-5:
The
Memorize
Report
dialog box.

QuickBooks memorizes the print orientation with the report, so if the print orientation isn't the way you want it for the report, you should first change it by choosing File⇨Printer Setup. Select the orientation you want to memorize, click OK, and then memorize the report.

E-mailing

If you click the E-Mail button, QuickBooks displays a drop-down list of commands that lets you e-mail either an Excel workbook or a PDF version of the report to someone else. When you choose the command that corresponds to the report file format you want to e-mail, QuickBooks displays the Edit E-Mail Information box. All you need to supply is the receiving person's e-mail address.

Exporting

If you click the Export button, QuickBooks displays the Export Report dialog box (see Figure 15-6). You can use this dialog box to create an Excel report that holds the same information as shown in the report. (To do this, just press Enter when you see the Export Report dialog box.) You can also get fancier in your exporting by exporting a comma-separated values file (these files can be opened by other electronic spreadsheet programs and by database programs), by exporting to a specific Excel workbook file, and by using the Advanced tab to control how the exported information is formatted.

A friendly suggestion, perhaps? Feel free to experiment with all the special exporting options. Just remember that after you export a QuickBooks report to a new, blank Excel workbook, you can also do any of this fancy-dancey stuff — special formatting and so on — there.

The other buttons and boxes

If you want to see how the Hide Header, Collapse, and Dates stuff work, just noodle around. You can't hurt anything.

If you change the report dates, click the Refresh button to update the report. (To set refresh options for reports, choose Edit➪Preferences. Then click the Reports & Graphs icon in the list on the left and click the My Preferences tab if necessary. Click one of the Reports and Graphs options and then click OK.)

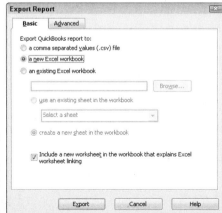

Figure 15-6:
The Export
Report
dialog box.

Reports Made to Order

If you intend to print a large number of reports — and, more important, if you intend to print a large number of reports and show them to customers, investors, and other significant people — you want your reports to look good and to be easy to understand. I believe that beauty is in the eye of the beholder, so I'm not going to get into the aesthetics of report layouts. What I am going to do is explain how you can make QuickBooks reports look exactly the way you want them to look.

Choose Edit➪Preferences. Click the Reports & Graphs icon in the list on the left and then click the Company Preferences tab to see the Preferences dialog box, as shown in Figure 15-7, for reports and graphs.

You need to be logged in to single-user mode as the administrator to change company preferences. Read how in Appendix C.

Figure 15-7:
The
Preferences
dialog box
for reports
and graphs.

Here are your options:

- **Accrual:** *Accrual* is one of those cruel accounting terms that are hard to understand at first. If you select the Accrual radio button in the Summary Reports Basis panel, you tell QuickBooks to include all your transactions, sales, purchases, expenses, and so on, from the moment they're recorded, not from the time you receive or pay cash for them.

  Accountants follow the accrual method because it gives a more accurate picture of profits. Also, the Internal Revenue Service (IRS) says that big corporations must use accrual accounting for their tax returns.

✔ **Cash:** If you select the Cash radio button, all the financial transactions in your reports are counted at the time you make your expense payments and you receive your customers' payments.

✔ **Age from Due Date:** If you select the Age from Due Date radio button in the Aging Reports panel, QuickBooks counts your expenses and invoices from the day that they fall due. Otherwise, QuickBooks counts them from the day they're recorded.

✔ **Format:** Click the Format button if you want to improve the look of your reports. In the Report Format Preferences dialog box that appears, as shown in Figure 15-8, you can use the Header/Footer tab to choose preferences for displaying the company name, the report title, the subtitle, and so on.

✔ **Reports – Show Accounts By:** You select a radio button in the Reports – Show Accounts By button group to indicate how you want QuickBooks to arrange account information on your reports: by name, by description, or by both name and description.

✔ **Statement of Cash Flows:** You click the Classify Cash button to tell QuickBooks how it should handle its accounts when it produces a picture-perfect statement of cash flows using generally accepted accounting principles. A suggestion? Leave this for your CPA.

You can use the Fonts & Numbers tab in the Report Format Preferences dialog box to choose preferences for displaying numbers, decimal fractions, and negative numbers. You also can fool around with different fonts and point sizes for labels, column headings, titles, and other things in your reports.

Figure 15-8:
The Report
Format
Preferences
dialog box.

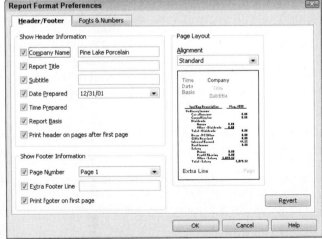

TIP

Click the Revert button in the Report Format Preferences dialog box to undo your customization changes.

Processing Multiple Reports

Want to print several reports at once? No problem. Choose Reports⇨Process Multiple Reports. When QuickBooks displays the Process Multiple Reports dialog box, as shown in Figure 15-9, select the reports that you want to print or display.

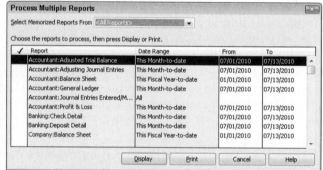

Figure 15-9:
The Process
Multiple
Reports
dialog box.

Last but Not Least: The QuickReport

The QuickReport is one of the best kinds of reports, so I saved it for last. You can generate a QuickReport from a list, from invoices and bills with names of people or items on them, and from account registers. QuickReports are especially useful when you're studying a list and see something that momentarily baffles you. Simply make sure that the item you're curious about is highlighted, click the Reports button, and choose the QuickReports command for the item from the drop-down list.

REMEMBER

You can also right-click an item and choose QuickReport from the shortcut menu to create a QuickReport of the item.

Figure 15-10 shows a QuickReport produced from a register. I clicked the QuickReport button to display this Register QuickReport window with the transaction information for a vendor: the fictitious Big Bertha's Workshop.

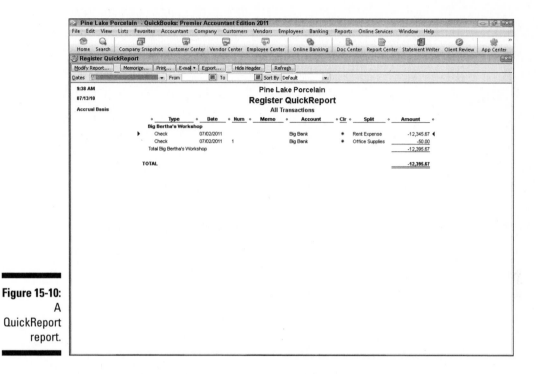

Figure 15-10:
A
QuickReport
report.

The QuickReport option is also on the Reports menu when you have a register or list open. Often times, then, you can display a QuickReport from a form — even though no QuickReport button appears — by choosing the menu option. For example, if you're writing a check to a vendor, you can enter the company's name on the check and choose Reports⇨QuickReport to see a report of transactions involving the company.

Chapter 16

Job Estimating, Billing, and Tracking

QuickBooks Pro and QuickBooks Premier have a feature that's very interesting for businesspeople — such as contractors, consultants, engineers, and architects — who do jobs or projects for their customers. QuickBooks Pro and QuickBooks Premier have the capability to do simple project or job costing. This capability means that your business can create project or job estimates, track costs by project or job, and bill invoices by project or job.

In this short chapter, I describe the QuickBooks job costing feature.

Turning On Job Costing

To turn on the job costing or estimating feature in QuickBooks, choose Edit⇨Preferences. Click the Jobs & Estimates icon on the left; click the Company Preferences tab (as shown in Figure 16-1); and then use the Do You Create Estimates? and Do You Do Progress Invoicing? radio buttons to tell QuickBooks whether, in fact, you want to do these things. You get this, right? You select the Yes radio button if you do, and select the No radio button if you don't.

Note: Progress billing or *progress invoicing* refers to the practice of billing or invoicing a client or customer as work on a project progresses. In other words, rather than invoice at the very end of a project, you might bill half the agreed-upon amount when work is roughly half done. And then you might bill the remaining half of the agreed-upon amount when the work is finally finished.

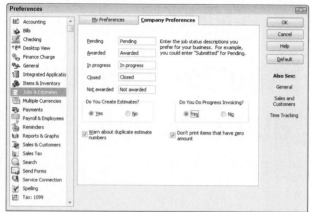

Figure 16-1:
The
Company
Preferences
tab show-
ing Jobs &
Estimates
options.

While you're looking at the Company Preferences tab (refer to Figure 16-1), let me also mention that as the figure shows, QuickBooks lets you categorize jobs as falling into several different status categories: Pending, Awarded, In Progress, Closed, and Not Awarded. As you might guess, you use these Job Status descriptions to categorize your jobs.

Setting Up a Job

If you want to use QuickBooks job costing, your first step is to set up a job. For example, if you're a contractor, you can use QuickBooks to track the invoices and costs of the remodeling jobs you do. You just need to set up a job every time you get ready to bid on a project.

To set up a job, first set up a customer in the usual way. Then set up a job also in the usual way. In Chapter 3, I describe how you do all this, so I don't repeat that information here. Just to save you time, however, all you need to do is choose Customers⇨Customer Center to display the Customer Center window, right-click the customer for whom you might do a job, and then choose Add Job from the Customer:Job pop-up menu. When QuickBooks displays the New Job window, describe the job by filling out the fields in the window that QuickBooks displays.

Creating a Job Estimate

In QuickBooks, job costing starts with an estimate. An *estimate* is just a list of the estimated costs you'll incur for some job you'll perform for some customer.

Assuming that you've already created a job and have told QuickBooks that you use estimates, here are the steps that you follow to create an estimate:

1. **Choose Customers➪Create Estimates.**

   QuickBooks opens a Create Estimates form (see Figure 16-2), which bears an uncanny resemblance to the Create Invoices form that you've seen if you've worked with QuickBooks at all. (Refer to Chapter 4 for more information about the Create Invoices form.)

2. **Start filling in the blanks.**

   Choose the appropriate Customer:Job from the drop-down list at the top of the form. QuickBooks automatically fills in as much information as it can — usually at least the Name/Address text box — on the form.

   If you configured QuickBooks to track classes, the appropriate drop-down list shows up in the top center of the form. Go ahead and use the box, if appropriate.

   Feel free to change the default settings — the Date and Estimate #, for example. The Date Setting tricks that you can find in Chapter 4 and on the online Cheat Sheet can be found at www.dummies.com/cheatsheet/quickbooks2011.

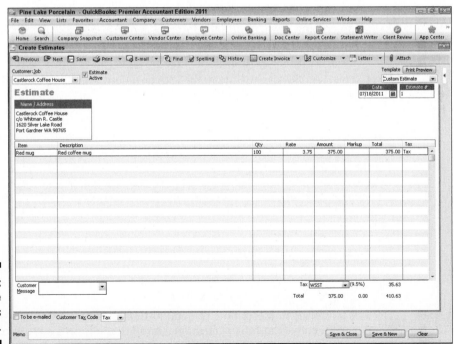

Figure 16-2: The Create Estimates window.

3. **Add the line items — details, details, details.**

   You fill in the details of a Create Estimates window in the same way that you fill in the details of a Create Invoices window. Read Chapter 4 if you have questions.

   One field that is unique to the Create Estimates window is Markup. The Markup field, which appears on some versions of the Create Estimates window, adds a specified percentage of the line item price total. Refer to Figure 16-2, where I specified the markup percentages as zero, so the Amount column values match the Total column values. However, if I had specified a 50 percent markup using the Markup column, the values shown in the Total column would all be 50 percent greater. The Markup field doesn't appear on all versions of the Estimates template: only the Custom Estimate and Proposal templates.

   In Chapter 3, I describe how to add items to the QuickBooks Items list. Each line item that you want to include on your job estimate needs to be described in the Items list. Note that because you often sell work to clients and customers by using, in part, an estimate, you'll typically want to include full descriptions of the items. (My construction-contractor clients, for example, often use several lines of descriptive text to fully explain each item that shows on the estimate.)

4. **(Optional) Add any optional information.**

   Use any of the other boxes available in the Create Estimates window to collect and store additional information. For example, just as with the Create Invoices window, you can click the Customer Message drop-down list and choose or write a friendly message.

   You can also use the Memo field to write a note to yourself regarding the job. Or maybe add some notes about the screenplay that you've been thinking about pitching to the studios. Whatever suits your fancy.

If you want to include other items in the Create Estimates window, you can customize that window. Choose Customize from the Template drop-down list in the upper-right corner of the Create Estimates window. QuickBooks gives you a list of your estimate forms. Choose the one you want to edit. (You may have only one estimate form on the list if you've never created a new one.) Click either the New or the Edit button. If you click New, QuickBooks displays the Customize Estimate dialog box.

In Chapter 4, I talk a bit about how to customize invoice forms. You may want to look there if you have questions about how to customize the Create Invoices form.

Before you print that estimate, remember that information in the Create Estimates window isn't the same information that appears on the written estimate. To see how the printed version looks, click the down arrow beside the Print button in the Create Estimates window, and choose Preview from the drop-down list. The result is a full-page image, shrunk to fit onscreen.

If you haven't saved your estimate yet, go ahead and click either the Save & New button or the Save & Close button.

To examine the estimate (or any onscreen QuickBooks form) more closely, either click the Zoom In button at the top of the Print Preview screen or move the mouse cursor over the image. When the cursor looks like a magnifying glass with a plus sign in it, click the left mouse button. Because you can see only part of the preview this way, use the scroll bars at the bottom and right of the windows to move around to the different areas.

Note that the magnifying glass now has a minus sign in it, and the Zoom In button toggles to Zoom Out. If you complete more than one estimate, you can use the Prev Page and Next Page buttons on the Print Preview screen to look at other estimates. When you finish, click the Close button.

When you get back to the Create Estimates window, click the Print button; QuickBooks Pro displays the Print One Estimate dialog box. Click Print to print the estimate without any further ado.

If you haven't used QuickBooks to print estimates before, you may need to set up your printer for this task first. To do so, choose File⇨Printer Setup and then choose Estimate from the Form Name drop-down list. Specify the printer settings that you want for printing estimates. (This process works the same way as it does for printing other forms, such as invoices, as I describe in Chapter 4.) Click OK when you're done. The Print One Estimate dialog box that QuickBooks displays after you click Print in the Create Estimates window also works the same way as the Print One Invoice dialog box does. Read Chapter 4 if you need help with this dialog box.

Revising an Estimate

To revise an estimate, display the Create Estimates window, as described earlier in this chapter. Then click the Previous button until you see the estimate.

Make your changes, and QuickBooks recalculates all the totals. Smile. Imagine doing this task by hand — the recalculations, the looking up of prices, the retyping, the inordinate amount of wasted time. Making these changes automatically with QuickBooks doesn't quite beat a hot dog with sauerkraut in the park on a sunny day, but it's pretty close.

You can keep only one estimate per job. After you click Save & New, any changes that you make automatically take the place of the old estimate. If you make changes to an estimate, though, you can tell QuickBooks to treat the revision as a change order. With a change order, the modifications to an existing estimate get added to the bottom of the estimate. Cool, right?

Turning an Estimate into an Invoice

You can easily turn the estimate into an invoice by following these steps:

1. **On the Customer Center screen, select your customer.**

   QuickBooks shows you a list of transactions for the customer, including any active estimates.

2. **Double-click the estimate you want to work with.**

   The Create Estimates window opens. (Refer to Figure 16-2.)

3. **Click the Create Invoice button at the top of the window.**

   If you indicated that you might progress-bill a customer or client, QuickBooks displays a dialog box that asks whether you want to invoice the entire estimate or just some portion of the estimate. Answer the question by marking the appropriate option button. Then click OK. QuickBooks creates an invoice based on your estimate (see Figure 16-3). If you need to make any changes, you edit the invoice directly and then click OK to continue.

   If you don't see the Create Invoice button at the top of your Create Estimates window, maximize the window's size so it fills the QuickBooks program window. If QuickBooks can't quite fit everything into the Create Estimates window, QuickBooks removes the Create Invoice button to make room. But increasing the window size should solve the problem.

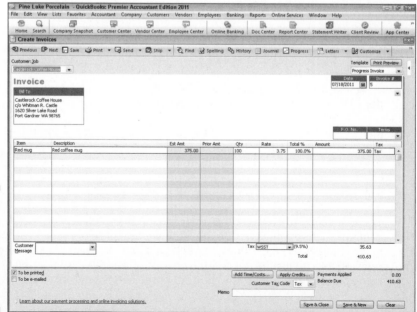

Figure 16-3:
The Create Invoices window with the data from Figure 16-2.

4. **(Optional) Make any necessary changes to the resulting invoice.**

   The invoice that you see is a regular QuickBooks invoice, and you can edit it the same way that you edit any invoice. Until you click Save & New, the invoice isn't recorded in your records.

5. **After you make all your changes, click Save & New or Save & Close to record the invoice.**

   If you want to print the invoice instead, you can click the Print button.

Comparing Estimated Item Amounts with Actual Item Amounts

In the previous paragraphs, I describe how you can take an estimate and create an invoice by using that estimate as a starting point. I also say that you can edit the numbers that come off the estimate. Now, here's an interesting job costing point: QuickBooks prints reports — like the one in Figure 16-4 — that let you compare the item estimates shown on the original estimates with the actual billed items shown on invoices.

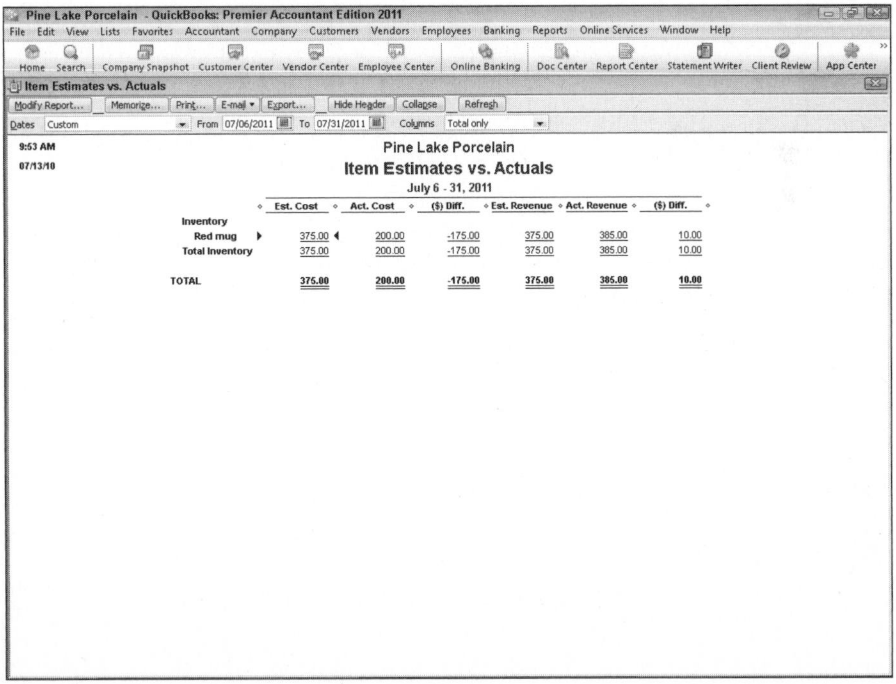

Figure 16-4: An Item Estimates vs. Actuals report.

To produce such a report, choose Report Center➪Jobs, Time & Mileage➪ Item Estimates vs. Actuals. QuickBooks displays a report that lets you compare estimated amounts with invoiced amounts. If you bid jobs by using estimates but must invoice with actual numbers, such a report is a great way to see how good of a job you're doing in your estimating.

Charging for Actual Time and Costs

If you charge a customer for actual costs and hours, you need to track the costs and time when you incur the charges for them. You assign the cost to the job by entering the customer and job information into the Customer:Job column that's shown in the form window used to record a particular cost or time charge. For example, if you use the Enter Bills window (refer to Chapter 6) to record a bill for a particular job, you use the Customer:Job column to designate the job.

To charge a customer for costs or time that you recorded, follow these steps:

1. **Choose Customers➪Create Invoices to open the Create Invoices window.**

2. **Change the name in the Customer:Job drop-down list to the proper customer.**

   This step is easy: Activate the drop-down list and choose the appropriate customer and job. If you've assigned time or costs to this customer, a screen pops up, asking you to click the Time/Costs button to include the charges in your invoice.

3. **Click the Add Time/Costs button.**

   QuickBooks displays the Choose Billable Time and Costs dialog box. The dialog box already shows the costs and time charges that you assigned to this customer and job combination.

4. **Select the billable time and costs that you want to add to the invoice.**

   Check the time charges and costs that you want to bill for. Note that the Choose Billable Time and Costs dialog box provides different tabs for Items, Expenses, and Mileage.

5. **(Optional, Expenses only) Indicate the markup.**

   The Expenses tab has a couple extra fields at the top of the tab to indicate the Markup Amount or % and the Markup Account. If applicable, fill in the fields with the appropriate information.

6. **(Optional) Indicate whether you want the charges to appear as a single item on the invoice.**

   If you want to avoid listing the gory details of the charges to your customer, check the Print Selected Time and Costs as One Invoice Item check box located in the bottom-left corner of the invoice.

7. **Click OK.**

   After you have everything the way you want it, click OK. As if by magic — even if it was by your hard work and the sweat of your own brow — the invoice appears.

8. **(Optional) Add anything else you want to include on the invoice.**

   This invoice is a regular QuickBooks invoice, remember? You may want to click the down arrow beside the Print button and choose Preview from the drop-down list to make sure that only the job costs that you want to appear do appear.

9. **Click Save & New or Save & Close.**

   That's how you record the invoice.

After you record the invoice, the job costs that have been billed are removed from the Choose Billable Time and Costs window. You're finished. Breathe easier.

You can also track the amount of time that you or other employees spend on clients or customers. To turn on time-tracking, choose Edit⇨Preferences, scroll down to and click the Time Tracking icon, and then select the Time Tracking Yes radio button. After you do this, you can track the time that you spend on a client or customer by choosing Customers⇨Enter Time⇨Use Weekly Timesheet or Customers⇨Enter Time⇨Time/Enter Single Activity. Either command displays an easy-to-understand window that lets you record time spent on a particular client or customer.

And a final important point: The time-tracker clock keeps ticking as long as the QuickBooks program runs. The program doesn't need to be the active Windows program to continue working. (I mention this because in some older versions of QuickBooks, the timer stops if you start working with another program, such as your word processor or e-mail program.)

Tracking Job Costs

To see the costs assigned or allocated to a project, use the Job, Time & Mileage Reports, which are available when you choose Reports⇨Jobs, Time & Mileage. You can experiment with the different reports to see which provides the information in a format and at a level of detail that works best for you. For example, if you're invoicing customers by job and collecting cost data by customer and job, you can produce great job-profitability reports that show what you've made by job. Also note that you can budget amounts by customer and job (using the same budgeting technique described in Chapter 12). If you do the extra work of budgeting by customer job, you can also compare actual job revenues and costs with budgeted job revenues and costs.

Chapter 17

File Management Tips

*O*kay, you don't need to worry about the data files that QuickBooks stores your financial information in. Pretty much, QuickBooks does all the dirty work. But that said, you do have a few housekeeping tasks to take care of. In this chapter, I describe these chores and how to do them correctly with minimal hassle.

Backing Up Is (Not That) Hard to Do

Sure, I can give you some tricky, technical examples of fancy backup strategies, but they have no point here. You want to know the basics, right?

The guiding rule is that you back up anytime you work on something that you wouldn't want to redo. Some people think that a week's worth of work is negligible, and others think that a month's worth of work is negligible.

So here's what I do to back up my files. I back up every week after I enter my data for the week. Then I stick the disk (you might use any removable disk, such as a USB flash drive, a Zip disk, or a writable CD) in my briefcase so that if something terrible happens (like a meteor hitting my office building), I don't lose both my computer and the backup disk with the data. (I carry my briefcase around with me — a sort of middle-age security blanket — so that it won't get destroyed in some after-hours disaster.)

Sounds like a pretty good system, huh? Actually, I admit that my strategy has its problems:

- ✔ Because I back up weekly, I might have to re-enter as much as a week's worth of data if the computer crashes toward the end of the week. In my case, I wouldn't lose all that much work. However, if you're someone with heavy transaction volumes — if you prepare hundreds of invoices or write hundreds of checks each week, for example — you probably want to back up more frequently, perhaps every day.

- ✔ A second problem with my strategy is only remotely possible but still worth mentioning: If something bad happens to the QuickBooks files stored on my computer's hard drive as well as the files stored on the backup flash drive, CD-R, CD-RW, or Zip disk, I'll be up the proverbial creek without a paddle. (I should also note that a removable disk — especially a floppy — is far more likely to fail than a hard drive and is easier to lose.) If this worst-case scenario actually occurs, I'll need to start over from scratch from the beginning of the year.

Some people, who are religiously careful, circulate three sets of backup disks to reduce the chance of this mishap. They also regularly move one copy off-site, such as to a safe deposit box. In this scenario, whenever you back up your data, you overwrite the oldest set of backup disks.

Say you back up your data every week, and your hard drive not only crashes, but also bursts into a ball of flames rising high into the night. To restore your files, you use the most recent set of backups — one-week old, max. If something is wrong with those, you use the next–most-recent set — two weeks old. If something is wrong with those, you use the last set — three weeks old. This way, you have three chances to get a set that works — a nice bit of security for the cost of a few extra disks or storage devices.

Backing up the quick-and-dirty way

You're busy. You don't have time to fool around. You just want to do a passable job of backing up, and you decided how often you plan to do it. Sound like your situation? Then follow these steps:

1. **Insert a blank disk/disc into the appropriate drive.**

   You can back up to any removable disk, including flash memory devices, floppy disks, Zip disks, and writable CDs. However, note that Intuit (the maker of QuickBooks) now recommends that you not use the QuickBooks backup command to move a backup file onto a CD. Instead, Intuit recommends you back up the file onto your hard drive and then use the Windows File Copy command to burn the file onto the disc. This workaround approach tends to solve some of the CD-writing problems people experience when backing up directly to a CD.

rock

Heck, I should admit that you can back up to any fixed disk, such as your hard drive or a network disk, but the advantage of a removable disk is that you can store it in some other location. As a compromise, you can also use a network disk. You typically don't want to use your hard drive (although this is better than nothing) because one of the disasters that might befall your QuickBooks data is a hard drive failure.

You can also back up your QuickBooks files to an online storage area. See the sidebar "Backing up files online" for more information.

2. **If you store data for more than one company, make sure that the company whose data you want to back up is the active company.**

   Yes, I know that all your companies are active; I'm hoping they're not dead in the water. My point is that you want to back up the correct company. To find out whether the correct company is active, just look at the QuickBooks application window title bar, which names the active company. (If you don't remember setting up multiple files, don't worry. You probably have only one file — the usual case.)

3. **Choose File⇨Create Back Up to begin the backup operation.**

   QuickBooks displays the first Save Backup dialog box (see Figure 17-1).

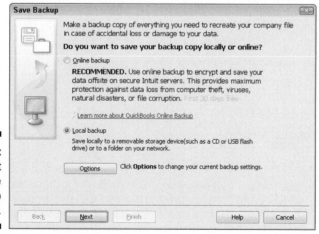

Figure 17-1: The first Save Backup dialog box.

If you use QuickBooks in multi-user mode, you need to switch to single-user mode before you back up your file. For more information on how to make this switch, see Appendix C.

4. **Tell QuickBooks where you want to back up the QuickBooks data file.**

   When QuickBooks displays the first Save Backup dialog box — the one shown previously in Figure 17-1 — specify the location for the backup by clicking either the Online Backup or Local Backup button.

To back up your QuickBooks file locally — this is my recommendation for new QuickBooks users, but do see the upcoming sidebar on backing up files online — select the Local Backup option.

5. **Describe how QuickBooks should back up your data file.**

With the first Save Backup dialog box still displayed, click the Options button. QuickBooks displays the Backup Options dialog box (see Figure 17-2), from which you specify how and when QuickBooks backs up your data file:

- *Pick a default location.* Specify where the backup file should be located. You can do this either by entering the pathname of the backup folder in the Tell Us Where to Save Your Backup Copies box (the hard way) or by clicking the Browse button and then using the Browse for Folder dialog box that Windows displays to pick a default backup location.

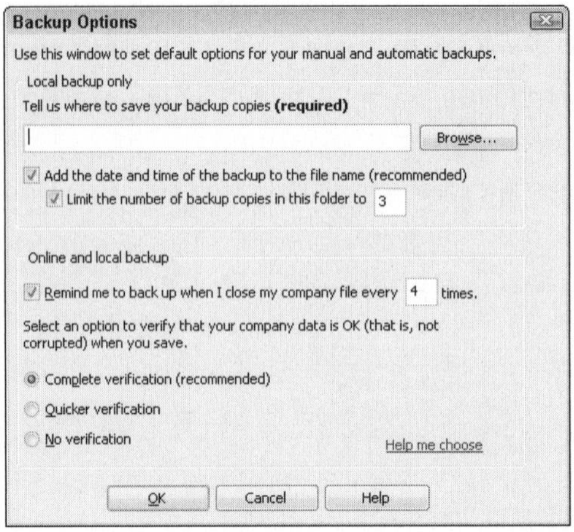

Figure 17-2:
The Backup
Options
dialog box.

- *Fine-tune the backup operation.* The Backup Options dialog box provides a couple check boxes that you can use to fine-tune the old QuickBooks backup operation. The Add the Date and Time of Backup to the File Name check box, if selected, does just what it says. The Limit the Number of Backup Copies in this Folder To [X] check box tells QuickBooks to limit the number of backup copies of your QuickBooks file it stores in the backup folder. The default number of backup copies kept on hand is three; that should be fine.

- *Specify the backup reminder rule.* You can select the Remind Me to Back Up When I Close My Company File Every [X] Times check box to tell QuickBooks it should remind you every so often to back up. By default, QuickBooks reminds you every fourth time you close a data file, but you can replace the value in the text box to specify some other backup reminder frequency.

- *Select a data verification option.* QuickBooks provides three data verification options, which appear as radio buttons on the Backup Options dialog box (refer to Figure 17-2). You can select the button that corresponds to the data verification method you want: Complete Verification (safe but slow), Quicker Verification (fast but not as thorough), and No Verification (saves you a bit of time now at the risk of huge problems later). The Complete Verification option is what QuickBooks and I both recommend.

When you finish with the Backup Options dialog box, click OK. QuickBooks displays the second Save Backup dialog box, Save Backup: When (see Figure 17-3).

Figure 17-3:
The second
Backup
Wizard
dialog box.

6. **Determine when QuickBooks should back up your data file.**

   The second Backup Wizard dialog box provides radio buttons that you use to schedule when you want to back up. For example, to indicate that you want to back up on the spot, select the Save It Now radio button.

7. **Confirm the backup file location and name.**

   With the second Backup Wizard dialog box displayed (refer to Figure 17-3), click Next. QuickBooks displays the Save Backup Copy dialog box (see Figure 17-4). If you successfully completed Step 5, you already specified the appropriate folder location for the backup file. Just to be on the safe side, confirm that the filename and folder location shown in the Save Backup Copy dialog box are correct. If the folder location isn't correct, select a new folder location from the Save In drop-down list. If the filename isn't correct, edit the name shown in the File Name text box.

Figure 17-4:
The Save
Backup
Copy dialog
box.

8. **Click Save.**

   QuickBooks backs up your data file and displays a message box that tells you it has backed up your file. The message also gives the backup filename and folder location.

Backing up files online

You can quickly and easily back up your data online. If you do so, you no longer need to remember to make backups and take them offsite. To find out more about online backup, choose File⇨Create Backup and click the Learn More about QuickBooks Online Backup link.

The Online Backup service is a pretty darn good idea if you have a fast Internet connection, but the service costs a little bit of money. You pay at least $50 yearly and as much as $220 yearly, depending on the level of service, but you can set up the service so that QuickBooks automatically backs up your data and even other important files on a regular basis. I think this is pretty cool.

Two final points about using the QuickBooks online backup option. First, and just for the record, I don't think you need to worry about security. (You can read more about the security measures at the QuickBooks Web site, but your data is as secure online as it is in your office.) Second, I think most folks should use the service. I use it. Online offsite backup at the prices that Intuit offers seems like a really excellent deal for any business where the QuickBooks data files are important.

Getting back the QuickBooks data you backed up

What happens if you lose all your QuickBooks data? First of all, I encourage you to feel smug. Get a cup of coffee. Lean back in your chair. Gloat for a couple minutes. You, my friend, have no problem. You have followed instructions.

Okay, you may have one or two problems, but you can probably blame PC gremlins for those. If the disaster that caused you to lose your data also trashed other parts of your computer, you may need to reinstall QuickBooks. You also may need to reinstall all your other software.

After you gloat sufficiently (and piece your computer back together again if it was the cause of the disaster), carefully do the following to reinstate your QuickBooks data:

1. **Get your backup disk.**

   Find the backup disk you created and carefully insert it into the appropriate disk drive or USB port.

2. **Start QuickBooks and choose File⇨Open or Restore Company.**

   QuickBooks displays the Open or Restore Company dialog box (see Figure 17-5).

Figure 17-5:
The Open or Restore Company dialog box.

3. **Indicate that you want to restore a backup copy of your QuickBooks data file.**

   How you do this is probably obvious, right? Select the Restore a Backup Copy option button.

4. **Tell QuickBooks whether you backed up locally or online.**

   Click Next to continue. QuickBooks displays the Restore Backup: Method dialog box (not shown). Select the Local Backup radio button to indicate that you made a local backup.

5. **Identify the backup file that you want to use.**

   Click Next to continue. QuickBooks displays the Open Backup Copy dialog box (see Figure 17-6). If you know the company filename and location, you can enter this information in the boxes provided. If you don't know this information, use the Look In drop-down list to identify the drive that contains the file you want to back up. Then choose the backup file you want to restore and click Open. QuickBooks displays the Open or Restore Company dialog box (not shown) telling you that the next step (where you specify the restoration location) is pretty darn important.

Figure 17-6:
The Open
Backup
Copy
dialog box.

6. **Specify where the restored file will be located.**

   Click Next again. QuickBooks displays the Save Company File As dialog box (see Figure 17-7). Use the File Name text box and Save In drop-down list in the Save Company File As dialog box to identify the file you want to replace.

   If you know the company filename and location, you can enter this information in the text boxes provided. If you don't know this information, use the Save In drop-down list to make sure that you place the restored file in the correct folder on the correct drive.

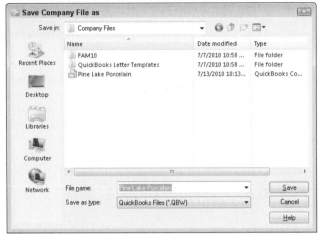

Figure 17-7:
The Save
Company
File As
dialog box.

7. Click Save.

If the file you're trying to restore already exists, you see a message box telling you so. Click Yes to overwrite and replace the file with the one stored on the backup disk, or click No to keep the original copy.

QuickBooks may ask you for your password to verify that you have administrative permission to restore the file. Then, if everything goes okay, you see a message box that says so. Breathe a deep sigh of relief and give thanks.

Oops. I almost forgot:

✔ When you restore a file, you replace the current version of the file with the backup version stored on the backup medium. Don't restore a file for fun. Restore a file only if the current version is trashed and you want to start over by using the version stored on the backup disk.

✔ You need to re-enter everything you entered since you made the backup copy. I know. You're bummed out. Hopefully, it hasn't been all that long since you backed up.

Accountant's Copy

Hey. While I'm on the subject of the housecleaning stuff that you can do with your QuickBooks files, let me mention the Accountant's Copy feature.

Accountant's Review allows your accountant to make adjustments in a special copy of your QuickBooks data file while you continue to enter your daily transactions in the master file. When your accountant returns the updated file, you can merge the changes back into the master file.

To use Accountant's Review, choose File➪Create Copy. Select the Accountant's Copy option and then follow the onscreen instructions. You can import the accountant's changes later. If you need help with this feature, talk to your accountant.

You should never upgrade to a newer version of QuickBooks while your accountant is still working with the accountant's copy. Or at least you shouldn't do this if you plan on using the accountant's changes. If an active accountant's copy is in use, your screen will state that at the very top, next to the company name.

Working with Portable Files

QuickBooks includes a portable-files feature. A *portable file* is a smaller, condensed version of the QuickBooks data file. The portable file is small enough, in fact, that you can probably e-mail it to your accountant, your sister in Portland, or me.

To create a portable file, choose File➪Create Copy. When QuickBooks displays the first Save Copy or Backup dialog box, select the Portable Company File radio button, click Next, and then follow the onscreen instructions. The process, by the way, resembles the backup process described earlier in this chapter. I find it really easy to save the file on the desktop. Then you can attach it easily to your e-mail and send it out. After the other party receives the file, you can just drag your copy to the Recycle Bin. Your real file remains intact. (A portable file must typically be 10 MB or less in size for transmission through most e-mail services.)

To open a portable file, a person (this could be your accountant, your sister in Portland, or me) should choose File➪Open or Restore Company. When QuickBooks displays the Open or Restore Company dialog box (refer to Figure 17-5), this other person just specifies the file that he or she wants to open as a portable file and then follows the onscreen instructions.

Using an Audit Trail

For some curious reason, in the post-Enron world of accounting, people are much more interested in the QuickBooks Audit Trail feature. In fact, some readers of past editions of this book have tracked me down as though I were a wounded animal so that they could ask about audit trails in QuickBooks. Because of this renewed interest, let me share the three things you need to know about using the QuickBooks Audit Trail feature:

✔ An *audit trail* is simply a list of changes. The QuickBooks Audit Trail — which is a simple report that lists the changes to the QuickBooks data file — lets you see who changed what.

✔ To turn on the Audit Trail feature in old versions of QuickBooks, you had to choose Edit⇨Preferences, click the Accounting icon, click the Company Preferences tab, and then select the Use Audit Trail check box. However, ever since QuickBooks 2006, you don't have to turn on the Audit Trail feature. It's always on, baby.

✔ You can print the Audit Trail report by choosing Reports⇨Accountant & Taxes⇨Audit Trail.

Using a Closing Password

QuickBooks doesn't require you to or even let you "close" months and years, the way old manual accounting systems did. (When you "closed" an old accounting period, you actually zeroed-out the revenue and expense accounts and transferred the net amount to the owner's equity accounts.)

However, QuickBooks does let you use a closing date and password. The closing date sort of prevents someone from entering transactions earlier than the specified date. If you set a closing password, for example, someone needs to supply that password before entering a transaction or changing a transaction dated before the closing date. If you don't set a closing password, someone trying to enter or change a transaction dated before the closing date is warned, but he or she can still create or change the entry.

To set a closing date, choose Edit⇨Preferences, click the Accounting icon, click the Company Preferences tab, click the Set Date/Password button, and then enter the closing date (probably the end of the most recently completed year) in the Date Through Which Books Are Closed box. To use a closing password, click the Set Password button and use the dialog box that QuickBooks displays to create the closing password. ***Note:*** QuickBooks lets you check the Exclude Estimates, Sales Orders and Purchase Orders from Closing Date Restrictions box to not lose access to these transactions as part of the closing.

Chapter 18

Fixed Assets and Vehicle Lists

*I*n this chapter, I cover two specialty topics of modest interest to a small handful of business owners: how the QuickBooks Fixed Asset list works and how the QuickBooks vehicle mileage-tracking tool works.

Let me say at the outset that you may not need these tools. QuickBooks users commonly think the tools do more than they really do. In some situations, though, business owners and accountants truly do find these two simple tools helpful.

But you know what? I'm getting ahead of myself. Let me start at the start.

What Is Fixed Assets Accounting?

So that you understand where the Fixed Asset list and vehicle mileage tracker fit into the scheme of things, let me begin by defining the term *fixed assets* and by explaining just what *fixed assets accounting* is.

Fixed assets historically refer to assets that are fixed in place. For example, a factory or building set into concrete is fixed. Likewise, a 20-ton piece of machinery bolted into the floor is also fixed.

In the context of QuickBooks and its Fixed Asset list, fixed assets also include items such as furniture, equipment, and vehicles — things that aren't so "fixed" but instead are assets that last a long time — that a business, therefore, must depreciate.

Now that you know what fixed assets is — at least according to Steve Nelson — let me define fixed assets accounting. *Fixed assets accounting,* I'm going to say, refers to three accounting tasks:

- ✔ Tracking your fixed assets' costs, descriptions, and other relevant information so that you can take proper care of your stuff

- ✔ Calculating and recording fixed assets' depreciation so that tax returns and financial statements can be prepared

- ✔ Calculating and recording the effect, including the gain or loss, stemming from the disposal of fixed assets so that tax returns and financial statements can be prepared

Obviously, this fixed assets accounting stuff is important, but let me throw you a curveball. I'm not sure you need to worry about this stuff.

Now, of course, you want to keep track of fixed assets so that you know what you own. This stuff-you-own information is pretty essential for thinking smartly about how much insurance you should purchase, for example. You may also pay property taxes on this stuff so that's another good reason to really know what you have.

And ditto on your need to be able to depreciate your fixed assets and to keep track of what happens when you sell a fixed asset. Shoot, you don't have to be in business more than about a year before you know that tax laws and generally accepted accounting principles say that you have to do this, regardless of whether you want to.

But here's my lazy-boy thinking. You know your accountant? The woman or man who does your taxes? She or he is already keeping such a list to calculate the correct amount of depreciation that you should enter onto your income tax returns. This makes me wonder why you need to maintain a second, duplicate list.

To me, you need to do the fixed assets accounting yourself in only two situations:

- ✔ **Because you have so much stuff that your poor accountant needs or would benefit from help in tracking the stuff:** This will be the case if you have hundreds or thousands of items.

- ✔ **Because you don't use an outside accountant:** You, therefore, are yourself the poor sap who has to do this fixed accounting work.

Hopefully, most readers can just quit their reading at this point. Most readers now realize that their accountants are almost certainly already doing their fixed assets accounting work. Most readers, in fact, will realize that they really don't need to worry about noodling around with the QuickBooks Fixed Asset list at all!

However, be cautious here. Perhaps a quick telephone call to your accountant can confirm that your fixed assets accounting is already being performed. Another way to check this is to look carefully at last year's tax return. Do you see, buried somewhere near the back of the return, a listing of your fixed assets? If so, skip this chapter.

If you realize that you need to handle the fixed assets accounting yourself, keep reading.

Fixed Assets Accounting in QuickBooks

Fixed assets accounting amounts to three things:

- ✔ Keeping a list of the assets that you own
- ✔ Recording depreciation on any depreciable assets
- ✔ Recording the disposal of an asset, including any gain or loss on disposal

The Fixed Asset list, which I describe in the next section, takes care of the first task. The Fixed Asset list doesn't directly help you with the second or third tasks shown in the preceding list, though. You need to understand this important point. You still need to calculate and then enter asset depreciation. And when you dispose of an asset, you still need to construct a journal entry that records the disposition.

Chapter 20 describes how depreciation works and how you go about recording the disposal of an asset. Read that chapter if you want to know how that stuff works.

Setting Up a Fixed Asset List

As noted earlier in the chapter, if your business owns a lot of stuff with long-lasting value, either you or your accountant needs to keep track of the items. If you need to track the items, you can do so by using the Fixed Asset list.

Adding items to the Fixed Asset list

To add a piece of furniture, some bit of equipment or machinery, or another item of long-lived value to the Fixed Asset list, follow these steps:

1. **Display the Fixed Asset list.**

   To display the Fixed Asset list, choose Lists⇨Fixed Asset Item List. QuickBooks displays the Fixed Asset Item List window, as shown in Figure 18-1. Initially, because you haven't yet added any assets, the list shows no assets.

   Have assets you've purchased already? You can edit the original purchase transaction and add the fixed asset to the list during editing.

2. **Tell QuickBooks that you want to add an item to the Fixed Asset list.**

   Click the Item button and then choose New from the menu that QuickBooks displays. QuickBooks displays the New Item window, as shown in Figure 18-2.

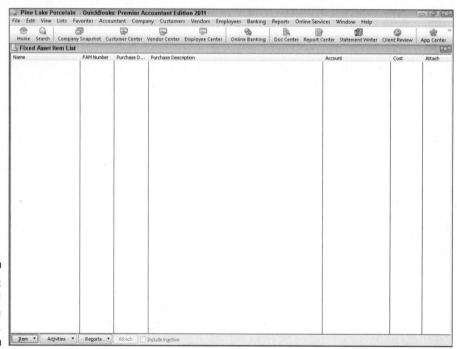

Figure 18-1:
The Fixed Asset Item List window.

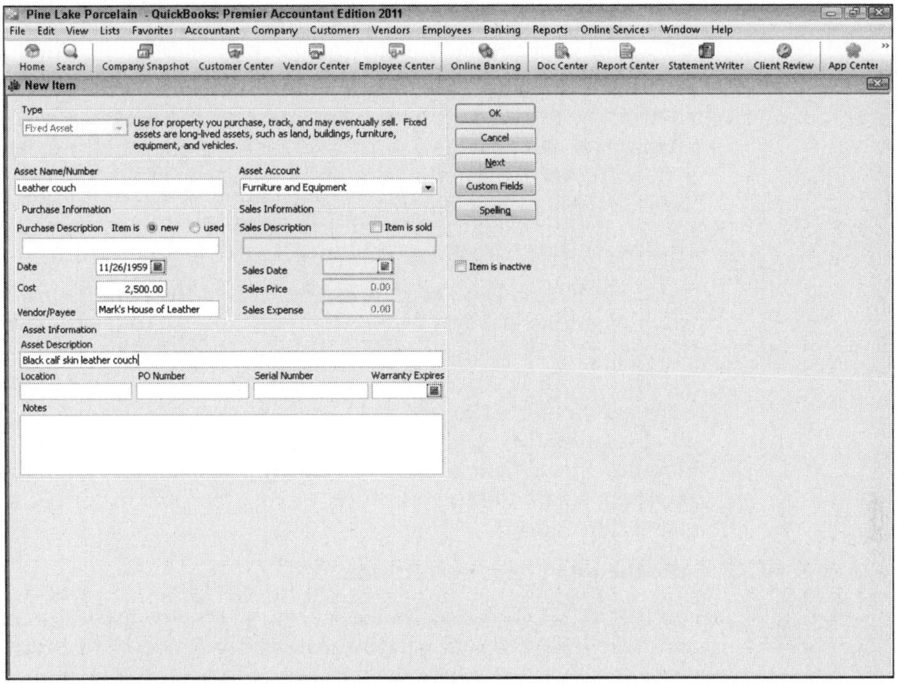

Figure 18-2:
The New
Item
window.

3. **Name the asset.**

   Give the asset a unique name. For example, you might give a piece of furniture a name like *Leather couch,* a computer a name like *HP Pavilion,* and a vehicle a name like *'02 Chevy S20 Pickup.*

4. **Select the appropriate fixed asset account.**

   From the Asset Account drop-down list, select the fixed asset account in which the asset you're describing should be placed. A leather couch used in your opulent reception area, for example, should probably be placed in a furniture fixed asset account. A piece of machinery should probably be placed in an equipment fixed asset account.

   QuickBooks, as you might guess, supplies a bunch of accounts automatically, but you may not see the account you need or want in the Asset Account drop-down list. You can add a new asset account on-the-fly, so to speak, by entering a new account name and pressing Enter. When QuickBooks sees that the fixed asset account isn't yet set up, it prompts you to set up the new fixed asset account.

5. **Describe the purchase terms.**

   Use the Purchase Information area to describe the item that you purchased and the purchase terms. For example, you want to indicate
   whether the item is new or used by marking the New or Used radio
   button. You can provide a purchase description, purchase date, purchase
   cost, and even identify the vendor by using the other, self-explanatory
   boxes in the Purchase Information area.

6. **(Optional) Describe the asset in further detail.**

   The Asset Information area at the bottom of the New Item window
   provides additional text boxes that you can use to describe the asset.
   The area provides a humongous field in which to place a lengthy asset
   description, for example. You also have fields you can use to identify
   the asset location, the original purchase order (PO) number, the asset's
   serial number, and the warranty expiration date. If these fields aren't
   adequate, heck, QuickBooks even supplies a Notes area that you can use
   to write a small ode to your asset or record some other bit of relevant
   asset information.

7. **Save the asset item description.**

   You can click OK to simultaneously save the new asset item description
   and close the New Item window. Alternatively, you can click Next to
   save the new asset item description but leave the New Item window
   displayed.

Adding fixed asset items on-the-fly

You can add items to the Fixed Asset list, as described in the preceding
paragraphs. Alternatively, you can add an item to the Fixed Asset list when
you record the bill that records the vendor invoice for the asset or when you
record the check that pays the vendor invoice for the asset.

Here's how this works: If you told QuickBooks that you want to maintain a
Fixed Asset list, QuickBooks prompts you to add a fixed asset item when you
categorize, or debit, a fixed asset account while entering a bill or recording
a check.

To collect the information required to set up the fixed asset item, QuickBooks
displays the same New Item window (refer to Figure 18-2). The steps that I
provide in the preceding section for filling in the New Item window also work
when adding fixed asset items on-the-fly.

Editing items on the Fixed Asset list

To edit a fixed asset item, follow these steps:

1. **Choose Lists⇨Fixed Asset Item List.**

   QuickBooks displays the Fixed Asset Item List window. (Refer to Figure 18-1.)

2. **Double-click the item that you want to edit.**

   QuickBooks displays the Edit Item window, as shown in Figure 18-3.

3. **Update the asset description.**

   As necessary, update the information shown in the Purchase Information and the Asset Information areas. Note, too, that if you want to record the disposal of an asset, you can select the Item Is Sold check box. Then QuickBooks enables the Sales Information area's text boxes. You can use these to identify the sales date, price, and amount of selling expenses.

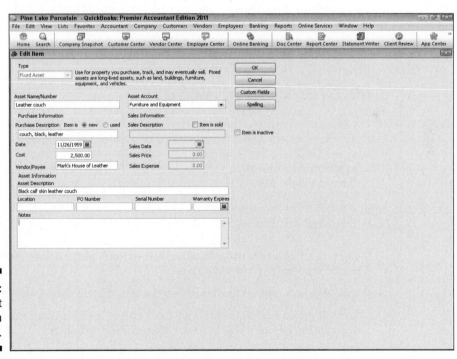

Figure 18-3:
The Edit
Item
window.

QuickBooks doesn't do any bookkeeping with the purchase and/or sales information shown on the New Item and Edit Item windows. For example, QuickBooks doesn't add an asset to the balance sheet because you set up a fixed asset item. And QuickBooks won't calculate the gain or loss on disposition of the asset because you enter sales information. You need to do that yourself — or have your accountant do that — by using either standard QuickBooks transactions or traditional journal entries. Read Chapter 6 for information on how to record a bill that stems from a vendor invoice and refer to Chapter 8 for information on how to record a check that pays for some asset. Peruse Chapter 20 for instructions on how to record depreciation and how to record asset dispositions.

Tracking Vehicle Mileage

QuickBooks supplies a business vehicle-mileage tracker that you can use to track and tally business mileage. As you may already know, you need to know both your total miles and your business miles to accurately deduct vehicle expenses on your tax return. (If you're not sure how this works, confer with your tax advisor. I also have a little write-up that explains how all this works, including how the notorious sport utility vehicle tax loophole works, at my Web site, www.stephenlnelson.com/faq.htm.)

Identifying your vehicles

By law, you're required to track your mileage by vehicle. QuickBooks, accordingly, provides a Vehicle list. To add items to the Vehicle list, follow these steps:

1. **To display the Vehicle list, choose Lists⇨Customer & Vendor Profile Lists⇨Vehicle List.**

   QuickBooks displays the Vehicle List window, as shown in Figure 18-4. Initially, because you haven't yet added any vehicles, the list shows no assets.

2. **Click the Vehicle button (bottom-left corner) and choose New from the menu that QuickBooks displays.**

   QuickBooks displays the New Vehicle window, as shown in Figure 18-5.

3. **Enter a name for the vehicle in the Vehicle text box and enter a description of the vehicle in the Description text box.**

   Identify the vehicle by its make and maybe the year of manufacture. I suppose if you have a fleet of cars or trucks, you may want to provide more identifying information than this.

4. **Save the vehicle description by clicking OK.**

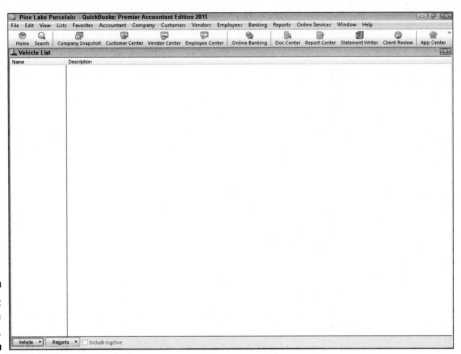

Figure 18-4:
The Vehicle List window.

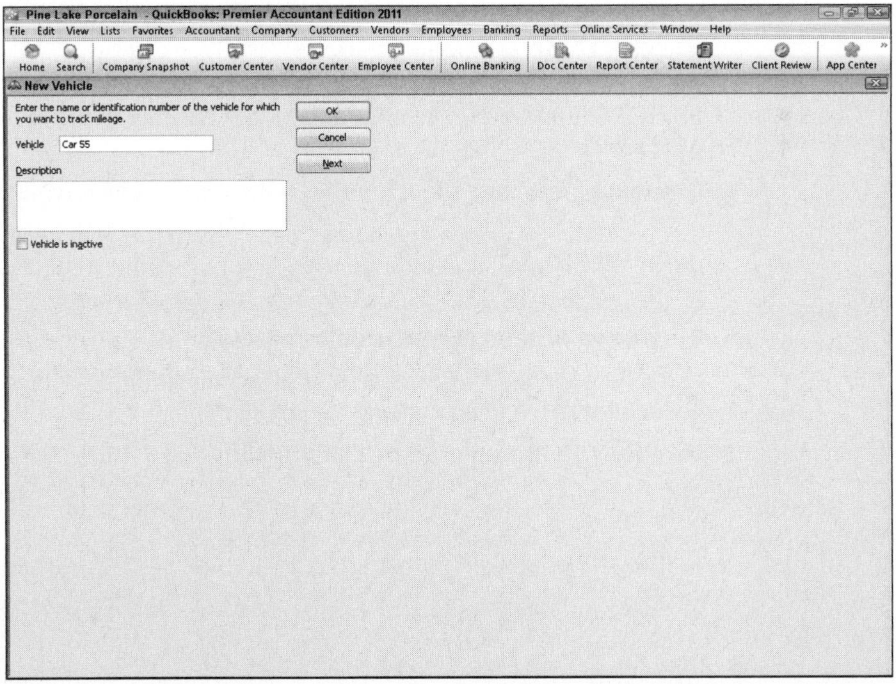

Figure 18-5:
The New Vehicle window.

Recording vehicle miles

After you add your business vehicles to the Vehicle list, you record each trip by using the Enter Vehicle Mileage window. To do this, follow these steps:

1. **Display the Enter Vehicle Mileage window by choosing Company➪Enter Vehicle Mileage.**

   QuickBooks displays the Enter Vehicle Mileage window, as shown in Figure 18-6.

2. **Select the vehicle in which you took the trip from the Vehicle drop-down list.**

3. **Provide the starting and ending dates of the trip.**

   Enter the starting date of the trip in the Trip Start Date text box and the ending date of the trip in the Trip End Date text box. Note that you can click the little calendar button at the right end of these two text boxes to display the QuickBooks pop-up calendar.

4. **Enter the starting mileage of the odometer into the Odometer Start box and the ending mileage of the odometer into the Odometer End box.**

   After you enter the two mileage readings, QuickBooks calculates the total trip miles.

5. **(Optional) Identify the customer and job.**

   If the trip's miles should be billed to or associated with a particular customer or job, select the customer or job from the Customer:Job drop-down list. For more information about how invoicing works, refer to Chapter 4.

6. **(Optional) Associate the trip miles with a particular invoice item.**

   If you bill the trip miles on an item, select from the Item drop-down list the invoice item that should be used. For more information about how invoice items work, refer to Chapter 4.

7. **Provide additional information as necessary.**

   Use the Notes text box to collect or store any additional information needed for the vehicle mileage record keeping.

8. **Save the trip information by clicking the Save & Close button.**

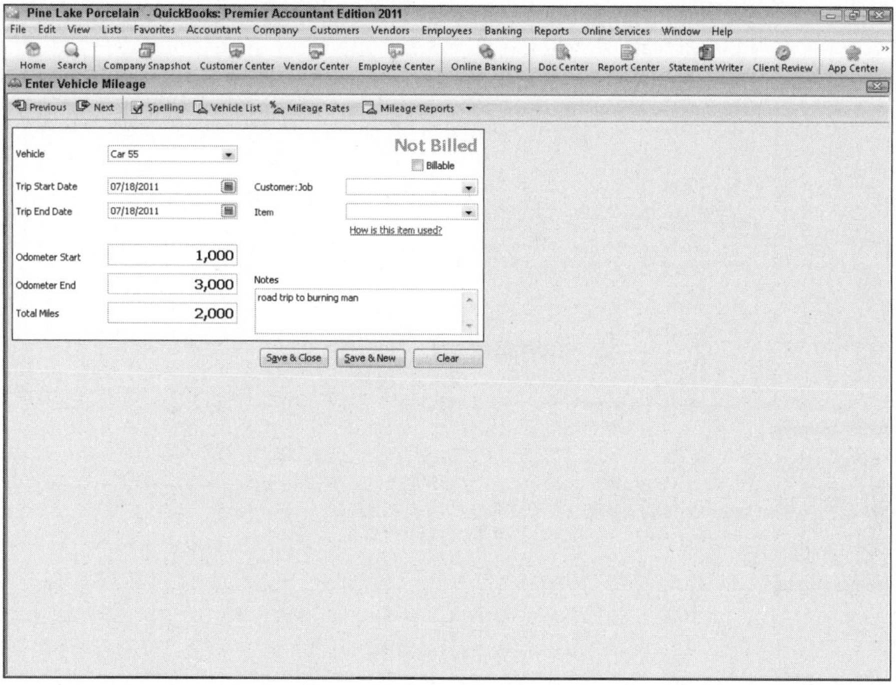

Figure 18-6:
The Enter
Vehicle
Mileage
window.

Using the vehicle reports

If you click the Reports button at the bottom of the Vehicle List window
(refer to Figure 18-4), QuickBooks displays a menu that lists four different
vehicle mileage reports: Mileage by Vehicle Summary, Mileage by Vehicle
Detail, Mileage by Job Summary, and Mileage by Job Detail.

You can access another menu of commands that produce these same reports
by clicking the Mileage Reports button that appears at the top of the Enter
Vehicle Mileage window (refer to Figure 18-6).

To produce a particular vehicle mileage report, choose one of the reports
from either of these menus.

Updating vehicle mileage rates

If you click the Mileage Rates button at the top of the Enter Vehicle Mileage
window (refer to Figure 18-6), QuickBooks displays the Mileage Rates dialog
box (see Figure 18-7). The Mileage Rates dialog box lists Internal Revenue

Service (IRS) mileage rates and their effective dates. You can enter a new mileage rate by clicking the next open row of the mileage rate schedule and then entering the effective date into the Effective Date column and the standard rate into the Rate column. You can find the current year's business mileage rate at the IRS Web site at `www.irs.gov`.

Figure 18-7:
The Mileage
Rates
dialog box.

Part V
The Part of Tens

The 5th Wave   By Rich Tennant

"I'm not sure — I like the mutual funds with rotating dollar signs, although the dancing stocks and bonds look good too."

In this part . . .

As a writing tool, laundry lists aren't something that high school English teachers encourage. But you know what? The old laundry list format is pretty handy for certain types of information.

With this in mind (and, of course, with deepest apologies to my high school English teacher, Mrs. O'Rourke), this part simply provides you with ten-item (or almost ten-item) lists of information about QuickBooks.

Chapter 19

(Almost) Ten Tips for Business Owners

*I*f you run a business and you use QuickBooks, you need to know the information in this chapter. You can get this information by sitting down with your certified public accountant (CPA) over a cup of coffee at $200 per hour. Or, you can read this chapter.

Sign All Your Own Checks

I have nothing against your bookkeeper. In a small business, however, people — especially full-charge bookkeepers — can bamboozle you too darn easily. By signing all the checks yourself, you keep your fingers on the pulse of your cash outflow.

Yeah, I know this practice can be a hassle. I know that you can't easily spend three months in Hawaii. I know that you have to wade through paperwork every time you sign a stack of checks.

By the way, if you're in a partnership, I think that you should have at least a couple of the partners co-sign checks.

Don't Sign a Check the Wrong Way

If you sign many checks, you may be tempted to use a John Hancock–like signature. Although scrawling your name illegibly makes great sense when you're autographing baseballs, don't do it when you're signing checks. A clear signature, especially one with a sense of personal style, is distinctive. A wavy line with a cross and a couple of dots is easy to forge.

Which leads me to my next tip. . . .

Review Canceled Checks Before Your Bookkeeper Does

Be sure that you review your canceled checks before anybody else sees the monthly bank statement.

This chapter isn't about browbeating bookkeepers. Still, a business owner can determine whether someone is forging signatures on checks only by being the first to open the bank statement and by reviewing each of the canceled-check signatures.

If you don't examine the checks, unscrupulous employees — especially book-keepers who can update the bank account records — can forge your signature with impunity. And they won't get caught if they never overdraw the account.

I won't continue this rant, but let me mention one last thing: Every time I teach CPAs about how to better help their clients with QuickBooks, I hear again and again about business owners who haven't been careful about keeping an eye on the bookkeeper — and have suffered embezzlement and forgery as a result.

If you don't follow these procedures, you — not the bank — will probably eat the losses.

Choose a Bookkeeper Who Is Familiar with Computers and Knows How to Do Payroll

Don't worry. You don't need to request an FBI background check.

In fact, if you use QuickBooks, you don't need to hire people who are familiar with small business accounting systems. Just find people who know how to keep a checkbook and work with a computer. They shouldn't have a problem understanding QuickBooks.

Of course, you don't want someone who just fell off the turnip truck. But even if you do hire someone who rode into town on one, you're not going to have much trouble getting that person up-to-speed with QuickBooks.

A bookkeeper who knows double-entry bookkeeping is super-helpful. But to be fair, such knowledge probably isn't essential. I will say this, however: When you're hiring, find someone who knows how to do payroll — and not just the federal payroll tax stuff (see Chapter 11), but also the state payroll tax monkey business.

Regularly Review Your Financial Statements

Truly, truly, I'm not trying to increase the headache factor of your running your small business. The whole *purpose* of this book is to make your small business's accounting flow more smoothly. But nevertheless I want to add a task to your to-do list: You need to regularly review your financial statements.

In other words, regularly produce and look over the profit and loss statement that QuickBooks effortlessly generates. Get habitual about looking over your balance sheet with its lists of assets and liabilities. Explore and find another report or two that gives you useful insights into the rhythms and rhymes of your business.

Probably, you can keep a pretty firm handle on the operation by looking at two or three easy-to-understand reports. And by regularly peeking at these financial statements — say a time or two a week — you turn your accounting system into a tool useful both for spotting tempting opportunities and for avoiding dangerous traps.

No kidding, I run my businesses by looking at three QuickBooks reports: a profit and loss statement that compares the current year's and previous year's year-to-date numbers (so I can see how I'm doing in the current year as compared to the previous year), the accounts receivable summary aging (so I can see which clients and customers are past due), and the balance sheet (so that I can monitor my cash and working capital and spot any funny stuff).

Choose an Appropriate Accounting System

When you use QuickBooks, you use either cash-basis accounting or accrual-basis accounting. (I describe the difference between these two methods in Appendix B.)

Cash-basis accounting is fine when a business's cash inflow mirrors its sales and its cash outflow mirrors its expenses. This situation isn't the case, however, in many businesses. A contractor of single-family homes, for example, may have cash coming in (by borrowing from banks) but may not make any money. Alternatively, a pawnshop owner who lends money at 22 percent might make scads of money, even if cash pours out of the business daily.

As a general rule, when you're buying and selling inventory, accrual-basis accounting works better than cash-basis accounting. However, cash-basis accounting typically defers income taxes.

If QuickBooks Doesn't Work for Your Business

QuickBooks is a great small business accounting program. In fact, I'd even go as far as to say that QuickBooks is probably the best small business accounting program available.

However, if QuickBooks doesn't seem to fit your needs — if, for example, you need a program that works better for a manufacturer or that includes some special industry-specific feature — you may want one of the more complicated (but also more powerful) small business accounting packages.

One possibility is the Enterprise Solutions version of QuickBooks, which costs more but also works for bigger businesses. The Enterprise version of QuickBooks looks and works almost identically to the "regular" versions of QuickBooks. If you know QuickBooks Premier, accordingly, you already know (or mostly know) QuickBooks Enterprise.

If the Enterprise version of QuickBooks doesn't work, you may want to talk to your accountant about industry-specific packages. (For example, if you're a commercial printer, some vendor may have developed a special accounting package just for commercial printers.)

I'm amazed that PC accounting software remains so affordable. You can buy a great accounting package — one that you can use to manage a $5-million or a $25-million business — for a few hundred bucks. Accounting software is truly one of the great bargains in life.

Keep Things Simple

Let me share one last comment about managing small business financial affairs: Keep things as simple as possible. In fact, keep your business affairs simple enough that you can easily tell whether you're making money and whether the business is healthy.

This advice may sound strange, but as a CPA, I've worked for some very bright people who have built monstrously complex financial structures for their businesses, including complicated leasing arrangements, labyrinthine partnership and corporate structures, and sophisticated profit-sharing and cost-sharing arrangements with other businesses.

I can only offer anecdotal evidence, of course, but I strongly believe that these super-sophisticated financial arrangements don't produce a profit when you consider all the costs. What's more, these super-sophisticated arrangements almost always turn into management and record-keeping headaches.

Of course, the one positive thing you can say about such arrangements is this: You'll make both your accountant and lawyer happy. And rich. So that's good for them, at least.

Chapter 20

Tips for Handling (Almost) Ten Tricky Situations

. . . .

. . . .

As your business grows and becomes more complex, your accounting does, too. I can't describe and discuss all the complexities you'll encounter, but I can give you some tips on handling (just about) ten tricky situations.

In QuickBooks, you make journal entries by using the General Journal Entry window, which you get to by choosing Company⇨Make Journal Entries. If you don't understand double-entry bookkeeping but want to, take a gander at Appendix B.

To track the depreciation of an asset that you already purchased (and added to the Chart of Accounts), you need two new accounts: a Fixed Asset type of account called something like *Accumulated Depreciation* and an Expense type account called something like *Depreciation Expense*.

If you have a large number of assets, keeping track of the accumulated depreciation associated with specific assets is a good idea. You can do this either outside QuickBooks (for example, in an Excel spreadsheet or with your tax return) or inside QuickBooks (by using individual accounts for each asset's original cost and accumulated depreciation).

After you set up these two accounts, you can record the asset depreciation with a journal entry, such as the following one that records $500 of depreciation expense:

	Debit	Credit
Depreciation expense	$500	
Accumulated depreciation		$500

The federal tax laws provide a special form of depreciation — *Section 179 depreciation* — which enables you to depreciate the entire cost of some assets. This is a big break for small businesses. You can't, however, use more than a certain amount of Section 179 depreciation in a year: $250,000 in 2008, for example. You also need to know some other nitty-gritty details, so confer with your tax advisor if you have questions.

Selling an Asset

When you sell an asset, you need to *back out* (get rid of) the asset's account balance, record the cash (or whatever) that somebody pays you for the asset, and record any difference between what you sell the asset for and its value as a gain or loss.

If you purchase a piece of land for $5,000 but later resell it for $4,000, for example, you use the following journal entry to record the sale of this asset:

	Debit	Credit
Cash	$4,000	
Loss	$1,000	
Asset		$5,000

You may need to set up another income account for the gain or another expense account for the loss. Read Chapter 2 for information on setting up new accounts.

Selling a Depreciable Asset

Selling a depreciable asset works almost identically to selling an asset that you haven't been depreciating. When you sell the asset, you need to back out the asset's account balance. You also need to back out the asset's accumulated depreciation (which is the only thing that's different from selling an asset that you haven't been depreciating). You need to record the cash (or whatever) that somebody pays you for the asset. Finally, you count as a gain or a loss any difference between what you sell the asset for and what its net-of-accumulated-depreciation (or *book value*) is.

This process sounds terribly complicated, but an example helps. Suppose that you purchased a $5,000 piece of machinery and have accumulated $500 of depreciation thus far. Consequently, the asset account shows a $5,000 debit balance, and the asset's accumulated depreciation account shows a $500 credit balance. Suppose also that you sell the machinery for $4,750 in cash.

To record the sale of this depreciable asset, you'd use the following journal entry:

	Debit	Credit
Cash	$4,750	
Accumulated depreciation	$500	
Asset		$5,000
Gain		$250

As I note earlier in the chapter, if you have a bunch of assets, you probably want to set up individual accounts for each asset's original cost and its accumulated depreciation. The individual accounts make it much easier to make the journal entry shown in the preceding paragraph. Also, be sure to record the amount of that asset's depreciation for the year of the sale before you make the entry for the sale itself.

Owner's Equity in a Sole Proprietorship

Actually, tracking owner's equity in a sole proprietorship is easy. You can use the single account that QuickBooks sets up for you, called Opening Bal Equity, to track what you've invested in the business. (You might want to rename this account something like *Contributed Capital.*)

To track the money you withdraw from the business, you can set up and use a new owner's equity account called something like *Owner's Draws.* Table 20-1 gives an example of owner's equity accounts in a sole proprietorship. Note that the numbers inside parentheses are negative values.

Table 20-1	An Example of Owner's Equity Accounts in a Sole Proprietorship
Account	*Amount*
Contributed capital	$5,000
Retained earnings	$8,000
Owner's draws	($2,000)
Owner's equity (total)	$11,000

Owner's Equity in a Partnership

To track the equity for each partner in a partnership, you need to create three accounts for each partner: one for the partner's contributed capital, one for the partner's draws, and one for the partner's share of the distributed income.

Amounts that a partner withdraws, of course, get tracked with the partner's draws account.

The partner's share of the partnership's profits gets allocated to the partner's profit share account. (Your partnership agreement, by the way, should say how the partnership income is distributed between the partners.) Table 20-2 gives an example of owner's equity accounts in a partnership.

Table 20-2	An Example of Owner's Equity Accounts in a Partnership	
Account	*Partner A's Amount*	*Partner B's Amount*
Contributed capital	$5,000	$7,000
Profit share	$6,000	$6,000
Draws	($3,000)	($4,000)
Equity (total)	$8,000	$9,000

Owner's Equity in a Corporation

Yikes! Accounting for the owner's equity in a corporation can get mighty tricky mighty fast. In fact, I don't mind telling you that college accounting textbooks often use several chapters to describe all the ins and outs of corporation owner's equity accounting.

As long as you keep things simple, however, you can probably use three or four accounts for your owner's equity:

✔ **A capital stock par value account,** for which you get the par value amount by multiplying the par value per share by the number of shares issued. The par value of the stock is written on the face of the actual stock certificate, and it's stated in the corporate Articles of Incorporation.

✔ **A paid-in capital in excess of par value account** for the amount investors paid for shares of stock in excess of par value. You get this amount by multiplying the price paid per share less the par value per share by the number of shares issued.

✔ **A retained earnings account** to track the business profits left invested in the business.

✔ **A dividends paid account** to track the amounts distributed to shareholders in the current year.

Table 20-3 shows an example of owner's equity accounts in a corporation.

Table 20-3   An Example of Owner's Equity in a Corporation

Account	Amount
Par value	$500
Paid-in capital in excess of par value	$4,500
Retained earnings	$8,000
Dividends paid	($3,000)
Shareholders' equity	$10,000

Multiple-State Accounting

For multiple-state accounting, you typically need to track sales, payroll, and property by state. I'm not going to get into too much detail here, but you need this level of granularity because state business tax returns require you to apportion your taxable income using state-level sales, payroll, and property data. (For more information about this, ask your accountant.)

To track sales, payroll, and property data by state, you can either use classes for each state or set up a Chart of Accounts that supplies state-specific income, payroll expense, and asset accounts. After you set up this Chart of Accounts, all you have to do is use the correct state's class or accounts to record transactions.

If you do business in both Washington and Oregon, for example, you record sales in Oregon as Oregon sales and sales in Washington as Washington sales. You'd treat other income accounts and all your payroll expense accounts the same way. If you use class tracking for sales in different states, you don't need duplicate accounts for each state.

If you will do business tax returns for multiple states, confer with your tax advisor. What I've said here only scratches the surface of the subject. And there are some details (quite likely specific to your states of operation) that you want to hear about from a local expert.

Getting a Loan

Getting a loan is the hard part. After you get the money, recording it in QuickBooks is easy. All you do is record a journal entry that increases cash and that recognizes the new loan liability. For example, if you get a $5,000 loan, you might record the following journal entry:

	Debit	*Credit*
Cash	$5,000	
Loan payable		$5,000

You'll already have a cash account set up, but you may need to set up a new liability account to track the loan.

Repaying a Loan

To record loan payments, you need to split each payment between two accounts: the interest expense account and the loan payable account.

Suppose that you make $75 monthly payments on a $5,000 loan. Also suppose that the lender charges 1 percent interest each month. The following journal entry records the first month's loan payment:

	Debit	*Credit*	*Explanation*
Interest expense	$50		Calculated as 1 percent of $5,000
Loan payable	$25		The amount left over and applied to principal
Cash		$75	The total payment amount

The next month, of course, the loan balance is slightly less (because you made a $25 dent in the loan principal, as shown in the preceding loan payment journal entry). The following journal entry records the second month's loan payment:

	Debit	Credit	Explanation
Interest expense	$49.75		Calculated as 1 percent of $4,975, the new loan balance
Loan payable	$25.25		The amount left over and applied to principal
Cash		$75.00	The total payment amount

Get the lender to provide you an amortization schedule that shows the breakdown of each payment into interest expense and loan principal reduction. If this doesn't work, choose Banking⇨Loan Manager. QuickBooks displays the Loan Manager window. If you click the Add a Loan button, QuickBooks collects a bit of information about the loan terms and builds an amortization schedule for you. Note, too, that you can tell QuickBooks to remind you of upcoming loan payments and even to schedule the payments.

You can record loan payments by using either the Write Checks window or the Enter Bills window. Just use the Expenses tab to specify the interest expense account and the loan liability account.

You can check your loan accounting whenever you get a loan statement from the bank. What the bank shows as the ending balance for a particular month should match what QuickBooks says is the balance for that month. To correct discrepancies between the loan balance that the bank shows and the loan balance that QuickBooks shows, make a general journal entry that adjusts both the interest expense and the loan principal at the same time. For example, if the loan balance is too low by say $8.76, you need to increase the loan balance and decrease the loan interest expense using the following journal entry:

	Debit	Credit	Explanation
Interest expense	$8.76		Adjusts the interest expense by the same amount as loan balance changes
Loan payable		$8.76	Increase the loan principal balance to match the lender's statement

Chapter 21

(Almost) Ten Secret Business Formulas

I have some good news and some bad news. The good news is that you can use some powerful formulas to better your chances of business success and increase your profits. No, I'm not joking. These formulas do exist. You can and should use them. And in the pages that follow, I explain the formulas and how to use them.

Now for the bad news: To use these formulas, you need to feel comfortable with a bit of arithmetic. You don't need to be a serious mathematician or anything, but you do need to feel comfortable using percentages and calculators. By the way, you can use the standard Windows Calculator, available from within QuickBooks by choosing Edit⇨Use Calculator to work with these secret formulas.

Even if you're not particularly fond of (or all that good at) math, I want to encourage you to skim this chapter. You can pick up some weird insights into the world of finance.

The First "Most Expensive Money You Can Borrow" Formula

Here's something you may not know: The most expensive money that you can borrow is from vendors who offer cash or early payment discounts that you don't take. For example, perhaps your friendly office supply store offers a 2 percent discount if you pay cash at the time of purchase instead of paying within the usual 30 days. You don't pay cash, so you pay the full amount (which is 2 percent more than the cash amount) 30 days later. In effect, you pay a 2 percent monthly interest charge. A 2 percent monthly interest charge works out to a 24 percent annual interest charge — and that's a great deal of money.

Here's another example that's only slightly more complicated. Many, many vendors offer a 2 percent discount if you pay within the first 10 days that an invoice is due rather than 30 days later. (These payment terms are often described and printed at the bottom of the invoice as 2/10, Net 30.)

In this case, you pay 2 percent more by paying 20 days later. (The 20 days later is the difference between 10 days and 30 days.) Two percent for 20 days is roughly equivalent to 3 percent for 30 days (one month). So, a 2 percent, 20-day interest charge works out to a 36 percent annual interest charge. Now you're talking *serious* money.

Table 21-1 shows how some common early payment discounts (including cash discounts) translate into annual interest rates. By the way, I am a bit more precise in my calculations for this table, so these numbers vary slightly from (and are larger than) those given in the preceding paragraph.

Table 21-1   Annual Interest Rates for Early Payment Discounts

Early Payment Discount	*For Paying 20 Days Early*	*For Paying 30 Days Early*
1%	18.43%	12.29%
2%	37.24%	24.83%
3%	56.44%	37.63%
4%	76.04%	50.69%
5%	96.05%	64.04%

Is it just me, or do those numbers blow you away? The 2 percent for 20 days early payment discount that you often see works out (if you do the math precisely) to more than 37 percent annual interest. Man, that hurts. And if you don't take a 5-percent-for-20-days-early payment discount when it's offered, you're effectively borrowing money at an annual rate of 96 percent. You didn't read that last number wrong. Yes, a 5-percent-for-20-days-early payment discount works out to an annual interest rate of almost 100 percent.

I want to make a couple more observations, too. Turning down a 1 percent discount for paying 30 days early isn't actually a bad deal in many cases. Look at Table 21-1. It shows that the 1 percent discount for paying 30 days early results in 12.29 percent. Sure, that rate is pretty high, but that interest rate is less than for many credit cards and is less than for some small business credit lines. If you have to borrow money some other way to pay 30 days early, making an early payment might not be cost effective.

The bottom line on all this ranting is that early payment discounts, if not taken, represent one of the truly expensive ways to borrow money. I'm not saying that you won't need to borrow money this way at times. I can guess that your cash flow gets pretty tight sometimes (a circumstance that is true in most businesses, as you probably know). I am saying, however, that you should never skip taking an early payment discount unless borrowing money at outrageous interest rates makes sense.

Oh, yes. The secret formula. To figure out the effective annual interest rate that you pay by not taking an early payment discount, use this formula:

Discount % / (1 – Discount %) × (365 / Number of Days of Early Payment)

To calculate the effective annual interest rate that you pay by not taking a 2 percent discount for paying 20 days early, calculate this formula:

.02 / (1 – .02) × (365 / 20)

Work out the math, and you get 0.3724, which is the same thing as a 37.24 percent interest rate. (Note that the discount percents are entered as their equivalent decimal values.)

The Scientific view of the Windows Calculator includes parenthesis keys that you can use to calculate this formula and the others I give in the chapter. Choose View➪Scientific to switch to the Scientific view of the calculator.

The Second "Most Expensive Money You Can Borrow" Formula

You know that "most expensive money you can borrow" stuff that I talk about in the preceding section? The very tragic flip side to that story occurs when you offer your customers an early payment discount, and they take it. In effect, you borrow money from your customers at the same outrageous interest rates. For example, if customer Joe Schmoe gets a 2 percent early payment discount for paying 20 days early, you, in effect, pay ol' Joe roughly 2 percent interest for a 20-day loan. Using the same formula I give for the first "most expensive money you can borrow" formula, the rate works out to 37.24 percent.

In some industries, customers expect early payment discounts. You may have to offer them, but you should never offer them willingly. You should never offer them just for fun. Borrowing money this way is just too expensive. A rate of 37.24 percent? Yikes!

Let me also offer a rather dour observation. In my experience, anytime someone offers big early payment discounts — I've seen them as big as 5 percent — he's either stupid or desperate, and probably both.

The "How Do 1 Break Even?" Formula

I know that you're not interested in just breaking even. I know that you want to make money in your business. But knowing what quantities you need to sell just to cover your expenses is often super-helpful. If you're a one-person accounting firm (or some other service business), for example, how many hours do you need to work to pay your expenses and perhaps pay yourself a small salary? Or if you're a retailer of, say, toys, how many toys do you need to sell to pay your overhead, rent, and sales clerks?

You see my point, right? Knowing how much revenue you need to generate just to stay in the game is essential. Knowing your break-even point enables you to establish a benchmark for your performance. (Any time you don't break even, you know that you have a serious problem that you need to resolve quickly to stay in business.) And considering break-even points is invaluable when you think about new businesses or new ventures.

As you ponder any new opportunity and its potential income and expenses, you need to know how much income you need to generate just to pay those expenses.

To calculate a break-even point, you need to know just three pieces of information: your *fixed costs* (the expenses you have to pay regardless of the business's revenue, or income), the revenue that you generate for each sale, and the variable costs that you incur in each sale. (These variable costs, which also are called *direct expenses,* aren't the same thing as the fixed costs.)

- ✔ Whatever you sell — be it thingamajigs, corporate jets, or hours of consulting services — has a price. That price is your revenue per item input.

- ✔ Most of the time, what you sell has a cost, too. If you buy and resell thingamajigs, those thingamajigs cost you some amount of money. The total of your thingamajigs' costs varies depending on how many thingamajigs you buy and sell, which is why these costs are referred to as *variable costs.* A couple examples of variable costs include hourly (or contract) labor and shipping. Sometimes, the variable cost per item is zero, however. (If you're a consultant, for example, you sell hours of your time, but you may not *pay* an hourly cost just because you consult for an hour.)

- ✔ Your fixed costs are all those costs that you pay regardless of whether you sell your product or service. For example, if you have to pay an employee a salary regardless of whether you sell anything, that salary is a fixed cost. Your rent is probably a fixed cost. Things like insurance and legal and accounting expenses are probably also fixed costs because they don't vary with fluctuations in your revenue.

Fixed costs may change a bit from year to year or bounce around a bit during a year. So maybe *fixed* isn't a very good adjective. People use the term *fixed costs,* however, to differentiate these costs from *variable costs,* which are those costs that do vary with the number of goods you sell.

Take the book-writing business as an example. Suppose that as you read this book, you think, "Man, that guy is having too much fun. Writing about accounting programs, working day in and day out with buggy beta software — yeah, that would be the life."

Further, suppose that for every book you write, you think that you can make $5,000, but you'll probably end up paying about $1,000 per book for such things as long distance telephone charges, overnight courier charges, and extra hardware and software. And suppose that you need to pay yourself a salary of $20,000 per year. (In this scenario, your salary is your only fixed cost because you plan to write at home at a small desk in your bedroom.) Table 21-2 shows how the situation breaks down.

Table 21-2		Costs and Revenue
Description	*Amount*	*Explanation*
Revenue	$5,000	What you can squeeze out of the publisher
Variable costs	$1,000	All the little things that add up
Fixed costs	$20,000	Someplace to live and food to eat

With these three bits of data, you can easily calculate how many books you need to write to break even. Here's the formula:

Fixed Costs / (Revenue – Variable Costs)

If you plug in the writing business example data, the formula looks like this:

$20,000 / ($5,000 – $1,000)

Work through the math, and you get 5. So you need to write (and get paid for) five books per year to pay the $1,000 per book variable costs and your $20,000 salary. Just to prove that I didn't make up this formula and that it really works, Table 21-3 shows how things look if you write five books.

Table 21-3		The Break-Even Point
Description	*Amount*	*Explanation*
Revenue	$25,000	Five books at $5,000 each.
Variable costs	($5,000)	Five books at $1,000 each.
Fixed costs	($20,000)	A little food money, a little rent money, a little beer money.
Profits	$0	Subtract the costs from the revenue, and nothing is left.

Accountants use parentheses to show negative numbers. That's why the $5,000 and the $20,000 in Table 21-3 are in parentheses.

But back to the game. To break even in a book-writing business like the one that I describe here, you need to write and sell five books per year. If you don't think that you can write and sell five books in a year, getting into the book-writing business makes no sense.

Your business is probably more complicated than book writing, but the same formula and logic for calculating your break-even point apply. You need just three pieces of information: the revenue that you receive from the sale of a single item, the variable costs of selling (and possibly making) the item, and the fixed costs that you pay just to be in business.

QuickBooks doesn't collect or present information in a way that enables you to easily pull the revenue per item and variable costs per item off some report. Neither does it provide a fixed-costs total on some report. However, if you understand the logic of the preceding discussion, you can easily massage the QuickBooks data to get the information you need.

The "You Can Grow Too Fast" Formula

Here's a weird little paradox: One of the easiest ways for a small business to fail is by being too successful. I know. It sounds crazy, but it's true. In fact, I'll even go out on a limb and say that business success is by far the most common reason that I see for business failure.

"Oh, geez," you say. "This nut is talking in circles."

Let me explain. Whether you realize it, you need a certain amount of financial horsepower, or net worth, to do business. (Your *net worth* is just the difference between your assets and your liabilities.) You need to have some cash in the bank to tide you over the rough times that everybody has at least occasionally. You probably need to have some office furniture and computers so that you can take care of the business end of the business. And if you make anything at all, you need to have adequate tools and machinery. This part all makes sense, right?

How net worth relates to growth

Okay, now on to the next reality. If your business grows and continues to grow, you need to increase your financial horsepower, or net worth. A bigger business, for example, needs more cash to make it through the tough times than a smaller business does — along with more office furniture and computers, and more tools and machinery. Oh, sure, you might be able to have one growth spurt because you started with more financial horsepower (more net worth) than you needed. But — and this is the key part — you can't sustain business growth without increasing your net worth. Now you may be saying things like "No way, man. That doesn't apply to me." I assure you, my new friend, that it does.

As long as your creditors will extend you additional credit as you grow your business — and they should, as long as the business is profitable and you don't have cash-flow problems — you can grow your business as fast as you can grow your net worth. If you can grow your net worth by 5 percent yearly, your business can grow at an easily sustained rate of only 5 percent per year. If you can grow your net worth by 50 percent yearly, your business can grow at an easily sustained rate of only (only?) 50 percent per year.

You grow your business's net worth in only two ways:

- ✔ **Reinvest profits in the business.** Note that any profits that you leave in the business instead of drawing them out — such as through dividends or draws — are reinvested.

- ✔ **Get people to invest money in the business.** If you're not in a position to continually raise money from new investors — and most small businesses aren't — the only practical way to grow is by reinvesting profits in the business.

How to calculate sustainable growth

You can calculate the growth rate that your business can sustain by using this formula:

Reinvested Profits / Net Worth

I should say, just for the record, that this formula is a very simple *sustainable growth* formula. But even so, it offers some amazingly interesting insights. For example, perhaps you're a commercial printer doing $500,000 in revenue yearly with a business net worth of $100,000; your business earns $50,000 per year, but you leave only $10,000 per year in the business. In other words, your reinvested profits are $10,000. In this case, your sustainable growth is calculated as follows:

$10,000 / $100,000

Work out the numbers, and you get 0.1, or 10 percent. In other words, you can grow your business by 10 percent yearly (as long as you grow the net worth by 10 percent per year by reinvesting profits). For example, you can easily go from $500,000 to $550,000 to $605,000 and continue growing annually at this 10 percent rate, but your business can't grow any faster than 10 percent per year. That is, you'll get into serious trouble if you try to go from $500,000 to $600,000 to $720,000 and continue growing at 20 percent per year.

You can convert a decimal value to a percentage by multiplying the value by 100. For example, 0.1 × 100 equals 10, so 0.1 equals 10 percent. You can convert a percentage to a decimal value by dividing the value by 100. For example, 25 (as in 25 percent) divided by 100 equals 0.25.

The sustainable-growth formula inputs are pretty easy to get after you have QuickBooks up and running. You can get the net worth figure off the balance sheet. You can calculate the reinvested profits by looking at the net income and deducting any amounts that you pulled out of the business.

I'm not going to go through the mathematical proof of why this sustainable-growth formula is true. My experience is that the formula makes intuitive sense to people who think about it for a few minutes. If you aren't into the intuition thing or if you don't believe me, get a college finance textbook, and look up its discussion of the sustainable-growth formula. Or do what all the kids today are doing — search online for *sustainable growth formula*.

The First "What Happens If . . . ?" Formula

One curiosity about small businesses is that small changes in revenue or income can have huge impacts on profits. A retailer who cruises along at $200,000 in revenue and struggles to live on $30,000 per year never realizes that boosting the sales volume by 20 percent to $250,000 might increase profits by 200 percent to $60,000.

If you take only one point away from this discussion, it should be this curious little truth: If fixed costs don't change, small changes in revenue can produce big changes in profits.

The following example shows how this point works and provides a secret formula. For starters, say that you currently generate $100,000 yearly in revenue and make $20,000 per year in profits. The revenue per item sold is $100, and the variable cost per item sold is $35. (In this case, the fixed costs happen to be $45,000 per year, but that figure isn't all that important to the analysis.)

Accountants like to whip up little tables that describe these sorts of things, so Table 21-4 gives the current story on your imaginary business.

Table 21-4		Your Business Profits
Description	*Amount*	*Explanation*
Revenue	$100,000	You sell 1,000 doohickeys at $100 a pop.
Variable costs	($35,000)	You buy 1,000 doohickeys at $35 a pop.
Fixed costs	($45,000)	All the little things: rent, your salary, and so on.
Profits	$20,000	What's left over.

Table 21-4 shows the current situation. Suppose that you want to know what will happen to your profits if revenue increases by 20 percent but your fixed costs don't change. Mere mortals, not knowing what you and I know, might assume that a 20 percent increase in revenue would produce an approximate 20 percent increase in profits. But you know that small changes in revenue can produce big changes in profits, right?

To estimate exactly how a change in revenue affects profits, use the following secret formula:

Percentage Change × Revenue × (1 – [Variable Cost per Item / Revenue per Item])

From the sample data provided in Table 21-4 (I'm sorry this example is starting to resemble those story problems from eighth-grade math), you make the following calculation:

0.20 × $100,000 × (1 – [35 / 100])

Work out the numbers, and you get $13,000. What does this figure mean? It means that a 20 percent increase in revenue produces a $13,000 increase in profits. As a percentage of profits, this $13,000 increase is 65 percent:

$13,000 / $20,000 = 65 percent

Let me stop here and make a quick observation. In my experience, entrepreneurs always seem to think that they need to grow big to make big money. They concentrate on doing things that will double or triple or quadruple their sales. Their logic, though, isn't always correct. If you can grow your business without having to increase your fixed costs, small changes in revenue can produce big changes in profits.

Before I stop talking about this first "What happens if . . . ?" formula, I want to quickly describe where you get the inputs you need for the formula:

✔ The percentage-change input is just a number that you pick. If you want to see what happens to your profits with a 25 percent increase in sales, for example, use 0.25.

✔ The revenue input is your total revenue. You can get it from your profit and loss statement. (In Chapter 15, I describe how you can create a profit and loss statement in QuickBooks.)

✔ The revenue per item sold and variable costs per item sold figures work the same way as I describe for the break-even formula earlier in this chapter.

The Second "What Happens If . . . ?" Formula

Maybe I shouldn't tell you this, but people in finance (like me) usually have a prejudice against people in sales. And it's not just because people who are good at sales usually make more money than people who are good at finance. It's really not. Honest to goodness.

Here's the prejudice: People in finance think that people in sales always want to reduce prices.

People in sales see things a bit differently. They say, in effect, "Hey, you worry too much. We'll make up the difference in additional sales volume." The argument is appealing: You just undercut your competitor's prices by a healthy chunk and make less on each sale. But because you sell your stuff so cheaply, your customers will beat a path to your door.

Just for the record, I love people who are good at sales. I think that someone who is good at sales is more important than someone who is good at finance.

But that painful admission aside, I have to tell you that I see a problem with the "Cut the prices; we'll make it up with volume" strategy. If you cut prices by a given percentage — perhaps by 10 percent — you usually need a much bigger percentage gain in revenue to break even.

The following example shows what I mean and how this strategy works. Suppose that you have a business that sells some doohickey or thingamajig. You generate $100,000 yearly in revenue and make $20,000 per year in profits. Your revenue per item (or doohickey) sold is $100, and your variable cost per item (or doohickey) sold is $35. Your fixed costs happen to be $45,000 yearly, but again, the fixed costs aren't all that important to the analysis. Table 21-5 summarizes the current situation.

Table 21-5		Your Current Situation
Description	*Amount*	*Explanation*
Revenue	$100,000	You sell 1,000 doohickeys at $100 a pop.
Variable costs	($35,000)	You buy 1,000 doohickeys at $35 a pop.
Fixed costs	($45,000)	All the little things: rent, your salary, and so on.
Profits	$20,000	What's left over.

Then business is particularly bad for one month. Joe-Bob, your sales guy, comes to you and says, "Boss, I have an idea. I think that we can cut prices by 15 percent to $85 per doohickey and get a truly massive boost in sales."

You're a good boss. You're a polite boss. Plus you're intrigued. So you think a bit. The idea has a certain appeal. You start wondering how much of an increase in sales you need to break even on the price reduction.

You're probably not surprised to read this, but I have another secret formula that can help. You can use the following formula to calculate how many items (doohickeys, in the example) you need to sell just to break even on the new, discounted price. Here's the formula:

(Current Profits + Fixed Costs) / (Revenue per Item – Variable Cost per Item)

From the example data provided earlier, you make the following calculation:

($20,000 + $45,000) / ($85 – $35)

Work out the numbers, and you get 1,300. What does this figure mean? It means that just to break even on the $85 doohickey price, Joe-Bob needs to sell 1,300 doohickeys. Currently, per Table 21-5 Joe-Bob sells 1,000 doohickeys yearly. As a percentage, then, this jump from 1,000 doohickeys to 1,300 doohickeys is exactly a 30 percent increase. (Remember that Joe-Bob proposes a 15 percent price cut.)

Okay, I don't know Joe-Bob. He may be a great guy. He may be a wonderful salesperson. But here's my guess: Joe-Bob isn't thinking about a 30 percent increase in sales volume. (Remember, with a 15 percent price reduction, you need a 30 percent increase just to break even!) And Joe-Bob almost certainly isn't thinking about a 50 percent or 75 percent increase in sales volume — which is what you need to make money on the whole deal, as shown in Table 21-6.

Table 21-6	How Profits Look at Various Sales Levels		
Description	*1,300 Units Sold*	*1,500 Units Sold*	*1,750 Units Sold*
Revenue	$110,500	$127,500	$148,750
Variable costs	($45,500)	($52,500)	($61,250)
Fixed costs	($45,000)	($45,000)	($45,000)
Profits	$20,000	$30,000	$42,500

In summary, you can't reduce prices by, say, 15 percent and then go for some penny-ante increase. You need huge increases in the sales volume to get big increases in profits. If you look at Table 21-6, you see that if you can increase the sales from 1,000 doohickeys to 1,750 doohickeys — a 75 percent increase — you can more than double the profits. This increase assumes that the fixed costs stay level, as the table shows.

I want to describe quickly where you get the inputs that you need for the formula:

- ✔ The profit figure can come right off the QuickBooks profit and loss statement.

- ✔ The fixed costs figure just tallies all your fixed costs. (I talk about fixed costs earlier in this chapter in "The 'How Do I Break Even?' Formula" section.)

- ✔ The revenue per item is just the new price that you're considering.

- ✔ Finally, the variable cost per item is the cost of the thing you sell. (I discuss this cost earlier in the chapter, too.)

Please don't construe the preceding discussion as proof that you should *never* listen to the Joe-Bobs of the world. The "cut prices to increase volume" strategy can work wonderfully well. The trick, however, is to increase the sales volume massively. Sam Walton, the late founder of Wal-Mart, used the strategy and became, at one point, the richest man in the world.

The Economic Order Quantity (Isaac Newton) Formula

Isaac Newton invented differential calculus, a fact that is truly amazing to me. I can't imagine how someone could just figure out calculus. I could never, in a hundred years, figure it out. But I'm getting off-track.

The neat thing about calculus — besides the fact that I'm not going to do any for you here — is that it enables you to create optimal values equations. One of the coolest such equations is the *economic order quantity,* or *EOQ,* model. I know that this stuff all sounds terribly confusing and totally boring, but stay with me for just another paragraph. (If you're not satisfied in another paragraph or so, skip ahead to the next secret formula.)

Perhaps you buy and then resell — oh, I don't know — 2,000 cases of vintage French wine every year. The EOQ model enables you to decide whether you should order all 2,000 cases at one time, order 1 case at a time, or order some number of cases in between 1 case and 2,000 cases.

Another way to say the same thing is that the EOQ model enables you to choose the best, or optimal, reorder quantity for items that you buy and then resell.

If you're still with me at this point, I figure that you want to know how this formula works. You need to know just three pieces of data to calculate the optimal order quantity: the annual sales volume, the cost of placing an order, and the annual cost of holding one unit in inventory. You plug this information into the following formula:

$$\sqrt{(2 \times \text{Sales Volume} \times \text{Order Cost})/\text{Annual Holding Cost per Item}}$$

You buy and resell 2,000 cases per year, so that amount is the sales volume. Every time you place an order for the wine, you need to buy an $800 round-trip ticket to Paris (just to sample the inventory) and pay $200 for a couple of nights at a hotel. So your cost per order is $1,000. Finally, with insurance; interest on a bank loan; and the cost of maintaining your hermetically sealed, temperature-controlled wine cellar, the cost of storing a case of wine is about $100 yearly. In this example, you can calculate the optimal order quantity as follows:

$$\sqrt{(2 \times 2{,}000 \times \$1{,}000)/\$100}$$

Work through the numbers, and you get 200. Therefore, the order quantity that minimizes the total cost of your trips to Paris and of holding your expensive wine inventory is 200 cases. You could, of course, make only one trip to Paris per year and buy 2,000 cases of wine at once, thereby saving travel money, but you'd spend more money on holding your expensive wine inventory than you would save on travel costs. And although you could reduce your wine inventory carrying costs by going to Paris every week and picking up a few cases, your travel costs would go way, way up. (Of course, you would get about a billion frequent-flyer miles yearly.)

You can use the Standard view of the Windows Calculator to compute economic order quantities. The trick is to click the √ (square root) key last. For example, to calculate the economic order quantity in the preceding example, you enter the following numbers and operators:

$$\sqrt{(2 \times 2{,}000 \times 1{,}000)/100} = \text{sqrt}$$

The Rule of 72

The Rule of 72 isn't exactly a secret formula. It's more like a general rule. Usually, people use this rule to figure out how long it will take for some investment or savings account to double in value. The Rule of 72 is a cool little trick, however, and it has several useful applications for businesspeople.

What the rule says is that if you divide the value 72 by an interest rate percentage, your result is approximately the number of years it will take to double your money. For example, if you can stick money into some investment that pays 12 percent interest, it will take roughly six years to double your money because 72 / 12 = 6.

The Rule of 72 isn't exact, but it's usually close enough for government work. For example, if you invest $1,000 for 6 years at 12 percent interest, what you really get after 6 years isn't $2,000 but $1,973.92.

If you're in business, you can use the Rule of 72 for a couple other forecasts, too:

- ✔ **To forecast how long it will take inflation to double the price of an item, divide 72 by the inflation rate.** For example, if you own a building with a value that you figure will at least keep up with inflation, and you wonder how long the building will take to double in value if inflation runs at 4 percent, you just divide 72 by 4. The result is 18, meaning that it will take roughly 18 years for the building to double in value. Again, the Rule of 72 isn't exactly on the money, but it's dang close. A $100,000 building increases in value to $202,581.65 over 18 years if the annual inflation rate is 4 percent.

- ✔ **To forecast how long it will take to double sales volume, divide 72 by the given annual growth rate.** For example, if you can grow your business by, say, 9 percent per year, you will roughly double the size of the business in 8 years because 72 / 9 = 8. (I'm becoming kind of compulsive about this point, I know, but let me say again that the rule isn't exact, but it's very close. If a $1,000,000-per-year business grows 9 percent annually, its sales equal $1,992,562.64 after eight years of 9 percent growth. This figure really means that the business will generate roughly $2,000,000 of sales in the ninth year.)

Part VI
Appendixes

The 5th Wave   By Rich Tennant

"He saw your laptop and wants to know
if he can install QuickBooks."

In this part . . .

Appendixes are like basements. Why? Authors use them to store stuff that they want to keep but don't know where else to put. The Appendixes that follow provide instructions for installing QuickBooks, an overview of accounting, and some help with how you share the QuickBooks data file in a multi-user setting.

Appendix A

Installing QuickBooks in Ten Easy Steps

*I*f you haven't already installed QuickBooks, get it over with right now:

1. **Turn on the PC.**

   Find and flip on the computer's power switch. (Depending on which version of Windows 2000, XP, Vista, or 7 you're using, your screen may look a little different from the figures here. I'm using Windows 7, by the way. Not that you care, or that it matters. . . .)

   If you're installing QuickBooks on a computer running a professional or business edition of Windows, you may need to log on as either the administrator or a user with administrator rights. With the business flavors of the Windows operating systems, Windows security features require an administrator to install the QuickBooks program.

2. **Get the QuickBooks CD.**

   Rip open the QuickBooks package and get out the CD (which looks exactly like the ones that play music).

   You can also purchase QuickBooks directly from Intuit using the www. quickbooks.intuit.com Web site and then download the software at the time of purchase. You need a fast Internet connection to download the QuickBooks software — the download requires close to an hour with a cable modem and even more time with a DSL connection. If you do download, skip ahead to step 4.

3. **Insert the CD into your CD-ROM drive.**

   Windows recognizes that you inserted the QuickBooks CD and displays a little message box that tells you "Welcome to QuickBooks." Click Next to really get things started. (You may need to click Next again.)

4. **Indicate that you accept the QuickBooks licensing agreement and then click Next.**

QuickBooks next asks whether you agree to play by its rules, as outlined in tedious detail in the licensing agreement displayed onscreen. Assuming you do — and you have to agree in order to install the software — select the I Accept The Terms of the License Agreement (But Only Because I Have No Other Choice) button and click Next.

5. **Select the Express installation option and click Next.**

   When the Choose Installation Type window appears (see Figure A-1), select the Express option and then click the Next button. The installation program begins using Intuit's default installation settings. (The default installation settings are fine for 999 of 1,000 users.)

You don't have to choose the Express installation option. You can, instead, choose the custom installation option, which lets you specify stuff such as where the QuickBooks program and data files get stored. I don't talk about these options here because most people won't want to (and shouldn't) make these customizations. What's more, if you're someone who can safely customize the QuickBooks installation settings, you don't need my help with figuring out how this stuff works.

6. **Provide the License and Product Number and then click Next.**

   When the License and Product Numbers window appears (see Figure A-2), enter these two bits of licensing information (they should be printed on a yellow sticker on the back of the CD sleeve) and then click Next.

7. **Begin the installation.**

   The installation program tells you, at long last, that it's ready to begin as soon as you click Install. Click Install. The program begins extracting files from the CD.

   While the installation program runs, you can see a little bar that shows your progress.

If you need to cancel the installation at any time, just click Cancel. QuickBooks warns you that the setup is incomplete. That's okay; just start the setup from scratch next time around.

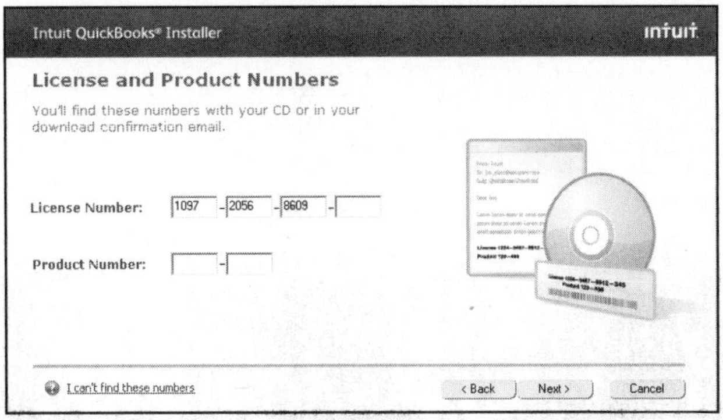

Figure A-2:
The License and Product Numbers window.

8. Take 15–20 minutes or so to contemplate the meaning of life or get a drink of water.

9. When the Install program finishes, click Finish.

Congratulations. You're finished with the installation. You have a new item on the Programs menu and probably new shortcuts on your desktop.

10. (Optional) Celebrate.

Stand up at your desk, click your heels together three times, and repeat the phrase, "There's no place like home." And watch out for flying houses.

As soon as you're done celebrating, you may want to flip to Chapter 2 and find out how to register the program. You'll probably want to register QuickBooks before you begin using it.

If you work on a network and want to share a QuickBooks file stored on one computer with another computer on the network, you need to install QuickBooks on all the other computers that you want to use to work with the file. *Note:* You need a separate copy of QuickBooks — such as from the five-pack version — for each computer on which you want to install QuickBooks.

By the way — and I mention this just because I had a couple of clients ask about this — running QuickBooks on a network with multiple QuickBooks users isn't super-tricky or terribly complicated. QuickBooks takes care of the hard stuff. If you have more than one person using QuickBooks, you owe it to yourself (and your business) to set up a network and then purchase and install multiple copies of QuickBooks. Read Appendix C for more information.

Appendix B

If Numbers Are Your Friends

You don't need to know much about accounting or about double-entry bookkeeping to use QuickBooks, which, as you know, is most of its appeal. If you're serious about this accounting business or serious about your business, consider finding out a bit more; setting up QuickBooks and understanding all the QuickBooks reports will be easier, and you'll be more sophisticated in your accounting, too.

Just because the accounting in this appendix is a little more complicated doesn't mean that you can't understand it. To make this whole discussion more concrete, I use one running example. I hope it helps you out! If nothing else, it'll inspire you to get into the rowboat rental business.

Keying In on Profit

Start with the big picture. The key purpose of an accounting system is to enable you to answer the burning question "Am I making any money?"

Accounting is that simple. Really. At least conceptually. So, throughout the rest of this appendix, I just talk about how to calculate a business's profits in a reasonably accurate but still practical manner.

Let me introduce you to the new you

You just moved to Montana for the laid-back living and fresh air. You live in a cute log cabin on Flathead Lake. To support yourself, you plan to purchase several rowboats and rent them to visiting fly fishermen. Of course, you'll probably need to do quite a bit of fly fishing, too, but just consider it the price you pay for being your own boss.

The first day in business

It's your first day in business. About 5 a.m., ol' Peter Gruntpaw shows up to deliver your three rowboats. He made them for you in his barn, but even so, they aren't cheap. He charges $1,500 apiece, so you write him a check for $4,500.

Peter's timing, as usual, is impeccable. About 5:15 a.m., your first customers arrive. Mr. and Mrs. Hamster (pronounced "ohm-stair") are visiting from Phoenix. They want to catch the big fish. You're a bit unsure of your pricing, but you suggest $25 per hour for the boat. They agree and pay $200 in cash for eight hours.

A few minutes later, another couple arrives. The Gerbils (pronounced "go-bells") are very agitated. They were supposed to meet the Hamsters and fish together, but the Hamsters are rowing farther and farther away from the dock. To speed the Gerbils' departure, you let them leave without paying, but you're not worried. As the Gerbils leave the dock, Ms. Gerbil shouts, "We'll pay you the $200 when we get back!"

Although you don't rent the third boat, you do enjoy a sleepy summer morning.

About 2 p.m., the Hamsters and Gerbils come rowing back into view. Obviously, though, a problem has occurred. You find out what it is when the first boat arrives. "Gerbil fell into the lake," laughs Mr. Hamster. "Lost his wallet, too." Everybody else seems to think that the lost wallet is funny. You secretly wonder how you're going to get paid. No wallet, no money.

You ask Mr. Gerbil whether he will come out to the lake tomorrow to pay you. He says he'll just write you a check when he gets home to Phoenix. Reluctantly, you agree.

Look at your cash flow first

I just described a fairly simple situation. But even so, answering the question "Did I make any money?" won't be easy. You start by looking at your cash flow: You wrote a check for $4,500, and you collected $200 in cash. Table B-1 shows your cash flow.

Table B-1	The First Day's Cash Flow	
	Cash In and Out	*Amount*
Add the cash.	Rent money from Hamsters (pronounced "ohm-stairs")	$200
	Rent money from Gerbils (pronounced "go-bells")	$0
Subtract the cash.	Money to purchase rowboats	($4,500)
Equals your cash flow:		($4,300)

To summarize, you had $200 come in but $4,500 go out. So your cash flow was –$4,300. (That's why the $4,300 is in parentheses.) From a cash-flow perspective, the first day doesn't look all that good, right? But does the cash-flow calculation show you whether you're making money? Can you look at it and gauge whether your little business is on the right track?

The answer to both questions is no. Your cash flow is important. You can't, for example, write a $4,500 check unless you have at least $4,500 in your checking account. Your cash flow doesn't tell you whether you're making money, though. In fact, you may see a couple problems with looking just at the cash flow of the rowboat rental business.

Depreciation is an accounting gimmick

Here's the first problem: If you take good care of the rowboats, you can use them every summer for the next few years. In fact, say that the rowboat rental season, which runs from early spring to late autumn, is 150 days long and that your well-made rowboats will last ten years.

✔ **You can probably rent the rowboats for 1,500 days.**

   (One-hundred-fifty days per year times ten years equals 1,500 days.)

✔ **Each rowboat costs $1,500.**

   The depreciation expense for each rowboat is only $1 per day over 1,500 days. That's a whopping $3 for all three boats.

Do you see what I'm saying? If you have something that costs a great deal of money but lasts for a long time, spreading out the cost makes sense. This spreading out is usually called *depreciation*. The little $1 chunks that are allocated to a day are the *depreciation expense*.

Different names, same logic

I don't see any point in hiding this nasty little accounting secret from you: Accountants call this cost-allocation process by different names, depending on what sort of cost is being spread out.

Most of the time, the cost allocation is called *depreciation.* You depreciate buildings,

machinery, furniture, and many other items as well. Allocating the cost of a natural resource — such as crude oil that you pump, coal that you dig, or minerals that you extract — is *depletion.* And allocating the cost of things that aren't tangible — copyrights and patents, for example — is *amortization.*

Accountants use the terms *cost* and *expense* to mean distinctly different things. A *cost* is the price that you pay for something. If you pay Peter Gruntpaw $1,500 for a rowboat, the rowboat's cost is $1,500. An *expense,* on the other hand, is what you use in a profit calculation. The little $1 chunks of the rowboat's $1,500 cost (that are allocated to individual days) are expenses.

If this depreciation stuff seems wacky, remember that what you're really trying to do is figure out whether you made any money your first day of business. And all I'm really saying is that you shouldn't include the whole cost of the rowboats as an expense in the first day's profit calculation. Some of the cost should be included as an expense in calculating the profit in future days. That's fair, right?

Accrual-basis accounting is cool

You don't want to forget about the $200 that the Gerbils owe you, either. Although Mr. Gerbil (remember that the name is pronounced "go-bell") may not send you the check for several days or even for several weeks, he will pay you. You earned the money.

The principles of accounting say that you should include sales in your profit calculations when you earn the money and not when you actually collect it. The logic behind this include-sales-when-they're-earned rule is that it produces a better estimate of the business you're doing.

Say that the day after the Gerbils and Hamsters rent the rowboats, you have no customers, but Mr. Gerbil comes out and pays you $200. If you use the include-sales-when-they're-earned rule — called *accrual-basis accounting* — your daily sales look like this:

	Day 1	Day 2
Sales	$400	$0

If you instead use *cash-basis accounting* (in which you count sales when you collect the cash), your daily sales look like this:

	Day 1	Day 2
Sales	$200	$200

The traditional accrual-based accounting method shows that you have a good day when you rent two boats and a terrible day when you don't rent any boats. In comparison, when you use cash-basis accounting, your sales record looks as though you rented a boat each day, even though you didn't. Now you know why accrual-basis accounting is a better way to measure profit.

Accrual-basis accounting also works for expenses. You should count an expense when you incur it, not when you pay it. For example, you call the local radio station and ask the people there to announce your new boat-rental business a couple times for a fee of $25. Although you don't have to pay the radio station the day your announcement airs, you should still count the $25 as an expense for that day.

Now you know how to measure profits

With what you now know, you're ready to measure the first day's profits. Table B-2 is a profit and loss statement for your first day in business.

Table B-2	A Profit and Loss Statement for the First Day	
Description	*Amount*	*Explanation*
Sales	$400	Rental money from the Hamsters and Gerbils
Expenses Depreciation Advertising	 $3 $25	 Three rowboats × $1/day depreciation Radio advertising
Total expenses	$28	Depreciation expense plus the advertising
Profit	$372	Sales minus the total expenses

Although the first day's cash flow was terrible, your little business is quite profitable. In fact, if you really do make about $370 per day, you'll recoup your entire $4,500 investment in less than three weeks. That's pretty darn good.

Some financial brain food

Now that you know how to measure profits, I can fill you in on some important conceptual stuff:

- ✔ **You measure profits for a specific period of time.**

  In the rowboat business example, you measured the profits for a day. Some people actually do measure profits (or they try to measure profits) on a daily basis. Most times, though, people use bigger chunks of time. Monthly chunks of time are common, for example, as are three-month chunks of time *(quarters)*. And everybody measures profits annually — if only because the government makes you do so for income tax accounting.

- ✔ **When people start talking about how often and for what chunks of time profits are measured, they use a couple terms.**

  The year that you calculate profits for is the *fiscal year.* The smaller chunks of time for which you measure profits over the year are *accounting periods* or *interim accounting periods.*

  You don't need to memorize these new terms. But now that you've read them, you'll probably remember them.

- ✔ **The length of your accounting periods involves an awkward trade-off.**

  Daily profit and loss calculations show you how well you did at the end of every day, but you have to collect the data and do the work every day. And preparing a profit and loss statement is a great deal of work.

  I made the example purposefully easy by including only a few transactions. In real life, you have many more transactions to worry about and fiddle with.

- ✔ **If you use a quarterly interim accounting period, you don't have to collect the raw data and do the arithmetic very often, but you know how you're doing only every once in a while.**

  In my mind, checking your profits only four times per year isn't enough. A lot can happen in three months.

In the Old Days, Things Were Different

If you're new to the arithmetic and logic of profit calculation — which is mostly what modern accounting is all about — you won't be surprised to hear that not all that long ago, most people couldn't and didn't do much profit calculating.

What they did instead was monitor a business's financial condition. They used — well, actually, they still use — a balance sheet to monitor the financial condition. A *balance sheet* just lists a business's assets and its liabilities at a particular point in time.

Say that at the start of your first day in the rowboat-rental business — before you pay Peter Gruntpaw — you have $5,000 in your checking account. To make the situation interesting, $4,000 of this money is a loan from your mother-in-law, and $1,000 is cash that you invested in your business.

Here's a key to help you understand the balance sheets and cash flow in this section:

- ✔ A business's *assets* are composed of things that the business owns.

- ✔ *Liabilities* consist of the amounts that the business owes.

- ✔ *Equity* is the difference between the business's assets and its liabilities. Interestingly, equity also shows the money that the owners or shareholders or partners have left in the business.

- ✔ If you correctly calculate each of the numbers that go on the balance sheet, the total assets value always equals the total liabilities plus total owner's equity value.

Your balance sheet at the beginning of the day looks like the one in Table B-3.

Table B-3	The Balance Sheet at the Beginning of the Day	
Description	*Amount*	*Explanation*
Assets	$5,000	The checking account balance.
Total assets	$5,000	Your only asset is cash, so it's your total, too.
Liabilities	$4,000	The loan from your mother-in-law.
Owner's equity	$1,000	The $1,000 you put in.
Total liabilities and owner's equity	$5,000	The total liabilities plus the owner's equity.

If you construct a balance sheet at the end of the first day, the financial picture is only slightly more complicated. Some of these explanations are too complicated to give in a sentence, so the paragraphs that follow describe how I got each number.

Even if you don't pay much attention, I recommend that you quickly read through the explanations. Mostly, I want you to understand that if you try to monitor a business's financial condition by using a balance sheet, as I've done here, the picture gets messy. Later in this appendix, I talk about how QuickBooks makes all this stuff easier.

Table B-4 shows the balance sheet at the end of the first day.

Table B-4	The Balance Sheet at the End of the Day	
	Description	*Amount*
Assets		
	Cash	$700
	Receivable	$200
	Rowboats	$4,497
Total assets		$5,397
Liabilities and owner's equity		
	Payable	$25
	Loan payable	$4,000
Total liabilities		$4,025
	Owner's equity	$1,000
	Retained earnings	$372
Total liabilities and owner's equity		$5,397

Cash, the first line item shown in Table B-4, is the most complicated line item to prove. If you were really in the rowboat-rental business, of course, you could just look at your checkbook. But if you were writing an appendix about being in the rowboat-rental business (as I am), you'd need to be able to calculate the cash balance. Table B-5 shows the calculation of the cash balance for your rowboat-rental business.

Table B-5	The First Day's Cash Flow		
Description	*Payment*	*Deposit*	*Balance*
Initial investment		$1,000	$1,000
Loan from mother-in-law		$4,000	$5,000
Rowboat purchase	$4,500		$500
Cash from the Hamsters		$200	$700

The $200 receivable, the second line item shown in Table B-4, is the money that the Gerbils owe you.

The third line shown in Table B-4, the Rowboats balance sheet value, is $4,497. This is weird, I'll grant you, but here's how you figure it: You deduct from the original cost of the asset all the depreciation expense that you charged to date. The original cost of the three rowboats was $4,500. You charged only $3 of depreciation for the first day, so the balance sheet value, or net book value, is $4,497.

The only liabilities are the $25 that you owe the radio station for those new business announcements (shown on the seventh line in Table B-4) and the $4,000 that you borrowed from your mother-in-law (shown on the eighth line in Table B-4). I won't even ask why you opened that can of worms.

Finally, the owner's equity section of the balance sheet shows the $1,000 that you originally contributed (see line 10 in Table B-4) and also the $372 you earned (see line 11 in Table B-4).

It's not a coincidence that the total assets value equals the total liabilities plus the total owner's equity value. If you correctly calculate each of the numbers that go on the balance sheet, the two totals are always equal.

A balance sheet lists asset, liability, and owner's equity balances as of a specific date. It gives you a financial snapshot at a point in time. Usually, you prepare a balance sheet whenever you prepare a profit and loss statement. The balance sheet shows account balances for the last day of the fiscal year and interim accounting period. (I think that it's kind of neat that after only a few pages of this appendix, you're reading and understanding such terms as *fiscal year* and *interim accounting period*.)

What Does an Italian Monk Have to Do with Anything?

So far, I've provided narrative descriptions of all the financial events that affect the balance sheet and the income statement. I describe how you started the business with $5,000 of cash (a $4,000 loan from your mother-in-law and $1,000 of cash that you yourself invested). At an even earlier point in this appendix, I noted how you rented a boat to the Hamsters for $200 and they paid you in cash.

Although the narrative descriptions of financial events — such as starting the business or renting to the Hamsters — make for just-bearable reading, they are unwieldy for accountants to use in practice. Partly, this awkwardness is because accountants are usually (or maybe always?) terrible writers. But an even bigger problem is that using the lots-and-lots-of-words approach makes describing all the little bits and pieces of information that you need difficult and downright tedious.

Fortunately, about 500 years ago, an Italian monk named Lucia Pacioli thought the same thing. No, I'm not making this up. What Pacioli really said was, "Hey, guys. Hello? Is anybody in there? You have to get more efficient in the way that you describe your financial transactions. You have to create a financial shorthand system that works when you have a large number of transactions to record."

Pacioli proceeded to describe a financial shorthand system that made it easy to collect all the little bits and pieces of information needed to prepare income statements and balance sheets. The shorthand system he described? *Double-entry bookkeeping.*

This system enabled people to name the income statement or balance sheet line items or accounts that are affected and then give the dollar amount of the effect. The profit and loss statement and the balance sheet line items are *accounts.* You need to remember this term.

A list of profit and loss statement and balance sheet line items is a *chart of accounts.* You might already know this term from using QuickBooks.

Pacioli also did one wacky thing: He used a couple new terms — *debit* and *credit* — to describe the increases and decreases in accounts:

> ✔ **Debit:** Increases in asset accounts and in expense accounts are *debits*. Decreases in liability, owner's equity, and income accounts are also debits.
>
> ✔ **Credit:** Decreases in asset and expense accounts are *credits*. Increases in liability, owner's equity, and income accounts are also credits.

Keeping these terms straight is a bit confusing, so see Table B-6 for help.

I'm sorry to have to tell you this, but if you want to use double-entry book-keeping, you need to memorize the information in Table B-6. If it's any consolation, this information is the only chunk of data in the entire book that I ask you to memorize. Or, failing that, dog-ear this page so that you can flip here quickly — or just refer to the online Cheat Sheet at www.dummies.com/cheatsheet/quickbooks2011.

Table B-6	The Only Stuff in This Book That I Ask You to Memorize	
Account Type	*Debits*	*Credits*
Assets	Increase asset accounts	Decrease asset accounts
Liabilities	Decrease liability accounts	Increase liability accounts
Owner's equity	Decrease owner's equity accounts	Increase owner's equity accounts
Income	Decrease income accounts	Increase income accounts
Expenses	Increase expense accounts	Decrease expense accounts

And now for the blow-by-blow

The best way to help you understand this double-entry bookkeeping stuff is to show you how to use it to record all the financial events that I've discussed thus far in this appendix. Start with the money that you invested in the business and the money that you foolishly borrowed from your mother-in-law. You invested $1,000 in cash, and you borrowed $4,000 in cash. Here are the double-entry bookkeeping transactions — the *journal entries* — that describe these financial events.

Journal Entry 1:	To record your $1,000 investment	
	Debit	**Credit**
Cash	$1,000	
Owner's equity		$1,000

Journal Entry 2:	To record the $4,000 loan from your mother-in-law	
	Debit	**Credit**
Cash	$4,000	
Loan payable to mother-in-law		$4,000

If you add all the debits and credits in a journal entry, you get a *trial balance*. A trial balance isn't all that special, but you use it to prepare profit and loss statements and balance sheets easily. If you add the debits and credits shown in journal entries 1 and 2, you get the trial balance shown in Table B-7.

Table B-7	Your First Trial Balance	
	Debit	**Credit**
Cash	$5,000	
Loan payable to mother-in-law		$4,000
Owner's equity		$1,000

This trial balance provides the raw data needed to construct the rowboat-business balance sheet at the start of the first day. If you don't believe me, take a peek at Table B-3. Oh, sure, the information shown in Table B-7 isn't as polished. Table B-7 doesn't provide labels, for example, that tell you that cash is an asset. And Table B-7 doesn't provide subtotals showing the total assets (equal to $5,000) and the total liabilities and owner's equity (also equal to $5,000). But it does provide the raw data.

Take a look at the journal entries you'd make to record the rest of the first day's financial events:

Journal Entry 3:	**To record the purchase of the three $1,500 rowboats**	
	Debit	*Credit*
Rowboats (fixed asset)	$4,500	
Cash		$4,500

Journal Entry 4:	**To record the rental to the Hamsters**	
	Debit	*Credit*
Cash	$200	
Sales		$200

Journal Entry 5:	**To record the rental to the Gerbils**	
	Debit	*Credit*
Receivable	$200	
Sales		$200

Journal Entry 6:	**To record the $25 radio advertisement**	
	Debit	*Credit*
Advertising expense	$25	
Payable		$25

Journal Entry 7:	**To record the $3 of rowboat depreciation**	
	Debit	*Credit*
Depreciation expense	$3	
Accumulated depreciation (fixed asset)		$3

To build a trial balance for the end of the first day, you add all the first-day journal entries to the trial balance shown in Table B-7. The result is the trial balance shown in Table B-8.

Table B-8	The Trial Balance at the End of the First Day	
	Debit	*Credit*
Balance sheet accounts		
Cash	$700	
Receivable	$200	
Rowboats — cost	$4,500	
Accumulated depreciation		$3
Payable		$25
Loan payable		$4,000
Owner's equity		$1,000
Profit and loss statement accounts		
Sales		$400
Depreciation expense	$3	
Advertising expense	$25	

The trial balance shown in Table B-8 provides the raw data used to prepare the balance sheet and profit and loss statement for the first day.

If you look at the accounts labeled *Balance sheet accounts* in Table B-8 and compare these with the balance sheet shown in Table B-4, you see that this trial balance provides all the raw numbers needed for the balance sheet. The only numbers in Table B-4 that aren't directly from Table B-8 are the subtotals that you get by adding other numbers.

If you look at the accounts labeled as *Profit and loss statement accounts* in Table B-8 and compare them with the profit and loss statement shown in Table B-2, you see that this trial balance also provides all the raw numbers needed for the profit and loss statement. Again, the only numbers in Table B-2 that aren't directly from Table B-8 are the subtotals that you get by adding other numbers.

Blow-by-blow, Part II

If you understand what I've discussed so far in this appendix, you grasp how accounting and double-entry bookkeeping work. I want to show you about a half-dozen more transaction examples, however, to plug a few minor holes in your knowledge.

When you collect money that you've previously billed, you record the transaction by debiting cash and crediting receivables (or accounts receivable). In the rowboat business, you make this basic entry when Mr. Gerbil later pays you the $200 that he owes you for the first day's rental.

Journal Entry 8:	To record a payment by a customer	
	Debit	Credit
Cash	$200	
Receivable		$200

Don't record a sale when you collect the cash. The sale has already been recorded in Journal Entry 5. When you pay the radio station for the advertising, you record the transaction by debiting accounts payable and crediting cash.

Journal Entry 9:	To record your payment of $25 to the radio station	
	Debit	Credit
Payable	$25	
Cash		$25

The one other thing I want to cover — ever so briefly — is *inventory accounting*. Accounting for items that you buy and resell or the items that you make and resell is a bit trickier, and I don't have room to go into a great deal of detail.

When you buy items to resell, you debit an asset account, often named Inventory. If you purchase 300 of the $10 thingamajigs that you hope to resell for $25 each, you record the following journal entry:

Journal Entry 10:	To record the cash purchase of thingamajigs	
	Debit	Credit
Inventory	$3,000	
Cash		$3,000

When you sell a thingamajig, you need to do two tasks: Record the sale and record the cost of the sale. If you need to record the sale of 100 thingamajigs for $25 each, for example, you record the following journal entry:

Journal Entry 11:	To record the sale of 100 thingamajigs for $25 apiece	
	Debit	**Credit**
Receivable	$2,500	
Sales		$2,500

You also need to record the cost of the thingamajigs that you sold as an expense and record the reduction in the value of your thingamajig inventory. That means that if you reduce your inventory count from 300 items to 200 items, you need to adjust your inventory's dollar value. You record the following journal entry:

Journal Entry 12:	To record the cost of the 100 thingamajigs sold	
	Debit	**Credit**
Cost of goods sold	$1,000	
Inventory		$1,000

The cost of goods sold account, by the way, is just another expense. It appears on your profit and loss statement.

How does QuickBooks help?

If you keep (or someone else keeps) the books for your business manually, you actually have to make these journal entries. When you use QuickBooks to keep the books, however, all this debiting and crediting business usually goes on behind the scenes. When you invoice a customer, QuickBooks debits accounts receivable and credits sales. When you write a check to pay some bill, QuickBooks debits the expense (or the accounts payable account) and credits cash.

In the few cases in which a financial transaction isn't recorded automatically when you fill in an onscreen form, you need to use the General Journal Entry window. To display the General Journal Entry window, choose Company➪Make General Journal Entries. You use the General Journal Entry window to create journal entries. An example of one of these noncash transactions is depreciation expense.

QuickBooks automatically builds a trial balance, using journal entries that it constructs automatically and any journal entries that you enter by using the General Journal Entry window. If you want to see the trial balance, just choose Reports➪Accountant & Taxes➪Trial Balance. QuickBooks prepares balance sheets, profit and loss statements, and several other reports by using the trial balance.

Two Dark Shadows in the World of Accounting

The real purpose of accounting systems, such as QuickBooks, is simple: Accounting systems are supposed to make succeeding in your business easier for you. You may think, therefore, that the world of accounting is a friendly place. Unfortunately, this scenario isn't quite true. I'm sorry to report that two dark shadows hang over the world of accounting: financial accounting standards and income tax laws.

The first dark shadow

"Financial accounting standards," you say. "What the heck are those?"

Here's the quick-and-dirty explanation: *Financial accounting standards* are accounting rules created by certified public accountants (CPAs). These rules are supposed to make reading financial statements and understanding what's going on easier for people. (I happen to believe that just the opposite is often true in the case of small businesses, in case you're interested.) But because of what financial accounting standards purport to do, some people — such as bank loan officers — want to see profit and loss statements and balance sheets that follow the rules. The exact catchphrase is one that you might have heard before: "Prepared in accordance with generally accepted accounting principles."

Unfortunately, the rules are very complicated, the rules are inconsistently interpreted, and actually applying the rules would soon run most small businesses into the ground. (And, as you were running your business into the ground — you'll be happy to know — your CPA would make a great deal of money helping you figure out what you were supposed to be doing.) So what should you do about this first dark shadow?

Glad you asked:

- ✔ **Know that it exists.** Know that people like your banker honestly think that you should follow a supercomplicated set of accounting rules.

- ✔ **Don't get sucked into the financial accounting standards tar pit.** Tell people — your banker included — that you do your accounting in the way that you think enables you to best manage your business. Tell people that a small business like yours can't afford to have an in-house staff of full-time CPAs. Finally, tell people that you don't necessarily prepare your financial statements "in accordance with generally accepted accounting principles."

Do attempt to fully and fairly disclose your financial affairs to people who need to know about them. Lying to a creditor or an investor about your financial affairs or getting sneaky with one of these people is a good way to end up in jail.

The second dark shadow

And now, here's the second dark shadow: income tax accounting laws. You know that Congress enacts tax legislation to raise revenue. And you know that it does so in a political environment strewn with all sorts of partisan voodoo economics and social overtones. So you won't be surprised to find out that the accounting rules that come out of the nation's capital and your state capital don't make much sense for running a business.

You need to apply the rules when you prepare your tax return, of course, but you don't have to use them the rest of the year. A far better approach is to do your accounting in a way that enables you to best run your business. That way, you don't use accounting tricks and gambits that make sense for income tax accounting but foul up your accounting system. At the end of the year, when you're preparing your tax return, have your tax preparer adjust your trial balance so that it conforms to income tax accounting laws.

The Danger of Shell Games

This appendix is longer than I initially intended. I'm sorry about that. I want to share one more thought with you, however. And I think that it's an important thought, so please stay with me.

You could use the accounting knowledge that this appendix imparts to do the bookkeeping for a very large business. As crazy as it sounds, if you had 3,000 rowboats for rent — perhaps you have rental outlets at dozens of lakes scattered all over the Rockies — you might actually be able to keep the books for a $200 million-per-year business. You'd have to enter many more transactions, and the numbers would all be bigger, but you wouldn't necessarily be doing anything more complicated than the transactions in this appendix.

Unfortunately, the temptation is great — especially on the part of financial advisors — to let the money stuff get more complicated as a business grows. People start talking about sophisticated leasing arrangements that make sense because of the tax laws. A customer or vendor suggests some complicated profit-sharing or cost-reimbursement agreement. Then your attorney talks you into setting up a couple new subsidiaries for legal reasons.

All these schemes make accounting for your business terribly complicated. If you choose to ignore this complexity and go on your merry way, very soon you won't know whether you're making money. (I've seen plenty of people go this route — and it isn't pretty.) On the other hand, if you truly want to do accurate accounting in a complex environment, you need to spend a great deal of cash for really smart accountants. (This tactic, of course, assumes that you can find, hire, and afford these really smart accountants.)

If you're unsure how to tell whether something is just too complicated, here's a general rule you can use: If you can't easily create the journal entries that quantify the financial essence of some event, you're in trouble.

So what should you do? I suggest that you don't complicate your business's finances — not even if you think that the newfangled, tax-incentivized, sale-leaseback profit plan is a sure winner. Keep things simple, my friend. To win the game, you have to keep score.

Appendix C

Sharing QuickBooks Files

● ●

In This Appendix

▶ Understanding how QuickBooks works on a network

▶ Installing QuickBooks for network use

▶ Setting up user permissions

▶ Specifying multi-user mode

▶ Working with a shared QuickBooks file

● ●

*O*kay, here's a cool deal: Within QuickBooks, you can set up user permissions, which enables you to specify who has access to which areas of your QuickBooks files. In fact, you can also work with your QuickBooks file on a network and in a multiple-user environment by using a powerful feature called *record locking*.

If you work on a network and need to use or just want to find out about the QuickBooks network features, read this appendix. If your computer isn't connected to a network, but you want to designate unique permissions for different people by using a QuickBooks file on a single computer, read the section, "Setting Up User Permissions," later in this appendix. And if you're the only one using QuickBooks, you can skip this appendix.

Sharing a QuickBooks File on a Network

Two important features power the QuickBooks multi-user network capability: user permissions and record locking. The *user permissions* feature lets multiple users of a QuickBooks file have unique permissions settings to access different areas of QuickBooks. *Record locking,* the second feature, allows more than one person to log on to and work with a QuickBooks file at the same time.

User permissions

QuickBooks enables you to set user permissions so that you can give different QuickBooks users different privileges. For example, Jane Owner may be able to do anything she wants because, metaphorically speaking, she's Da Man. Joe Clerk, though, may be able to enter only bills. Joe, a lowly clerk of perhaps dubious judgment and discretion, may not have the ability to view the company's profit and loss statement, print checks, or record customer payments. This idea makes sense at a practical level, right? In a situation where a bunch of people access the QuickBooks file, you want to make sure that confidential information remains confidential.

You also want to make sure that people can't intentionally or unintentionally corrupt your financial records. For example, you don't want someone to enter incorrect data (perhaps because they stumble into some area of the QuickBooks program where they have no business). And you don't want someone fraudulently recording transactions — such as fake checks— that they can go cash.

I think that if you reflect on this user permissions stuff, you'll realize, "Hey, yeah, that makes sense!" So I'm not going to talk a bunch more about it. Let me conclude by throwing out a couple general observations about how you decide which user permissions are appropriate:

✔ **Data confidentiality:** This issue probably has the most to do with your management philosophy. The more open you are about stuff, the less you probably have to worry about people snooping for stuff. I want to point out, however, that payroll is always a touchy subject. If everybody knows what everyone else is paid, some interesting discussions occur — but you already knew that.

✔ **Data corruption:** Regarding data corruption, you need to know that people usually apply two general rules:

  • Don't give people access to tools they don't know how to use. That's only asking for trouble.

  • Make sure that no one person can muck around unsupervised in some area of the accounting system — especially if that person records or handles cash.

If at all possible, employ a buddy system whereby people do stuff together so that people always double-check — even if only indirectly — other people's work. Maybe Joe records a bill, for example, but Jane always cuts the check to pay the bill. Maybe Raul records customer invoices, but Chang sends them out. Maybe Saul records cash receipts, but Beth deposits them. You see the pattern, right? If two people deal with a particular economic event — again, especially one that involves cash — it's a really good idea for Joe and Jane, Raul and Chang, and Saul and Beth to look over each other's shoulders.

Just what is a network, anyway?

A *network* is a set of connected computers so that the people who use the computers can share information. Uh, well, this is somewhat self-serving, but let me say that if you don't currently use a network, *Networking For Dummies,* 9th Edition, by Doug Lowe, and *Home Networking For Dummies,* 4th Edition, by Kathy Ivens, and *Wireless Home Networking For Dummies*, 3rd Edition, by Danny Briere, Pat Hurley, and Edward Ferris, explain how to set up a small business network in a couple hours and live to tell about it.

Record locking

The easiest way to understand record locking is to compare it with the other variety of locking: *file locking.* Most of the other programs that you use — perhaps every one but QuickBooks — use file locking. What file locking means is this: If one person on the network has, for instance, a word processing document open, nobody else on the network can open that document. Others may be able to open a copy of the document that they can save on their computers, but they can't edit the original document. The operating system locks the original document (the file) so that only one person can fool around with the file at a time. This locking ensures the integrity of the data and the changes that people make to the data. (If this business about ensuring integrity seems weird, think about the difficulty of making sure that both people's changes end up in a word processing document that both people are editing simultaneously.)

Record locking works differently. With record locking, more than one person on the network can open and edit the same file at once, but only one person can work with a specific record.

A *record* is a part of a file. For example, in a file of bills that you owe to vendors, the file is the entire collection of bills. The individual bills are records within the file, and more than one person can open the file of bills. Individual bills, though — the individual records that make up the file — are locked when a person grabs a record.

This information sounds like too much confusion, but differentiating between files and the records *within* a file is what makes sharing files possible. In QuickBooks, for example, if Jane is entering one bill for the Alpha Company in a file, Joe can edit a bill for Beta Corporation because the two bills are different records. However, Jane can't — because of record locking — fool around with the Beta Corporation bill that Joe is editing. And Joe can't — again, because of record locking — fiddle with the Alpha Company bill that Jane's entering.

Restated more generally, no two people can edit the same record in a file at the same time. Record locking enables employees to use a file in a multi-user environment because it lets more than one person work with a file.

Installing QuickBooks for Network Use

To install QuickBooks for network use, you must first install QuickBooks on all the computers on the network that need to access and work with the QuickBooks file. This task isn't tricky. You don't need to install QuickBooks in any fancy way to be able to share QuickBooks files.

You need to purchase a copy of QuickBooks for each computer that's going to run the program. If you have five computers on which you want to use QuickBooks, you need to buy five copies of QuickBooks. Or you can buy the special five-license version of QuickBooks. If you attempt to install a single copy of QuickBooks (with a single key code) on multiple computers, QuickBooks won't allow two computers using the same key code to share a file in multi-user mode.

When you create the file that you want to share, you need to make sure that you store the file in a location where the other QuickBooks users can access it. You may need to store the file on a server. You can also store the file on a client computer as long as you designate sharing permissions for either the folder or the drive on which you save the QuickBooks file.

Choosing a good password

The administrator has access to all areas of QuickBooks, so picking a good password is especially important. Other users (especially those with higher levels of access permission) also need to select their passwords carefully.

A good password is one that you can easily remember but that other people can't easily guess. Combinations of letters and numbers are the best way to go. For example, use your grade school nickname plus the number of your favorite basketball player. Or use a random number combined with the name of your favorite

restaurant (as long as you don't walk around all day muttering "Number nine, number nine, number nine" and raving about your love of this particular eatery). Avoid using telephone numbers, family names, and family dates (such as the birthday of a family member). And *absolutely do not* use banking PINs or Social Security numbers.

One last tip: QuickBooks lets you create passwords from 0–16 characters in length. As a general rule, choose a password that's five or more characters long.

Another important thing: Whoever creates the QuickBooks file automatically becomes the file administrator. The *file administrator* has access to all areas of the file and sets up the other file users, so you don't want just anybody setting up the QuickBooks file. Either the business owner or the head of accounting is well suited for this job. In any case, the person who sets up the file should be trustworthy, regularly around the office, and easy to reach for any questions or problems that arise. And this person probably should have a strong background in accounting. See the following section for more details.

Setting Up User Permissions

You can tell QuickBooks who else will use the file and set permissions for these other people during the EasyStep Interview (see Chapter 2). I'm going to assume that you give QuickBooks this information later. To do it later, use the User List dialog box, as shown in Figure C-1. To display this dialog box, choose Company⇨Set Up Users and Passwords⇨Set Up Users.

Figure C-1:
The User List dialog box.

1. **Click the Add User button.**

   Doing so displays the first page of the Set Up User Password and Access Wizard (see Figure C-2). You use this wizard to add new users and specify user permissions.

2. **Type a username and password for the additional person who you want to be able to use the QuickBooks file; type the password again in the Confirm Password text box.**

   Re-entering the password confirms that you typed the password correctly the first time.

   From this point, when someone opens the QuickBooks file, QuickBooks asks for a username and password. So for another person to access the QuickBooks file, he or she must enter the username and password that you set.

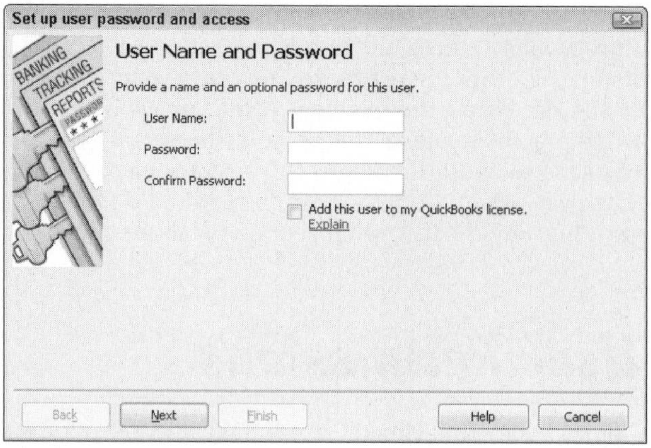

Figure C-2:
The first
Set Up User
Password
and Access
Wizard
page.

3. **Click Next.**

   QuickBooks displays a dialog box (not shown here) asking whether you want the person to have access to all areas of the QuickBooks file or only some areas.

4. **Click All Areas or click Selected Areas; then click Next.**

   If you specify that you want to give access to only some areas, QuickBooks displays a series of dialog boxes that allow you to set permissions for each area. Figure C-3, for example, shows the Set Up User Password and Access Wizard page that specifies what the new employee, Beth, can do with sales and accounts receivable accounting.

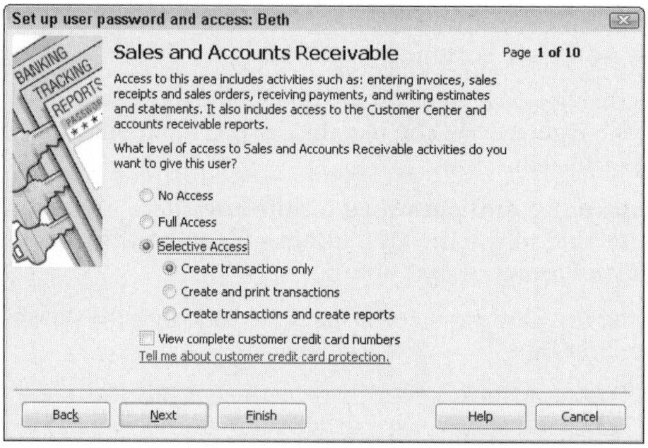

Figure C-3:
The Sales
and
Accounts
Receivable
screen of
the Set
Up User
Password
and Access
Wizard.

5. **Designate the access permission level for each area in the Set Up User Password and Access Wizard.**

   Select the No Access radio button to make the area off-limits for the user. Select the Full Access radio button to give the user permission to create and print transactions and reports in the area, or mark the Selective Access radio button to give partial access to the area. If you mark Selective Access, specify the limited access. Click Next after supplying each area's access information to proceed to the next area. The other areas' wizard pages look and work the same way.

6. **Tell QuickBooks whether you want the user to be able to change or delete existing transactions and those recorded before the closing date that you specify.**

   After you go through the access permissions for all the areas, QuickBooks displays a wizard page that provides option buttons for restricting user access to existing transactions. By specifying a closing date, you can prevent users — for example, new QuickBooks users or new employees — from altering data before a given date.

   To set a closing date, log on to the QuickBooks file as the administrator. Make sure that you're working in single-user mode. (If you aren't, choose File⇨Switch to Single-User Mode.) Choose Company⇨Set Up Users and Passwords⇨Set Up Users. When QuickBooks displays the Set Closing Date and Password window, enter a closing date password into the Closing Date text box. Then click OK.

7. **Click Next.**

   Specify whether you want the user to be able to access QuickBooks data from another application, such as TurboTax.

8. **Review the permissions that you granted the new user.**

   After you finish stepping through the Set Up User Password and Access Wizard, QuickBooks shows a summary of the permissions for a user. Click the Prev button if you need to go back and change permissions for an area.

9. **Click Finish to finish setting up the new user.**

   QuickBooks displays the User List dialog box again but with the new user added. Click Add User to add another new user, click Edit User to edit the selected user, or click Close to close the dialog box.

A user can log on and open a QuickBooks file from any computer on the network as long as the computer has QuickBooks installed and has network access to the QuickBooks file. If a person attempts to open a restricted area or perform an unauthorized action, QuickBooks displays a message box indicating that the person lacks the permissions necessary to perform the action.

Individual users can specify and save their preferences for working with QuickBooks. For example, a user can decide to display and even customize the QuickBooks icon bar or set options for graphs, reminders, and warnings. Users can access their preference settings by choosing Edit⇨Preferences. Select an area by clicking an icon (such as General) on the left. Click the My Preferences tab, if it isn't already selected.

Specifying Multi-User Mode

For more than one person to work with a QuickBooks file at once, users must work with the QuickBooks file in *multi-user mode.* The first person who opens the file needs to specify multi-user mode for others to be able to open the file. To specify multi-user mode, choose File⇨Switch to Multi-User Mode. You can tell that you're working in multi-user mode because the QuickBooks title bar indicates so. When other people open the QuickBooks file, it automatically opens in multi-user mode. For another user to work in single-user mode, the other users must close the QuickBooks file and the user wanting to work in single-user mode needs (or may need) to choose File⇨Switch to Single-User Mode command.

Working in Multi-User Mode

Sharing a QuickBooks file over a network involves a couple tricks. First, you need to make sure that no one who is in single-user mode is using the file that you want to open. If someone is and you try to open the file, QuickBooks displays a message indicating that someone is using the company file in single-user mode. Tell the person to switch to multi-user mode and then click Try Again.

As soon as you begin creating or editing a transaction, QuickBooks locks the transaction. This way, no one else can edit the transaction while you work on it. You can tell whether you have a transaction open in edit mode by what QuickBooks indicates on the title bar at the top of the form: QuickBooks displays `Editing Transaction` on the title bar. Other users can open the transaction while you edit it in edit mode, but they can't make changes to it until you're through.

For example, if you attempt to edit a transaction that your co-worker Harriet already has open in edit mode, QuickBooks displays a message that reads (and here, I paraphrase), "Excuse me, Bubba? Harriet is working with that transaction. You need to come back later."

Index